Oliver St. John Gogarty (1878-1957) is regarded as one of the leading characters of the Irish literary renaissance. Born in Dublin, he was educated at Mungret, Stonyhurst, Clongowes Wood College, the Royal University and the medical school of Trinity College, Dublin.

A man of many talents, poet, writer, Senator, successful ENT surgeon and legendary wit, he was closely associated with W.B. Yeats, George Moore, AE and James Joyce, with whom he shared the Martello tower at Sandycove in 1904, and who irreverently portrayed him as Buck Mulligan in *Ulysses*.

As I Was Going Down Sackville Street is possibly Gogarty's best known book. Other prose works include *I Follow St. Patrick*, *Rolling Down the Lea*, *It Isn't This Time of Year At All*, *Going Native*, *Intimations*, and *Mr. Petunia*. His three plays, *Blight*, *A Serious Thing* and *The Enchanted Trousers*, were produced at the Abbey Theatre, under a pseudonym.

Yeats described him as 'one of the greatest poets of our age' and his poetic works include *An Offering of Swans* and *Wild Apples*.

During the Civil War Gogarty was kidnapped by republicans and escaped by diving into the river Liffey. His country house at Renvyle, Co. Galway was burned down. In 1939 Gogarty went to the United States, and lived there until his death in New York in 1957.

ROGER GREENE

An independent film-maker, Roger Greene produces documentaries through his own company Charlemont Films for, amongst other broadcasters, the BBC, UTV and RTE. In 1987 he produced *Silence Would Never Do*, a biographical documentary on the life of Oliver St. John Gogarty for the BBC/RTE, which was also broadcast on American and Australian television.

As I Was Going Down Sackville Street

Oliver St. John Gogarty

THE O'BRIEN PRESS

DUBLIN

This edition first published 1994 by The O'Brien Press Ltd.,
20 Victoria Road, Rathgar, Dublin 6, Ireland.

First published 1937

Copyright © text Oliver D. Gogarty

All rights reserved. No part of this book may be reproduced or
utilised in any form or by any means, including photocopying,
recording or by any information storage and retrieval system without
permission in writing from the publisher. This book may not be sold
as a bargain book or at a reduced price without permission in
writing from the publisher.

10 9 8 7 6 5 4 3 2 1

British Library Cataloguing-in-publication Data
Gogarty, Oliver St. John
As I Was Going Down Sackville Street
New ed.
I. Title
941.835082092

ISBN 0-86278-394-1

Cover design: The O'Brien Press
Cover separations: DOTS Ltd., Dublin
Printing: Cox & Wyman Ltd., Reading

"We Irishmen are apt to think something and nothing are near neighbours." BISHOP BERKELEY

To Mrs Clifton
of Lytham Hall, Lancs.

NOTE
The names in this book are real,
the characters are fictitious.

Introduction

Oliver St. John Gogarty is unique amongst Irish literary renaissance figures for many reasons, not least of which is that his own celebrity has tended to obscure his accomplishments in print. His notoriety as a Rabelaisian wit and his associations with the leading literary and political figures of his day are by now well chronicled. By comparison little attention has been given to his writings over the decades since his death in 1957. It has been stated that Ulick O'Connor's perceptive biography of Gogarty in 1964 saved both the man and his works from oblivion. Later biographies by Professor J.B. Lyons of the Royal College of Surgeons, Dublin, and Professor James Carens of Bucknell University, Pennsylvania, have ensured a continuing understanding, in the wake of O'Connor's work, of Gogarty's important contributions to both the literary and political influences in the founding years of the Irish nation.

In his biography of W.B. Yeats, the distinguished academic of Anglo-Irish literature, A. Norman Jeffares refers to Gogarty as 'an unduly neglected minor poet'. This is in the context of the 1936 *Oxford Book of Modern Verse*, wherein its editor, Yeats, included seventeen of Gogarty's poems. It is held by some that this generous representation of Gogarty's poetry in the volume was a pay-off and acknowledgement by Yeats of their long-standing friendship and a demonstration of gratitude to Gogarty for instigating Yeats's inclusion in the first Irish Senate.

It is perhaps as a result of this representation in the *Oxford Book of Modern Verse* that, to whatever extent he is known in literary terms, Gogarty is regarded more as a poet than a writer of prose. But either way it remains a conundrum that his writings – poetry and prose – have, for the most part, been overlooked by publishers and by critics since his death.

Following the publication of the Yeats edition of the *Oxford Book of Modern Verse*, James Stephens wrote to Gogarty observing: '. . . that, perhaps, you will not be praised as you should be until about 50 years after you're dead'. The O'Brien Press is to be congratulated for anticipating Stephens's prophecy by some thirteen years in publishing this first-ever Irish edition of *As I was Going Down Sackville Street*, thereby reviving literary interest in, and acknowledgement of, Gogarty the writer.

Sub-titled 'A Phantasy in Fact', *Sackville Street* appeared in 1937 when the author was in his sixtieth year – late by any standards for the publication of a first prose work. Gogarty had been encouraged by a US columnist and publicist to produce 'a book of memoirs for an American publishing firm'. If this was indeed the brief, then Gogarty adhered to it to the letter. *Sackville Street* is just that, a collection of memoirs assembled without conventional construction, presented in an almost haphazard format with single thoughts triggering a multiplicity of observations which, in some instances, give scant recognition to their origins. The result is a book which starts in the present (the late 1930s) and works backwards some twenty years to its ending in an idyllic setting of place and mind at a picnic by Lough Bray in the Wicklow mountains. In its journey backwards *Sackville Street*, the most profound of Gogarty's autobiographical memoirs, takes the reader from a present state of weariness with modern Ireland, political disillusionment and resentment, back to a mental perception of an ideal start to adulthood in the company of Macran (McGurk), Tyrell, Mahaffy, Orpen, Vera Hone and Endymion in the sunlit setting of a lazy picnic gathering, where the conversation is peppered with Greek literary allusion and intellectual aggrandizement.

In a letter to Dorothy Wellesley after the first publication of *Sackville Street*, Yeats wrote: 'Have you read Gogarty's book? Here everybody is reading it. A publican down the quays told a customer, "You can open it anywhere, like the *Imitation of Christ*". It is not all wit, one can say much of it, as somebody said, I think of Raleigh, it is "high, insolent and passionate". None of its attacks on things I approve vex me, and that is because they are passionate. His only attacks are on modern Ireland. He is passionate not self complacent so we forgive him.'

At times Gogarty's 'passion' in the book verges on straight-forward vitriol about the newly formed Irish State, its emerging politics, its revitalised cultural identity and the ineluctable potency of De Valera in whom he was incapable of finding any virtue. These vituperative attacks can be excused within their context in *Sackville Street*, particularly as Gogarty's early political beliefs had been rooted in the IRB and he had aligned his subsequent ideals and allegiances with those of Arthur Griffith and Michael Collins.

A further illustration of Gogarty's passion is evidenced in an early chapter of *Sackville Street* set in the Shelbourne Hotel, where Kurt Kelner, the publicist and columnist, urges the Gogarty persona to write his memoirs. In conversation, Kelner states: 'there is a mighty lot that has not been told about your country. You are not all dreamers.' The Gogarty persona replies: 'Maybe not, but woe betide the reputation of anyone who wakens us up from our dreams. It is worse for you in the United States. There you have got the permanent dreams of half-a-dozen nations who are the hyphens, to deal with. In order to avoid loss of national homeland identity in the great merger of humanity, the newcomers rally round and cling to the totem-poles of their country of origin. The Lutheran becomes more Lutheran, and the Irish Nationalist never moves from the politics of a hundred years ago. The reactions of this on Ireland, whose politics are supported by the American-Irish, can be imagined. It leads to a perpetuation of the politics of the Famine. It keeps alive resentment and encourages the demagogues here to hawk Hate. And Hate is anything but a policy of progress. It keeps us back, and the more backward we become the more we hate those who present us with object-lessons of success and prosperity. We save our faces by hating England . . .'

It is fifty-seven years since these words were first published – in the light of certain political representations made to the United States at the beginning of this year, they still remain relevant.

Gogarty's reminiscences in *Sackville Street* can be divided into the two broad categories of politics and literature. And it is under these two unwritten headings that he devotes the majority of his work, in memoirs of an observational genre imbued with, we hope, for the most part accurate accounts of, and conversations with, amongst others, Arthur Griffith, Michael Collins and Tim Healy on the political front and W.B. Yeats, James Joyce, George Russell (AE), George Moore and Lord Dunsany on the literary side. There are, of course, many parts of the book where the two sectors merge.

Having stated that *Sackville Street* is presented in a haphazard format, it must be acknowledged that this is not a disparaging criticism of its literary merits. On the contrary, its 'haphazard' nature works to the reader's advantage and turns, sometimes within a line, a tragic, destructive event with bitter and resentful memories, into one of great hilarity. Such is the unusual style that the chapter devoted to the burning of the author's Connemara home, Renvyle House, by De Valera's supporters in 1923, starts out with helpless regret and bitterness. Then, within a sentence, it becomes both an hilarious and chilling account of a ghost hunt in the past involving Yeats, Mrs Yeats, Lord Conyngham, Seymour Leslie and Welshman Evan Morgan, the hapless victim rendered speechless and breathless as a result of being locked in the room haunted by Renvyle's resident child ghost, Athelstone Blake. Throughout, the Gogarty persona attempts, like an erstwhile Basil Fawlty, to present a veneer of normality on the whole proceedings.

It is necessary in an introduction to *Sackville Street* to mention two factors surrounding its first publication: the ensuing libel case by the Sinclairs and, more tangentially, the author's relationship with Joyce. I say tangentially for, their relationship apart, comparisons can and have been drawn between Joyce's *Ulysses* and Gogarty's *As I Was Going Down Sackville Street*.

In his introduction to the first publication of *Sackville Street*, the critic, historian and novelist Francis Hackett gives recognition to this comparison when he describes Gogarty as: 'Being something of a chameleon, he begins as if he were to write another *Ulysses*. I rather trembled.' Here Hackett alludes to the great rivalry between Joyce and Gogarty, a rivalry which began on Joyce's departure from the Martello tower (where he had lived for a brief period with Gogarty) and lasted until his death. In his 'trembling', Hackett expresses an unwarranted fear that Gogarty is, in *Sackville Street*, attempting to duplicate Joyce's great work with another odyssey of Dublin. The comparison is drawn in the similarity of openings. But, in relief, Hackett continues: 'Then he slips from the Joycean Endymion . . . It is only as he warms up that he forgets Joyce.'

It is evident that Joyce resented Gogarty and probably disliked him. His depiction of Gogarty in *Ulysses* as Buck Mulligan is less than complimentary and the first description of the character is disparaging. 'Stately, plump Buck Mulligan . . .', when analysed, is nothing short of offensive. 'Stately' is not a compliment, but a slur on Gogarty's establishment status and the 'plump' is more a reference to Gogarty's purveyance of success or self-satisfaction than to any criticism of his physique.

However, in *Sackville Street* there is evidence to suggest that rather than avenge the portrait painted of him by Joyce, Gogarty offers admiration of his former friend. This is particularly prevalent towards the latter half of the book in his deliberations on the state of Irish theatre and the unwarranted exclusion of Joyce by Lady Gregory from the Abbey Theatre. In this sequence Gogarty pays tribute to Joyce's expertise with: 'Joyce knew far better than I what was in the air, and what was likely to be the future of the theatre in Ireland . . . Who can measure how great was its loss when Lady Gregory gave him the cold shoulder?'

In the same section Gogarty takes a swipe at Lady Gregory: 'Her namby-pamby humour deadens my spirits.' He then continues to question her talents and abilities as a playwright by asking: 'How much of her plays did she write?' This question he puts in the context of the many visits by Yeats to Coole Park and gives further evidence to his suspicions by adding: 'I about got him [Yeats] to acknowledge his authorship of *The Rising of the Moon*. He then observes that 'the perpetual presentation of Lady Gregory's plays nearly ruined the Abbey'. Leaving his remarks about Lady Gregory to one side, Gogarty quite firmly pays tribute to Joyce.

A great many accounts have been recorded of the libel action taken against Gogarty and *Sackville Street* by the

Sinclairs, wherein Samuel Beckett was just one who took the stand on behalf of the plaintiff. At the time, the court action succeeded in having the book withdrawn from sale and the offending verses removed before further publication. As was the case in the banning of *Ulysses*, the notoriety surrounding the withdrawal of *Sackville Street* did more in the creation of demand than any publicity generated by its publishers.

The case was founded on grounds of anti-Semitism through the inclusion in *Sackville Street* of verse (written, not by Gogarty, but by George Redding) of which, it was claimed, two passages were an 'indecent and foul libel' on the Sinclair twins. The justification of the outcome of the case can now be assessed by the reader, as the offending verses are included in this edition.

It could be stated that De Valera had far greater grounds for libel action when one reads some of the sentiments expressed about him by Gogarty in *Sackville Street*. For example: 'He who has done more damage in a decade to our country than England did in seven hundred years' or 'He is more Irish perhaps than any of us, seeing that he looks like something uncoiled from the Book of Kells' – both attacks more incisive and potentially libellous than the verses about the Sinclair twins.

But it wasn't just his attacks on people living and dead that caused a degree of resentment towards Gogarty on the publication of the book. Much of the anti-Gogarty feelings in Dublin surrounded his own personality and character traits, particularly his reverential depiction of and admiration for the English nobility. It can be argued that this has no validity as a criticism, for Gogarty was happy to admit and even censured his own personality failings – as he states in relation to the Duke of Connaught: 'There must be something if not the courtier, then at least the flunkey in my composition. I like to have people better than myself about me.'

And in this sentiment we have, perhaps, the essence of Gogarty – his courage in self-recognition and honesty. By his own admission he was a snob, so his accusers largely wasted their breath. In his defence it can be stated that, if a snob, then he was a snob with a social conscience. This is borne out by his work in the Senate to improve the deplorable living standards in Dublin's slums and to advance the state of public health and education. He also argued for the equality of women in the workplace. In these and other issues he was, for the most part, a lone voice.

Of all his prose works *Sackville Street* is the closest one gets to knowing Gogarty, for here the mask of social buoyancy and Rabelaisian wit is lowered and, at times, may reveal the man. It also includes a discord of political and social sentiments, diametrically opposite at times in their support of Irish nationalism on the one hand and British nobility on the other. But as a vivid account of political and literary leaders and events in Ireland during the first quarter of this century, *As I Was Going Down Sackville Street* is a thought-provoking, relevant work full of historical reference, sadness and some wonderful humour.

Roger Greene
Dublin 1994

CHAPTER I

QUAINTLY HE CAME RAIKING OUT OF MOLESWORTH STREET INTO Kildare Street, an odd figure moidered by memories, and driven mad by dreams which had overflowed into life, making him turn himself into a merry mockery of all he had once held dear. He wore a tail-coat over white cricket trousers which were caught in at the ankles by a pair of cuffs. A cuff-like collar sloped upwards to keep erect a little sandy head, crowned by a black bowler some sizes too small. An aquiline nose high in the arch gave a note of distinction to a face all the more pathetic for its plight. Under his left arm he carried two sabres in shining scabbards of patent leather. His right hand grasped a hunting crop such as whippers-in use for hounds. His small, sharp blue eyes took in the ash-dark façade, topped by a green-white-and-orange flag, of that which had been the Duke of Leinster's town house; but it held the Senate now. He saw a sentry dressed in green, staring at the green pillar-box which stood a few yards in front of him, near the angle of the footpath where two tall T.D.'s, heavily moustached and carelessly tailored and coiffeured, were bidding good-bye to each other, hiding in the fervour of their handshake all the contempt they mutually reserved.

" Slaun-lath, now. And there I leave you."

" Bannacht lath, Shaun. I'll be seeing you soon again."

The sentry stared on at the letter-box, his eyes not raised to the martial cricketer, for Dublin had accepted him as the present representative and chief of those eccentric and genial characters whom it never fails to produce in every generation. Only when he muttered close to the ornamental iron gates which the sentry guarded, did he disturb his brown study.

What were the memories he " represented " by his accoutrements and his dress? What turned him into his present lunatic condition? To answer these questions we must go back to the days when the great Lord Lieutenant, the Earl Cadogan, held state in the Phœnix Park. That Viceroy, hearing of an act of gallantry which had cost the man his reason, sought him out, and finding that he was but slightly " touched," gave him the run of the viceregal grounds, with their pageants of state and their cricket matches. He was but slightly " touched," for he had wit enough to realise his trouble. So, when his doctor told him that his mental disability was likely to become progressive, but that he would never be violently unbalanced, he remarked : " Endymion, whom the moon loved : a lunatic . . ."

So " Endymion " he became. There was method in his madness, and more than method. But let that more reveal itself to those with eyes to see. This, however, will not be contested ; the sabres are his cavalry escort, for he must have been impressed by the cavalcade of sixty well-mounted troopers who attended the viceregal carriages ; and the cricket flannels—his memories of summer evenings on the smooth pitch ; the whip, his runs in winter with the stag-hounds of the Ward. All gone now ; alive only in memory and regret those peaceful, prosperous days when life was fair and easy and man's thoughts were the thoughts of sports-men. If he be held treasonable now for regretting those days, all the more reason for this investiture in motley. Dublin saw him only a man gone " natural," and Dublin has out-standing examples in every generation.

Endymion was preceded by Professor Maginniss, who turned himself into an Italian professor of deportment by eliding the two terminal letters of his name. But what if Endymion were a Dean Swift *aneu malakias* ; a gentle Dean gone genial and given more to mockery than to fierce indigna-tion ? There is evidence that this theory in no way exaggerates his worth. But let us not delay him by considering his pose or its significance.

With a word to the sentry, he passed into the National Library.

Up the street a tall figure, blond as a sun of Italy, could be seen approaching—the figure of a young man who walked thoughtfully, as if dictating to himself. He was walking past the National Museum, for there is a museum at each end of Kildare Street. Coming along, he must have seen the merry droll.

I will ask him a question which I wish to have solved, for he is the brainiest fellow in Dublin, an honest man, and what is more, an honest solicitor.

" Austin," I said, " tell me, am I right if I see in the cuffs on Endymion's ankles the proclamation to all who run and can read such signs, that he is standing on his head and walking on his hands, as it were—upside-down ? "

A smile flickered, but he answered as if considering the matter profoundly.

" You are right.   And what is more, if Endymion's world is upside-down, then he becomes the only one who can be said to be related to it correctly.   What is the use of our walking upright if the world is upside-down ?   If we stood on our heads in a topsy-turvy world, there would be no disharmony.   Endymion becomes the only sane creature in the world as he sees it."

" I guessed it.   By God !   A good fellow and a fantastic fellow to boot.   He shouted ' Noom ' to the sentry as he passed.   ' Noom to me, and moon to you.' "

Austin pondered a little while.   " You see, he may be symbolising his ideas or theories more thoroughly than either of us imagines.   He may be going backwards in Time as well as reversing in Space.   Just let us see if it be a crescent or a waning moon."

" I have thought of that," I said ; " waning it should be. Just let us look down the street and see."   The ghostly crescent appeared.   " Of course, that is a last quarter. . . . He is more thorough than we think.   I wonder if he is mad at all ? "

" Well, he is allied to great wit.   It must be wonderful to believe yourself to be the only sane man in the world.   More wonderful still to have your past before you again, and becoming your future.   Having been completely reversed, he is going back with the moon to the fullness and the foison. We are declining to darkening days."

" To think of my having laughed at him !   He has outsoared the shadow of our night.   Envy and calumny and hate and *gain* can touch him not.   And I laughed at him ! "

" He would like you to do so.   He does not want to lessen, he wants to increase the amount of mirth in the town.   There certainly is room for more mirth in Dublin.   His pose has the advantage of silence for the most part.   He cannot be held up for being captious.   He cannot be held up for anything, in fact ; for who can prove that he is a symbolistical critic of our time ?   At most we can only say that he is amusing himself and us too, and this is a kinder form of amusement than the more common, which is at the expense of someone else."

I thought for a while, envying Endymion, who had achieved an attitude towards things that had made him not only a laughing philosopher, but an amusing one. That transient envy, itself a form of flattery, which never fails to touch me when I see great work, now assailed me momentarily. Why had I not thought of that? To be Endymion, to speak—if not my mind—to act my part protected from the hates, jealousies and trickeries of the days about us now; to scorn them symbolically . . . to turn myself right about, not only right about face, but upside-down, and journey ever onward to the Golden Age.

" *Prætulerim delirus inersque videri.*"

As Horace, Rome's less sententious Kipling, has it. What a wonderful thing it would be if we could choose and control our madness! Not that awful insanity which King Lear prayed Heaven to withhold: that uprooting of the Reason from storms within as destructive as the ruin of the elements outside: breaking the age-stiffened oak: a brain set adrift by the ingratitude of its own flesh and blood. Not that, sweet Heaven! But to be able to adjust the Reason to the phantasmagoria of Life. And, while maintaining the steadfast lapis lazuli within, to have it played upon by every delicate shading of the weather, deepening its azure now and lighting it again in tone with the luminous and magical haze which is tremulous with life. To be magical as Life itself, and as irresponsible: to be lunatic enough to take the hard edge from knowledge, to be irrational enough to temper Justice with Mercy, and to be able to adjust oneself to the changes in intensity which the waxings and wanings of Reality assume in the shimmerings of its cloud—this would be an ideal adjustment and a poetic opposition to outrageous Fortune.

"But surely he could not have been symbolising when he jumped into the empty vat in the brewery, when his companion fell in? They say that he thought that it was full of some fluid, and that his friend was in danger of drowning. But it was only full of carbon dioxide gas."

"Are you so very sure that he may not have meant something by his plunge into the gas? Anyway, retrospectively I am sure he means it now. For all we know, he may intend in the course of this cavalcade backwards of Dublin life, when he reaches again the point in time when he fell in, to fall out—in fact, to regain his sanity. But we should not insist too much on the appositeness of symbols. Their value lies in the breadth of interpretation they allow."

" A cavalcade of Dublin life backwards for thirty years!
When was it he fell into the vat of gas ? Thirty years ago.
Shall I ask him ? "

" No, no. Leave him to his studies, whatever they may
be," said Austin, smiling.

" Yes, indeed, whatever they may be." I knew that if
I could arouse a curiosity in those " studies," that I might
get Austin to look into the Library—that home of the Dublin
Muses and its Sybil . . . that porticoed place which has made
so many philosophers but so few of them Stoics.   I wondered,
would Endymion ask for books such as those which walled
the library of Pantagruel ?   What books would he ask for ?
. . . it was a matter for investigation.   My imagination could
not supply the authors who would be likely to interest so
strange a fellow.

" If we go in there, there is no knowing whom we may
meet. . . ."

" But they cannot talk to us, and we can slip out again.
I will merely glance at the form he has filled to get a book,
and the name of the book on it."

" It's not improbable that he brought some book or even
a newspaper to read in the library—yesterday's *Evening Mail*."

I remembered the fissure on the left of the wayside at
Delphi, as you ascend the Sacred Way, whence the gaseous
vapour still issues that at the time when the Oracle was at
its best used to intoxicate the fasting priestess and induce the
prophetic frenzy. It is by the roadside, only moved by an
earthquake a little distant from the ancient cella of the god.
After all, I mused, if a whole nation, if the wisest nation
of the world once, set its course by noxious fumes, why not
Endymion ?

I described the finding of the fissure in the ditch beside the
Sacred Way.   I told how I bent down and leaned my head to
inhale the very breath of those hysterical hexameters which
steered old states and kings.   It smelt as a hothouse smells—
of deep earth and warmth.   It did me little good, probably
because I am a prophet in my own country (which accounts
for my being a nobody), and, anyway, the last Oracle
announced its own extinction.

Speaking my thought aloud, I said, " Is it not strange how
reputable the Oracle was ? "

" Almost any form of words may prove oracular, provided
the soul is sufficiently agitated. On the morning of any

momentous day, do we not begin by looking out for signs of good luck or bad, the left shoe to the foot first, the white horse, the red-haired woman ? . . . These cannot help as much as, if we are anxious enough to notice and attach value to them, their presence or absence may mar. It was the direction of the mind inward to the business in hand that made the reputation of the Oracle. If an Oracle to-day said, ' Please keep off the grass,' we might take it as a warning against investing in Land Bonds, or a hint that a sea voyage would prevent a nervous breakdown."

" The priestess had to be a woman of the canonical age, as we call it in Ireland. Apparently no pretty flapper would do. . . . Greece, like Ireland, was, therefore, immoderately influenced by hags."

Austin raised his hat.

" Who was that who passed ? "

" Miss Bellowson. Surely you know her ? "

" Let us cross the street. I am somewhat superstitious. I have a strange idea that certain spots of earth are fey or haunted ; certain houses are unlucky. This street corner is evocative. . . . Yeats holds that to speak of ghosts is to conjure them up. Let us move along on the other side."

" Stop ; look ! There's Endymion. He did not stay long in the National Library."

We watched him emerge, cross into the middle of the street and halt. From his pocket he produced a large compass. He scrutinised it carefully through his monocle. He turned it, looking up now and then as he did so. He set his course for home. " He goes home by compass ! He cannot trust the ebbing town." He raised his whip-hand to the north, and entered Molesworth Street again.

" Going home by compass ! Was there ever such a fellow ? I wonder where he is off to now ? "

" He lives in Pleasants Street. I hardly like to mention it. Things are getting so appropriate to him that I feel slightly moonstruck myself. What an idea to live in Pleasants Street ! I should have thought of that."

" Where is Pleasants Street ? "

" Off Camden Street. It is a charming street full of old-world two-storeyed cottages ; steps ascend to hall doors on the first floor, they are all the same pattern save one, which has a pagoda-roof-like shade of green above its window. It is a sunny street, and the yellow bricks seem to catch the sun, for it is more sunny than any street in Dublin.   Round the corner you can see, as the light grows fine or thickens, green and blue, the Dublin Mountains with their hanging fields. Endymion's house has a white horse in the fanlight.   But, for Heaven's sake, let us not inquire into what that may mean, or what he may mean by that.   It is our chance to see what he has been reading."

The Reading Room is a large building roofed by a cylinder arch.   George says that the National Library has two domes, the second being the bald head of its librarian, Lyster.   One of the attendants, who sits at the inquiry desk, provides a third dome.   His head sends heliographs of warning when the light beats down to those who disturb the silence of the place.

The great Reading Room was almost empty.   Two lady medicos, with their fair heads together, were studying Gray's *Anatomy*, and shaking with suppressed mirth.   Opposite to them, surrounded by little blocks on which " Silence " was printed in large letters, sat a clergyman with a " fire-red, cherubini face."   From time to time, in regular intervals which synchronised with the maximum pressure and suffusion wrath produced on his countenance, he hissed out " Whist ! " like escaping steam.   Another clergyman wandered, lonely, round the shelves which held the dictionaries.   He looked like a parchment-pale Oliver Goldsmith.   He moved his lips silently, as if quoting to himself.   In truth, he was gently masticating a small piece of carrot, which is full of vitamins.

" The saints are equal to the doctors—two of each."

" Whist ! " said Father McQuisten.

We turned to the desk.   In the Signature Book, spreading fully in purple pencil across a page, was the signature of Endymion.   It read, to our amazement :

JAMES BOYLE TISDELL BURKE STEWART FITZSIMONS FARRELL

" Damn his symbolism," said I ; " he's got my name and the names of my friends and acquaintances included in his title.   There's George's, Joe's, and the Shamuses'.   You've escaped.   What's the idea ? "

" Whist ! " said Father McQuisten.

" He cannot have been christened in all the surnames he has included in that line—that almost reads like one of Phœbus Apollo's gaseous hexameters ! "

" No one can say for certain why he has made a conglomeration of the present-day well-known citizens, and taken their

names to himself, unless . . . well, what's the use? You
cannot prove a surmise. He may mean that he represents in
his person an amalgam of the ingredient races that go to make
up the nation."

" He means that he is Ireland? Poor devil ! "

" Its countless Jameses, the Norman, Elizabethan, Crom-
wellian conquerors, merchants and mediocrities—all the in-
comers, in short, that make the Irish mosaic."

" That he is a walking amalgam ? "

" Or that the Irish Farrell has to bear on his back all the
rest of them—Normans, Elizabethans, etc. Or that he is
leading them in triumph—settlers, planters, merchants and
mediocrities, as well as the Shamuses of the people. So he is
a nation in himself."

" Whist ! " said Father McQuisten.

A red-nosed little rat of a man with sooty eyes, who wore a
long, faded overcoat for shirt, waistcoat and jacket, and had
just seated himself, looked up, and answered " Whist ! "
antiphonally.

Perhaps it was hearing this profane voice subconsciously
that brought the Librarian to the desk. His bright scalp,
added to the light from the attendant's dome, sent double rays
of warning towards the little man, who sank into his great-
coat, and remained motionless as a hibernating rodent.

Lyster is a lovable man, and I felt grateful when he beckoned
us to his Librarian's office. His brown beard moved a little as
he smiled, with cheeks fresh as a child's, while his whispering,
diffident, feminine voice invited us.

I saw him better when we had passed the barrier; a large,
broad, short, soft, suave man in a greyish-blue suit. He
indicated two arm-chairs and fussed about, though it was
evident that they could not be moved. With a sigh, he
prayed us to be seated.

" It is trying work, conducting a National Library," he
said. " You can have no idea of the difficulties which confront me. I am worn to a shadow, as one might say, endeavouring to keep the peace. I am at the disposal, at the mercy of
a public, some of whom are not trained for a room, not to
speak of a library. And then, even the students who come
here from the Universities are wholly undirected in their
reading. Without direction among so many books from the
different ages and countries, it is as if (nay, worse, since a
library is undying) the young students were suddenly to be

exposed in an arena to any danger. That is, if left undirected.
Any country can be an arena, without culture. And who is to
lead the mind in the direction of educational reading but I,
the Librarian? I believe that, next to the irremediable harm
of a general education by which they are left open to any
influence, any sinister author, the second grievous thing is
undirected reading. Do I bore you? No. Then let me
give you a few instances and examples of my difficulties.
They are equal to and almost—I will be bold to say it—quite
on a par with the responsibilities an Ambassador has to bear,
and charged with as great import for his nation. Think of
the harm Nietzsche could do to the half-informed minds of
some of our undergraduates. And yet, because doubtless of
some ' review,' I find his name put down not once but twice,
for those authors which are to be acquired by us. Some little
undeveloped fellow wants to glory vicariously in Battle!

"A medical student called the other day and demanded
the latest book on Surgery. We required that he fill in the
name of the author or, in these cases, editor. He said he did
not know it, but that we at least should know what were the
latest books. Do I bore you? No. Happily, I heard the
argument with the attendant at the desk. Infinite tact, as
you will see, is so necessary when dealing with a surly person.
The last thing is to be resentful, and our much-tried attendants
are apt so to be. ' If you don't know the name of the book
you want,' said one, ' how can you expect us to get it for you?
This is not a thought-reading salon you are in.' Gentlemen,
we were on the verge of a scene . . . a scene in a library!
Unthinkable!

"' But it is a thought-reading salon—what else is a library?
May I help you, sir?' I said. He seemed rather taken aback.
I merely meant that the thoughts of all the greatest minds are
here to be read. But either that appealed to him or did not,
or he had deeper forebodings than I could fathom. Much to
our relief, he left. If this is boring, pray interrupt me. . . .

"An engineering student fills in a form for Stott on Strains
and Stresses. What strange and invariably monosyllabic
names these writers have! I interpose: ' May I just offer
for your consideration—and I know it is cultivated—this most
appropriate poem of Kipling? After reading it, I am quite
convinced that you will have no time, nor, indeed, inclination,
for mere stresses.' The sons of Martha! How beautifully
and fully, without trigonometry, he indicates their function!

Not for a moment, mark you—and this is important—hinting or indicating that they are dissatisfied with their lot in life. Do I bore you? No. ' It is their care that the gear engages, it is their care that the switches lock.' What book on engineering could be so satisfying? Turn to his picture of the sons of Mary, the first-class passengers through life. Let us look at them lolling in a Pullman to Bath or Penzance. We see the lighted windows of the restaurant coach. We see the sons of Mary sipping in careless ease the good things of this world. Outside, the sons of Martha in the reasty tunnel! Is it not a masterpiece? If I bore you, stop me. So many schoolmasters are unable to realise the help I have given, the fillip I have endeavoured, in this my responsible post, to impart to higher education. Think of asking for a book on mathematics!

"Worst of all, perhaps, are the little uniformed fellows who are studying to be bank clerks. I commend them to Browning. Other brands saved from the burning."

"But not saved from the Browning," Austin whispered.

"To-day, Mr. Farrell had the grace to call in. He is interested in mediæval astronomy. He presented himself before the attendant, muttering ' Lytel Lewis, Lytel Lewis.' Did I allow my subordinates to put him to the question? No. The moment he quoted the title of Chaucer's dedication to his son, the ' Lytel Lewis ' of his essay on the Astrolabe, I was there to have it sent for. This is one of the few consolations of the librarian—to direct reading, not merely to serve it. Do I? No? Well, then, never forgetting that without my efforts this great library might easily degenerate into a mere annex of the Alexandra School or Wesley College, you will realise my difficulties. I am not . . .? Put my problems another way. A medical student has pawned his books. I have actually known it occur. He comes here. But what is my position? If I am to offer sanctuary from the Dublin pawnshops, I must wean him from the mere unimaginative side of his medical work, and take him into the higher realms and romantic fields of that great and noble profession. Rose and Carless on Surgery, or Osler on Medicine! One or other of these books are all he can envisage as being representative of the great tradition of medicine, wide as the ages! What are our educators doing? What an account shall they not have to render, deprecating imagination and degrading medicine to a rule of thumb! Separating man from the

Universe, from his starry bourne.   I say to medical students,
' Before perusing Osler, who is quite a modern author and
divorced from European tradition, might I not '—Do I bore
you ?—' suggest that you dip for a little into Paracelsus, that
Doctor of both Faculties, neither of which he deigns to
define ?   Surely your mind is not impervious to the charm of
those inadequately appreciated Middle Ages ? '   He signs a
docket, gentlemen, for Theophrastus von Hohenheim, that
' Para ' which, as you know from your Greek, is derived in the
sense of ' beyond ' Celsus, who held the medicine of the Mittel
Zeit in fee.   These students rarely revert, once having tasted
Castalia, otherwise this great library would be the ante-room
of the dissecting-room, a morgue, or, but for my vigilance, a
pathological department.   We are under the protection of the
Muses and the Minister for Education."

Of whom does he remind me, I wondered, as I watched the
Librarian ?   Not of the skipper on a Thames lighter, nor the
captain of a trawler in the North Sea.   His burly body and
that pleasant beard, the brow of a philosopher above the
broad shoulders of an athlete, and then that diffident, whispering, virginal voice.   I have it !   Plato, of course.   He is
Plato, the Broad.   And his subtile, inquiring, reasonable, if
fantastic, mind !   Will he reveal a tendency towards myths ?
Out of his time ; but yet associated in character with a Library,
an Academy for the whole town.   I should have thought of it
long ago !   Plato !

" You are very silent, gentlemen.   If I am boring you,
do not hesitate for one moment to call me to account.   But to
continue : If I am in difficulties with the lay and those untrained in thinking, imagine how multiplied those difficulties
must be when I am dealing with the theologian and minds
which are both subtile and sensitive.   But if I were to retreat
or to shirk my duties, I might as well abdicate.   Instead of
coming here for books, the danger would be that books would
be brought in to be perused here.   Then why a library ?
Exactly !   And books of the same kind as those in the library
of the late Boss Croker, who ordered a thousand volumes of
Algebra to decorate his walls.   Breviaries, not Algebras.
That was the possibility until, with the most delicate tact, I
met a situation which indeed wanted it.   A clergyman—a
friend of mine since the incident—called one day and, without
filling in any form, took up his place by the radiator and
proceeded to immerse himself in his Breviary.   Had I not

known of the spiritual problem which beset poor Father
McQuisten, of his struggles with the Fiend, his wrestlings with
visions of lingerie, or rather with the thoughts which a lady's
underclothing gave rise to, I could not have been in a position
to extend to him my help.   A very delicate position indeed!
I could not have had the advantage of his understanding of
my difficulty had he not been a man of wide reading and
common sense.   He was no Mr. Pepys and she was no Lady
Castlemaine.   Merely the bride of the neighbouring rector.

    " ' You read your Breviary by the radiator,' I said.   ' Well,
what about it?' said he, challengingly.   ' Nothing, that is
nothing of import,' said I, ' but I mean . . .'—You know
how easily one becomes confused in affairs of eschatology?—
' I do not mean to imply that reading of your Breviary means
nothing to me; but I was about to ask if your learning extends to a catholic appreciation of our treasures.'   Now here,
gentlemen, you observe my tact—' We have a very early
edition of the controversy regarding the Priscilliantists and
other Docetic heresiarchs with whose work you are doubtless
well acquainted.'   ' Docetic '—let us keep our Greek constantly
in repair as Dr. Johnson advises us to keep our friendship—
comes, as you gentlemen know, from ' δόκειν,' to appear.
These heretics held that our Divine Lord was a mere apparition, a wraith.   A dreadful heresy!   To some extent encouraged, of course, by the importance of His appearances
after death.   But yet, a dreadful heresy!   Our library rather
prides itself on its heresies, of which we have most erudite
commentaries.   The Ages of Faith—do I bore you?—when
hearts believed and built, one should couple with religious
reading, works on architecture: Byzantine, Transitional,
Gothic and Baroque.

    " ' But, Father, if you would care to have a table set apart
for your deeper studies I shall arrange it if you please, where
you would not be disturbed by the more frivolous and female
students of Medicine.   I find it so hard to make them read
anything but mere note-books, one might call them enchiridion
of Medicine: but your table, I will see to it myself, will be
kept well supplied with the more authentic records of the
heresies; and of what befell Pelagius, who opposed the view
that God's grace was destined for all men, but that man must
make himself worthy of it.   St. Augustine, who, as you are
doubtless aware, " endears himself to us by his mistress and
his illegitimate child."   I quote not myself—far be it from

me—but George Moore, a frequenter of this library and a
friend of our wistful stylist John Eglinton, who rebutted him.
Moore had the Dark Ages in his mind so far as a sense of
historical perspective went.   Yes, there is a translation of the
Confessions.   What Latin!   Only to be compared with
Lyly's Euphues . . . " *Nondum amarem sed amare amabam* . . ."
quite an obsession. . . .'   Do I bore you ?   Ah yes, the book
will be with you in a moment.

" Father McQuisten is a charming man, charming and
scholarly.   If you already know his story, forgive me—or,
rather, the story of his tragedy.   I am demanding too much
of your attention ?   No ?   How shall I explain it ?   Let me
put it like this.   He was as much the victim of propinquity
as of delinquency.

" The Vicarage and Parochial House, as is natural in
Ireland, were separated as far as could be considering the
size of the village ; but their gardens abutted on each other
at the end of their sheltered walks.   Their gardens abutted !
The Vicarage garden ended in a clothes'-line, the Parish
priest's garden ended in a privet hedge over which the clothes'-
line was clearly to be seen.   Clothes hung out to dry !   So
long as they were bachelor's garments they could by no means
be regarded as sails of escape from the daily round of un-
romantic fancies.   Oh, do I bore you ?   The Vicar married,
the Vicar married !   When his young bride was brought
home and her undies waved in the winnowing airs at the end
of the Vicarage garden, how futile must it have seemed to
Father McQuisten to read, ' *ne nos inducas in tentationem* ' when
the herbaceous border led directly down thereto !   There was a
disembodied ballet dancing in mid-air, where the sparrows of
Venus fly (you remember the first of Sappho ?) ' like an un-
bodied joy,' as that exquisite fellow Shelley has it, ' whose race
has just begun.'   Do I bore you ?   Can you forgive the over-
zeal of the devotee who, after three days' distraction, loaded
his twelve bore with double cracks and let fly, not at the para-
virginal cami-knickers, but at four of the Vicar's shirts which
in the interval good taste and modesty perhaps had interposed
for his lady's lingerie.   The shirts hung upside-down !
The outrage could be forgiven, the mistake never.
Imagine taking a shirt for a chemise ! "

" Appearances were against him," I ventured to suggest.

" Ah, of course—I relied on you to see it !   A form of
Docetism, nothing else !   A form of Docetism !

"That recasts the creed of the Phantasiasts."

"All we want is to be understood." And he smiled suavely with a twinkle of mischief, as I thought.

At length we escaped.

"What an extraordinary fellow!" I said to Austin. "One is never allowed to get a word in."

"No, nor the book one wants."

"Why should one be? I thought the fellow most amusing: saving engineers by Kipling; budding bankers by bad verse; suspended priests by heresies. He calls it snatching brands from the burning. I heard you whisper that it would be better to snatch the bank clerks from Browning."

"I did not quite say that. Why are you so hard on Browning?"

"Because he didn't keep on banking. He introduced jazz into English verse, on account of his mixed blood no doubt. There is black blood in him somewhere, that is why he was called Browning—it comes out in the tom-tom of his verse.

'Beautiful Evelyn Hope is dead,
    Rumptity, rum pity; don't look dour!
This was her table, that was her bed;
    And here her last leaf of geranium flower.'"

"I rather like it. The economy with which he makes a scene is amazing."

"But, then, the cross-word puzzles of his poems. He anticipated cross-words. He kept so many people guessing that he got a reputation for depth and for poetry out of all proportion to the beauty he evoked in words. Instead of 'fundamental brainwork,' there is only something foundered beneath the surface. What porridge!

"The nearest he got to poetry was 'A chorus-ending of Euripides,' and Mrs. Browning. He depends for half his effect on our associations of ideas with the Greek; for the rest on his wife. His inspiration is rarely original. It is literature begotten on literature, Caliban upon Mrs. Browning. Where is his equivalent to what is created out of nothing :—

'Come unto these yellow sands'?

"His muse is as much invalid as his wife was invalide. I much prefer Longfellow, who does not turn your mind into a war dance, but he leaves it cool and smooth.

'As he leaned upon the railing,
    And his ships came sailing, sailing,
    Northward into Drontheim fjord.'

And smoothness is one of the three indispensables of poetry.
Yes.   Browning is only suited for reading in banks.   There is
a Browning Society in England whose members assure each
other that they understand him.   When I read his translation
of Æschylus, I find it very useful to have the Greek beside me
so that I may find out what the English means.   He does not
write poetry, but his prose pulsates.

" Then those medical students for whom he has prescribed
a course of mediæval quackery!   And his priest studying
heresy!   What an amusing fellow ! "

" I never listened to more suave and childlike irreverence
in my life."

" I saw nothing irreverent in it."

" You would not be likely to, being irreverent yourself."

" So you have succumbed to the Pelagian heresy, which
would deny me God's grace.   A heresy whose chief was an
Irishman from, as Dr. Macalister suggests, Tibroney, where a
lot of ' Fly Boys ' from Roman persecutions had collected.
An archetype of Bray.   The people who think that priests
must be regarded as dehumanised sicken me.   You would
respect the butler more than the nutriment, the barometer
more than the weather, and would be afraid to tap at it. . . . I
am, as I have often sadly realised, the only true Catholic in
this town, who lives his religion and does not excommunicate
the clergy, who are a large part of our life, from a share in that
life, as if they were already relics.   If we are to have a living
Catholicism, you must not treat the clergy as outside life.
You may have the Faith but, like a score of Irishmen, you
have lost the tradition and the great amplitude of the Church.
You are as bad as ex-President Cosgrave, whose piety greatly
embarrassed His Holiness the Pope."

" Is that why the ex-President took you to Rome ? "

" Precisely.   He knew that I had been there before and
that I had lived in Austria when that great Catholic country
was a living Empire.   The Holy Roman Empire, in effect.
There one could see the clergy sharing the lives of the
people."

" That does not explain why it was necessary to take you
to Rome."

" He wanted somebody who would not be considered to be
bringing coals to Newcastle.   Had there been the least
doubt about my orthodoxy, do you think I would have been
given a large gold medal by the Pope ? "

"You got it by mistake. He probably intended it for the President."

"Nonsense. Have you lost your faith in Infallibility? The Holy Father is infallible as I have reason to believe. It is you who are heterodox, and not I."

"You are irreverent."

"It makes me sad to hear people, who never went to Rome, talking of irreverence in Ireland. They are all suffering from a feeling of inferiority to Protestantism yet. They deny themselves joy in religion, and they conduct themselves as if their clergy were a lot of old maids or parsons' wives. They forget that the Devil is the Spirit who Denies."

At that moment a strange desk-deformed figure appeared, leaning to one side with head cast down sideways over a despatch case: the despatch case, the invariable sign of revolutions which end successfully for the petty intriguers and bureaux rats. He was low sized, in a blue double-breasted overcoat and the usual black trilby hat. His face was thin, with loose, lemon-coloured flesh hanging down on each side from his mouth, which looked as if someone had suspended a bat upside down from his nose. His eyes were like zinc.

"Who is that?"

"That's Cascara the Economist, the greatest catabolite of the new system. I don't care whether you think me superstitious or not, but I'm off now! This place is uncanny."

"That's the way you went on when Miss Bellowson appeared. . . . Don't let me think that you really are, after all, only a figure in the mind of a lunatic."

"Forgive me, old man, but I really must be going. What are any of us but figures in the National mind?"

I had to remove myself. I should have had too much hatred to sustain, and contempt, had I remained in the precincts of the Government building, with that nasty little Cassius hard by. All that is scheming, mean, humourless and vile resides in that sinister figure: all that makes for the eternal ineffectuality of the native. The little bagman, the Firbolg, with his sinister little lack-lustre eye on the look-out for recognition he had never earned. That's the first phase of Communism in this country. His teeth are black from mouthing "The Republic." Soon it will be the Union of Soviets. Ireland a Society of gullible slaves dominated by an over-salaried hypocritical bureaucrat. There is, I am glad to say, but one other scoundrel in Dublin equal to that fellow. He is the undersized, big-skulled, streamy-eyed solicitor, who is making up by an old age of viciousness for a middle age gone grey in regularity and religious duties, which he found an unwelcome but indispensable preliminary to stalking rich widows in Gardiner Street. Even now, I suppose he is sneaking to Mount Street on his way to take out in kind what he can no longer extract in cash from some poor woman whom his tentacles surround. This is known as " being kind to his clients " !

My mind cannot entertain hatred long. It upsets the physicochemical equilibrium of my blood. . . . Mount Street : Pleasants Street, Mount Pleasant Avenue ! What a wonderful town ! There was one thing that made Our Lord lose His patience, and that was hypocrisy. Then who can blame me for my Christian attitude to these humbugging sneaks ? That coffin-worm of a solicitor devouring widows and orphans, and the little yellow leprechaun who stole power through a confidence trick on the ignorance and illusions of an electorate equally narrow, and who now persecute the Irish people in the name of The Irish People, and seek for a continuance of power by bringing about catastrophic collapse of all the old honest forms of profit-making.

Get this into your head, Austin : it behoves us more than ever to support the Church at this moment, seeing that it was never before so gravely threatened, and by self-seeking deceptive curs such as that. I would be the last to weaken it, seeing that the alternative to it in this country is a reign of plague-bearing rats.

> O Signor mio, quando saro in lieto
>   a veder la vendetta, che, nascosa,
>   fa dolce l'ira tua nel tuo segreto ?

The heresy politicians suffer from is belief in themselves.

§

The three best streets in Dublin are those that run from south to north parallel from St. Stephen's Green to Trinity College—Grafton Street, Dawson Street and Kildare Street. Grafton Street is connected to Dawson Street transversely by Duke Street, and likewise Dawson Street to Kildare Street by Molesworth Street. These streets are a little over one hundred yards in length. The three first-named streets are closed by three different views of Trinity College, which redeems their present-day drabness by the grey, substantial dignity of the Eighteenth Century. It is hard to say which street has the loveliest vista. Grafton Street shows the great window, wreathed in roses of sculptured stone, of Professor Tyrrell's spacious rooms. The campanile beyond, with its beautiful cupola of newer stone, leaves dark the shoulder and the mighty roof of the library in the full majesty of its age. But Kildare Street has to pay for its two museums, its Government Houses and its Royal College of Physicians, by giving up any vista but that of the railings of the College Park and the roofs of rickety houses beyond. Dublin, on the north, is bounded by the Eighteenth Century, as Seumas O'Sullivan says.

Pointing to Trinity, " That is where all the trouble originated," I said to O'Duffy, one of the few men left who can understand a reference, and debate a theory without flying into a rage or seething with hushed hate. " That is where it all began in the early Seventeenth Century, when the Virgin Queen founded Trinity College—the College of the Holy and Undivided Trinity. The very term ' Undivided ' is almost a prophetic cynicism."

" The Virgin Queen," he repeated. " I saw somewhere how a little girl in a history paper said, ' Queen Elizabeth was the Virgin Queen. As a Queen she was a great success.'

" She succeeded in throwing a pretty apple of discord into Ireland when she founded a college and promulgated the idea of ' Freedom ' to break up the native Chieftains. There was no word in the Irish language for Freedom as she wished it to be understood, or as she wanted it for purposes of disruption. And it was not very hard to win the native from his ' allegiance ' to his Chief, or to send that Chief on the run before his ' tenants.' She made him about as popular as a latter-day landlord by suggesting the new idea—and any new idea, no matter whence it comes or how rotten it may be, will stampede the Irish into enthusiasm. We have Moscow's anti-God and anti-mother love and anti-family. Our little Dermot McMurroughs invite not the Normans now, but Friends of the World to Ireland. So she told them first of ' fixity of tenure.' Instead of merely having grazing lands annually allotted to them, on which it was not worth while and probably forbidden to build, she said, ' Pay me a shilling and your Chiefs cannot shift you,' or words to that effect. Why, it was as disastrous as a Methodist Mission to the naked and non-venereal natives of the South Seas. The mere Irish became infected with Freedom, but they quite characteristically cornered it for themselves, as they do to the present day. Every tribe became a monopolist of ' True Freedom.' Whether they fought with each other mattered little to the Chieftain, who was not included when the new-found panacea was being dispensed. But they all fell into Elizabeth's hands and the hands of England : ' enslaved,' as they call it now ; but it was ' freed ' while it suited them."

"Poor devils ! " I said, " at the mercy of an unexamined catch-cry !—as they are down to the present day."

"I have not the least pity for them. They may be poor devils, but they can still make those connected with them devilishly poor. Look at them now, they are trying to ' free ' themselves from civilisation : ' to be self-contained ' like a wild cat with an imperforate anus. We are told that it is an impertinence to call us British. It is we who are to be made *remotos ab orbe*, by ourselves.

"Politics is the chloroform of the Irish People or, rather, the hashish."

"They are the stock-in-trade of that little skunk, what's-his-name. He will soon be discredited."

"He is discredited already in my mind in the term of your description. He is not a skunk. That animal, as you know——"

"I know."

"But it is the other end with him."

"I saw him the other day with a despatch box. The usual symbol of sovereignty of these little commissars. He secretly was on the look out for a salute from a policeman. There is nothing more sinister than the humility of the mean. The earliest natives were ' bagmen ' too. The low-grade Firbolgs, the Plain Men ! "

" His bag is probably full of notes on a Catholic Socialist Republic and other deceptive contradictions. He would prohibit the sale of contraceptives, and yet in mercy to his wife not wear a gas-mask. We are ready to impose on others the shortcomings of ourselves."

"You remember how those citizens in *Julius Cæsar* ' threw up their sweaty night-caps, and . . .' "

" Oh, my dear fellow, don't go on with it. How Shakespeare hated the plain men! He knew too much about them. He had to live too closely to them when he was side-stepping the Puritans, to whom he was a public enemy. Professor Hotson, who discovered more about him from Harvard than all England from London, showed that he was what we would call a gunman of sorts with steel on hip, an associate of Falstaff's ' harlotry players ' and touts. How he got time and peace to write amazes me. ' Sometimes he excused himself as one in pain.' He would not go the way Jack Green went. He had to be sober sometimes, and yet he had time to indulge in whatever gave him that stroke which is apparent in his last signatures : hemiplegia. Otherwise, why retire and die at fifty-two ? Eighty would be more like it nowadays : Tennyson, Bridges, Watson. . . . Only the other day Yeats pointed out to me the curious fact that Shakespeare never praised Elizabeth."

" What about ' Who is Sylvia ? ' ? "

" Yes, who and what (the hell) is she, that swains commend her ? How he escaped from being drawn into politics is a mystery. He must have had a close squeak when Essex was discredited. He must have been a kind of George Russell, one recognised as a literary man and one of whom politics is no more to be expected than meanness from a parish priest."

" Perhaps you have met a mean politician ? "

By this, we were come to College Green. Grattan in bronze hailed with uplifted right hand the statues of Burke and Goldsmith, the gentle Irish Virgil, but who, of course, now cannot be acknowledged as Irish by the little unreckonable rats who have done nothing for Ireland save use the word as a fool-trap for votes and office from the uninformed and unemployed. " Ireland " has come to be as deadly and as degenerating an incantation as " Freedom " was in the days of the Virgin Queen. Virgins have done a deal of harm in this island. And marriage does nothing to soften their dissatisfaction with life. It cannot be all the fault of the men. It must be the hardness of our women that is driving men to politics. A little slogan formed itself in my mind, a cry to the women of Ireland : " More petting, less politics." I was able to tell it to O'Duffy. I find it so hard to withhold what seems to me to be a witticism, especially when it is just born. But O'Duffy is bad enough on the Present State of Ireland, without drawing him out further on the subject of all the old trots who go about wreaking their insatiable illusions and desire for exhibitionism on the youth of the land. No, I said to myself, I will wait until I meet Hackett. He's the lad that will laugh. Or O'Connor, when he comes up again. His nose will cream and wrinkle when he expatiates on Our Hard Women. . . .

While I absented myself momentarily in thought from my friend, he was looking down Dame Street.

" What are they doing over there ? " he asked, pointing to a platform of timber which was being put up.

" There is to be an address by the True Republicans this evening, I believe. I saw it in a copy of their paper, which has since been suppressed."

" Suppressed ? "

" By the less true, because more prosperous, Republicans. Once Republicans get into office, it becomes the turn of the disgruntled to delve deeper for the pay-dirt of the ' Republic ' through adits so narrow that they can be counted on to defy anyone drawing a salary as a Minister. They become *truer* Republicans . . . so inaccessibly true that the only way one can co-operate with them is by giving them a vote towards office and a thousand pounds a year less Income Tax and free motoring. Then they hand on the baton, or rather, the baton is taken up by a still lower stratum, who in turn become inaccessible, or rather, in what is to be the next turn, unapproachable. . . ."

" Which Truists are holding the meeting this evening, did you hear ? "

" Naturally the ones with an axe to grind. . . . Let us come to it."

" My dear sir, not for worlds would I listen to those scoundrels. I would put them into a labour battalion with no labour leader, but a British infantry sergeant instead. And when one of them had done even one honest day's work— voluntarily, mind you—then that one could go out. He would have been handled and made.   The only good Irishman is an ex-Service man."

Now, why did I not think of that ? I asked myself, envious again because, without the friction of my mind, where would O'Duffy's flint have been ?   However, I will remember it : I shall say it, as Whistler prophesied of Oscar Wilde in like circumstances.   But what good is an epigram if it lacks a receptive hearer ?   To whom shall I repeat ' The only good Irishman is an ex-Service man ' ? I don't care from what army. Will I be brave enough to father it or to put it back on O'Duffy ? That's a good idea ! If it be not too well received, I shall take the authorship on my own shoulders ; whereas if it score a success, I will give credit where credit is due. There is this truth in it, anyway : Discipline is our greatest need.   Otherwise we are only yeast to raise other people, among whom we are transplanted, to prominence, if not success. . . .

§

So I shall have to go alone to the show.   I will not stay long.   The crowd is always more interesting to me than the speakers.   I cannot help regarding politicians as that genius, poor Tom Kettle, saw them, " partly mountebanks." But the crowd.   There is nowhere a wittier, or cheerfuller, or more good-natured crowd than in Dublin.   Profane, obscene, they come out of the Seventeenth Century with a power of expression that rivals, or rather, is that of the English of Elizabeth, a language in which it was possible to say more with a few words than we can say now with all the abused words in our swollen vocabulary.   I will try the effect of this on O'Duffy.   I waved my finger as if marking time for a quotation.   I caught his attention.   " Listen :

' The natives leave the right arms of their infant males unchristened, as they call it, to the end that they may give a more ungracious and ungodly blow when they strike, which things not only show how they are carried away by traditious obscurities, but do also intimate how full their hearts are of inveterate revenge.' "

He picked it out at once with a little mocking laugh.

" ' Traditious obscurities '—the very words to describe what it would take a page to demonstrate : the mutterings, ill-feelings, that ' hushed hate ' which, as Shane Leslie declares, is the root of Irish melancholy, the withheld minds, emotions instead of reasons—all that goes to the make-up of the soul of a race that never beat anybody but itself and hates itself for others' excellence, is summed in ' obscurities.' And as for ' traditious,' I suppose it means treasons of sorts, or perhaps traditional and race inability to fling words straight and true. . . ."

We were stopped by a sudden figure, a stout, middle-aged man, with an immense W-shaped black moustache like the horns of an aurochs, under a green Tyrolean hat.

" Ha, ha ! " he said. " And to what problem of the time are my eminent friends devoting themselves ?   I am waiting for the White Terror. I have not shot anybody for ages. I must begin again ! "

" The White Terror, Marshal, I never heard of that ? "

" Never heard of the White Terror ?   Ah, my good friend, it is well for you that you did not. But I have heard of it and experienced it. It comes after the Red Terror. Have you never heard of Bela Kuhn ? "

He closed one eye and moved his right arm in a martial gesture which made me see him, a sole survivor, surrounded by innumerable dead in some quite unaccountable battlefield. I tried to feel impressed, but I could not spur myself into an ardour for a terror, which had a terror interposed. I gazed at the Ionic pillars on the curved bulk of the edifice, which Shelley regretted had degenerated from the Temple of Liberty to the Halls of Mammon. The light caught the bayonet of the sentry and shone on his " Nugget "-polished gaiters. The leather leggings of the Free State soldiers are the brightest things in the town. I found myself ignored and my companion, possibly for his greater credulity and access to enthusiasm, not to mention admiration, preferred.

After some time the Marshal observed my inattention and noticed that my eye was on a soldier of the guard. He bade farewell to O'Duffy, but to me he said on parting :

" Ha ! the bayonets will be flashing. Wait until you see."

He marched away, leaving me feeling that soon, through some obscure fault of mine, I was to witness and even be involved in some hosting of bayonets which boded me no good.

What am I to do ? I asked myself. Am I to believe in all his nonsense, or make an enemy of him for life ? He

always alarms me with his ancestral voices " prophesying war."
I saw the bemused look O'Duffy wore.

"Does that man really exist?" he asked. "Do you think
we are in for another revolution?"

"My whole field of vision is unreal," I said. "It is
peopled by extraordinary beings. The moment I begin to
think martially, this absurd impersonation of militarism
appears, but his presence here somehow reassures me. You
see, I met him some years ago when he was just about to
march in triumph through Hyde Park. But do you mind if
we turn into Trinity? We can emerge by the Lincoln Place
Gate."

"Have you met the O'Donovan of the Glens?"

"Yes."

"And you know the Glen of the Downs in wooded
Wicklow?"

"Who does not?"

"Well, the Marshal and the O'Donovan announced themselves full-titled to a nervous parlour-maid in Kingstown,
who opened her mistress's door in a hurry and called: ' The
Glen of the Downs, ma'am.' "

" *Intonsi montes !* "

The red brick behind the campanile fulfilled the note of
warmth amid the grey stone of the College quads which the
pink hawthorns lend it in Spring.

The way through the Front Gate divides the great quad
of Trinity College, which opens on a large cobbled space on
the third side, into two equal squares. In the lawn of each
stands a great oak. Old grey houses with windows framed
in lighter stone shelter the immense trees. In front, the
graceful campanile stands between the library and the
Graduates' Memorial, backed by two lawns and the Queen
Anne wing. Nearer, the Chapel faces the Examination Hall.
Equal lawns intervene. It took me a long time to accept
the intrusion of red brick among the grey walls, but now it
lends a warm background to the campanile and tones with
the hawthorns in the grassy spaces.

Is there any College in the world that for its size has sent
within the few centuries since it was founded more famous
men near and far? I asked. Sterne, Burke, Goldsmith,
Hamilton of Quaternion fame, Fitzgerald who anticipated
Marconi and was the first who had the courage to put his
convictions of flight to the test in a glider from the parapet

of the Engineering School. Her degrees are honoured farther afield than many colleges go.

Untidy undergraduates were grouped about the chains. Lady undergraduates unwilling to relinquish cap and gown floated across the path.

Left and right the dark portals of the house gloomed sullenly. That one over there, the last next to the Examination Hall, leads to the Provost's house, but no figure emerges. I remember the time when in full light on the cobbles stood the greatest Provost of them all—Sir John Pentland Mahaffy. Over six-foot and over seventy, unbowed, with head slightly inclined, I see him talking to some attentive Fellow, and I await the dismissal with a wave of the hand and the supercilious smile. " If they must learn Irish, teach them that beautiful pre-Gaelic speech of which only three words remain. Anyone with a little aptitude can learn them in a week . . ." and he would walk away slowly with the right toe turned in somewhat, as if he stood at a wicket. But nothing appears in the doorway, and I try to realise my feelings. Yes. I know to what to compare my disappointment at the loss of animation at the doorway. It is as when I went to the Zoo as a child and, wandering round in the overheated house, I came to a cage with a little box with a black opening. The tenant hid within. Where is the Marmoset ? " Ah, you should come here, sonny, at feeding-time." Why are there no Mahaffys now and none to take their place ? Because great figures belong to great periods, and great periods are those in which the eternal truths are assured. There is no slithering of the very cardinal points of life, nor is religion regarded as a mere historical phenomenon subject to waxing and waning. There is no one left now to point out with a sneer, with that thing the Greeks called eutrephelia, well-bred arrogance, the fallacy of all this modernism and Bolshevic " philosophy," no one to draw the student's attention to the answer to sidelong truths such as these modernist professors of history teach. We ourselves wax and wane, but that alters not our nature or the value of our beliefs.

A space between the buildings revealed Botany Bay.

" Just look at that slum, built after the Union. It is enough to justify any Revolution. The misery began in Trinity College the moment the Irish Parliament left College Green. And not a word of protest. They haven't the daring to say a word for themselves even now, or to raise a voice against the travesty of Freedom which has come to be more disastrous to Trinity College than the Union of 1800. If the Botany Bay quad was justifiably called after the Penal settlements more than one hundred years ago, what should they call it now?"

"It ought to be the first object for clearance by the College Society for demolition of the slums. What culture can penetrate such hideousness? It is almost as great an eyesore as the Rotunda Gardens. What is the Provost doing?"

"He is engaged in the study of old Irish."

"I cannot quite see the connection."

"No, but you can see the slob land of Botany Bay."

We pass under the Library, one of the five great Libraries which can lay claim to a free copy of every book printed in Great Britain or Ireland. We passed the results of Ruskin's *Stones of Venice*, the Engineering School. They were open to intimations in those days. A beautiful building—perhaps the most beautiful modern building in Dublin. The sweet smell of new-mown grass flowed from the spacious Park.

"What a beautiful space in the grimy city! A kind of sunken plain between the raised rampart of Nassau Street, which was made when the Thing-mote was demolished. This Park must be very wide."

"It extends, roughly, from the wall over there to the place where the first Norse founders of the city landed and erected their stone. It stood where the Crampton Monument now stands."

"Oh, the Crampton Monument. I know it—in Brunswick Street. Strange, that a monument should be erected to Crampton. You know the story of his rather unfortunate marriage? His wife and he suffered more from incompatibility of stature than of temperament. So she left him *a mensa et thoro*, to stand, as it were, 'on the floor,' like my grandfather's clock. I always think of my grandfather's clock when I think of Crampton and his monument."

"Surely you do not mean 'it was taller by half'?"

"No. It is much taller. It dwarfs his bust as the Parnell obelisk dwarfs Parnell."

"And there was Coffee, with a reputation like Crampton's, who took part in private theatricals, but classic drama would have made him. He was cast for a lead in the Lysistrata playing opposite to the widow of a late Lord Mayor. His funeral was magnificent. It is a pity that these warriors who have fought in love *non sine gloria* should not have a funeral with military observances instead of a plain lid to their coffins."

" With music."

" And to be buried at St. Satyr, like Michel, as Villon has it ! "

" I see that they are rolling the pitch. We shall have cricket soon. I like to drop in of a summer evening to watch the cricket here. What town has so central a playing-field ? I was amused one day—I forget the match—to see Endymion solemnly stalking round the field. He said, ' I must walk round four times sun-wise so that the other side may win.' "

Endymion again ! I thought ; will I never get away from him ? How can I, if I believe the uncomfortable innuendo of Austin that I am but a figment of his mind ?

Recovering my good spirits, I said : " I bet one thing, and that is that Endymion never revealed for which side he was circling the field."

" Now that I come to think of it, I really believe he did not. Isn't that odd ? "

" Quite, quite," I said. " Oh yes, quite odd, and maybe more so. . . ."

O'Duffy looked disturbed : " Have I ? Is there anything wrong ? I meant nothing more than what is on the surface, Endymion. . . ."

" Oh, let us drop cricket . . . prepare for the Black Death. We are passing the Pathological Laboratory. They had a goose there once with enough diseases, tropical and otherwise, to kill half Dublin. The yard of the Laboratory abuts on the back of Fanning's snug (as it used to be then) in Lincoln Place. About Christmas we snared the goose with the blind-cord and hauled it up, *pâté de foie gras* and all ; and, having quietly dispatched it, presented it to Fanning."

" But surely he must have heard the row ? "

" It made very little row. You are not allowing for its reservoir of sleeping sickness. Our gift was gratefully received and lavishly reciprocated."

" It laid the Golden Egg ; but what happened to Fanning ? "

" It did more. If you saw Fanning you would realise that nothing ever happens to him. Even Time has not happened to him. He has not lost a hair of his head, the best head of hair in Dublin, a sable silvered, and he is as straight as a cricket

stump; lively too, though seventy. Not to be caught nap-
ping. I attribute it all to our antidotal Christmas present.
That goose laid the Golden Age in Lincoln Place. Perhaps
you would like to drop in and have a word with Senator
Fanning. We can put his vintage to the proof. You will
then be able to verify my miracle." But the dapper little
man drew away. He was afraid of entering a public-house.
So few of us are really emancipated. And yet we have more
freedom than we can dare use. It is our bogies that enslave
us, not England. " Cannot I have mine ease in mine inn ? "
The most pathetic cry in all literature. And now in the
1105th year from the founding of this City of the Taverns
by the great Wassailers from the North a Dublin citizen
fights shy of an inn. You might think that this city was
Belfast.

As we entered Lincoln Place my eye caught on the opposite
side of Leinster Street a spare figure of a man about sixty.
His back was turned. His arms were outstretched at full
length sideways from his shoulders and his hands, upturned
at right angles to his wrists, followed each other in parallel
movements like those of a figure on the wall in a tomb in
Egypt.

" What is that fellow doing ? "

" Too well I know (I'll say good-bye to you here): he is
explaining to a friend a patent device for motor signals."

" Good heavens ! "

" Good-bye."

I dived into Fanning's.

The Senator looked up from his evening paper.

" Good-evening, Boss. A moment now ? "

A bolt slid back, and a door of a snug opened immediately
on my left. " Come into the fire," and he waved his hand to
the sun which lit the cosy.

" And how has the world been using you ? "

" The world's all right, if it were not for this Government."

He was started. He refrains from speaking in the Senate,
for he is choleric and eloquent. But——. " Gyroscope
yourself down into a region of calm now for a moment ! "

Surprised, I subsided, I who imagined myself to be tranquil.

" Lookit here, now. Those flounderers have the country
bloody well ruined. Do you know the latest ? They have
issued permits to send cattle across to England, and there's a
regular trade in these permits most of which have got into the

hands of Jewmen and blackguards who never had anything on more than two feet in their houses except a cockroach!"

" Is it as bad as that?"

" Worse!"

" But why should there be permits at all?"

" Now you're talking! The country's fallen into the hands of a bunch of gutties whose knowledge of land is confined to the clay of the geranium in the tenements in which they were born. Then they talk of factories! Then they talk of factories, and they have taken the backbone out of the best factory in the world, the land of Ireland, and lodged it up in Mountjoy prison—that's where the real farmers are!"

" I blame it on the Long Fellow listening to that little yellow bittern," I said. " Look at us now! We have lost in fourteen years what it took forty to achieve: fixity of tenure for farmers and our fiscal freedom. Freedom is hard to come by, but harder still to hold. If De Valera was in the pay of England's secret service he couldn't do Ireland half the harm that he is doing it now."

The dark eyes blazed with indignation. Words failed him. He shook his head. Suddenly the fresh face relaxed: " What are you having?"

" Some of your excellent sherry."

He called to an attendant. " That's all right. This is on the house."

" I wouldn't hear of it. You must let me . . ."

" Well, the next one, then. Pay of England. He's worse! England never leaves a country so crippled that she cannot do business with it, but this——"

He was called away, but I knew that between calls he would look in at the first lull. He reappeared bodily.

" So that's what ' Freedom ' did for us: made us poorer under a native Government than when we were being ' robbed and held in bondage ' by Great Britain?"

" Aye. And they haven't got enough of it yet. It's a Republic they want for the thirty-two counties, when they are afraid of taking it for the twenty-six. ' Bring in the North ' me neck! Think of the chance they have of bringing in Ulster when Ulster sees those it threw out as failures and mischief-makers running this country to worse mischief and greater failure still! ' Bring in the North ' indeed!"

A lull. I sipped my sherry. He returned.

" There was a fellow telling me the other day that the

real reason Guinness is leaving Dublin is that they are afraid of the Communism that this Government is letting grow up from its blundering and incapacity.   Lord Iveagh's responsibility is so great that he cannot risk stoppage of supplies even for a week.   And with the recovery of England that we are supposed to be bankrupting, he must go where he has an increasing market.   There has been a transport strike going on now for two months.   Who is it that would be bankrupt ? "

" It's what they are accustomed to that they extend to others, bankruptcy and failure."

" And what are strikes but the preliminaries of Bolshevism ? "

" They certainly have succeeded in making politics incompatible with prosperity," I ventured.

" There'll be plenty of prosperity for Mesopotamian rats and mongrels that are sneaking into this country to benefit by the countless tariffs and Orders-in-(bloody)-Council. God, it's awful to see a fine rich country turned into a poorhouse for manufactured paupers and unemployed."

" I cannot see a grain of hope anywhere," I said sadly.

" Hope, is it ?   You might as well be looking for an earwig in the Phœnix Park."

" With the Silk of the Kine slaughtered, the slums increasing, and the cream of our youth transported by thousands, De Valera is about as good a nation-builder as an advocate of birth-control."

" Abso-bloody-lutely ! " said Mr. Fanning.

CHAPTER II

AS I LEFT THE HOSPITABLE HOUSE WHICH WAS "TOO CLEAN" FOR James Joyce I thought I saw a movement in an incredible place. High up in the blank wall of a house, the first letter in Oxo opened to disclose a window, and revealed a head with the lined, vexatious, aquiline face of a clean-shaven, middle-aged man. It looked like the head of a cavalry officer. "Dammit!" it said; and the window was closed. It was Thwackhurst, a collector of graffiti. As I went, I thought I heard the mewing of a cat.

Debating what this apparition might mean—was he looking for his cat, only to find it in the precipitous yard from which it could not escape; or was he merely giving vent to emotions necessarily pent up during a conversation with his landlady? I passed the Kildare Street Club, the landlords' Club, the Club that "dear Edward" used to call the cod bank, from the silver heads shoaled high in its great windows. It is a museum of such as are left now; where the old ornaments from the past century compare with the gold ornaments of more archaic days. "With silver and gold. . . ." So that is where Yeats found at last the Land of Heart's Desire. I wondered what possessed that wise man to become a member of such an establishment. His wish must have come from that protective and self-inspiring dream of his which exalted the Anglo-Irish in his mind to become the "greatest breed in Europe." We have to sing our own Magnificats, or go mad. I thought of the poet of Sicily "pasturing his visionary flocks," and it explained the poet of Sligo's wish to patronise his visionary tenants. A safe proceeding, provided it occurs only retrospectively in imagination. The old landlords betrayed their country, so the popular rumour has it. But nobody can betray Ireland: it does not give him the chance; it betrays him first. The landowners merely fell between two stools and two railway stations—Kingstown and Euston. Since Lord Dunraven died and Horace Plunkett, they have not left a notable name in their Club, save that of their last comer, Yeats, and he will be about as sib to them as Daniel O'Connell's memory is to the Masonic Lodge round the corner in Molesworth Street, where his regalia are still preserved. Between these thoughts and considerations whether I should attend the meeting fixed for the late evening in College Green, I lost my alertness.

A voice challenged: "You were trying to cut me," and, looking up, I saw the Bud smiling. His arms were by his side and his attitude was full of quiet hopefulness. "You have a chance to come in on it now. There never was such a time as the present for initiative and enterprise. There are hundreds of thousands of tons of it; and a deep-sea harbour at Port na Cloy. The world's market is about a hundred thousand tons short every year. Mullin is interested, and has gone over to study the problem in Cornwall, where they are finding ever-increasing difficulties as they go down. I can let you in on it if you can put up the money at once. I have to be off to Paris to make arrangements. . . . I may have to be away for a fortnight. It's practically now or never. We have an option on Mrs. McNulty's holding."

"But," I asked, confused and yet trying to retain my reason, "what is it?"

He stood back and regarded me sternly for a moment before letting the righteous contempt, which his regard expressed, melt into commiseration.

"You don't mean to say you don't know? You don't know that there are about three hundred million tons of it, of the finest quality in the world, lying untouched in Mayo and the deep-sea slip at Port na Cloy! One hundred pounds a ton f.o.b., and there you go."

I knew that if I asked again, again the pantomime. I hoped he would think I guessed. I replied as if considering a revelation.

"But why must you go to Paris if the stuff is in Mayo? Can't you ring them up?"

"My dear sir, my very dear sir, who could do business with Paris satisfactorily by long-distance telephone? Most unsatisfactory, not to add impossible. I might take a specimen with me, but business—no, sir, nothing doing on the line."

If I had stayed where I was happy at Fanning's this would not have happened, I thought. I will certainly tell George about it. This is a matter for that stern daughter of the voice of George—his Muse.

"I have no money," I faltered. "Who has, these times?"

"Then you or they will never have it, and never deserve to have it, if chances like this are let slip."

A bright thought: "What is it for?"

"What is it for? Why, for all high-temperature cement, for 'gilling' paper—for making anything, in fact, that is to be made out of kaolin."

(So it's kaolin.)   Nevertheless I'll tell George.

" Was it you I saw demonstrating the robot signalling apparatus half-an-hour ago ? "

" Now don't get off the subject.   There is a world shortage of a hundred thousand tons, and the Cornish mines are petering out.   They may be ballsed up already for all I know. We just want to get a few of us together and to form a syndi- cate : not a Company, mind you—that will come later, but we must all be in first on the ground floor."

" Why don't you apply to the Government under the Trades' Accommodation Development Grant ? "

" The Government !   Is there one of them what knows what China clay is ? "

" Kaolin," said I, glibly.

" But you're an educated man, quick on the uptake ; and you understand things.   (A twinge of hypocrisy made me more tolerant : maybe I will not tell George after all.)   And you realise the importance of keeping it to ourselves."

" Well, I wish you luck.   But as things are at present there is no hope for anything that requires foresight and enterprise developing, while there is so much uncertainty as to the future."   I was going to sketch the difficulties of getting a market, but I wanted to be off.

" I will walk as far as your corner," he said.

We turned the corner.   I made a minatory sign as I pointed to the bank.   It suggested that I could not pay the expenses of his specific visit to Paris.

" I'll be hopping off."   And he was gone.   A good- hearted fellow caught in the dream that there was any- thing left that had not been skinned long ago from the country.

After all, curiosity brought me to the Republicans' meeting—that is, the meeting of the true Republicans.   As I guessed, all signs of the platform had gone.   The speeches were to be delivered from a lorry which would drive up without advertising itself to the Guards.

There was little trace of a crowd, but that one would form as quickly when the lorry did arrive as it forms when you are swearing at a collided motor, I was aware.

Down Trinity Street it came.   It halted where once the statue to King William stood, destroyed by those as regardless of historical landmarks as the Vandals who seized the Four

Courts and burned their country's records—records which had been spared even by the Danes.

There were six men, and, of course, the inevitable pair of hard women, seated on a bench which was secured midway in the lorry. One stood up. He had a long, dark coat which was buttoned close about his neck. This made him, by hiding linen he may have had, a Plain Man, a Man of the People. This is what he said. He said it three times, addressing the swiftly arriving newcomers as they collected :

> " Fellow citizens of the Republic of Eireann, we have come to address you in the cause of Freedom and Democracy, in spite of the interference of the paid assassins of Liberty. . . ."

Behind me two women were describing a scene, gaining much in the telling by the slowly charging atmosphere of indignation. I knew the overtures of Liberty speeches by heart, so I lost nothing by turning to more interesting eavesdropping.

" I said to her, that is when they got him snugly into the accident ward and she was sending for her sons to break up Mrs. Durkin's husband. . . . ' You know. . . .' I soothed her. ' Hands off me ! ' sez she, ' till I quench the bastard.' ' Now, now, Mrs. D.,' sez I, ' take my advice,' I sez, ' and lave him to Gentle Jayshus; and he'll play bloody hell with him. . . .' " Vengeance is mine, I thought. The brawler above me on the platform continued :

> " The present Free State Government, in attempting to coerce us into recognising Free State institutions, is no more entitled to describe itself as Republican than Michael Collins was . . ."

(Cheers : " Up Collins ! God bless the Big Fellah and may the Lord have mercy on him.")

> " There can be no compromise between Freedom and bondage."

(A voice : " Take it out of bond, and we'll all share it ! Won't we, be Jayshus ! ")

> The plainer Dubliners amaze us
> By their so frequent use of ' Jayshus !'
> Which makes me entertain the notion
> It is not always from devotion.

Behind me the women asked each other: "Who's the fellow in the long coat?   One of them new Politicals?"

A feeling that the police had finished supper and were apt to emerge from the barracks hard by, damped the curiosity of the listeners.   In the expectant lull his voice grew louder.   I was able to draw nearer to the platform.   I gazed in horror at the faces of the two women who sat grimly behind the orator. Is the harem life so reprehensible, after all?

> "Your duty is clear.   There can be no wavering in this crisis, no turning back.   It must be onward to the United Front. . . ."

His voice rose to a scream.   The two grim women clapped their hands, but what they shrieked was inaudible.   The speaker was working himself up, and as he gesticulated his coat opened and, after a little, fell down to his elbows, showing his shirt-sleeves. . . . The applause was more deafening now.   I realised then that the more inaudible he became the greater the effect he was producing.   I thought of Wesley, who, when his voice failed in the pulpit, kept on moving his lips and hands and affecting his audience, who thought that they heard him more by his inaudibility than by his eloquence.

> "Rally," (he cried it) "O men, O citizens, don't let what cost us so much, down.   Close the ranks of the United Front!   Rally round the flag.   Rally, ral . . . raw . . . the flag!"

He raised his arm, and sat down suddenly.   The silence that held the mesmerised mob was ludicrously broken by a little girl of eight or so, who emerged from under the wagon with a rusty tin of Jacob's biscuits suspended from her neck.   One side bore the faded legend: "Digestive."   On the top of it she beat a brisk tattoo breaking the silence, singing in a shrill innocent treble:

> "Rally, men, rally,
> Irishmen rally!
> Rattle a fart in a band-box!"

As the women stretched to seize her, she disappeared.

While the next speaker was disappointing the crowd by her immobility, I stood pondering in my mind the more serious problem presented by the little girl's adjuration.   Mixed with this in my mind was Yeats' advice to his daughter never to take up politics, never to become "opinionated."

Have I not seen the loveliest woman born
Out of the mouth of Plenty's horn,
Because of her opinionated mind
Become an old bellows full of angry wind?

But the wind in a band-box! There were frozen words which fell on the deck of a certain ship which was voyaging among enchanted islands before Dean Swift wrote *Gulliver*. One of these frosted things when thawed emitted a loud noise and was gone. Now that in a band-box, provided always that there was residual air in sufficient quantity, might possibly enable Irishmen to perform that rattling feat. What an orator, then, and appropriate leader would not he be whom St. Augustine mentions in his *De Civitate Dei* (XIV. 24), who could make such sounds at will? Like a pied piper he would, haloed by halitosis, lead the " Irish People " by adjusted detonations to—a bombinating Republic.

The applause was disappointing. Women speakers are not popular with the men in Dublin. Maybe they are too mindful of oratory at home.

While there were consultations going on between the speakers on the lorry, I listened carefully to the effect on the crowd.

" A cook should be able to rule Russia. That's what Lenin said. He meant that government should be so simple that any member of the country should be able to take over if needed."

" But who would do the cooking? "

" Ah, Jayshus! What's the use of explaining things to the likes of you? "

Evidently there was a convert already, and one whose intellect only required clearing, or in lieu of brains some wild enthusiasm.

" Look on both sides of you " (said the next speaker, a short man with the accent of the ' Glasgow Irish,' a muffler on throat), " look on both sides and what do you see? Banks extravagantly built. The palaces and strongholds of the Capitalists, built with our sweat to be debtors' prisons. We must take over these workers' Bastilles. (Applause.) Or lie rotting in their grip. They will be turned into Clubs " (more clubs!) " and Recreation Rooms for those whose sweat of blood allowed them to be reared. Where did the money come from that went into their stone

and mortar ? From usury, from the interest on money.
What it cost to build them would build decent houses for
you, US ALL. The day is not far distant . . ."

The best statue of an orator drawing fire from the central
flame of the land that bore him is in the National Bank, I
remembered. I hope they will appreciate that, when the
Communists take the banks, at least as much as the ignoramuses
ignorant as those in England who set up a committee to assess
the Elgin marbles, who have put it aside in a corner instead of
making it the central ornament of their hall. Their one
justification cast aside! Thereby the bank fell off the gold
standard in the immortal standards of great art—O'Connell's
statue by O'Connor. Of course, the sculptor has to live and
work in Paris. If he lived here he would be in debt to the
Bank. I thought of the £4,000,000 spent on Gaelic culture
which consisted in bemusing children with Esperantisised
Irish and making them fall more readily victims to the
Communist and Demagogue. And I thought of the fate of
Harry Clarke, that supreme colourist in glass, who lived in
Frederick Street, to see the window he did for the Irish
Hall at Geneva (of course it had to be Geneva, for the eyes of a
fool of a Nation are on the ends of the earth) turned down by
the Government who commissioned it because a figure or two
celebrating Irish exiled authors were in the nude. The money
spent in attempting to turn this nation into a race of bi-lin-
gualists ignorant and gullible in two languages, would have
given Dublin spacious streets and boulevards and restored it
to the place it held as the Seventh City of Christendom
before Napoleonic Paris was built. It could provide, if not
" houses for you, us, all," at least homes for O'Connor and
Harry Clarke.

As I looked up at the brawling demagogue, I thought of the
régime he would usher in : a state of horror in comparison
with which the muddlers from whom we suffer would appear
ideal ; a state of things that would involve a ruin of loveliness
and beauty widespread enough to make the horrors in the
lorry ideals of femininity !
Again a speaker :

" Money is not wealth, no more than your hat-check
is your hat when you go to a meeting in the Mansion House.
But by juggling with the tickets and tallies of wealth—

always a point or two of interest higher here than across the water—you get the paradox of wealth and want. Why? Why? Why? Because they can hold up your hat which is your food and clothing, and they can hold up production and transport of goods and decent housing while they are taking a rake off on the tickets of your wealth which is not money."

And from the walls of the street of the Banks came back the echo—Money!

It will take more than a band-box to hold that, I said, for now he is telling the truth.

And that is the way it goes. With Good and Bad, Truth and Falsehood in unequal fermentation, there will always be a rumble in the bowels of Life.

CHAPTER III

DUBLIN HAS ONE ADVANTAGE: IT IS EASY TO GET OUT OF IT.
Unlike London, which is bottled on three sides and un-
interesting on the fourth, Dublin has the country and the
streamy hills very near, and nearer still the sea.

It is but three minutes' drive to Ballsbridge, which was
widened recently by " Contractors," which is about as much of
a "Bull" as the statement that the Sussex heights are downs.
And Ballsbridge is by Serpentine Avenue, in which you can get
a horse for an hour's canter on the wide sands of Merrion.
One must choose the time when the tide is out, or at least not
fully in. And as the tides—uncharacteristically—of Dublin
are predictable and punctual, there is very rarely an hour of a
morning when the sands are covered. The morning sky is a
sight worth more than a morning's sleep. Before the reek
ascends from the old houses in which now nearly every room
holds a fire—so different from the days when one family
held a whole house—there is always a glint of sunlight to
be found at the edge of the distant tide. The little waves
that cannot rise to any height on the level sands may be the
better part of a mile away, and you can canter for five minutes
before you meet them and watch them bearing rainbows and
spreading on the tawny sands their exquisite treasures brought,
as it were, overseas from the inexhaustible and sunny East.

On the right is the smooth outline of the Dublin mountains,
rising like cones and rippling into nipples like the paps of
Jura, where Wicklow shows Bray Head. The Golden
Spears are softened and magnified in the golden morning
haze and the greater nearer mass of the Two and Three Rock
mountains is half translucent and unreal. Far away, twin
steeples catch the light at Kingstown; and the great house at
Monkstown, built where the Dun or stronghold of Leary stood,
begins to blink its windows at the sun. The outline of the
little granite town between the hills and the sea is the colour of
the sand, and recalls some such sight as must have gladdened
pilgrims' eyes when dawn showed them Florence or Fiesole.
But the irregular formation of the Wicklow Hills preserves
the mind from forming a pattern or formula for their formation. They are subject to no one design as the herring-bone
ridges of the Apennines; and they will never by repetition
offend or limit imagination. And yet in the morning light

they rival the hills of Italy in the beauty of their form; at other times their beauty must depend, like all Irish mountain scenes, on the play of shade and light. The uncontaminated breezes flow in with the gentle tide. Howth is amethystine yet, and the long, high horizon is unbroken by a sail. I can see the parallel valleys shared out from a central ridge running along half Italy, steeped in monotonous and assured sun. Here, before I turn, all may be changed. The luminous mass may be angry brown and fuming at its edges with luminous vapour. The whole canvas may be erased.

The morning sky along the coast may be seen as late as 9 a.m. on a morning of February or March. Dublin is, during the months from October to March, a winter resort. The summer gives us delights in their proper season. It is only the winter months that would lie heavy were it not for the advantages the town has of egress to the wilds. We inhale the Atlantic vapours and they turn us into mystics, poets, politicians and unemployables with school-girl complexions; thus these vapours have lost their enervating and transforming powers before they reach England. And yet her only thanks is to send us for April her eastern winds, whose influence is influenza. No one makes allowance enough for us who live in this vat of fumes from the lost Atlantis.

You must not think that Merrion is like this every morning at the beginning of the year; certainly not, but I have seen it thus on occasions when beauty reigned in the air and made it receptive. All we have to do is to dwell on such moments of beauty. The other moments matter little, and should be dismissed as interlopers and of evil origin. It is the same with life: few moments are allotted to us free from concerns or boredom. These can be counted on the fingers, but as they shall have to stand for us for whatever is desirable and tolerable in life, engrave them in golden letters on the marble of memory and let the rest be forgotten, or remembered, by the happy moments' foil.

It costs one hour's sleep and half-a-crown to ride out to meet the winnowing tide at Merrion. You could not do it for that in Rotten Row, nor there, for all the money in the Treasury, could you make sure of being alone. There may be a corpulent and cheery bookmaker striding the foundation of his profession along by the sea wall, but he will not come near you. He will think that you are melancholy mad or that your horse is restive: that you are better left alone. One thing is sure : you will not waken Dublin, which insists on nursing its misery while shutting its eyes to its delights. Your horse will be hard to hold once he is turned. He sees the squat tower of Irishtown Church. He knows the slip that leads to the roadway. He wants to get back to his stables. No matter how far you may take him beyond them, he will gallop back.

It will not take me long to get through my hospital work this morning, I thought, as I was breakfasting. I shall have time to read the morning papers, particularly the *Daily Express*, for things have come to such a pass now that we have to look into an English paper for uncoloured news and for news suppressed at home. Either through pity for the Government, or an endeavour to leave it unembarrassed, the two untied papers " go easy with the news." A leader or two criticising finance, or such impersonal theme, is the furthest the criticism goes. The Government here has freedom from the Press. This is compensated for by the fact that it owns a Press which has no freedom from the Government, and so the whole round earth is every way . . .

If I am late I shall have to talk to Sir Chalmers, the historical surgeon at the hospital. He is an asset to us, for without him the tradition of surgery which comes down from Nelson's hard-battling fleets would be broken. He is a type of the old and lost school of the days when a doctor had first of all to be a gentleman. After that he could be qualified. How few could be qualified were such a condition to be made primary! A genial man, a great host. " That's sloke and piping hot . . . with the mutton . . . with the mutton. . . . What was this I was about to say ? Oh, yes ! I believe in top-dressing women, and in helping them, if occasion arises afterwards. And why not, poor creatures ? The under sex."

Sir Frederick will be there, he whose memory goes back so far that he has forgotten his survival in the present. And the " workers " of the Staff will, mercifully, be engaged. Thank goodness, my line of work seldom involves calamities. In the scramble for beds no one has as yet suggested " slabs " for me. I will be discreet and ask no questions about the winner of the over-night's Sweep. Well, I know, but unofficially— which covers a multitude of inquiries—that there is a Sweep nightly in most of the wards, and he who draws the " stiff "— the first to die in the morning—wins. Thus it is differentiated from horse-racing, which is gambling ; but Death is certain ! " When we beat the Incurables, I was in the Hospice for the

Dying. We beat them by nearly ten degrees." The degrees were degrees of temperature. Rival nurses took the temperatures of a selected team from the ward in each hospital, added them up and reported. " We beat them by ten degrees, and if Mr. Purvis Puris is operating to-day, we'll knock hell out of the Fever Hospital next week." Such are the advantages of Surgery over Medicine !

There are nineteen hospitals in Dublin, and all of them unmergeable into one. That is due to the fact that many grants and endowments were denominational. There is a greater vested interest in disease than in Guinness's Brewery. This explains why it would give rise to far more trouble than it is worth to run the nineteen into one. Besides the unemployment it would create and the disease it would end ! Disease is not always a heartbreaking and melancholy affair, as might be supposed. Where there are so many hospitals for so small a city the diseases thin out, as it were, in proportion to their deadliness ; they tend to become chronic and tolerable. The cheeriest people I have come across are cripples or invalids of some sort. A robust or " hearty " person is looked on somewhat as askancely as he would be in Magdalen or " The House." The same applies to an independent spirit. . . . I sometimes feel that even I am wanting in popularity.

" So St. Vincent's beat us. I am sorry to hear that, Sister. Who had we running against them ? "

" The Grattan Ward."

" And they ? "

" Their Gynæcological."

" They must have had a few puerperals, for they won by 6.80° over our side : we were playing eleven. I hope none of them rubbed their thermometers on their sleeves or put them on the hot-water bottles. . . . I have known that kind of thing to happen, and it's not fair. When patients take such an interest in these inter-hospital sports competitions, which help them to bear their trouble and add interest to the weary hours, they should at least play the game."

" There was no cheating. I took the temperatures with my own thermometer."

" Sister, that is an excellent report."

" But, sir, I am afraid there is to be a Board inquiry."

I was puzzled. I felt that I had been putting my foot into it if the inquiry involved the sister.

" A Board inquiry ? What about ? "

" About these inter-hospital matches.   Matron says they are disgraceful, undignified and full of unbecoming levity."

" I will make a point to attend that meeting."

" We'll all be grateful if you will, sir.   I need not say how grateful I will be, for it was I who took the temperatures."

But I had no time to compose a defence because one of the physicians came in, with " Look here, I'd be glad of a word with you."

" Yes.   Out with it."

" The hospitals are going to blazes.   It seems that for months most unseemly competitions in temperatures have been going on : whole wards vying with each other, not only in their own hospitals, but against wards in other hospitals. It will bring us into disrepute and lead to a collision with the other Staffs.   We are holding a meeting in the Board Room this afternoon at four o'clock. . . ."   (Just as I might have guessed, when I cannot be there, I said to myself.)   " A Board meeting to find out what is to be done."

" It's quite clear : reduce your temperatures on the medical side, and we will look after our surgical side, so that our hospital will be scouted out of the Senior League or whatever it is ; and let the others set their own houses in order."

" That's all very well ; but Matron says we must show our authority and maintain discipline by administering a stern rebuke."

" I'm perfectly sick of authorities and administrations of stern rebukes.   If I go to that meeting, I warn you I will blow it sky high.   What sort of Sadists are you, that you must stuff your authority into patients, when probably all they want is a clyster ?   Anyway, this department, which was built for me by the Irish Hospitals' Sweep, is hardly the place to deprecate sweeps in hospitals.   If it ever occurred to you to ask yourself whence comes the amazing courage of the half-fed sick poor that makes ailing and terrorised patients face operations—all the more appalling because of ignorance exaggerating terror—and makes them ' frivolous,' as you call it, in the face of Death, you will find it is due to this camaraderie and good-human-natured joking among the patients them-selves.   The alternative is disciplined efficiency run to such lengths as would turn the establishments for the relief of pain and the cure of disease into vivisection societies.   Let them have all the fun they can, and good luck to them.   They are better men than I would be if faced with half of their disabilities—of which not the least is the arbitrary discipline planned to exalt ' Authority.' Every little pettifogging (no, no, that is not the word, for they don't leap as to the tabor's sound and they have no joy in the jumping), every trumpery little commissar is trying to bolster up his lack of personality and character by becoming a disciplinarian and an authority. And now they want to put a stop to the only game in which it may be truly said that the side which is beaten is not disgraced. Some women have no gumption ; they would offer to nurse St. Anthony through his struggles with the flesh."

" Well, you are busy now, but we can go into the matter thoroughly at four o'clock."

My own character must be weak somewhere, I thought, after Crowningshield had taken himself off. The moment I gain a point I feel like a bully and I want to apologise. Now, Crowningshield is a nice fellow if not driven by " Authority." I do not want to hurt his feelings. The more I dwelt on that the more I saw he was right in a way : most of us are—because there is something to be said for discipline in hospitals, something to be said for measures against frivolity in the ante-room of Death.

I remembered what happened to a beautiful young woman whose father took up Spiritism, or whatever they call it, late in life. The growing girl was taught that Death is not, and that the supersession of breath was no more than " passing over." After two attempts to poison herself, she jumped from a high bridge into a shallow stream and drove her splintered thigh-bones into her beautiful body. Once we relax the fear of Death something happens to Life. It would appear, then, that Death is an astringent to Life. It is verily. This is borne out by the fact that those who are near to Death fear it not so much as those who are in the fulness of health and the enjoyment of life. These are conscious of what they have to lose, and so the contemplation of the opposite condition becomes frightful. Death holds life together. We are borne onwards by the black and white horses.

Long ago I was greatly shocked when I saw patients for operations being trundled on a tumbril of sorts into the anæsthetic room *en route* to the theatre, where they would be operated on by a man whose job it was, and who neither knew their names nor circumstances. But the reverse of the picture converted me. Were the surgeon to know that perhaps he had under his knife the breadwinner of a family of eight, would it help or hinder him? It would be in degree like operating on a relative. And where was the sympathy to end? Surely you could not permit dirty friends to accompany the sick man up to the moment he was put to sleep. There is plenty of discipline where it is wanted. Try to relax it where it is not. The whole problem of the treatment of the sick appeared at one time to me to be full of wastes, overlappings and abuses. Suppose, for example, forty little hunchbacks are gathered together under the new disease description of " Surgical tuberculosis " in a mansion sold for the sake of the rates. Any syndicate who owned the premises could call it the only hospital for the exclusive treatment of bone tuber-culosis, a staff of sixty could congregate—proprietors, doctors, nurses, laundry-maids, porters, wardmaids, etc. That is one and a half supers carried on each little hump! Why is this not scandalous? Because the expense falls on no one in particular, and one and a half persons to serve each hump is not as good as two, or even three would be. The more, the sooner the hump may disappear. . . . No one in particular is paying for the upkeep of this imaginary example of a hospital. But many get their living out of it, and each child gets an extra chance of life. So long as we consider life precious, this must continue. Humaneness is our claim to existence in a civilised mode. The higher the type the more humane. Humanity is all that matters to human beings. There is so much of it among the British people that it overflows into the animal world, as is witnessed by the Societies for the Prevention of Cruelty to Animals and the pampering of dogs. The corollary: disregard of animal suffering is a disregard for human life; as soon as animals are maltreated it will not be far until children, women and men will suffer. It is a good thing to have an overplus of humane feelings. The multi-plication of small hospitals might be objected to if they were a drain on the community. The Empire of Austria had but one for the whole of its wide and mixed territory. The conditions there were the next thing to inhuman. There were no nurses, as we know them, for there were no middle-classes whose daughters would enlist. Old street-walkers took their places, and, what is worse, took the places and performed the duties of qualified men. And if a student wished to get into personal relationship with a teacher, with-out which it is hard to learn, he had to go round the corner to a little half-private hospital run by the nuns of some Order.

Any personal sympathy with the patients was out of the question because of the system and because of the multiplicity of languages. The different departments were marked by coloured stakes : red for surgery, blue for midwifery, yellow for eyes, etc. And the flag that announced no deaths was never flown. . . . We have discovered a way to deal with diseases and to subordinate them to man. We keep disease in its proper place. If Death walks the world, why not make it walk the streets and suffer us to be its souteneurs like George Moore's *Alfred aux belles dents* ? Yes ! We must meet it with a serious aspect. Let us make disease " keep " us all.

Thus we make disease pay for its own upkeep, but keep those concerned with its cure or treatment. Those who fell victims to suffering—the dead—have endowed most of our hospitals. The rest of the upkeep of hospitals falls now on sportsmen, no longer on the Banks. The Banks have thus lost the last link that bound them to humanity, and sportsmen gained the first links which give them possibly something in common with religion—Hope and Charity. The Archbishop of Canterbury points to an eternal reward after death, and bids his followers live in Hope. The Hospitals' Sweep sells us Hope of an earthly reward three times a year. Thus the Archbishop and the Bookmakers have a common interest : both hawk Hope ; but the hoping sportsmen, seeing that they are not required to die tri-annually before chancing into their reward, endow the dying so that they may take their eternal chance. The Archbishop requires that men should spend their lives righteously and in corporal works of mercy. The horsey people propose that you should live your own life and spend ten shillings, and the Sweep will look after the mercy by endowing charities. It is Cantuar *v.* Centaur.

Three great inventions came from Ireland—the invention of soda water whereby whiskey outdoes champagne, the invention of the pneumatic tyre whereby was made possible the evolution of an engine to scale the blue, and the invention of the system whereby disease is made to support patient, nurse and doctor, and horses to carry hospitals !

There are proportionally to population not half so many hospitals in London, and this in spite of the many vocations which lead to disease. This is only apparent. The truth is that every Englishman's house is his hospital, particularly

the bathroom. Patent medicine is the English patent.
Liverpool to London, judging by advertisements for food,
sauces, soups, purgatives and hygienic porcelain, is an
intestinal tract. Millions have been made out of patents
for purgatives, not to include the patent medicines which are
intended to deal with the various results of eating too much.
And most of these patent medicines, very nearly all of them,
are taken in the bathroom. The most amazing results are
advertised. You can lose pounds of flesh by taking a patent
form of Glauber's Salts, or put on pounds (only if you are a
lady) by the same taking. Agonising aches in people unseen
and unheard of by the patentees disappear, regardless of
idiosyncrasy, or a positive Wassermann. And the Englishman believes all this. He believes that a purgative can fatten
or make him thin; he believes that either there is only one
kind of ache or that one medicine can cure various kinds.
His empty churches would be filled twice over by the faith
he wastes on the permutations and importance of his lower
bowel. And yet, in spite of his faith in one medicine for
many unseen and unknown diseases, he cannot accept miracles;
he burks at the infallibility of the Pope, but unquestioningly
accepts the infallibility of the pill. " Just as much as will fit
on a threepenny-piece " instead of as many angels as will stand
on the point of a needle. So Faith has fallen in England to
the level of the lavatory. And yet it cannot be said that it
gives rise to less appreciation of love of righteousness, for it
makes *Mens conscia recti*. But it saddens me to think of the
pent-up faith misdirected that liberated could rise to Heaven
in minsters with flying buttress, curious pinnacle and soaring
belfry. Perhaps, fearing lest he be made to hop on the Day
of Judgment, the Englishman is keeping something in
reserve.

CHAPTER IV

IT IS TIME I MOVED ONWARDS BY HORSE-POWER OF A DIFFERENT and non-metaphorical kind.

If I go by canal, I will be at the aerodrome in twenty minutes and the banks of the canal, which must have been the ornaments of Dublin when this greatest of its " Shannon Schemes " was engineered. They are lovely even now, in spite of their neglected elms and the garish hoardings which are allowed to deface the only boulevards we possess. Old elms, open and half hollow, which were planted to be conduits for water in days before cast-iron or earthenware could be made, gauntly stand in their decay, more sinned against than sinning, and shelter by night the fugitive loves of a city, as the Bard said when he compared a lady whose reputation was disputed to the trees on the canal. The path is lovely because it runs beside the long water over-arched by bridges of cut stone which complete their ellipse by reflection in the calm water. From Dublin to the Shannon, one hundred miles away, these two great examples of Eighteenth-century engineering extend. They cross valleys and enter marshes, such as those which alone could hold up the onsweep of the Roman roads. Lonely through the rich brown bogs they run, to little towns whose white cottages brighten the pale green water, and on through short borders of sheltering trees. Reliable, unleaking, linking Dublin to the largest river of the three kingdoms, to the " lordly Shannon spreading like a sea. . . ."

When my mind longs for that peace which is Death's overture, I think of myself as a lock master at one of the country locks beyond the edge of Dublin, where the sound of living water never ceaseth. I would appoint myself to the Ninth Lock, which is not far from Clondalkin. There is a great stretch of water on one side and a well-appointed public-house where one might rest and spend some of the three pounds a week between boats. With a well-chosen form of peculiarity or moroseness one might preserve the privacy of the inner man . . . until you opened the great gates for the last time, and the skipper of one later boat would say: " Lift the coffin over here and I'll cover it with turf. He was all right in his way, and it will save something to float him down to Harolds Cross, and that's handy for

Mt. Jerome." . . . "And on the mere the wailing died away."

"Contact." That is the thing I wish to be rid of—contact with earth, for a while, but contact it is. The brown shallows pooled far beneath are in the circuitous River Liffey; where it steps down in white water are the weirs. Leixlip Castle on its mound is there, with the dark, paneless windows of its ancient heronry. Save for that at Rathfarnham Castle, there are few of these remaining. How winding the river is! If it ran straight it could reach the sea in ten miles, and it takes seventy-three. None of us wants to reach his end straight away. That great white-fronted house is Castletown, said to have a window for every day in the year. And those ruined walls the walls of a great mill. The mill-race runs through Celbridge Abbey, owned and decorated worthily now by Lady Gregory's daughter-in-law, famous for her good taste. Hidden in the laurels is the maze, and beside the river running under the private bridge is Grattan's Walk. In the days when *ex tempore* speeches were considered bad form, Grattan thought out his speeches by the softly-singing river. And in those stables Dublin's edition of the Gloomy Dean, Dean Swift, tethered his horse before his brutal interview with Vanessa. Under the Abbey's embattled roof her heart broke and she died. What was the matter with the Dean? I wish Yeats had given his mind to that, even though he forgot George Moore. I had a chance to ask that question of an expert on such subjects and the inventor of explanations on everything germane to sex "problems" when William Bullit, the late President Wilson's unofficial ambassador, was going to Vienna to see his friend Sigismund Freud. "Take the *Journal to Stella* with you," I implored, "and ask him to give you his opinion on the enigma of Dean Swift's amours." But I heard no more of the enterprise. Maybe it appeared to that citizen of the United States to be no more than an attempt on my part to substitute old loves for new. To bring love problems to Vienna may have seemed to be the latest and most delicate cynicism. So the Dean's libido remains undiagnosed. It is gone now; the Abbey and Lyons come into view below its hillside lake and woods. There Lord Cloncurry's daughter, Emily Lawless, wrote her *Bog Myrtle and Peat*.

The great mansion is yet held by her sister: one of the few lovely places left in the family which planned and cherished

and preserved them. I wish I had asked the pilot to come
along. I may spin if I let my mind wander from the machine.
It may be as well to seek safety in height. It needs about
three thousand feet to separate oneself from the coil of earth
and petty concerns. Up here, were it not for the noise, there
is heavenly peace. Swinging to the east, the bright buff-
coloured Hill of Howth and the sands of the two Bulls can
be seen. The Danes " took a great prey of women from
Howth " somewhere in the Tenth Century. Such raids are
discontinued now that each woman has become a host in herself : such is the development of individuality. A great prey of
women. . . . The finely-drawn hills are on the right, lighted
on their southern side. And at the end of the range, where
it falls to make the plain of Dublin, can be seen Dundrum and
Rathfarnham, where Yeats lives. I will look him up this
evening. There is nowhere to land if the engine conked
except on Leopardstown or the Phœnix Park when one
flies over the city. It is worth noticing the roof-like, flat,
floating island of smoke which, seen sidelong, looks as opaque
as plank or as a piece of plate-glass. We can see through
it from beneath, but it diminishes the brightness of the stars
and refracts the violet rays. However, there is the great
brewery that has done more for Dublin than any of its institutions. It cleared the fœtid liberties long before philanthropists
took to improving the houses of the poor. It provided one
of the loveliest *volks garten* in Europe, and it set the model
to employers long before Henry Ford expounded his theory
of high wages. It went beyond that, for what happens in
the U.S.A. to employees after the wage-earning age ?—too
old at forty : in Guinness's you are in your prime. If I
were beginning life again—(oh ! a pretty bad bump from
the smoke of the chimneys to remind me that I must hold on
to the life I have, such as it is)—if I were beginning life
again I would seek a job in the brewery. I have often longed
not only to take, but to make drink. And by making Guinness
you make so many other things as well—garden villages,
dependable workers and the " brew that savours of content."
Like dark sleep, it knits up the ravelled sleeve of care, and,
what is an achievement, it wastes the time that might, if we
were not drinking, be devoted to scheming, posing, hypocrisy
and money-making.

    " The silted Nile mouths and the Moeritic Lake " : Clouds.
What a wonderful communion Guinness provides ! You

can drink yourself into helping the poor by better housing; you can drink yourself into St. Stephen's Green, or at least into appreciation of those who gave it to the city; and you can, if you like, drink yourself into poverty and become an object, if not a dispenser of charity. Old martyrs fought with beasts in the arena and those tore out their victim's viscera in a minute; now you can dedicate your liver, fair and softly as they did whose custom provided the sums that went to the restoration of Christ Church, to the erection or maintenance of holy fanes. When you see a face that would act as a bed-warmer, as Will Shakespeare has it, scorn it not. Salute the *bon nez* to which went so much drink in the making. And think of the Rose window of some great cathedral, gules and purple, wing on wing. Drink to the Lord Ardilaun who gave us the Green. Drink until you see the ducks swimming in your tankard. Drink your liver into martyrdom . . . take your time: there are no Neros here. Where is my funnel?

Where am I? At three thousand feet, and instead of over the great brewery, I am near the Hill of Howth. It is time to turn. "Rudder and bank together," as that best of instructors, Elliot, used to sing out. But all his skill could not save him from a fellow who ran into him at a thousand feet. Back over the Fifteen Acres, the most wonderful aerodrome any city could ask for, only seven minutes from Dublin's centre. But it is not open spaces that make aerodromes, but open minds and enterprise. There are twin chimneys of Clondalkin that beckoned me home—in gratitude to them I confess it, no matter how it reflects on my " navigation "— many and many a time. What I want is a balloon.

And now for the landing. There is a chance of a three-pointer, since there is no acknowledgeable and critical head in the front cockpit, to make me self-conscious. Just let her in at sixty-three. Crab a bit of height off and . . . Back, back! Yes, poor Elliot! Your old pupil's remembering. Stick *right* back! Just my luck! When I do land well, there is nobody about to see it.

And now for lunch.

What would Dublin do without the Shelbourne Hotel? The host of fashion and of whatever interesting visitors arrive from overseas. Well-dressed women with vivacious voices; tall men with shining hair and rubicund faces, who order things. The Boers call them *rooi-necks*, but they are the Boers' master in spite of—no, on account of—their colour scheme. For it is the beef-eaters and the beer-and-whiskey-drinkers that inherit the earth. It does me good to see them, tall and carefree, walking about as if they owned the hotel with the rest of the Empire. Careless and carefree people, for whom the best is about good enough. They hate no one, for they consider the world their household. They have built an Empire and ruled it, and they have attained that air of carelessness by having so many subject nations to master by disregard. This quality of the Britisher drew the attention and criticism of a German philosopher, who reflected that the English rule as the best lovers of women succeed, by a certain amount of casualness. But it is not with one of them I am lunching.

My host is an American " columnist," and he represents a large publishing firm in the U.S.A. I do not know him by sight, but George, the hall porter, who knows everyone, will point him out. It was George who first noticed our Decline and Fall when he saw the new Minister in a morning suit with turned-up trousers and *yellow* boots. He was quite right, it was the beginning of the end : but what puzzles me is, why should such solecisms make such a difference ? It may be because there is something of subjection and flattery in imitating the fashions of another people, or is it not that the nation that sets the fashion rules the world ? That must be the reason. But there is something deeper yet. I remember being given a great compliment—an hour's talk with Doctor Lowell, the founder of modern Harvard. He wore a frock coat and *brown* shoes. No matter what he said of interest or wisdom, it was lost on me. I only remember those brown shoes. . . . Now, why should the wrong colour in shoes discredit his words and take away any good from whatever message he was conveying ? No one but myself would have been light-witted enough to care. That is not quite the reason. The reason is that observance instead of observation, manners—that is, ' *mores* ' from which ' *morals* ' is derived—instead of knowledge are the marks of the older Universities. Founded, like Greece's foundations, on the crystalline sea of Thought, they are aware that there is nothing new, unprecedented nor likely to be, so that having drunk deep of Castalia, the next thing is to observe the *convenances*. The blue serge on Sunday, the bowler and the cherry cane. . . . I did not exactly weep tears of pity on the Principal's polished shoes, but I came away in a confused state of mind, annoyed at myself for being unable to remember what my hour with Lowell should have given to me, and angry that I was the victim of feelings which I could not analyse. I have it now! His shoes were *immoral!*

A columnist is a person who writes like this in American papers and earns, or draws, five thousand pounds a year or more :—

> New York:
>> The age of magnificent contrasts:
>> An ex-Bank President hailing a Street car.
>> Dave Apollon's King of Heart's hair cut.
>> Wonder how John D. Jnr. would look in a beret.
>> Look alikes: Bud Kelland and his son.
>> What became of Zelma O'Neal?

He shall have my sympathy for it. It must be harder to write like that than to do brainwork. It is a hard thing to make the trivial significant, or to make mediocrities interesting. And yet the Press, by thrusting publicity on people, gives them a significance in publicity. No! It gives Publicity a significance. The Press becomes a Temple of Fame. And those whose names are written on its columns achieve a momentary immortality, an ephemeral fame. And, strange to say, even those who are quizzed are pleased: notoriety at any cost, as was the early way with Ford's motors.

But it was easy to find Kurt Kelner, for he was with my friend, Captain McLoren—clipped moustache, trim figure, grey eyes and straight. He is always the gallant captain to me since I was made aware of his sad story. It might be called " The Vengeance of Shiva." He was stationed in India, and one day he had the chance of saving the life of a priest of a sequestered temple. Curiosity born of the apparent contradiction to Western minds by which it seemed incomprehensible that courtesans should be associated with a holy shrine, made him ask as a favour if he could visit one of those ladies who had dedicated themselves to religion in so strange a way. The priest was evidently in a difficulty. He was caught between his gratitude and his fidelity to his trust. He explained that the women were really girls of high rank who devoted their bodies to the service of the Temple and that, as it would be clear to them that he could not possibly share their belief or approach them except from the most obvious motives, he would leave the matter to his better judgment. But judgment in a man of twenty-three can be obscured by concupiscence, especially in the absence of officers' ladies who had dedicated themselves to arms. He had his wish, and will.

"She saw through me at once," McLoren said. "'You only come here out of lust and curiosity. You have no prayer to the god.'" He acknowledged that he had not. 'This is a form of prayer. We have dedicated our bodies to the service of those who have neither the leisure, the philosophy nor the power to remove from their minds the veils of the flesh. We drain their concupiscence from them. They are then in a better frame of mind in which to reach communion with the deity.'

"That was pretty hard on me. I thought at first that the priest had put her up to it, but no. She insisted on me going through with it; said it was her vow. And I never experienced anything like it in my life, before or since. That's why European women are utterly without interest for me. A bit of a tragedy, you know."

How much of a tragedy I learned later, when from two sources I heard of the despair of my friend obsessed by maddening memories. He forgot that he was overlooking the fact that his youth, at the time of this meeting with the priestess, added to the transports; and he failed to take it into account when brooding on his lost delights.

"If it had been love at first sight, I could understand it," one of my informants confided.

"But it was, and far more," said I.

"Yes, but what I mean is, that I have heard of men never marrying because the woman they loved died or married some-one else; but to be dreaming still as McLoren is carrying on, twenty years after, of some coloured woman. . . . It's incomprehensible."

"I have learned that she was not coloured, but had an ivory sort of skin. . . ."

"Oh, he told you that, did he? But what about the snowy skins that he turns down? He groans when a really good-looking girl meets him. The prettier, the worse it takes him. Sometimes he's damned rude."

"Perhaps it is that women in Ireland are not a form of prayer?" Let it not be thought that I was heartless or that I did not do my best for McLoren. At the risk of being misunderstood, I wrote to India to a Diotima whom I knew, to a lady who "had intelligence in love," asking what might be done. This is her reply:

"Should your friend indeed have had ingress to a priestess learned in the art and practice of the African Aphrodite and Diana of the Ephesians and Venus of the Triple Gate, whose mysteries are alive in India alone to-day, then truly would he go sighing for evermore after that memory of unendurable pleasure indefinitely prolonged. And certainly would he find the women of the West amorously inept."

What more could I do ?   But I was all the more interested in watching McLoren.

"I want you to meet Mrs. Kelner, Miss Babette Vyse, Kelner.   And now we will go in and have lunch at last. . . . Hold on : I was told to ask you if you'd care for a cocktail."

The mixed drink of a mixed race and yet more characteristic than the drink of any other nation save, perhaps, absinthe or the vodka of the Russians and the butter tea of Thibet. . . . And yet how preferable to any of these ! . . .

"Yes, a cocktail."

"What kind ?"

"Oh, the yellow one with lemon juice in it . . . it has a faintly green look.   I used to get it in New York."

"You have been in New York ?"

"Yes.   And what surprises me is that I am able to answer that embracing question which someone is sure to ask : What do you think of New York ?"

Irony, however slight, is either not understood or misunderstood and the subject of suspicion to an American.

"I was going to ask that very question," said Mrs. Kelner. "Well, what do you think of it ?"

"Seen from the air, or from over the Hudson in the evening purple, it is by far the loveliest city I have beheld.   It rises like fabulous Troy . . . there is no city in the world to compare with it. . . . It is greater than Troy not only in its buildings, but also in the beauty of its Helens.   The most characteristic thing in America, mechanical America, is that it can make poetry out of material things.   America's poetry is not in literature, but in architecture.   But one must have seen the sun from the East River on the dark, silvery pinnacle of the Singer Building, to believe it.   I lived with a friend for weeks in Number Two Beekman Place, and I saw, through the clear winter morning, that marvellous sight.   Like newly-cut lead the pointed roof shone. . . . The sight

was as new to me as my first sight of the slender pillar of a
mosque. . . ."

" Where did you see a mosque ? "

" When I went to Crete . . . the pillar stood out against
a calm, apple-green sky. It was unusual, and full of alien
romance to me."

" Yes. It is refreshing to get away from our traditions
for a while. . . . They are apt to be overwhelming if they are
not interrupted occasionally. Getting away from them
accounts for the popularity of touring, and that itself is a new
development of the last twenty years."

" Do you think that explains why Germany went off
Christianity this year ? "

" I don't get you."

" To assist her tourist traffic. I can imagine hundreds
of clergymen rushing there in mufti."

The way a waiter sticks up conversation with a dish is
most annoying. That is one reason why I hate food. It
interrupts good talk, and just as I was making an impression
(whether favourable or not does not matter), or just as I
thought I was doing well with my " reactions " to architecture,
the waiter hisses, " Sauce tartare ? " I must have shown
my temper on my face. . . . Is it any wonder I prefer drink
to food ? It promotes, or at least does not hinder, conversation. And it limits the waiters' chances of asking questions.
A man can give an order. The initiative is with him. He is
not at the mercy of a man who has to fill him up with comestibles
within a limited time.

When he had smeared my plate and departed, I said :
" Sorry I interrupted you," to one of the ladies. It was I
who had been interrupted, but in the pause it occurred to
me that I was probably talking too much and taking advantage
of other people's weakness for food.

" We were talking about the wine list."

Splendid !

" It would be an awful thing if the ancient drinks were
forgotten during the tyranny of the chocolate-makers, Quakers,
or whoever they were who dried a great nation. Gin is the
enemy of good drink. I suppose no American can remember
what good claret tasted like. To whom would he go to
recover the lost information ? If there was one good drinker
left in London, and if he were endowed by the American
Senate to come over and to preach on the merits of Château

Latour, that would not help : you cannot tell people about taste, any more than you can explain light to the blind.   Now, before you forget its flavour, drink thoroughly of some red or amber wine."

McLoren said, " I prefer a whiskey-and-soda."

That is one of Dublin's famous inventions—soda.   It was invented in Sackville Street.   The well is under Nelson's Pillar.   It is a temperance drink, but it is fated to be associated with whiskey until the end of time.   A perfect proof that not only is there a Providence, but that Providence disapproves of teetotallers.

" Large or small ? " interrupted the waiter.

I had a dear old friend who detested that disastrous question. He often rebuked the fool who asked it, with, " There is no such thing as a *large* whiskey."   He could always imagine and drink a larger one ; but a small whiskey did exist, to the detriment of all good drinkers. . . .

" What are you drinking ? "

" Oh, something from the Valley of the Moselle.   It is one of the loveliest valleys of the world.   I always think of that quotation from Claudian when I drink Moselle :—

' Immemorial vines embower the white houses,
  The earth yields to the labour of the slaves ;
  The incense rises from the temples where the distant Emperor is honoured :
  Fortune is seldom invoked, for men desire no change.'

That shows that there was at least one period in the world's history when people knew they were well off.

" ' Fortune is seldom invoked, for men desire no change.' Our peak point as a nation was reached about the time of Queen Victoria's Jubilee.   Even in the public-houses there was no talk of politics then."

" Oh, nonsense ! " McLoren exclaimed.   " What about Parnell and Healy, and all the bad blood ? "

" What I mean is that we had no politics thrust upon us.   We were not responsible for our condition.   We had always England to blame.   Now we have only ourselves. Politics and prosperity go in inverse ratio to one another. This town will soon be another modern Athens, dirty and full of lawyers.   A gong should have announced forty years ago : ' The golden pomp is come.' "

Mrs. Kelner whispered : " Kurt wants to get you for a book for his firm.   He represents a big syndicate in the States."

" Sure.   We must have your book."

" What kind of a book and on what subject ? "

" Why, the whole show."   He looked out of the window.
" All your memoirs."

" Alas, a medical man has no memoirs.   It isn't done."

" Now, come.   Was not Axel Munthe a medical doctor ?
And he wrote *San Michele* to get money for a Bird Sanctuary."

" I am a Bird Sanctuary.   Any of my little sisters, the birds,
will find my sanctuary inviolable and their confidences respected.   If I write, it will be to win a sanctuary for myself."

The ladies did not quite " get " this.   Our slang differs
from the American, which aims more at statement than
innuendo.   I feared to explain, knowing how poorly my
effort about the Germans going off Christianity to improve
their tourist traffic had been received, and so forbore to
point the reference to St. Francis and his sisters, the birds.

" But, sure, Doc., you could do a book that would not
give away any medical secrets.   You have been right through
the whole movement and you knew all the figures of your own
time.   You could include an historical perspective from the
inside that would be a valuable contribution when the history
of the time comes to be written."

" Don't expect me to write a perspective.   The only way
to treat this town is the way the Chineses treat their pictures :
eschew   perspective.   Perspective   is   too   facile.   Read
Desmond MacCarthy's wonderful description of a Chinese
landscape in his ' Experiences ' to realise my idea.   Taking
a point of view, any point of view, is certain to fill one with
sorrow.   But if you make Dublin the hero of a book and let
it portray itself as it is every day, you may get an effect
such as the wisest of Masters, the Chinese artists, achieved."

"Well, I hardly know.   I guess you know best.   But it seems
to me that you would be throwing a lot away if you were not to
give the history of the men you met as they appeared to you
and the effect of their new-found liberty on the Irish people."

" The effect of their new-found liberty on me is easy to
perceive.   I did not grow fantastic deliberately : I thought
I was going towards Freedom and breaking down a Bastille ;
it was only opening a lunatic asylum.   So I have, in order to
protect the ego, or whatever you call that which likes peace
of mind, accepted my *rôle* : I am a mere figment in the
National mind, and that mind is not quite sane.   And, by
the way, what is Freedom ? "

They thought that this was a joke, and a good one.   That is my fate : to be misunderstood jocularly.   But what of it ? So much depends on those who misunderstand.   Would it be worth while to set them right ?

" What do you think of the present situation ? "

" Remember I faced your question, what did I think of the U.S.A., but this is altogether beyond me.   I can tell you some facts.   We have less than three million inhabitants in the Free State, and more than three hundred thousand whom you will not permit any longer to enter the United States and to enjoy its fuller life and its higher standard of existence.   These unemigrated hate Ireland because it is not the U.S.A.   They look upon it as a prison, and the position of any government which depends on so many adult votes is somewhat similar to that of warders when the convicts have taken over the prison.   But the most ephemeral things are politics.   They are the passwords to oblivion. . . .

" Ireland at present is parallel to what Greece was in the age of myths.   We never had, as England had, the Roman schoolmaster to teach us logic.   Therefore, fairy-tales are our politics.   I am not anxious to compose fairy-tales : I can always send out for a daily paper."

Kelner smiled and said, " Yet I am not sure.   I still think that there is a mighty lot that has not yet been told about your country.   You are not all dreamers."

" Maybe not, but woe betide the reputation of anyone who wakens us up from our dreams.   It is worse for you in the United States.   There you have got the permanent dreams of half-a-dozen nations who are the hyphens, to deal with. In order to avoid loss of national or homeland identity in the great merger of humanity, the newcomers rally round and cling to the totem-poles of their country of origin.   The Lutheran becomes more Lutheran, and the Irish Nationalist never moves from the politics of a hundred years ago.   The reaction of this on Ireland, whose politics are supported by the American-Irish, can be imagined.   It leads to a perpetua-tion of the politics of the Famine.   It keeps alive resentment and encourages the demagogues here to hawk Hate.   And Hate is anything but a policy of progress.   It keeps us back, and the more backward we become the more we hate those who present us with object-lessons of success and prosperity. We save our faces by hating England.   It would be far better to shave them and to emulate."

"We'll talk about this another time."

"Those men think only of themselves and their plans, and it's always at some meal that they do business." Mrs. Kelner was feeling left out.

"It is altogether my fault," I said. "I am as bad as a friend of mine, a barrister, who went to condole with the widow of one of our presidents. He spoke for an hour without a break and without giving her a chance even of a sigh ; and then, coming out, remarked : 'A nice chatty little woman.' Now be as chatty as you can."

"Thanks, but I am a complete owner of myself, and you could never succeed in snowing me under. I only refrained from talking because I had nothing but questions to ask. And it's rude to ask questions ? "

"No. It would be worse if you took so little interest in us that you asked none."

Babette began to laugh. "She has them all arranged originally. They are original kind of questions. We drew them up between us this morning."

"Oh, don't betray me. But if you don't mind "—turning to me—" do tell me what are the things you would regret most if you left this town ? "

"Now, isn't that a swell way of finding out what we ought to see ! " Babette exclaimed.

"I would probably regret the informality of life here. I hate dressing up vocationally. In London the medical men are as distinctly got up as the chimney-sweeps."

"But here you cannot tell the difference ? "—from McLoren.

"Now, that is a nasty one. A bull's eye ! But even at the risk of being taken for a sweep, I prefer not to be judged by the cover exclusively, even if it is an old college or regimental tie."

"Humph ! " said Mac.

"Next to the formality, the easy egress to the country. We have wild geese two hundred yards from Merrion in the mornings, and the dells of the Dublin mountains are not ten miles away. Hills, rivers and sea, and an almost winter resort temperature. And perhaps it would be my greatest regret leaving the best water and water supply in the world : the Varty water."

"Millie's questionnaire has not taken us very far. What she wants to know is what we ought to see."

"Just round the corner from this hotel the Gold ornaments are to be seen at the Museum. What they have to do with the Muses, or why a building for housing antiques and not poets should be called a Museum, beats me," said McLoren. "But don't let me deter you from inspecting the most interesting native ornaments evolved by a nation which lived apart from Europe for centuries, almost as far off as the Government is trying to put it to-day. They are made of pure gold, which may have been plentiful until worked out on the surface of the Wicklow Hills. But they cannot compare as objects of Art with the Cretan and Greek cups, daggers and ornaments, earlier by one thousand five hundred years."

"Listen to me," I said; "you are under the curse of tradition. You expect that you will add to your statures and gain a feeling of superiority by borrowing from the poor unhistorical dead. If you find in the country into which you are born certain examples of a 'culture,' no matter whence it comes, you immediately take unto yourselves all the little tradition it may be presumed to bring you, at the same time withholding yourselves from any primitiveness with which it might identify you. Let us be truthful for about ten minutes. There is nothing to be gained from this dream of our superiority in some Golden Age, except an excuse to shirk life in this age in which we find ourselves."

"You don't say!" said Kelner.

"But I do. I would tell you all about the foreshortening fallacy of History. Mrs. Stopford Green was our best example. Her history of Ireland left you under the impression that Ireland was as colourful and as humane as *The Pilgrim's Progress* but for—but for—but for . . . anything except hard fact. . . . The Gold ornaments mean nothing more than a date in decadence from what was reached in Greece fifteen hundred years earlier and more marvellously."

"But, say, what are we to see after these barbaric ornaments in the Museum?"

"Ask Dr. Mahr, whose appointment was a miracle because it meant modern science in archæology, what his opinion is of the 'Gael' in contributing to modern civilisation. But don't embarrass him by asking him to describe that sole specimen of pre-Christian 'Art,' or of even collateral Christian Art, the quaint wooden figure he discovered in Mayo. 'Up, Mayo!'"

"Don't mind him when he scents some racial contradiction between the ancient observances and those of our day. He is so mischievous that he loves to expose any proof of contradiction he can find," said McLoren.

"Well, I know this much about Irish archæology: there has been only one example of pre-Christian sculpture found in the country except the Phallic deity of Northern Mayo. I grant you that it argues badly for a people who had to 'say it with' a wooden image instead of with the orchids of Fifth Avenue. Don't mind McLoren. Let us admit that the age of the Irish Gold Ornaments was a bad time for Blondes. There is one exhibit not from the Golden Age. It is the present President's boots."

"Boots?"

"Yes. Upstairs in a glass case to prevent anyone else stepping into them. They are long, thin boots with fallen arches."

"Fallen arches?"

"Possibly symbolical: to commemorate the fallen arches of the Mallow Viaduct destroyed in his civil war."

"I don't quite get that."

"Certain Rakes of Mallow blew it a quarter of a million pounds' worth to make Cork a Republic by isolation. If they were triumphal arches, it would suggest Empire and Imperialism. But these boots are calculated to appeal to the flat-footed man in the street."

"That is if the man in the street has boots."

"The Museum is not open to the barefooted. Besides, these boots have already a semi-sacred character, exhibited as they are in the Nation's Invalides. They may yet be regarded as relics and touched to cure corns."

"But not 'cold feet'!" said McLoren.

> 'Who dares the pair of boots displace
> Must meet Bombastes face to face.'"

"We must see these boots!"

"A cult of the Boots may down the arches of the years arise; the Order of the Boot, its insignia. The boots in which the President went to America only to hear them called 'shoes.' This will provide the characteristic schism. The boots may be taken out at the annual, triennial, or even bi-annual election of the President and used as a test of his fitness for the post, somewhat in the way the Tanist was

elected of old.   Then the Lia Fail or stone of Destiny sang
approval, now the Fitting of the Boots."

"Shoes" would be anathema even though it might bring
in the United States, to which in immemorial times the President took his departure.   It would be too suggestive of that
Old Woman (Eire) who lived in a shoe.

She had so many children *he* did not know what to do.
It would distract the devout by statistics of unemployment.

I noted that the boots were placed parallel to each other.
A somewhat more divergent attitude would have given
them character.

"I will not take coffee, thank you.   And really, Kelner,
you ought to know why.   I tried in vain for three days on an
American train to get white coffee, because the tea was a sort
of half-hearted poison and the black coffee too racking on the
nerves.   I hate all coffee since.   And I would hate your
trains, only you make up for your earth-bound, slow and overheated furnaces by your futurist air services.   The U.S.A.
owes its air-mindedness to its insufferable trains.   What the
phrase ' air-minded ' means, I leave . . ."

"But, Doc., what are we to see after the Museum ?"

It is strange how much it takes to make me drunk in boring
company;   I can get drunk without a glass with my good
companions.   But to be unable to shelter the mind from
questioning friends gave me to think . . . seriously.

"Well, when we have done the Gold Ornaments in the
Museum ?"

Yes, yes, I thought, the Museum . . . the Museum . . .
Museum . . . House of the Muses.   "Oh, you must go
straight ahead down the street in front of the Museum until
you come to the Royal Hibernian Hotel . . . a bonny
hostelry in its way.   I could tell you of a night with a few
Scotsmen there, but . . . You won't lose it.   I'll die dictating. . . : Take a bayonet turn to the right; half-way down
Duke Street is the Bailey.   Its windows are nearly flush
with its walls.   That spells the Seventeenth Century.   Scylla
and Charybdis prove its desirability.   They are the horrid
flower-sellers which haunt its portals. . . . Of them anon, no
later.   But the Bailey is the true Museum of Dublin because
it is the House of the Muses.   If you are lucky and if you can
work yourself into the confidence of James or Lewis, you
may be given a glimpse of the Symposium.   You remember

how Plato placed all the best of Athens at, what we in our degenerate and envious days would call a ' Drunk.'   He called it a banquet.   He does not, if you notice, interrupt good talk by food.   They called for larger cups.

" The Bailey entertained Parnell ; and, because of that tradition, Arthur Griffith, ' the greatest Irishman of all time,' according to Deputy Belton.   I always thought it detracted somewhat from Griffith's sense that he should judge a hostelry by its old patrons rather than by its mellow beverages.   The Bailey has the best whiskey and the best food in Dublin.   I took a young friend of mine, a wealthy fellow, and between the unreality of riches and his chef, he declared in the Bailey, and at the bar, mind you : ' You have the best eating-houses and drinking-houses in the world.'   He knew what food could be.   We know what food is.   Good cooking is an excuse for bad food.   But our prime beef defies camouflage and our Jameson . . . Well, you can see it in the hall of the Bailey, with its silver label on its barrel before it is consumed.   Later, those for whom whiskey is the chief event of their day come in. ' Its Protestants to be.'   The smoke-room upstairs, where Griffith took his ease after his day in the slum of Crow Street, is now a dining-room, but there is a room behind it with a corner fireplace.   There you may meet a bard or two, but they are on the wing."

A light touch on the arm.   A tall figure bent and whispered : " Is that George ? "   She went away, looking back with a laugh over her shoulder like a figure in Botticelli.

" Who was that woman with the clear skin and eyes like grey ice ? " Miss Vyse asked.

" If ladies praise her she must be beautiful," I said.

" Why, sure.   And she seems to know you pretty well. Surely you must see that she is lovely ?   We are wondering what she whispered in your ear."

" I'll tell you without the least hesitation, but it will take some explaining."

" She asked if you were George."

" If I was George ? "

" I heard her," said Miss Vyse.

" I don't want to puzzle you, but the meaning is this : I have a great friend who is a stout poet and a good writer. He does not publish nor advertise.   When I quote him, people pretend to think that I am trying to pass some of my own lucubrations under the name of a character I have in-

vented.   I cannot get the wife of one of our Consuls to believe
that George exists. So, mockingly she asked, ' Is that
George ? '   It's very annoying to be given credit for a character you have not invented and to meet with no recognition
for the characters you endeavour to create."

" Why not bring him in to call ? "

" I did !   But he is shy, and, as I failed to draw him out,
she still insists that he is a ' false creation.' "

" Say, I'd rather meet George than see the Gold
Ornaments."

" But you cannot meet him to-day, so———"

" Well, before we leave for ' The Chieftain Harrington.' "

" I have never heard of the Chieftain Harrington.   Who
is he ? "

Now what had I said ?   Their faces fell.

" Oh, but we met him on the boat.   He is the hereditary
Chieftain down somewhere—you have the address ?—in Cork.
He invited us to see his stronghold.   How extraordinary ! "

" Oh, I just thought that ' Harrington ' was not an Irish
name.   But so many Irishmen have odd names now, one cannot
be sure."

" But an hereditary Chieftain ? "

" I will inquire and let you know ? "

Now who the hell is Harrington ?

" And one thing more—where can we buy antiques ? "

" Nassau Street, Sackville Street, Liffey Street, where
Naylor's is and all along the quays.   Have you not heard ? "

'Two Jews grew in Sackville Street
  And not in Piccadilly.
One was gaitered on the feet,
  The other one was Willie.

'And if you took your pick of them,
  Whichever one you choose,
You'd like the other more than him,
  So wistful were these Jews.

'They kept a shop for objects wrought
  By masters famed of old,
Where you, no matter what you bought
  Were *genuinely* sold.

'But Willie spent the sesterces
  And brought on strange disasters
Because he sought new mistresses
  More keenly than old masters.

'The other...' "

It is hard to break away from those who have infinite leisure,
but I closed the entertainment as soon as I could.   Going
forth, I met Butterly, a spruce little barrister with a large red
face who always seemed to be leaving in a hurry, though no
one knew where he went or where he slept.   He was now
leaving the scene of one of his famous jokes, the lounge where
he gave his well-known advice to the two young officers who
were complaining about conditions on the Gold Coast. . . .

"It is all darn fine, but think of having to wake up with a negress's head each side of you on the pillow."

"Think imperially," said Butterly.

He was mysterious now. He beckoned me and took my arm as we walked out.

"I saw you pointing at the bank when you were talking to the Bud," he remarked. "It's in there you should be . . . or I should be."

I looked at him closely. I saw that the redness of his cheeks was composed of countless tiny purple veins which looked like little star-fish under the skin. There are places, I thought, from which he does not hurry away in time.

"I in a bank?" I asked, surprised.

"Of course you will : in your next incarnation any way," he said. "Your friend Æ must have told you long ago that we all become our own opposites after a cycle or an era or one of those things."

"It will take more than the Great Platonic Year to get me into a bank."

"Platonic? Ho, Ho! I don't know so much about that, but what I do know is that that is the greatest bank in Dublin. Don't mind its reserves, but just look at the view there is of all the finest women in Dublin. They pass along by the wall there twice a day. Twenty-three steps on an average to the sixteen yards." The little eyes gleamed with mirth. He dug me in the ribs. "I'll run you down to the green room in the Abbey and fix you up, as a typical bank manager. A little more silver in the hair, a little more tightness about the mouth until it suggests a savings' box, a little hint of parchment about your skin, ' this indenture witnesseth ' and a fund of meaningless small talk. We would call you Chitchat the bank manager."

I toyed with the idea, I might for a moment and count up. Five, six, seven, eight, nine. . . . "Her little heel fits in a shoe!" No! I could never do it! I could never keep myself from distractions : were they numerals or steps I was counting? . . . ten, eleven pounds and tuppence . . . a damn fine figure of a woman . . . and one halfpenny! She is stopping. . . . It was not at me she was looking, but at that fellow crossing the street. . . . Who is that fat little man? Then aloud : "It's only nonsense, after all."

"It's far from being nonsense," he said. "Just as the Orange pogroms in the North are a direct result of the hypocrisy of Belfast, which has its middle classes suppressed with so much respectability that they are afraid of being seen in public with a woman or a whiskey for 364 days in the year . . . they have to break out and take it out by beating drums and their fellow citizens on the feast day of that King who was financed by a Pope. It's far worse among the bankers of Dublin. They have no one to whom to look up. Lives of great men do not remind them that their mistresses were fine.

" Nelson, Wellington, O'Connell, Parnell: saviours of civilisation, empire-makers, liberators, statesmen. Sailor, soldier, liberator, statesman . . . but where, oh, where are the bawdy bankers? Can it be that because none of them is truly bawdy, none is truly great? Can it be that the further men remove themselves or are removed from the opposite sex the further they are removed from the service of humanity? And they have not even got a ' Twalfth.' That's what makes them so Sadistic. They have to take to helping fair clients with ' The Authorities,' who, of course, never see the letter. . . . I doubt if they exist—but it's great sport having the pretty girls writing letters to yourself. If you cannot work that you can write: ' Madam, I trust that you will be in a position by the 1st. prox.' God! Man, you've missed your vocation! There's a new movement in English prose there. You could be counting the girls' steps if you were in that bank."

And put it in the ledger, I thought, at the close of the day. A little grey elfin creature with a peaked hat took up her position squatting on the curb in front of the bank window. She never raised her head from her banjo, but, playing to herself, glanced sideways along the strings as if to follow the little notes in their flight from an indifferent town.

Butterly looked at his watch, evinced surprise, and was gone.

My hostess dispensed cocktails. The room was full of laughter, which is not the least of the contributions that alcohol makes to conviviality. A great, blue-clad figure dominated the scene as he moved lavishing the good cheer, an engine of mighty force to dispel the gloom of endless icy forests and immeasurable wastes, but over-strong for the little islands. Breast to breast the ladies whispered. A laugh rang out. " Let's all hear it. That's not fair ! "

Too far away to hear the explanation, I realised what it must be; as laughter is some form of short triumph, and what would make a woman laugh more than a short or long triumph over the male sex? She can rarely see fun in men's jokes, unless she is degraded, because, before they can amuse her, she has to accept some measure of degradation for her sex. Was it, I asked myself, what I took for maternal instinct, aggressive though I felt it to be, an outcome of the concern Mrs. Gallagher felt constrained to show for our failing? Had her husband's weakness strengthened her? Had she, from the transitory (and the trumpery), been transformed into the Eternal Feminine—that is, into a representative of the Feminine element in Nature? And her deep wisdom that suggested no more than her knowledge of the inherent weakness of men. Was she not endeavouring to dry Nature's tears at my expense? Nature has tears, that's the way to translate " rerum ": " Galen calls it ' natura.' "

" By introducing contra-conception to the Vistula? Here are half a million unborn sturgeons. No lemon with caviare."

" Silence! " roared Mr. Shillington. " I see an obvious pun which I want to anticipate, while there is still time. It might easily have been ' Caviare to the General Public.' Thank me for saving the assembly from the lower form of wit, which is the pun."

" The Doctor is now about to recite. I crave silence for the Doctor."

" Do you indeed? " said I. " When the Grand Duke has danced his Bear Dance, I will consider dispensing with what little reason remains to me. . . ."

" Clear the floor! And carry on! "

With arms folded in front of his face, the Grand Duke danced his bear dance, revolving heavily and grunting as he lifted himself up and down. Now and then he moved forward as if threatening; again he retreated into himself, symbolising the hibernation of winter sleep. He growled ominously in his awakened mood. Over his thick nose his honest blue eyes affected surliness, which was contradicted by his cheerful intellectual face; his bulky and apparently unwieldy body plopped up and down with the nimbleness none could have expected of a bear. Mrs. Gallagher, whose husband manufactured soap, retreated from his proffered embrace. The men of the party had by this become enlisted on his side; it was as if he were restoring them to self-respect; the very indifference of his growls awakened a wonder in her and an uncertainty, a wonder changing to a wild desire; were men justified in their aggressiveness? Her experience was the

experience of a maternity nurse. Hush-a-bye, baby! But
the Grand Duke growled. The married women took his
dance and all it suggested for matter of fact as it were. Why
was she the only woman in the room to whom it was left, by
implication of fault, to maintain a kind of obscure objection
to all that the bear dance implied? The Grand Duke was
hugging imaginary mates. Ladies who had intelligence in
love were withholding themselves and, thereby, egging the
dancer on to the suggestion of inaccessible ecstasies. Mrs.
Shillington clapped her hands. Mrs. Gallagher, still sipping
Schnapps and chewing caviare, saw the room suddenly filled
with sturgeons. They were swimming by her, and as each
passed, each regarded her with a reproachful eye. " College
of Sturgeons! "

" Francis wishes to speak on the newly-discovered Fifth
Gospel."

" But we got it all in Dawson Street before it was discovered
in Oxyrhynchus. Æ gave it to those who believed in him."

" Yes. But Æ probably believed in a Fifth Gospel.
Francis's claim to a hearing is his capacity to disbelieve twice
as much as any orthodox Hermetic. If a man is to get credit
for belief in something that does not exist, all the more is he
worthy of approbation who does not believe in the non-
existent. And this in spite of the fact that it is much easier
to believe in the non-existence of Nothing than to pin your
faith to the nothingness of existence."

When a Viennese girl of twenty sits on your knee and you
are finding reasons why you should be considered an exception, even though you are fifty, from the category of the middle-
aged, it is time that you considered your sanity and, if she is
not your daughter, hers.

" Dementia Præcox," I said, releasing her.

" Amazing person," said she, letting her pupils dilate.

> " ' Der stolze Dom—
> Dass ist mien Wien
> Die Stadt für Lieder,' "

I remarked, trusting to its inconsequence to save me. Vain
hope! Entranced, she continued:

> " ' Am schönen blauen Donaustrom.' "

Two sharp words in the German of Vienna's dialect recalled
her to herself. I saw her glide away, and I could not help
recalling a somewhat similar incident, when a charming girl

in a great house in Hesse was sent to the servants' quarters before midnight after having dined as an equal with the family. Morganatic, they called it. But Morgan, the Pirate, was surely less punctilious.

I was asked for a recitation or a song. I said, " I have none of my own, but if you like I'll give you one of George's poems. You know him ? He is the Juvenal of Dublin. Better, indeed ; for his work is more learned, smoother and more restrained."

Mrs. Shillington laughed. " George ! " she cried, ' George ! Of course you all know there is no such person. He is one of the Doctor's inventions. When he does not wish to speak in his own name he calls up ' George.' "

I raised my hand in a gesture of futility.

" If I could only write his verse, I would gladly accept the soft impeachment, and your flattering belief."

" We had a great deal of ' George ' from the Doctor at the wonderful dinner the new Irish Academy of Letters gave."

" Oh, do let's have him again ! " some young woman gushed.

" Yes, yes, yes, yes ! We want George ! "

" Provided you give him at least the credit for his own existence. I cannot imagine anything more exasperating than to turn up in the flesh and blood and find no one to take you seriously ; that is, your existence seriously. I know to what use I would put such a position. I know that if you all insisted on disbelieving that I was in the room now, it would suit me very comfortably. But, alas ! we are all held responsible both for our existence and, what is worse, our actions. If you are not apologetic I will produce George before the end of this orgy."

" This what ? " asked Mrs. Shillington.

" Orgy," I repeated. " When there is any pleasant and private feast from which a few who think that they should have been invited are excluded, they invariably call it an orgy. I have always regretted that I was never at an orgy ; I am trying to repair that shortcoming now. As I say, I will produce George. . . ."

" Well, until you do, just recite his latest."

" Very well," said I. " You must know that George is not only the *arbiter elegantiae* of Dublin, but a critic of the grosser forms of licence. Now, there was an old usurer who had eyes like a pair of periwinkles on which somebody had

been experimenting with a pin, and a nose like a shrunken
tomato, one side of which swung independently of the other.
The older he grew the more he pursued the immature, and
enticed little girls into his office.   That was bad enough;
but he had grandsons, and these directed the steps of their
youth to follow in grandfather's footsteps, with more zeal
than discrimination.   I explained the position to George, who,
after due fermentation, produced the following pronuncia-
mento :

'It is a thing to wonder at, but hardly to admire,
    How they who do desire the most, guard most against desire :
    They chose their friend or mistress so that none may yearn to touch her.
    Thus did the twin grandchildren of the ancient Chicken Butcher . . .'

I like the roll and oracular sound of ' Thus did,' etc., and the
play on the meanings of wonder and admire.—*Nil admirari !*—
And the organ-note in that ' Twin grandchildren ' which
endows their infamy with grandeur until it almost equals the
fame of the Great Twin Brethren, Castor and beneficent
Pollux.   ' Verse calls them forth ' from vulgar obloquy."
    " Another laurel or burden for ' George ' to bear," said
Mrs. Shillington.   " Who are the Great Twin Brethren ? "
    " Consummations of the poet's dream.   Shadows invoked
by sound.   Men who do not exist.   I thought I made that
clear ? "
    Sidelong I could see, across the angle of the hawthorn-
bordered square, George's car, outside his house.   As no one
believed in him, no one believed that he lived not far away
from where we were junketing.   I made up my mind to slip
away for ten minutes and return with George.   Judging by
the noise that human beings make when a little alcohol
loosens a lot of languages, the party would go on for an hour
or two yet and few would notice my movements.
    " I suppose that I may bring a friend in ? "
    " You are not going out ? "
    " As a matter of fact I promised to introduce George to
you, and if he is not too shy, I can bring him in in ten minutes."
    " Still insisting on George ? "
    " That settles it, then.   I will leave your hall-door ajar and
be back again in a moment."
    As I went out I hoped that George would not be too shy
for his *rôle* of gate-crasher.   Ha, there he is, leaving his house.
His evening stroll.   How to circumvent it ?
    " Hello," said I.

" Where did you spring from ? " he inquired.

" Oh, I was in that house across the way, having a cocktail or so at a party.   It is full of jolly people."

" Do I know any of them ? "

" You do.   There is one odd thing about it, I warn you.
There is a Viennese of twenty or younger who sits on the knees
of those she imagines are poets.   And she kisses them.   Fame
always wins women irrespective of men's looks.   Let us give
thanks for women's lack of the æsthetic sense !   The older I
grow, the more the truth is borne in upon me. . . . I am
beyond the age of self-deception."

" Where is all this ? "

" Oh, just in that house there.   Drop in with me and
have a drink.   They asked me to bring as many friends as I
could and I feel that I have failed them.   Besides, I have
been stealing your thunder.   The little lady thought that
I was you."

George snorted.   I knew that he was saying to himself,
" I must see about this."   He pulled the handles of his car to
make sure that it was locked.

" Promise to get me out of it in half-an-hour ? "

Dear, dependable George !   That great, well-formed head
of his, complemented by a full face, reminds me both of
Mahaffy and Walter Pater.   The grizzled moustache was
more a reminder of Pater, for it was more juvenile, than of the
full Saxon, arched head of the great Provost.   George has
great planes and ' values ' in his countenance.   He is *sehr
solide*.   Under middle height, as were Julius and Napoleon,
he moves like a bear in action.

" How have you been stealing my thunder ? " he asked
uneasily.

" Just this, George.   When I recite a poem of yours,
Mrs. Shillington and Mrs. Skafting insist on its being mine.
I am too honest . . . well, hang it all . . . you know I
don't want to rob any man.   ' Who steals my purse . . . '
But his verse !   That is a far more serious matter. . . ."

" How did my name come into this ? " George asked.

" Oh ! "—I felt embarrassed.   " Well, Mrs. Shillington
and Mrs. Skafting—they both persist in believing that I am
trying to pull their legs by pretending that the best satirical
verse of modern times is by you and not by me."

" By you and not by me ? "

" They think that you do not exist."

" And who writes my verse ? "

" That's just it.   They insist on believing that I am the author of all your verse ; and that I use your name to save my own from the fame which it deserves but which in Dublin is merely my reputation for more ' intimations of immorality.' "

" I must see about this."

The hubbub had not diminished a jot when we got back to the great front drawing-room.   We were unnoticed.   Mrs. Liddle, whose husband printed most of the primary school books, nearly made George self-conscious.

" The ' Side-cars ' are nearly finished.   Try ' Une rêve d'amour.' "

" Mrs. Shillington, this is George.   And Mrs. Skafting, this is George.   And Miss Hoult, this is George.   And Madame Meyler, this is George.   If I hear anyone laughing at me when the poet is quoted, here he will be for the next ten minutes to establish his own existence."

" Whom has he got now ? " asked Mrs. Shillington.

I was in a nice position.   If I let George realise the extent to which I was dependent on him for any notoriety I possessed, all the more would I have to explain to him how far I had been drawing on him, and also the absurd incredulity which attributed not only his fame but his existence to myself.

McViking said, " Glad to receive you, Mr. Boyle.   Don't mind my friend.   I am the Guest Master, and a large vodka with a small sandwich is what I condemn you to.   Boy, attend here !   Mr. Boyle is here as a guest the first——"

" I am not, I fear——"

" He says he isn't here," Mrs. Shillington whispered.

" I am not a gate-crasher, but my friend drags me about."

Six-foot-three, bald, youthful, bellied, our host bore down on us.   " Only what you call a tumblerful."

" When in Rome," I said.

George gulped half of the white liquor.

Mrs. Shillington and a barrister gathered around, awaiting epigrams.   I felt that anything I said in the circumstances of expectancy would be taken for witticisms, just as the banalities of the obsolescent jarvies are accepted by holiday-makers as *merum sal*.   So I left it to George.

He held his glass steadily, unmoved, while he said, " Thanks, thanks," and sought a quiet corner.

" You think that you will get away with it ? " Mrs. Shillington asked. Mrs. Skafting said, " The Minister for the Interior."

" Whose ? " asked I, getting rattled.

" In Vienna we have men *sehr solide*, just as your friend is, but we do not attribute to them our verses."

George drifted away to a low arm-chair by the hearth. He was farthest from the prawns and the many kinds of liqueurs. What I have achieved, I thought, is simply this. I have lost the ear of the company by going when I set out for George. Now the company has doubled, and it is more out of accord with a personal and topical note. Almost as tall as the Consul, the finer figure of the Flemish Minister, rapier against battle-axe, rose. His Excellency from the U.S.A. was announced. And all the better, for there was now no danger of being asked to address the company. It is aggressive to monopolise the attention of a free conversatione. As bad as the intrusion of comic songs on good talks, when it can be heard, at an official dinner. Miss Purser asked why there was no protection for stained glass. Why is there no tax on French saints made of plaster of Paris ?

" I think there is," someone said. " That accounts for the increase in robustness. Not robots, but robustness."

" What do you mean ? " asked Miss Purser, who financed a stained-glass factory, kept many girls and pretended that it was not one of the many disguised charities of the great family of Purser.

Monty fumbled. Someone said :

" It's high time that we were allowed to design our own saints, and not take them in plaster of Paris from a lot of French sculptors. I believe the increase of tuberculosis amongst our peasantry is traceable to chapels which depend on Parisians for their pious images. You cannot dwell long on or with anything without becoming like it, or to like it."

This shocked Miss Purser.

I caught Cunegunde. " Do you see that grave man near the window ? Go over to him. Wrap yourself round his neck. Kiss him, and say, ' But are you really you ? ' "

" Why should I do that ? " the child inquired.

" Just for fun. For a joke ; for a charade. But don't leave him too long alone, or he will go home."

I tried to avoid the Marshal's Pilsudski-looking eye.

" Hah, a little touch of grey attracts them. I saw her rapt

attention as she gazed." With his fingers he indicated the
hair above his ear.

" Don't be jealous," I implored. " It leads to duels, and I
am a bad correspondent."

His eyes converged as he made a mental note of continuous
hate, but he said blandly, " We cannot spare our able-bodied
men."

I did not like to jibe too openly with, " Ah, soon the
bayonets will be flashing." " I have seen the red field of
Carrhae," was all I said, " and ' the Balbian funeral torches.' "

" Every telephone pole has a white wire decoration to
prevent him running into them on his way home."

Now, to whom is that referring ? But, returning, Cunegunde said, " I nibbled his ear."

" Good girl ! What did he say ? "

" He said that I had eyes like ice."

To my hostess, as I was departing, I said, " Thanks for the
quiet orgy. I told you I'd bring him."

" I'm still unconvinced."

" Then you are as good (or as bad) a Berkleian as Yeats,
who holds that all existence depends on the observer, or rather
he held it until Æ pointed out an objection with, ' Very well,
Willie, then I am responsible for both your existence and your
poems.' "

Outside, the first thing I noticed was a certain pensiveness
in George. Lilacs before the hawthorn, pink and white,
the laburnum gilding both. The men of old knew how to
enfold their squares and city gardens. The sward of velvet
green glowed through the breaks in the railings. I respected
the pensiveness of George. Heavily, my most dependable
friend walked on. I sense brooding in another perhaps as
quickly as a woman. Was he labouring a resentment to grow
against me ?

" That girl is no nymphomaniac," George at last said, with
deep conviction.

How relieved I felt ! Had he said, " Why don't you recite
yourself and not me ? " that would have been a difficulty. But
all that was on his mind was Cunegunde.

" Sorry," I said. " But she is in good company. I left her
with Captain McLoren looking after her, and he knows
European women's weaknesses and their shortcomings. I
only meant to express the bewilderment I felt when she sat on
the knee of a fellow as old as I."

" You are always parading your age."

" But a kid like that ! "

" She is old enough to choose her friends."

" Yes ! Yes ! "   Distractingly : " Did you notice how they appreciate prawns ? "

" So would we if we were two thousand miles away.   So would everyone if what they were offered were exotic."

" So would I," said I.

Step by step along the deep brown granite footpath we walked, aware of the rose-red city in its evening glow ; George deep in thought on some moral problem, or deep in composition of a satire of other men's lapses from the curbing line.

Had I offended him by taking him to a drawing-room that was, after all, but a vaudeville of the Dublin of old ? . . . " They told me, Heraclitus ! " . . . but if we remember it, what does it matter who forgets it ?

West against the sunset the roofs of Mercer's shone : Union Street, Aberdeen is its counterpart.   Again, on our left the glory of the Spring, as the men of Dublin of old knew it : purple with lilac and gold with laburnum ; and the hawthorn about to whiten.   Old enough now to be acceptable as natural and not artificial, these old squares must have represented the height of landscape gardening in the days when they were laid out.   Powder and peruke and sedan chairs : as gracious as Versailles.   The façade of the College of Surgeons gleamed like a Greek temple beyond the lake and waterfall of Stephen's Green.   What a magnifying lens was that country that made Parthenons for those who had eyes to see in every city !   The pillars on the Acropolis are honey-coloured in the bright air, but these are white and grey, through moving veils of green. How soft is the yellow-green of Spring ! I thought.   Dante has no Spring in his *Inferno*.

" Shall we go down Grafton Street ? "

" Not unless you want to hear how kaolin in Mayo can be developed by a fortnight in the Boul' Mich."

" So you have heard our latest scheme for developing the country's resources ? "

" Many times," said George.

As we emerged by the Dawson Street gate, I saw across the road a trim figure in a blue reefer jacket who looked like a sea-faring man.   It was Monty, and he was smiling as one who had seen us first.   Monty is the wittiest man and the kindliest wit in the town.   But it is I who have to bear the laurel for him.   He censors films and compensates for this by making jokes for me.   I like it, for they are better and kinder, perhaps, than any I repeat.

But look at the position in which I find myself!   Between George, whose excellent verse and solid presence are attributed to me, and Monty, who wants to make me into a kind of George for himself.   I am the author of their poetry ?

" We are going to the Bailey," I said.

" I can't," said Monty.   " She is waiting for me at Mit-chell's.   She is not in too good a humour.   When we were walking past the Bailey it reminded her that we were twenty-three years married to-day!   ' What do you propose ? ' she asked.   ' Three minutes' silence,' said I."

" I hope you did not tell her it was my suggestion.   I hope it's you she's angry with and not me."

Monty went off through King Street.   The best Dubliner of us all, James Montgomery : Welsh-Norman or Norman-Welsh in descent, with no dismal heritage of resentment : witty without pathos.   His wit is light and no cover for self-evasion.   I wish I were called " Montgomery," for then I could sing to myself with more relish that catch from Burns :

> Ye banks and braes and streams aroun'
> The Castle o' Montgomerie.

What a lovely scene it calls up !   The grey walls and the fresh braes below.

" We will go down Dawson Street."

In the space before the Mansion House, with its potted shrubs and suburban rock-garden, we met Thwackhurst, the collector of graffiti.

" Did ye see that ? " he said without preliminaries.   " That bloody budget report ?   That's where we are landed by the Dago.   Taxes and taxes, and no tax on their own incomes !   What an abscess Griffith opened when he took up the sword for Irish freedom !   Freedom, me neck !   Freedom to be bled white by a gang that keeps in power by codding poor country louts with : ' John Bull, the enemy ! ' "

" I do not think you are correct in calling the President a Dago.   He is no more a Dago than Deputy Nugget.   A Dago is a citizen of San Diego, and one who would certainly think it an impertinence if you called him an Irishman or held him responsible for the present mess.   He is more Irish perhaps than any of us, seeing that he looks like something uncoiled from the Book of Kells. Besides," I asked, " which of the gang possesses the grand manner of a San Diegoite or is capable of a chivalrous gesture ? "

"It is true what a man from Waterford said yesterday— 'the English refused freedom to gentlemen like Parnell and Redmond, and gave it to a bunch of louts, knowing bloody well they could do nothing with it that would be any good.' "

"You are as bad as the old charwoman who blamed the English, first for living in the country and then for leaving it, and herself without a job."

"I'm sick of politics," said George.

"God blast you and them, anyway," said Thwackhurst cheerily. "You have ruined all the graffiti. You can't find anything in a piss-house now but political remarks. It's always a sign of decline in the fortunes of a country. Even at their moments of ease the people are obsessed with thoughts of politics. Instead of thinking of the matter in hand. And just when the spread of popular education was bringing the graffiti lower on the walls."

"Lower on the walls ? "

"Sure. Don't you see the little children were beginning to add their quota, when all this damn politics comes along."

"What would you consider as a graffito of the Golden Age ? "

Thwackhurst fumbled for a note-book, but before he found it he started reciting :

> "'Here lies the grave of Keelin,
> And on it his wife is kneeling;
> If he were alive, she would be lying,
> And he would be kneeling.'"

He waved his unopened note-book, saying : "It is funda-mental. It expresses the difference between Life and Death, Love and Loss. It is touched with the *lacrimæ rerum* above the Weeping Wall. Terse as a Greek epitaph," he murmured, fondling the words in his mind.

He must be thinking of the Wailing Wall. But I said :

"There is one about Shanks's patent in Trinity College."

"Is there ? " he asked eagerly. "In the Muses ? "

"Yes," I said.

"I must get the Provost's permission to go in and photograph it."

" There is no need for that.   Anyone can go in."

" The Provost likes formality," Thwackhurst said, with a twinkle in his wrinkling eye.

" The Baths of Caracalla," I remarked.

" For God's sake, come on," said George.

" They must have had their walls covered with wonderful graffiti scribbled by the young men as they lay cooling.   It was the Silver Age of Rome.   But tell me, where did you find Keelin's epitaph ? "

" In the lavatory behind Nelson's pillar.   There is a version in a pub in Dalkey, but it is corrupt."

" God blast you and your politics," Thwackhurst repeated. " They are as bad as glazed tiles !   You have ruined the finest town for graffiti in Europe, and ended its Elizabethan Age." He was gone.

" The Writing on the Wall," said George, restored to humour.   He had forgiven me for suggesting that his admirer, our admirer, little Cunegunde, was mad.

The furies which we ward off from Griffith's memory, the flower-sellers whom he encouraged by his largesse, beside his inn, attacked us.   We paid toll.   Joe was awaiting us. Joe with the forehead of a Spanish grandee.

" You took your time."

" This fellow brought me to a party and kept me there when I wanted to be here," said George.

" So, that was it," said Joe.

" Don't blame me."

" Listen," I said.   " Do you know what I found out to-day ? Endymion has all our names in his list of his Christian names. If you doubt it, go to the National Library and look in the signature book.   ' James, Boyle, Tisdell, Burke, Stewart, Fitzsimons, Farrell.'   We are all included . . . in his lunatic make-up."

" Figments in the mind of a lunatic !   I like that," Joe commented.

" Where do I come in ? " George asked.

" I have not instigated him," said I.

" I never did him any harm," said Joe.

" It is his way of aggrandising himself and of paying us a compliment.   He includes the life of Dublin at the moment in himself.   He regards us as all that is worth anything in the town."

" I wonder.   What a ' final famous victory '—we end not

as ideas burning on the hand of the Creator, but as loonies in the mind of a lunatic ! "

" You are somewhat pessimistic," I replied.

" Even in the Irish Free State there is room for pessimism."

" Gentlemen ? " large-nosed, red-haired Lewis inquired.

" Two tankards and a small one."

The Bailey is the only tavern where there still are tankards of pure silver. A few now, but one time one hundred and sixty. Trophy collecting and other forms of theft have reduced their number to seven or eight.

The fire in the corner fireplace was smouldering. The north light fell on the mirror which closed what had once been the folding-door to the smoke-room where Arthur Griffith held his sway, and before him, Charles Stewart Parnell. Joe sat sideways across the little room, George in the corner at his left, and I faced the fireplace and the mirror. Doors to the left and right of us.

" It's very quiet here," said Joe.

" If we're not interrupted by the famous bores, we'll be right enough," George remarked.

" We can ascend," said Joe.

In Arthur Griffith's day Mr. Hogan gave us the use of a reserved room one storey higher. In it, some of Griffith's messages to the Irish people were composed. Solemnly, when invaded by the town's tiresome ones, we were wont to bid ourselves good-evening publicly and to go up privately and unobtrusively to the privileged room. There we could sit *laudatores temporis acti* : living in the imagined successes of our past.

Now no Whelan holds the gate against intruders on Arthur. Griffith was dead and we, his disciples, meet but rarely in the upper chamber. We can let our talk range freely in the smoking-room until we are driven out by some insufferable but respectful bore, who calls us ' Sir.'

" We met Thwackhurst on our way here. That delayed us."

" He is one of those who cannot be accused of being *cupidus rerum novarum*," Joe said quietly.

" Nor quite satisfied with their results."

" He prefers poverty and freedom to observance and respectability. I like him well. Seumas brought me to his digs high up in a gable, where he lives with his cat. It was the morning of Christ's nativity. He got out of bed, put on a short reefer jacket over his naked form, stepped into his boots and, nether naked, squatted before his fireless grate with : ' It was the winter wild. . . . God blast my old huer of a landlady. Which of yez has a match ? ' ''

" Has she forgotten the mistletoe ? ''

" She has forgotten the bloody fire.''

" I saw him looking out of his window in Oxo after his cat this morning," said I.

" Another character, Maturnin, the best authority the *Encyclopædia Britannica* could enlist, used to do his work at the bar downstairs.''

" It's a great tavern right enough.''

" What amazes me," said George, " is that the Germans are sending over professors of English to trace out the imaginary itinerary of Joyce's imaginary Mr. Bloom through the different pubs he is supposed to have visited. They all miss the one that Joyce liked.''

" The Bloom that never was on sea or land ! He is quite unconvincing. A mere chorus to Joyce.''

" Was he Elwood ? ''

" Lord, no ! '' said I.

" I should hate to have my pubs stalked by German professors who took pub-crawling seriously. The moment our pubs become the subject of literature, that is the moment they are undone. Even we who patronise them would become self-conscious. The last thing drink should do is to make one self-conscious. We would become actors, as it were, in a play, and not simply patrons of our pub.''

" Even in our ashes live their Reuter's wires.''

" Talking of ashes, we saw that wonderful doctor who thinks that he is the cigar. He passed us in Dawson Street in a hurry, in his Ford.''

" Probably he was going to lay another wreath on the grave of the ' Unknown Soldier '.''

" To whom he was related.''

" In that he was more or less unknown.''

" Just the same again, Lewis," said I.

" Right you are, sir. Fawcus rode another winner to-day, sir.''

The unnecessary boy who makes a noise with the grate lingered to overhear, but left the fire slacked.

" How's Yeats to-day ? ''

"I heard he is better. Hackett is preparing a festival celebration of his seventieth birthday. I hope he'll be all right for it."

"When he's gone, the next in line is O'Sullivan," George affirmed.

"What about Stephens?"

"No. The Bard is the next best. Listen to this:

> 'Have thou no fear, though round this heart
>   The winds of passion are.
> The image of your love is set
>   Within, serene and far;
> As in some lonely mountain lake
>   The reflex of a star.'"

"My idea of lyrical poetry is different. I like it earth-free like a lark and devoid of sadness. James Stephens' is a good example.

> 'Lovely and airy the view from the hill
>   That looks down Ballylee;
> But no good sight is good until,
>   By great good luck I see
> The blossom of the branches
>   Walking towards me
>   Airily.'

It is light, bright and echoes with 'lovely' and 'good.' Or take that light and witty stave born out of merriment—if the Bard would adopt that style, he would be as witty as Willie Shakespeare. You know the stanza about the intermittent wife of a learned ornithologist who spent her week-ends with a tramp.

> 'That two-backed beast of which you speak
> He has no horns upon his beak
> And the reason is not far to seek—
> She needs strong back where a back is weak
> And there's wisdom yet in the ancient rann:
> "She's away with the gaberlunzie man!"
>
> Then guard your foreheads whatever befall
> For the tallest forehead amongst you all
> And the wisest scholar that ever was born—
> He yet may wear the cuckhold's horn.'

How gay it is and in the great tradition!—'a word of fear.' Why should wit be inadmissible to great verse? But you would have a little sermon concealed somewhere in a song. You stand for Wordsworth . . . I'm 'light as leaf on linde,'

and I stand for Burns.   There is always a hint of hypocrisy in
Wordsworth :

'Will no one tell me what she sings ? '

He doesn't want to know.   If he did, he would run off from
his love-making as he did once before from the girl in France.
He is the one person who does not ' Endear himself to us by
his mistress and his illegitimate child.'   He certainly does not.
Yet he had both.   He never wrote a love song. . . . He
never put up a fight."

"Burns' fight against hypocrisy does not necessarily make
him greater than Wordsworth."

"Not his fight essentially, but his attitude towards life.
The ease and clarity of his song.   Honestly now, George,
would you prefer a thousand Wordsworths in this pub to a
thousand Burnses ? "

"You have drawn a red herring of religion and the rest of
it in."

"No.   But I'm trying to show that your judgment of
poetry is basically religious.   You want the pulpit in the poem.
You have not got over your public school and Matthew
Arnold's influence yet.   Your poet must be a preacher as well
as a teacher.   However, Shakespeare diddles you all.   What
does he preach ?   Is it not significant that Wordsworth took
after Milton, and that Milton took after that arch-hypocrite,
Cromwell ?   Give me the pre-Cromwellian poets, no ' stern
daughters,' but ' Doxies over the dale.'   The English people
are afraid of Willie Shakespeare, and yet Wanton Willie and
Rantin', Rovin' Robin are the best poets in the English
language.   James Stephens is no black-leg in the domain of
the parsons ; he's a great spirit, one that outsoared the shadow
of his youth and outlived it unsoured. . . . After your pals
are dead and buried, ' he will hoist his flag and go,' as his
reincarnated Rafferty went with the Spring always at his back.

'Now with the coming in of Spring, the days will stretch a bit ;
    And after the Feast of Bridget, I will hoist my flag and go :
    For since the thought got into my head, I can neither stand nor sit,
    Till I find myself in the middle of the county of Mayo.' "

Joe, who cared little for either of us, said, " I believe in
George."
I was left confronting a silent George with an arsenal of
unexpostulated energy.   He kept so silent that somehow I
felt wrong and was beginning to feel concerned when he

smacked his lips. I thought he was about to speak. But George is a great friend. The minute that he found that the discussion was turning into an argument of conviction and that the position was about to drift from that most delightful of all communions when friends are found ' affirming each his own philosophy,' he suddenly changed the whole front by producing a little manuscript from his pocket-book. Silently he handed the page to me. I read:

> "Yes, you are right. There is no doubt. No balance sheet
> Will be made out; A call, maybe, On you and me.
> We shall not see A Company At God knows where In Far Mayo.
> But should the Bud to Paris go, Oh, there will be
> The Company Of hearts' desire, That stings like fire,
> Of sweet young things In silken hose, And others with-
> Out any clothes; When shapely limbs Are twirled in air,
> He will not know, He will not care; They will not run
> Before him there—When he goes down, A fervid man,
> To plump Louise Or swift Susanne, He will not know
> Or care a pin, If China clay Or Kaolin Be white as snow
> Or black as sin ! "

"Splendid ! " I shouted. I looked over it to find what caught my eye as I read . . . the verse mastery:

> "Of sweet young things
> In silken hose,
> And others with-
> Out any clothes."

The jerk between the " with " and " out " is like the pull off of the last stocking.

"Great writing, George ! It would keep Cook occupied touring this town to Paris if he used your verse as publicity for ' The White town far away,' as George Moore calls it."

"I liked ' twirled in air.' "

"More of the French actresses," said Joe.

"Where did George get ' Susanne ' ? " I asked.

"That reminds me," said Joe. "They are all Susannes."

"Are they ? "

"At Boulogne, at Rouen and Amiens, I never met anyone who was not Susanne."

"Why ? "

"*Nom de guerre*, I presume."

Gently the influence of Bacchus, that divinity who convinced the world of old that he was indeed a god and one whose influence could be proved; on whom unbelief needed no help, who suffered not from atheists, but only from fanatics, overcame us with his gift of peace.   Past grew as considerable as present : more important, too, magnified by the mists of time.   I gazed at my reflection in the mirror ; and I haloed it with clouds of smoke.

" Talking of ashes and Unknown Soldiers, Monty got a good one in to-day.   When the Bailey reminded his wife, whose eloquence is well-sustained, that they were twenty-three years married, she asked, ' How do you propose to celebrate the anniversary ? '—' By three minutes' silence.' "

" Oh, you told us that before ! "

" We may repeat our drinks, but not ourselves."

" Repeat ! " said Batt, as he entered suddenly.

" Repeat ?   What we want in this country is a vomitorium so that we can vomit out all the bloody fools who are ruining it.   England has a puke-point, but we have not.   That is why we cannot get rid of the sickening fools who try to boss us.   The worse we get the more we revel in despair.   Look at us now.   Thirteen years or more of home rule.   Who gets the rule but the poor bloody fools who have to stay at home ?   The fattest and most easy country in the world wrecked by selfish government in half a decade, and turned into a Spartan Helot's warning to the Commonwealth."

" But if we were totally free ? "

" When were we ?   If there was a when, when we were ? The first gang from overseas could walk through us.   Was there ever a conquest we resisted ?   Was there ever a con-quest by which we benefited ?   Whom did we kick out ? Only the men who could have made men of us as they were themselves.   Arthur Griffith's Ireland costing twice its revenue for one year's government.   And the Government afraid to send criminals before juries unless they want to get them off. We're half-beggared and twice taxed.

" When it comes to governing under democratic conditions you have either to reduce the people to your own level of mediocrity or reduce yourself to theirs.   As a rule it is a com-promise which brings both to a lower level than either held."

" We were just discussing verse," I murmured in expostu-lation.   I was not heard.

" I know, I know," said Joe.   " I would prefer to hand the whole place over to Bohane, who manages the Spring Show and the Horse Show.   He would make an excellent Dictator.   He knows the country and we know him."

" We know that he comes from Yorkshire."

" Where does De Valera come from ? "

" The Devil only knows ! That's his strong point, that he's unreckonable. We won't be ruled even by one of ourselves. A native would be too wise to try, or too harassed by jealousies to succeed. We simply are not a ruling race. Politically we are fodder for any foreigner to exploit : culture beds for any political microbe."

" Bohane could run the country rationally first, but he would need to have been cast ashore from the unknown, like Arthur Pendragon."

George said, " No country is run rationally. Even rationalist Russia has to stage pageants of force and to use the sex symbols of the Hammer and the Sickle."

" I see McGinty has been talking about the Sickle in his latest speech."

" So I saw," said Joe. " What's the idea ? "

" He has probably been dallying with it of late in its relation to the ' social transition ' he mentioned. We are drifting straight for Celtic Communism."

" Griffith said, ' I believe in the Irish people.' Well, I disbelieve in them."

" Why then, you will be asked, do you go on living here ? "

" To go on disbelieving. I should hate this country to be ruled by reason, and the certainty that it never shall be tempts me to remain. If this place were to be run in the interests of reason, do you think that we should ever get a drink ? "

Suddenly the golden light of the door-panes was shadowed. A heavy figure, with a mop of hair hanging over one shoulder, literally blew into the room. He lurched down the three-inch step, straightened himself, and shouted :

" Bring me a cup of sack, boy, I would be merry."

We raised a little welcoming cheer, and at once began to babble. Blue-eyed, vigorous, generous and reckless, Shamus takes the drabness from life. He has an open face and a winning smile that shows his fine teeth.

Turning to us, he inquired in a loud voice :

" How are all you huers ? " (It seems that in Dublin that word is bi-sexual. Or is it a relic of the Elizabethan days when " whoreson knave " was quite common ?) " I'm writing a book on Richard Cœur de Lion ; he was a great huer. He was the real artist. He bloody well laid them all out. He knew his stuff. He knew how to fight. Fancy being called ' Lion Heart' in days when every man was brave! A great huer, and a relative of mine. He was the hell of a lad. He bloody well forked them all up on his thirty-foot spear. He was the real Norman. The de Burgoes came over with him."

" With Cœur de Leeon ? " Joe inquired.

" De Leeon or de Lion, it's all the same. . . . What other Richard is there ? "

" There is Richard Lynam, who was King of the Kips," said Joe.

" Blast you, anyway. You are nearly as bad a cod as my old friend here."

" Thanks," said I.

" But he was always a cod; you're only coming into it. As I was saying, Richard Cœur de Lion forked them all up, and so did Eustace, the Monk. He sent the boys over with de Burgoes to Ireland, and we had our thirty-foot spears and we bloody well forked the natives up."

" I was waiting for that," said Joe.

" ' He fought with Love even to the end,' " I quoted. " Like the great Achilles."

The blue eyes flashed and smiled.

" Well, you are right. But no one else waited for the spear of the de Burgoes. We went through the country: ' Men who rode upon horses!' Yeats has us right enough. We came in and conquered the whole place in half-an-hour. And we forked all the natives to hell."

" Tell me, Shamus," I asked, " has the spear any phallic significance in your family ? "

Shamus laughed. He could laugh at himself, which is perhaps a proof of his non-Celtic origin. But his fine phrensy was not finished.

" On the distaff side I'm a descendant of Kubla Khan."

" In Xanadu ? "

" No, you idiot, in the thirteenth century. . . . Where's that bloody waiter ? "

" He has gone off, thinking that this is de Burgoes' day."

" If that waiter thinks that he is getting the day off on account of the victories of my family, he is bloody well mis-taken. What's yours ? "

" Shamus," I said, " I am so overcome thinking of the

' pleasure domes ' of your ancestors-in-law that I do not think I can sustain another drink. But don't mind me; I can become as intoxicated on good company as on drinks. I am thinking of the ' twice ten miles of fertile ground where Alph the Sacred River ran.' . . ."

" You bloody well ran into the River Liffey. What's wrong with that? And you scrambled out at Liffey Bank because you couldn't pass Guinness's."

" Surely you could not be expecting him to be looking for another wet ? " said Joe.

" Another wet ? Where's that waiter gone ? "

" To caverns measureless to man."

" ' What's wrong with that ? ' reminds me," George said, " I met Endymion the other day, and he told me that he had invented a cure for constipation."

" What is it ? "

" Take salt, take salt."

" But that will give you a thirst."

" Well, what's wrong with that ? "

" What's wrong with Lewis ? Hah ! mine ancient, here thou art ! Get us something to keep the intellect afloat over these shoaling tides."

" Right, sir. Right, sir. Fawcus won again to-day."

" We were never a very militant nation," said Joe—" that is, compared with the Scots. As late as 1746 they fought Culloden, where one thousand of the Clansmen went down in one battle for the House of Stuart. Where is Scotland now ? Dominating, directing and leading the British Empire. And where is King George ? Down at Balmoral every summer, dressing himself up in a kilt and wearing a—what d'ye call it—a sporran. And his son married to a Scots-woman. The Scots were wise enough to get a share of what they built. They are as honoured as the English now."

" Winning battles in the spirit in which they were lost ? " I asked, thinking of Æ.

" Do you suggest," said Batt, " that if Ireland lost more men and had a better beating than the Scots at Drumossie Muir, that the King would come over here every year and dress in a caubeen and knee-breeches and twirl a Shillelagh and stay with Buckley near the gas-works in Monkstown ? "

" I don't know what you are talking about, but I do know that a wise nation can fit into the team which is the British nation without losing its identity or self-respect."

" He'd look better as a National Forester," George thought.

" What's the good of singing ' Soldiers are we ' when we hate the very sight of the results of soldiering and all that it implies : conquest and Empire ?   It's time we gave ourselves a chance to do something else than wail and hate. We are the only nation in Europe who were never in a European war, hence we have to assure ourselves that we are soldiers."

" If we were totally free——" I began.

" By heavens," said Shamus, " if we get any more freedom we may as well all become teetotallers, for we will then be free to develop our spiritual side, which is to allow no one to do as they please.   If we get any more freedom we'll all be chained together.   I didn't notice any slave-driving British names among the Executive Council.   They are all Irish but two. . . . There's only one thing to do, and that is to go on the dole and eat out of these fellows' hands and degrade yourself so far that even they will be superior to you and feel what mighty monarchs they are."

" What about becoming one of them ? "

" Not so good.   You would have to associate with them and see Irishmen dominated by a foreigner in their own rooms.   Besides, who wants to be guilty of having fooled and betrayed so many of the kindly Irish ?   If our countrymen can stand such slave-driving from a home Government, the wonder is that they lost any men at all against the outsider."

" Perhaps we like the privilege of enslaving ourselves," Joe remarked.

" Our idea of Freedom," said Batt, " is unrestricted opportunity for victimisation."

" Well," I said, repeating an old thought, " politics is the rumble in the bowels of a nation.   I will now leave this intestinal tract.   Let me solace myself with song.

> ' There's nothing left but ruin now
> Where once the crazy cabfuls roared,
> Where new-come sailors turned the prow
> And love-logged cattle-dealers snored :
> The room where old Luke Irwin whored
> The stairs on which John Elwood fell—
> Somethings are better un-encored :
> There's only left —— ' "

I quoted.

" Jayshus !   What kind of a kip have I come into at

all ? " Shamus inquired, smiling.   The very question Odysseus asked of his homeland.

" There's only one kind of a kip or brothel and that is mentioned by Goldsmith.   Farewell all."

" Hold on a minute ! " Shamus shouted.

" He doesn't believe in the Irish people," Joe remarked. " That's why he's going."

" I want to be out of the way when the Irish people start believing in themselves."

" Where's that guy of a waiter ? "

" Guy Fawcus ? " Joe remarked.

We were just getting into the mood when laughter was beginning to come as readily as the drinks.   I was sorry to leave.   Suddenly the golden glass was darkened for a moment. A bright-eyed, intelligent face appeared and disappeared.

" Come in, Cahal ! " I said.

" Well, aren't you a cook's blind bastard ! " Shamus shouted, angry at being deprived of female society.   " That wasn't Cahal O'Shannon.   That was Norah Hoult ! "

" I never saw more intelligent eyes in a human face."

" The Bagmen are up.   Don't let the little Firbolgs get you on your way home.   The Bagmen broke out before in this country, but we always put them back in their places, and we'll have to do it again.   Do it again with the spear of de Burgoes ! " and Shamus lunged at the incoming waiter with an imaginary spear.   " ' Those " natives " will never rule,' as Paddy Hogan said."

I quoted

> " ' But I, the last, go forth companionless.
>   And the days darken round me, and the years,
>   Among new men, strange faces, other minds.' "

The problem confronted me.   Why does every educated Irishman regret that he is Irish ?   Is it the education, the country or himself that is wrong ?   Or is it wrong to be educated ?   Or is it wrong to regret ?   Perhaps regretting is a sign of grace.   Shamus is right in his instinctive wish to be differentiated from the herd among which he finds himself.   Why is it that most Irishmen seek that differentiation ? The cleavage is not wholly between Norman and native nor between gentleman and farmer.   There is no difference here between the gentlemen, such as are allowed to live in their land, and the men who live on the land.   I remembered

what McLoren once said to me : " Most of the peasants are
gentlemen and have an immemorial courtesy that can only
have come from a ruling race." What has happened to our
race ? Who are the race ? For the most part they resemble
Shamus, big, blond and blue-eyed. These are the remnants
of conquerors and a conquest of time out of mind. They
are descendants of that Milesian stock which conquered a
country inhabited as parts of isolated Africa are inhabited, by
little pigmy fellows, the Firbolgs, or Bagmen. We resent
identification with the defeated. The Bagmen with their
little despatch cases are for the moment in insurrection, and
it is against Milesians they are revolting. And they are in
the ascendancy just now. This explains a great deal. It
explains the desire not to be thought " Irish " in the narrow
and narrowing sense which that word has come at present to
have. They do not wish to be identified with all that is
small, narrow, vindictive, cowardly, and vile. Irishmen, be
they de Burgoes or Milesians, are not happy with this " Freedom " which has only thrown them to the mercy of the
tinkers in the land. I wondered how many of the Government were of the Atticotti type of mind. Was there one of
them worth Shamus de Burgoes' little finger ? It was his
like who were in ascendancy when Ireland was getting its
name for spontaneous courage, generosity and the open hand.
His history may be at fault, but his instinct is not. I longed
for that magical spear, no matter who wielded it, that could
" fork them all to blazes."

Up Shamus ! You are of the true and sterling stuff.
The Bagmen must be put back in their place, which is the
Republic of the ditches. And the magnanimous Milesian
must come into his own once more. An end to this Tinkers'
Dream ! The problem is solved, if there ever was one.
The problem why an Irishman is reluctant to be considered
as an Irishman. Why ? Because he is loth to be identified
with the defeated, and with dirt and defeat and multitude.
Before history recorded battles he was a conqueror. Now
that there is a record, he is an under-dog to his immemorial
inferiors. What is this I smell ? Class conflict ? What does
it mean when only one class, and that the lowest, is alone
to be paramount ?—Communism ! Of course ! I should
have known this long before, and not have been confusing
myself by obstinate questionings about the meaning of an
Irishman's reluctance to be thought an Irishman. He does

not resent being considered Irish. What he does resent, and what I more than most resent, is identification with Communism. I am in two minds whether to go back and ask the liberating Lyæus, Seumas, if he still is in the mood for a pint of sack. *Par le splendeur Dex!*

One of the harpies selling matches approached.

" Buy a box, Sir."

" I'll do nothing until Ireland's free!"

She looked puzzled. Then she broke out—

" Ireland me neck! A Dago President, an English King, an Eyetalian Pope! Ireland me neck! Up the United Front!"

" That two-backed beast."

The queues were forming up outside the cinema house in Grafton Street: Dubliners willing to buy a dream that will let them escape for an hour from their surroundings. I passed the prosperous betting house of Jack Martin.

" Fortune was seldom invoked, for they desired no change," I remembered grimly.

I turned into the Green, and left Grafton Street behind me, with its temple of Fortune and its cinema crowds seeking solace in their shadowy " stars."

CHAPTER V

TO GAIN ADMISSION TO THE VICE-REGAL LODGE IT WAS NECESSARY
to stop your car at the guarded gate and remain stationary
until a policeman had examined it and questioned you. He
would then inquire at the sentry's box if anyone of your name
was expected at the Lodge. This was before De Valera
invested himself with the functions of the Governor-General.

I was met by His Excellency's Major-domo, the tall and
impressive Mr. Doyle, late of the Gresham Hotel. His
fidelity to Collins and his help in the movement as well as
his undoubted ability placed him where he was.

" He is upstairs," said Doyle.

" *Vidi presso di me un veglio solo.*"

The First Governor-General of the Irish Free State, Tim
Healy, walked across to the window of one of the upper
rooms, and pointing to the view, said sepulchrally : " Louis
le Grand Monarque had nothing better than that."

Immediately underneath red geraniums blazed in their
formal beds ; the beautiful greensward was bordered by a
paling of graceful stone pillars. On either side, trees threw
up their fountains of young green. From the plateau of the
Phœnix Park the shallow vale of the Liffey appeared deeper
than it is. Afar through silver mists the Dublin mountains
rolled smooth as a dim wave. The smoke belt which roofs
the city was transparent and roofs and spires looked like a
mirage.

> " ' The people of Pa do not care for flowers ;
>   All the Spring no one has come to look.
> But their Governor-General, alone with his cup of wine,
> Sits till evening and will not move from the place.' "

I quoted, having gazed my fill.

" What audacity ! " Tim exclaimed, and smiled. " They
have not come so far," said he, thinking of his well-guarded
gates. " Where did you get that ? "

" That is a translation of the Chinese of Po-Chu-I when
he was Governor-General of Chung-Chou."

" Chung-Chou," mumbled Tim into his beard. " I don't
think I will invite them to look at my geraniums. Not even
for the Jubilee Nurses' Fund."

I said, " Well, the Vice-Regents who lived here knew how

to live.   They chose the highest and nearest open space to the city."

"They took it over," said Tim.

I thought of the spacious days of Lord Wimborne's Lieutenancy; of the stir when he, himself a Grand Monarch, and his escort "came sounding through the town"; of the bustle when her Ladyship went a-shopping in Grafton Street, and of the many cars walling the polo-ground of a summer's evening; the diners gay with uniforms every night.

I looked at the ivory face, the black-and-white beard and the high brow above the bright eyes of liquid brown, such as some Chief Rabbi might possess.   I thought of his marvellous and astute career.   *He* "took it over," I thought, and he sits with his collection of Waterford glass in the corner of the morning-room where he entertains his old cronies and new friends to lunch.

"Most cities extend in a westward direction.   Dublin is an exception to this rule.   Why?   Because of this Park, Guinness's Brewery and the Kingsbridge Railway Station. There is also the valley of the Camac and the gloomy bulk of Kilmainham to prevent the speculating builder."

"What a blessing!" I exclaimed.

"I suppose it is.   They would be overwhelming my house at Glenaulyn but for these safeguards."

"No city neglects its river as Dublin does.   There is not a pleasure-boat on the Liffey from Butt Bridge to Lucan. If the river and town were in England there would be water-gardens and boat-houses and people delighting themselves in the lovely amenities of the water."

"And drowning themselves," said Tim, in a comic sepulchral voice.   "You can see, but the trees are grown, the edge of the road where Joe Brady killed Lord Cavendish and Mr. Burke."

Was he thinking of his far insecurer position than that of the Vice-Royalists of 1882 ?

"That was a terrible affair," I said.

I remembered hearing, as a child, the story of the deed, and of how it was done with an ' amputation knife.'   I remembered the fascination which made me take out my father's surgical case when his back was turned, and examine the longest of the four or five long, narrow knives, so narrow and with such thick backs that their blades were almost triangular. . . .

" With a terrible weapon," said Tim.

" And a terrible end for Joe Brady. Marwood, the executioner, had to go down into the pit and hold on to his legs to kill him : he was so strong, and they miscalculated the drop."

I let my mind dwell on the other side of the question. What strong sense of overwhelming wrong had constrained a man of such good character as Brady to put his head into the halter ? But Tim's politics were in abeyance in the Lodge.

No man who ever practised at the Irish Bar had a more deadly simplicity of phrase than Tim Healy. He knew the popular way of thinking, as if every juryman took him into his confidence and confessed his point of view. The story of his defence of the Insurance Company that resisted payment because of the suspicious way in which a timber-yard they insured was burned, is an example. The two night watchmen, Tim told the jury, ' neither saw a spark nor heard a crackle or even smelt smoke, and yet during the hours of their guardianship the whole timber-yard of acres and acres is destroyed. Gentlemen of the Jury, the Babes in the Wood.'

We left the room and descended by the lift to the great drawing-room where he had put in two antique Georgian mantel-pieces at his own expense. He showed them to me and began a history of the Lodge. Then, without finishing it : " For fear I forget it, if you are doing nothing better to-night, come here for a lantern show of an attempt to ascend Mount Everest. And we will have a little dinner first. Another invitation—will you bring your friend Yeats, the Sally gardener, to my box at the Spring Show ? I have asked the Army Band, so I must entertain some of the officers and their ladies, who may want to dance afterwards. Some of them are Generals."

" They have attained suddenly very high rank ? "

" Now, don't be too sure of that. Their mothers may have been ' generals ' before them."

He smiled rather grimly as he was wont to do when he let his memories criticise the present state of things ; not dwelling for the time on the fact that but for the fighting of these ' generals ' he would never have sat in the House of the Satraps. I wondered why his intimate knowledge of the Irish mind should allow this contempt. Was it because he

could not emerge from the generation which he knew?
Was it because he could not forgive Griffith for his policy
of ignoring Westminster and all that it meant to Tim?
Honoured, trusted, consulted at Westminster, Tim Healy
sought for and accepted the position of Governor-General of
the Irish Free State and all it connoted merely as a compensation of sorts for all that he had lost? Was he the
first to foresee the futility of the future and the earliest to
cash in on his losses by making the better of them? He
had a profound knowledge of the popular mind, of its temperament, its character, its limitations and shortcomings.
Therefore, immediately after his appointment there were
rumours of his resignation. Knowing as I did the energy
and the influence he brought to bear in London to obtain
his appointment and his gratitude to Lord Beaverbrook for
his decisive aid, I asked him what he meant by threatening
to resign. " Nothing, Oliver, but the minute these fellows
here think I am enjoying myself, that is the moment they
will begin to undermine me."

He believed that his was a life appointment. He set
about furnishing the Lodge as a home, making it a liaison
office and a bridge between irreconcilable and uncouth
elements and those who had already, with Scotland and
Wales, nations with national features more marked than ours,
been content to join in the Celtic hegemony which built that
Empire which is Rome's successor. " *Ab orbe terrarum
remoti* " once: but now making the orb of the world revolve
round them. I do not say that he condemned or had little
faith in what the undefining politicians call " Gaelic Culture,"
but he knew the difference between Culture and Civilisation.
He knew that folklore, native dances, cottage life and the
Gaelic language could never fulfil the proper destiny of the
different classes of the Irishmen or bring Ireland to take its
place once again as a contributor to the civilisation of a
Europe far beyond it in progress.

To offer our island as a funk-hole or a retreat from the
wars and ambitions of Europe might be quite in character
with the tendency of the representatives of that part of the
Irish race which seeks sheltered occupations and longs for
ease when it grows tired of belligerency, or, rather, irrespon-
sibility after disturbance. It may never have appeared to
him in terms as succinct as these, but his instinct for " sizing
up " a jury made him size up his own countrymen and act

according to his perceptions. He did his best to heal the
' split ' : " As an expert of splits, take it from me that there
are some fellows who are depending for a livelihood on dis-
union. And one of them is De Valera." He could only
bring those together who were already in one camp. To
wean men away from the hopes of gain to be derived from
opposition was beyond him. He called himself the " Invisible Mender," but what he might regard as a rent or a
hole in his seat was a *modus vivendi* to De Valera and the
Irish who took up arms against the majority of their countrymen. Mending an Ireland split in two from the Vice-regal
Lodge was about as hopeful a proposition as that of a tailor
would be, who offered to sew from the Escurial the rents of
the garments of the beggars who lived by exposing their
sores. He had few delusions. I think that he was gratified
by being able to rise from the dead of the Redmond *régime*
which Griffith ended, and to take the plum from Griffith in
the end. He would have an added satisfaction had he heard
Griffith's " I don't want Healy ; he betrayed Parnell." This
was said to me by Griffith as we walked along Nassau Street
some months before Tim Healy's appointment to the richest
office in the New State. In certain ways, by his non-aggres-
sive astuteness, by his leaning on forces greater than himself,
and, like a glider pilot, getting a lift from any cloudy formation, he resembled De Valera. The Rabbi-like eyes and skin
they had in common, but for deep-hearted and sympathetic
understanding, for the ready hand that had not to be sought
but was proffered, for loyalty to Ireland as far as he was
akin to it, and for a faith that envied only those whose faith
was simpler, Tim Healy had no equal. He was too wise to
let it be seen that he enjoyed the Vice-regality while he had
it, though he must have known that it was a transient and,
to the new Ireland, an unkindred thing. How could an
Irish Viceroy improve on the genuine article ? Worse, he
took the shilling of the Sassenach, without spending in the
city the Sassenach's pound.

Henry Curt Mantel was shocked by the familiarity of
chief and serf in the Dublin of the Twelfth Century. He
sent over his professors of decorum, his royal tutors, to show
the chiefs the unwisdom of their ways and their want of a
dais and a withdrawing room. Uncle Tim's Cabin, as Lady
Lavery called it, had no withdrawing room. You met all
the founders of the new *régime* ; and they could meet you on

level terms.   If any signs of inferiority were manifested they were due to artificial and arbitrary rules of conduct, British in origin, which sought to lay down laws even for eating asparagus.   The asparagus, to give it its due, revolted and refused to be hung up by the green end.   Lady Lavery, who was usually at the banquets, could be counted on to come to the rescue by demonstrating by dainty gesticulation the nice conduct of the flail-like food.   But woe betide you if you thought that your ways with asparagus were enough to con- stitute " a national record."   Table manners could be con- fused with the habits of, or with attempts at apeing the Ascendancy.   There were days when Tim would not have hesitated by his contempt for such pomps.

As I drove away I went over in memory the few visits I had paid the Vice-regal Lodge of old.   When the Aberdeens first held Office I was taken, a very small boy, to some " drive " of theirs for Irish goods, dressed as an " Irishman "—knee breeches, top hat and the legendary shillelagh; the real article I have never seen in the hands of any Irishman since that day.   Then, the Wimbornes' *régime*, full of imperial hospitality to a little clan.   I pass over the second coming of the Campbells.   I prefer the liberality of Conservatives. The Dudleys and the Wimbornes spent £50,000 a year or more above the salary attached to the office of Lord Lieutenant.

I recalled the last time I was at the Vice-regal Lodge before the change of Government.   I drove there in one of Lord Fitzalan's cars; I returned on foot.   As far as guards and precautions against assassination went, they were some- what the same then as now.   Can it be that all governments have to be protected from the governed ?   Is the multitude never at ease ?   In Sweden, I believe, the King can walk about unguarded and also unmobbed.

As I drove along the Liffey towards O'Connell Bridge I thought of two journeys I had made in that way before.   One through the firing with Hugh Law; the other when, rescued at midnight and escorted by many gun-turreted tanks, I sat in an armoured car listening to desultory rifle-firing, and was driven to the Government buildings.   To how few is it given to have the sensation of driving headlong through a supine city !

> What a thing it were
> To ride in triumph through Persepolis !

True, it was easier for me to visit now the Lodge than

in the days before the change. Did this mean that the Lodge had come down, or that I had gone up in the world? That is one of those questions which are best answered by having a Yes on, " each way." One thing was certain : it could never be a bridge between the warring factions in the biggest faction fight Ireland has had for centuries, particularly since almost half the country was " out on its keeping." The Lodge had to go in the course of De Valera's march to Cloud Cuckoo Town, towards that City of Contradictions, his Irish Catholic Socialist Republic. But was Collins's dream any more realisable? It had not the elements and the makings of Communism, but it was just as inadequate and . . . but he was capable of seeing facts and of adjusting his position in the course of events. So, he would have enlarged on his ideal Ireland. Had he not written :—

> We must be true to facts if we would achieve anything in this life. . . . The true devotion lies not in melodramatic defiance or self-sacrifice for something falsely said to exist, or for mere words or formulas which are empty, and which might be but the house swept and garnished to which seven worse devils entered in.

And one a foreign devil!

Who could blame a man who had dared and done so much for an ideal to be still somewhat led by his dream?

> One may see processions of young women riding down on the island ponies to collect sand from the sea-shore, or gathering in the turf, dressed in their shawls and in their brilliantly coloured skirts made of material spun, woven and dyed by themselves, as it had been spun, woven and dyed for over a thousand years. Their cottages also are little changed. They remain simple and picturesque. It is only in such places one gets a glimpse of what Ireland may become again. . . .

He forgot the brothers of the young women! He was assassinated by his fellow-countrymen not far from his birthplace ; and he died in Emmet Dalton's arms :—

" The much-loved and trusted ' Big Fellow '—statesman and soldier too—now leaned against me in the darkness, rigid and dead, with the piteous stain on him, Ireland's stain, darkening my tunic as we jolted over the road. . . ."

There were no Englishmen about when that occurred, but Mr. De Valera was not far away, he who has done more damage in a decade to our country than England did in seven hundred years. England never sapped Ireland's morale. De Valera and degeneration are synonymous.

The south light was on the beautiful dome of the Custom House behind its hideous grid of loop-line railway. O'Connell and his four lady guardian angels looked after me as I turned to cross his bridge; how they would fly away were his monument to come to life! I looked along the curving river of the seven bridges to the city's steeples on its southern bank. At evening this is one of the loveliest views. The steeples gain in height; and, if the tide be full, the seagulls brighten the river as they float with their breasts held high against the current to the sun.

A crowd collected at the Ballast Office clock; that clock, by which all watches are set, caught my eye. I saw that the crowd was looking at Endymion the cricketer, as he saluted the clock with drawn sword. The ceremony over, he took from the tail of his coat a large alarm clock, set it carefully and replaced it in his pocket, from which it began to ring loudly as he walked, greatly to the crowd's delight. The people cheered good-humouredly. It was high noon!

I passed the bulging bank of Ireland, that squats on the city like a usurer with his money-bags, and so home.

A bulky figure was being assisted outside my house on to a side-car, that almost lost conveyance; a bulky figure with a dark Trilby hat above a mane of unkempt hair. I saw the sackcloth on his chest and belly. What a narrow escape! The reigning bore of the moment was leaving my house, doubtless having been told that I was not at home. A narrow escape! If I retain any of my youth in age, it is chiefly due to my avoidance of bores. My bore-point is very low. I flash off and I am gone. But this was the most tiring and, to women and young girls, the most offensive bore in Dublin. He owed his impunity to the religious attitude he adopted to bully women about their clothes. It made the police tolerant when they saw him with his apron of sacking and his girdle cord. He would sit in a tram and accost the passengers roughly about their low necks, bare arms or legs: was a self-appointed censor. He was one of those cases that suffer from frustration of sex . . . and to whom all sex is anathema. Also, it should be persecuted. This is not an uncommon attitude of mind in elderly adults who have nothing left to think about when the flesh is ignored. Subjugating their sex becomes an object in itself, as if gelding were godliness. This explains their hatred of women and the desire to make them suffer, as was apparent in the attempt of the Boston Methodists to persecute the beneficent inventor of ether the moment he applied it to the relief of birth throes. But Philip Francis Little was calling on me, not to call me to the sackcloth, but to leave me a book of his poems.

Philip Francis modelled himself, so far as his way of speaking went, on old Dr. Sigerson, and Dr. Sigerson, conscious always of his Danish or Scandinavian origin, used to speak as if he were translating a rune.

The amazing thing was that the poems were quite competent. This is the foreword:

> The aim that all we poets have in writing is of pleasing
> Ourselves, which is the object each one has when he is sneezing.

After all, he is more interesting than Gerald Manley Hopkins, who fooled Robert Bridges with his tricks with language. Philip Francis Little's

> No throstle cock, no blackbird
> Chrysostome upon a tree,
> Could sing a song of saxpence
> So merrily as he.

Chrysostome, golden-mouthed! Of course he got it from his religious studies, but it must have been almost profane to him to employ it for the " Ousel cock so black of hue, With orange tawny bill." What a pity he didn't stick to rhyming and leave preaching alone! He is taking his immortal soul too seriously; already he is eccentric; soon he will go mad. And now he was heaving off on a side-car, leaning over to talk to the jarvey who kept humouring him. Often as I have heard of that humour, I always took it with a grain of salt, with the suspicion that it was assessed by tourists who came prepared to see fun in anything Irish. But the remark from the quayside hazard to the men on the Guinness lighters, who comported themselves as shepherds of Ocean though their voyages were limited to a few miles of the river, " Eh! Bring us back a monkey or a parrot! " justifies them. And the jarvey who asked the famous surgeon who defended a divorce action for alleged misconduct in a cab, leading his bride in *secondes noces* out on his arm from Church *en route* for a honeymoon, " Cab, sir ? " had a terse turn of phrase.

CHAPTER VI

SIR HORACE WAS DISSATISFIED WITH HIS DEATH, OF WHICH the Press notices were quite unworthy. He had just died in New York, so that his loss would be all the greater in Ireland, which could not compensate itself by a public funeral. But so inadequate were the obituaries that, without waiting for the Irish Mail, he wrote on the fourth day to the newspapers pointing out certain omissions and misunderstandings, and assuring "those who worked with him" that the announcement of his death was premature, but that they and his country would have whatever years were left to him, devoted selflessly to their service. He then collected enough money in America to found in Dublin a paper of his own.

The reason of the paucity of cables of regret from Dublin was simply that "those who worked with him" were incredulous. They knew that there was so much of his usefulness still undemonstrated that his death was, at the worst, merely a means of getting a public assessment of his life-work and a criticism of their help—a method as it were of reporting progress. So, unimaginatively, they resented more than mourned him.

Therefore, I was all the better able to sustain the shock when I discovered that the Session of the Senate was about to open with a letter from Sir Horace sending in his resignation. He succeeded in hitching the Senate to his retirement, a thing that many could not do in the course of their full activities.

The Chairman read:

" MY DEAR GLENAVY,
          After too protracted and earnest thought, I have come to the definite conclusion that I am no longer justified in remaining upon the Senate. I therefore place my resignation in your hands and ask you to take the proper steps to have the vacancy filled. I wish to tender to you, to the Vice-Chairman and the members my grateful thanks for your kindness to me at my two attendances and your indulgence in regard to my many absences. To you all, as well as to myself, it is due that I should state the reasons for the course I have taken. They are two and can be briefly summarised:
          1. The Senate may, if its members give sufficient

thought to the problem submitted to them for discussion and disinterested advice to the Government and the people, build up and exercise great influence for good. It is a small body, and cannot afford to have members who are unable to attend at least a majority of its sittings. I could not do this for reasons of health in the near future, and do not believe that such attendance will ever be the best way of rendering that service to my country which will continue to be the chief aim and object of my life for the days I may be spared to see.

2. My work lies in spheres of voluntary effort—especially organised voluntary effort—and not in that of legislation or public administration. It is true that when much younger I represented an Irish constituency for eight years in the British Parliament. I presided over the Irish Convention, worked for the Dominion Settlement (without the Partition that had to be) and accepted the honour of a nomination to the Senate. But in the first case I was seeking State assistance for agriculture and industry. This came with the creation and endowment of the Department of Agriculture and Technical Instruction of which I was the working head for its first seven years. The other political activities were dictated by the recognition that, failing an Irish settlement, all the work I wished to do had come to nought.

I joined the Senate from a wish to take some small part in supporting the Free State Government, well knowing the personal inconvenience my doing so would cause. I would not leave it now if I could be reasonably suspected to be thereby safeguarding my person or my property. But, as things are, I do not wish to make a bad precedent in our public life by occupying a position the duties of which I cannot adequately discharge.

I need only add my earnest wish that the fellow-countrymen with whom I shall no longer be officially associated will realise the high ideal of public service they have set before them.

> Yours sincerely,
> HORACE PLUNKETT."

" To that letter," said Lord Glenavy, " I replied :

" MY DEAR SIR HORACE,

I read your letter with very great regret, in which, I am certain, every member of the Senate will share. I should have asked you to reconsider your determination were it not for your statement that your conclusion was definite. I shall, of course, communicate the contents of your letter to the Senate, and have only to add that I welcome your assurance that the resignation of your seat will not involve any interruption of your constant devotion and unselfish services in the interests of your country. . . ."

Mr. Bennet said:

"I think we might consider whether it might not be reasonable to ask Sir Horace Plunkett to reconsider his determination to resign. . . ."

That is better, thought I. That short letter of Glenavy accepting, almost with alacrity, Sir Horace's resignation, will never be forgotten as long as Sir Horace lives; and Sir Horace is likely to outlive Glenavy, for, not content with founding his own paper, he is bringing to Dublin his sanatorium from Battle Creek.

The Earl of Mayo said:

"I should like to say a few words with regard to the resignation of my old friend Sir Horace Plunkett. We were boys together. I have known him for many years. . . . We in this Senate must remember that Sir Horace Plunkett has been consulted with regard to co-operation by almost every leading man in Europe and America, except, of course, from Denmark, where the system of co-operation has been carried on successfully for many years. . . .

"I am glad to tell you his health is very much better. I think it must be better, because I saw an excellent letter from him in *The Times* the other day, dated from his house in London. . . ."

The idea of Sir Horace's health having the same curve as his letters to *The Times* was something I had not considered. But the Earl has just assured us that " it must be better ! "

Colonel Moore did not like to let the occasion pass. He had not always been in entire agreement, but——

Sir Thomas Grattan Esmonde, waving the lanyard of his eye-glasses, said:

"May I say how deeply I regret that Sir Horace Plunkett's health has compelled him to sever his connection with the Senate? I think it is a great pity when our country is struggling to her feet that the Senate should lose the services of a man who has given his whole life with absolute disinterestedness to further Irish interests."

Sir Nugent Everard said:

" As one of Sir Horace Plunkett's old colleagues in his co-operative work, I think it would ill become me if I did not add my voice, as I believe it is the wish of the Senate to ask him to reconsider his resignation. . . ."

This brought the Chairman, Lord Glenavy, into the discussion again:

" Of course, personally, no one would more sincerely welcome Sir Horace Plunkett back but . . . Perhaps I might suggest to Senator Bennet that he would consider that it might be more dignified and complimentary to Sir Horace Plunkett if he would frame a resolution somewhat to the following effect: ' That the Senate, while accepting his resignation with regret, desires to place on record its appreciation of the pre-eminent services he has for so many years rendered to his country.' I only throw that out as a suggestion. It is entirely in the hands of the Senate."

Mr. Bennet:

" I am quite in your hands and the hands of the Senate."

Who was it muttered: ' A washing of hands '?

The passage in Sir Horace's letter that referred to the wild state of things when Senators' houses were sent up in flames, not by any Englishman remaining in the country, but by the natives themselves; when losses of irrecoverable treasures were being inflicted daily, when the Record Office that contained irreplaceable records of our country went up in smoke burned by men of the class that never makes history, was the most remarkable because of its modesty. " I would not leave it now if I could be reasonably suspected to be thereby safeguarding my person or my property."

No man could reasonably suspect Sir Horace Plunkett of lack of courage. His drive right up to the kneeling British soldiers who were holding Dublin put any such thoughts out of my mind. Sir Horace was intrepid. He may have had a high disdain for danger, but it seemed that it never occurred to him to notice it. His passenger had cause to regret Sir Horace's intrepidity. He was beside Sir Horace in his two-seater when the British opened fire. There were traffic regulations which Sir Horace had disregarded—after all, he was on his way to the Plunkett House—so they opened fire without warning. Sir Horace drove on. His passenger was shot through the kidney. The mascot on the car was drilled. A few bullets pierced Sir Horace's clothing, but Sir Horace drove on, hastening slowly. " *Festina lente* " is the motto of his family.

" My dear fellow, I will see about this." He asked the kneeling rifleman : " Where is your officer? This is scandalous. I will have him here at once ! "

Men of the race of Plunkett cannot be reasonably expected to stampede.

CHAPTER VII

TO-DAY I WILL BE A MILLIONAIRE.   I WILL DO JUST AS I PLEASE.
Have I come into millions? Yes. The heavens have endowed me: it is a fine day in Dublin, and my tastes are more
than money can buy. I have never confused money with
wealth, that is why I am a millionaire: I am as wealthy as
any, though not as monied as the least. What are my wants?
Already I have the first of them gratified—it is a fine day in
Dublin; and the second, which needs a high barometric
pressure to fulfil, has got it. Freedom from the tyranny of
meals, appointments and even friends, any man can have by
embracing Sister Poverty; but there is one thing that she
must give me in return for my attentions, and that she cannot
give—the power of unimpeded movement. Her vehicles
are the ambulance or the Black Maria. I would desert her
for a Baby Ford.

A child has an extra appetite; one in addition at least to
those a grown person has—it is the necessity for movement.
To keep a child motionless would as assuredly kill it as it
would kill an old man to confine him to bed. Young and old
must move; and the desire for movement is overflowing into
the hunger for speed. The eternal feminine, the female force
in Nature, led the men of old upward; speed is taking her
place in this generation. What is at the back of this hunger
for and need of speed?

Just as there are tribes who are unacquainted with the facts
of parenthood, with children who do not know their fathers,
so we are unaware of our heavenly descent, our cosmic relationship. And yet the thrill of the electric atoms which
make up the substance of our bodies is slowly being felt and
interpreted in terms of Speed. Our bodies are desirous of
swift movement now: Speed for speed's sake. Soon our
minds will realise the electric nature of our being and deliberately direct our bodies' movements towards the All-mover,
the *Primum Mobile* whose glory thrills and penetrates the
universe.

Call them profanely protons and electrons, these are but
names for matter in the immeasurable Mystery of Being
which vibrates through the whole of space, or rather of
creation. The body is vibrating in harmony with the universe.
The more we grow conscious of this, the more we will to move.

Movement is the ritual and recognition of the divine nature of our substance. It is a recoil from that which is dead, an act of life. To satisfy the desire and to make an action of recognition, the power to move must be provided. Else we remain still as death.

My motor, therefore, takes me far to-day from the Eternal Feminine of the Vice-regal Lodge with her *gentil babil*, into the hills or even into the air. I will arise and go into the granite mountains, and sit on a stone in the middle of a little yard-wide rill, and watch the water move over the clean golden sands, or by a heathery stream watch the sub-aqueous grasses wave, while far above go the high cumulus clouds that look down upon it all.

I remember Talbot Clifton once asking me, " What the devil were you doing on that hill ? You had no gun."

There was not the least use in trying to answer him. The answer would, for peace and for understanding's sake, have to be ' nothing.' And that would seem an offensive and unsatisfactory reply. He did not know that I was a million-aire and can let others shoot my imaginary birds and catch all my fish but the Salmon of Knowledge.

With these blanketing clouds there will be a warm dell above Ticknock, where I can do nothing until it is time to fall down on Dundrum and give Yeats the Governor-General's invitation. Will he accept it ? Of course not, at first ; but a little strategy, a little strategy. I have already in my mind a little scheme to endow him with the necessary distinction. He must be made to see that he has an opportunity to take up the position which he likes beyond all others : the position from which he can both dominate and endow.

His mind provides me with a realm of beauty beyond the beauty of Woman. It will be a relief to be independent in thought for an hour or two while I sail in the shadowy waters or sit with Cuchulainn grown old. Seven lean years he en-dured of love, only to win at the end emancipation from— what was it the aged Sophocles called Love ?—" a relentless master."

Now he leaves to Love the perfervid sunlight. He has refracted his rays, as it were, through the pearl of Paradise, and they fall with so gentle a softness that they are only visible under the moon. How different this from George Moore, caught in the ugly snare and wry-twisted with curios-ity ; how different even from Keats, whom he makes to appear somewhat treacly and relaxed. Keats, Gates, Yeats: etymologically these three names are one and the same. They are names found in Cornwall. So Keats and Yeats are neither English nor Irish originally, but Cornish. And Yeats' mother being a Pollexfen makes Yeats closer to Cornwall than Keats, and closer to Parnassus as it rises to our modern eyes. I must remember that: Cornish! He will be delighted to hear it. He is growing somewhat tired of being irretrievably Irish, which has come lately to mean Gaelic, which means nothing. He wants a change. But with Yeats a Cornishman! He shall have sailed with Tristram, sung hopelessly of Iseult for seven long years and reproved the facetious Dinadan. And he shall disapprove of present times. Already I hear the sailors singing the oldest of sea shanties as they near Tintagel, where Yeats is waiting beside King Mark.

> They rowèd hard, and sung thereto
> With Heveloe, and Rumbaloo!

It's enough to give him, with this new outlook, a new lease of life. And that is the function of anyone who is a well-wisher of the Muses' son. And he can find an excuse to escape from boredom, which is the only thing that ages, an excuse to get out of the Kildare Street Club.

I will gather myself up and hurry down. I can see the old grey mole of De Lacy's Castle from here, and past it the Yellow House; a mile this side is Yeats. Yes. Yes. How pleased he will be! But, of course, he has to discover this lineage for himself.

Why did I not think of this before? There could not be a Gaelic Yeats. It won't take 'O' or 'Mac' as a prefix. Now that he is recovering from a cold, is the very time to complete the cure and put him up for the Round Table. He will elect himself. Merlin will not be in it with me as a magician! He had better be Sir Lancelot than Sir Tristram, for "Lancelot was better breathed."

Yeats lives in Rathfarnham in an old house in lovely grounds, a house built before cement took the place of stone and thin-walled clangour for the stately repose and long silence of continuous dwelling. His gate is on a bridge which spans a stream fresh from the golden granite of the hills. The walk rises through a well-gardened wilderness of flowering shrubs, and the old grey house is screened by a blossoming orchard. His croquet lawn is beside it, and the hills form an ever-changing picture as deep and as glowing in colour as a picture by his brother, Jack Yeats, in his latest style. The door faces you. "Yeats" on a heart-shaped brass knocker. As it used to be simply "Yeats" on his London house in Woburn Place before the place was demolished.

"I am glad you have come," he said, "you are the very man I want to see. I have just been reading George Moore's *Memoirs of my Dead Life*. And a question keeps rising in my mind which you can answer. Take that seat there. This is the question: Do you think George Moore was impotent?"

The great Cornishman was sitting up among his pillows, his magnificent head, with its crown of white hair and satin-like brown skin, toning well with the fawn dressing-gown he wore. His nose, like an eagle's, was broadest between the eyes. At the foot of the bed a gas-fire burned; outside the open window birds were seeking food in a coco-nut shell which he had fastened to the sill. He was recovering from a cold and "enjoying his illness" for the peace it provided and for the immunity it gave him from his friends.

Good Lord! but aloud: "I don't know. It is rare for a man to be impotent. He may be unable to propagate, but organic impotence must be very rare."

"Was he a man?"

"He had the pelvis of a woman, as artists are said to have. There is little to be deduced from that. The only arguments that come to my mind are based on deduction more than on facts physical or otherwise."

"Well, go on."

"Take the evidence of women. Susan Mitchell sensed something lacking. Women are like that. She wrote 'Some men kiss and do not tell, some kiss and tell; but George Moore told and did not kiss.' Kiss may mean . . . Well, she was hardly likely to say more."

"Go on."

"You remember Goethe says"—how well Yeats remembered, I knew, for I remembered long ago mentioning Goethe to Moore, and Moore pointing to Eckermann's *Life of Goethe* and saying with a snigger: 'That's where Yeats gets all his information. That's his text-book'—"that the 'passing of a genius is measured by the woman it leaves behind.' Now, where are Moore's surviving lady friends?"

"There's one."

"Oh, we all know! But did Moore hold her exclusive

affection ?   He did not.   She was faithful to him only in her infidelities, *splendide mendax.*   ' I could not love thee, Moore, so much, loved I not others more.'   That's argument number one.   Then, one evening I sat with him in his bedroom in Ebury Street.   He was recounting with a reminiscence so devoid of melancholy that I suspected it was but a work of the creative imagination.   Suddenly he looked at the rug in front of the fire and addressed it and me : ' O rug, thou could'st tell many a pleasant tale of love ! '   What's wrong with the bed ? thought I.

" Exactly," Yeats exclaimed, with the excitement of a triumphant detective, jerking himself up in the bed. " Exactly !   His accounts of his adventures are all one-sided. There never is,—he never gives one, a distinct feeling for the woman in the case.   I have just been reading these Memoirs, and I am wondering more than ever what form his impotence took.   I remembered this : He was passing along Merrion Square one night with Best and he saw couples standing upright, immobile, speechless with heads on one another's shoulders.   ' But they are not saying a word ! ' he exclaimed. ' I wish I could do that !   Best, could you do that ? '   Best said that it was about the only thing anyone could do.   But psychologically it reveals that Moore never felt the silence of love.   His scenes leave you with no account of the woman. It is only of his own sensations he talks.   Now we all know a woman has far fiercer sensations than a man.   She cannot conceal them.   She cries out.   Moore never tells what the woman did.   Why ? "—pointing and shaking his finger at me—" Because she was not there !

" A woman in Paris told me that the earlier emotions are apt to become obliterated by the later.   Moore only recounts his earlier emotions ! "

I said : " I consulted a woman novelist about the Moore problem and I put the objection regarding the one-sidedness of his love scenes.   ' *The Lovers of Orelay,*' for instance, where there is more writing about the locale than the love."

" What did she say ? "

" That Moore was an artist and was both sided, woman and man, as artists should be."

" She was a woman novelist, you say ?   That accounts for her defending him.   His works are admired particularly by women."

" Wait !   I begin to see a further argument for your

thesis in that. Women admire him because they feel instinctively that he can never give them away."

"Admirable!"

"Love must have ever been to Moore ' All a wonder and a wild desire.' His curiosity was undiminished, and yet, it could be argued that that was chiefly a proof that his interest in women was undiminished. An argument in his favour."

"Would you mind closing that window? The birds will not come back until it's down. I interrupted you?"

"Not at all. I remember since we spoke of the absence of the woman from Moore's description of his love scenes, his telling me of something a lover—no, he preferred to call her a mistress—of his was supposed to remark . . . it is so much on the lines of the ignorance he revealed to Best that I forbear telling it; but you may take it that now I come to think of it, it bears out the conclusion we come to from what he said to Best."

"What was that?"

"Oh, never mind. But don't you remember the way in which he tried to make me to personate him in Vienna shortly after I had returned from that most delightful of cities?"

"When the lady that admired his work threatened to come to Dublin so that she might bear a child of his?"

"Precisely. She was, according to Moore, a beautiful Viennese . . ."

"And you had just come back from Vienna. That's what gave him the idea. The idea of the Viennese admirer. You had been extolling Vienna?"

"Very likely."

"Go on."

"' How am I to know her? And do you imagine for a moment that she will not find me out?' 'My dear fellow, I will show you her photograph. And as for finding you out, she only admires my work, she does not know me, and that is why she insists on bearing a child to me.'"

"Yes! Yes! Go on."

"Having, so to speak, screwed my courage to the sticking-place, I asked to see the photograph."

"And did you see it?"

"I cannot remember."

"Try to think."

"I did see a photograph, but he might have forgotten that he had shown it to me before I left for Vienna the year before.   It may have been the photograph he used for Pearl Craigie. . . ."

"Now, listen to me.   I saw that photograph, yellow with age.   It had become, when I saw it, the photograph of a beautiful Virginian who was threatening to come to him from America desirous of his services.   He wrote a play about it. That was all."

Yeats lit the lamp beside his bed.   The birds were twitter-ing in his apple-trees, settling for the night.   I might open the window now.

"After all, he was a great artist and greatly loved art," I said.   "He was a devotee to that and creative in that sphere at all events.   He was a great person and he never forgot it. His air of perpetual cantankerousness was to defend himself from rational little critics 'while the work was in progress'; to defend himself from Reality and common-sense.   Had he not said, 'We must keep up the illusion'?   And while he attended to his garden, the garden of his prose, he resented what anyone can have if they bear fools gladly—comments."

But while Moore wrote much about Yeats, Yeats remained silent about his contemporary.   Why was this?   I think that Moore's inordinate jealousy, a jealousy which flew at the fame of Hardy like a pettish child, realised a greater genius in Yeats than he possessed, and so he tried to subject by ridicule what he could never have outshone.   Yeats disliked Moore, first of all for his " position,"—a landlord—and then because he was attacked by Moore before his friends for taking a Civil List pension.   Also, Yeats feels that his words may easily confer fame, since he has never allowed his literary judgment to be persuaded.   Making your rival ridiculous is the chief aim of Irish opponents since the duel was abolished.   And in his trilogy *Ave, Salve, Vale*, Moore mocked at Yeats.   *Ave atque Vale*, I have recorded it was at first, until he pilloried Professor Tyrrell, who, aware of Moore's ignorance, remarked on hearing of his portrait drawn by Moore, " Moore is one of those fellows who think that ' Atque ' is a Roman centurion."

The problems that confront the mind of man are innumer-able, some of them incalculable.   My problem was not one of those which may be described somewhat hyperbolically as vital ; nevertheless it was, considered from the point of view of Art, a cardinal one on which much hinged.   And I was nearly forgetting it !   I had to persuade a real poet to accept a invitation to a pseudo court.   Yeats is the greatest poet of this and of most of the last generation. Tennyson, his pre-decessor, built a world of song on ready-made foundations. Yeats had to create it all from 'airy nothing'; and to protect it from marauding hands. I had to persuade him to accept a word-of-mouth invitation to the opening ceremony of the Spring Show. The Show might have opened itself, but its success was contributed to by the presence of His Majesty's representative. Dublin is loyal at Ballsbridge. Horses connote knights, "Men who ride upon horses" (I will quote Yeats to himself), and therefore courtliness. This may help me to persuade the poet to join the "Distinguished Visitors" in the "Royal" box.

"By the way, Yeats, the Governor-General has asked me to invite you to the opening of the Spring Show. He will be in his private box, and we can go up to it or take tea under it in his private apartments.

"I will not go. I am suffering from a cold."

"You are not, but you are making your friends suffer from your cold."

"I will not abet this trumpery mockery of a throne. I will not meet Tim Healy or Lady Lavery in the Royal box. Really I am surprised that you take this mummery of kingship seriously."

"No. I do not; but I think that in the Decline and Fall of the British Empire in Ireland, and Ireland with it, you and I should stand like your Triton in the stream, and resist the lapse from grandeur with dignity. I am going in a tall hat, as it were crowned by remembering happier things. I am sure that mine will be the only tall hat at the Spring Show. Half the Kildare Street Club will be there, but they will hesitate to honour the King lest they offend Democracy by meeting his Viceroy suitably attired. I, as you know, have not the least concern for popular opinion."

"Neither have I!"

"I am going in what I hope will be the only silk hat to be seen at the first official function of the Free State. We must not conform to the unceremonious."

This roused him. "Look here, I think you are right. Unless we are to let the country drift without a protest into the loutish ways of the bog, we must stand for the observances of good manners. We must wear tall hats." The grandeur innate in the man was coming out. Quietly now! Leave him the tiller.

" You are quite right. If we do not give our countrymen the lead, who is there left courageous to sport a tall hat ? "

I hope, I said to myself, that the proposition will not appear to his mind as " Silk hats save Ireland ! "

He was agreeing, but it did not mean that he was coming to the Show.

" Quite so. But it is neither here nor there this mock court held by a barrister, in what is no more important than an agricultural show in one of the shires. I will not go. I am not well enough. It is a travesty : a revolution in a palace."

My last card : " Yeats, we need not ascend the grandstand at all. As poet of the Lake Isle, you ought to see the country girls producing the island's fare. It is a goodly sight. I saw some of the dairy-maids at work in the last Spring Show, and they were very comely. The butter-girls are so clean and wholesome you would think that they were personally selected by Dr. Russell of the Department of Public Health. Wonderful sight, the churning ! Lassies of seventeen, with white elbows."

" Why white elbows ? "

" You must know that the skin of the elbow retains to the last any trace of pigment that there may be in the racial species. If there is the least Eurasian, Arabian or Semitic blood, for instance, it shows in the browning of the skin of the elbow : some skin diseases are diagnosed by a spot or two at the elbows. Now the dairy-maids I saw churning have snow-white and ruddy arms like strawberries and cream. Their work at the churning had made them rosy, and still they kept on with the old-fashioned churns, plunging up and down the long handle. It is a very graceful attitude. I wonder why your brother Jack has not caught them at their work. In a year or two there will be no more churns with long upright handles, nothing but revolving barrels with glass windows. The old and homely things are ebbing away, ebbing away."

" You do not expect me to rise from my bed to see Tim Healy ; and a few country girls churning ? "

" Whoever suggested it ? I merely threw out a hint that you and I could attend the Spring Show, wear silk hats where no one else dared, and slip away from the Royal box in time for the butter-making competition. I will drive you home."

" Perfectly preposterous ! "

" Very well—you are missing a lot."

" What am I missing ? "

" Oh nothing, perhaps. But I am deep in the folk-lore of the churn. Most of the treasure trove from Irish bogs is butter, and we get that unique and beautiful form of vessel the mether from the bogs. The three- or four-handed goblet. The descendants of those who made the mether and put butter into firkins are churning at the present moment, unconscious of the long tradition of the churn ; and the awful tragedy of it is that no one realises what is being lost. The sea chanties were nearly all gone until a few late-comers collected half-a-dozen Bowdlerised stanzas or so. But the churn ! Only one song of butter-making remains."

" Have you got it ? "

" Father Claude overheard it in Tipperary, when a buxom maid was churning as she thought all alone. She had buttocks like a pair of beautiful melons. Her sleeves were rolled up. She had churned from early morning. Her neck was pink with exercise. Her bosom laboured, but she could not desist, for the milk was at the turn. Up and down, desperately she drove the long handle : up and down, up and down and up and up for a greater drive. The resistance grew against the plunger. Her hips and bosom seemed to increase in size while her waist grew thin. In front of her ears the sweat broke into drops of dew. She prayed in the crisis to old forgotten gods of the homestead ! Twenty strokes for ten ! Gasping, she sang :

> ' Come, butter !
> Come, butter !
> Come, butter,
> Come !
> Every lump
> As big as
> My bum ! '

You are missing not one, but many milk-maids' songs. And when we are dead, they too shall be ; and the folk-lore lost forever of the dairy and the byre."

" How does it go ? "—He beat time to recall the rhythm. " ' Every lump As big as My bum ! ' "

" Yes. You are correct. But my proposal is that we get these chants at first-hand and be not depending on Father Claude for such songs."

" When does Tim expect us ? "

" Any time from four to six."

" ' Come, butter, come, butter,' " he murmured. " I think I will join you. Let me know when you can send a car. And there's my hat to be brushed."

" Sir John and Lady Simon are the guests of honour."

" There was not a word about them when I was out at the Lodge this morning."

" They arrived by the evening boat. Can you call for me to take me out to dinner ? "

" With pleasure."

" At eight o'clock."

Lady Fingall put down the telephone. Now what is up ? I wondered. What brings Sir John Simon over here ?

The telephone rang again. Lady Fingall, it seemed, had been cut off.

" You know that Hazel is staying there and acting Lady Vice-Reine in the Lodge ? Lord Lovat is there and some American friend of Hazel's. It is a very private dinner; quite informal, but not informal enough for you to tell my stories. I am quite able to tell them myself. But you may remind me if I forget."

" Telling other people's stories ? I suppose I do, when they are not other people's stories about other people. We shall see."

" We will see how it goes. We may have a pleasant evening. No decorations ! " she laughed. " Eight o'clock."

I am presumed to know all Lady Fingall's stories by heart. Perhaps I heard them independently from other sources. I will tell no stories. I detest the set story which is brought to dinner, as obvious as a stud on one's shirt. I prefer personalities, for what are stories without characters whom we neither know nor are made alive for us ?

I thought of the last time I heard Tim speaking in public. It was at the dinner of the Tailltean Games. The Committee were undecided until the last moment whether they would invite the Governor-General or not. . . . When they had made up their minds as to the exact amount of vice-royalty athletes could sustain, it was almost too late to invite him with any propriety. In fact, it took a great deal of diplomacy on my part to persuade him to accept the half-hearted invitation.

There were almost a thousand guests in the Metropole. On the right of the Governor-General sat Prince Ranjitsinhji, the famous cricketer, magnificent in his jewelled turban. When Tim arose to speak, I marvelled at his rhetorical, or rather histrionic device for commanding attention. It is hard to hold an audience, particularly from the outset. They do not prick up their ears until the first quip or telling phrase. But Tim arose and putting his hands behind his back, leaning his head forwards and swaying it from side to side as if about to utter an incantation, he waited, then made his voice assume a dismal and sepulchral sound like the echoes in church. The effect was to make his audience as attentive as a congregation. Thus he held us from the first word.

"Your Highness, Ladies and Gentlemen, I don't know why I have been invited here to a banquet of the Tailltean Games. The only game I ever played was a game of marbles. But we have here on our right a splendid and world-famous sportsman, and deservedly so—His Highness, Prince Ranjitsinhji of Nawanagar. He is, as you know, a great sportsman, a wielder not alone of the cricket-bat, but of the salmon rod. . . . His presence here is a sign of the affection he bears our country. Gentlemen, he might have fished in the Ganges ; but he prefers the river at Ballinahinch ! "

The laughter and applause were deafening. The company saw the absurd vision of the Prince casting a fly and raising a crocodile. Only the praise and applause reached the Prince.

Another great Irishman who adopted this subterfuge in public speaking was our dear Tom Kettle. He had as great a force of genius and as great a gift for concentrating his force in a phrase. He is the only orator whose loss is a national deprivation. His fine gift for friendship sounded in his voice, which was the sonorous proclamation of the presence of a great soul.

"I went 'Home' to one of the ruined drawing-rooms of Eighteenth-century Dublin with a girl whom circumstances, all remediable, have turned into what is called a prostitute. There was a family living in every corner but one of that dilapidated *salon*. As we approached the prostitute's corner, we approached civilisation. There was a screen round her bed."

He said this to shock the apathetic and venal mismanaging Housing Committees of the day into dealing with the awful tenements which still fill up as soon as a family is housed elsewhere and sap the lives of the incoming countrymen.

It was useless to seek to divert him by pretending to be shocked by his meeting a prostitute. Kettle was too big to be affected by the calumnies of hypocrisy or of those who had not only the prostitute on their conscience, but also the lives of the three Christian families. He condemned the Committee with, " It's your housing makes whores."

Lady Lavery was acting as Vice-Reine. So far so good. She was one of those Londonised Americans who are adept hostesses. She could make a funeral feast entertaining. Wherein lay her accomplishment? In thoughtfulness for others and a genius for tact. How often have I left her hospitable house feeling as elated with myself as that guest described by my friend Pearsall Smith, but without the reaction which the cool evening caused. Women such as these know the knack, not necessarily of flattering men, but of standing aside and acting as prompters with the certain knowledge that men will do their own flattery in their own way. That makes them great entertainers.

In her own drawing-room she would have jumped up and half crossed the floor to meet us, arms outstretched. Things were stiffer at Tim's uncertain court. The ladies were casting about for some indication of Tim's attitude. Would he expect them to curtsey? Would it embarrass him if they did not do it before Sir John? Would he be cynical if they did? Lady Lavery's tact saved the entrance problem. She got in the way and led us to His Excellency. Soon he led us, with Lady Simon on his arm, to the small dining- or breakfast-room. As usual when he was in private, the table was decorated with his Waterford glass.

The American London hostess friend of Lady Lavery sat on my right. I never catch names, so, for all I knew or remembered, she might have been " Prudence." To heap coals of fire upon my head, she remembered me. Had we not met in London? Yes, of course. (My Lord, but where?) " . . . And what an amusing evening it turned out to be in the end ! "

" But was the issue ever in doubt ? "

" Well, I was not too confident of my powers to entertain."

This is where I flounder, I thought, if I say one word. But I was saved—or was I ?—by Lady Fingall, who asked me in a loud voice with everyone's attention already captured : " Tell us about the party you were at in London where Sargent was, and what he said to you when the negro minstrels sang."

In a flash I remembered the identity of the lady on my right who " was not too confident of her powers to entertain." It was to the big party she gave us in Chelsea she referred. I was a guest, but so unobtrusive was my hostess that I might just as well have been a gate-crasher. And I was by no means saved. Lady Fingall is hardly a lifeboat from a social predicament. I found myself now in danger of being represented as ungrateful enough to mock in Dublin the hospitality accepted and enjoyed in London. After all, it was Sargent's remarks I repeated to Lady Fingall. Had these become one of her stories? My face is not very expressive but I tried to make it register—Fire! No use! " I heard it from the Duchess of Rutland, who was there," said Lady Fingall; " I'll tell it if you don't."

" Is there any mystery ? " asked Tim.

I said, " I met Sargent, or rather, I was in a room with him. I noticed how tall and portly he was, and I remember the iron-grey on the back of his head and the light coming through his rather large and rosy ears."

" What was it the nigger sang ? "

" Oh, something from Shakespeare," said I, and dropped my voice and wriggled as one loth to continue.

" I remember it now," cried Lady Fingall. " He sang ' Take, O take those lips away.' And Sargent said, ' Yes, do. They are nine inches long.' "

" You must forgive me for Sargent's jokes," I said, turning to my neighbour.

" I am glad you enjoyed your evening," was her reply.

Ah me !

" Sargent made another joke about the other black man's song," persisted Lady Fingall.

" What was the other black man's song ? " Tim asked, cavernously.

" He sang about journeys ending in lovers' meeting; and Sargent said : ' Lynchings end such lovers' meetings in our Southern States.' "

" I did not think that Sargent had such an outlook. I thought that he had become as British as Henry James," said I, hoping to reinstate myself. But to my rescue nobody came. It was hardly a tempting speculation. No one cared what Sargent thought. They knew him as a painter. . . .

" I want to hear the story of Baldy Doody's Pig," said Tim.

" That is not my story."

" Has he never a story of his own ? " Lady Lavery asked. " But you cannot escape from telling it. It is his Excellency's command."

" Well, I don't want to steal Joseph Conlon's story, but here it is."

" That ruffian ? " asked Tim. " Go on."

" He said he was told to investigate on the spot a complaint from a village near Cloughjordan about an outrage of the Black-and-Tans. In order to get accurate details he approached the parish priest, who was a fine specimen of a man about nineteen stone weight.

" ' That'll do you, Mr. Conlon,' he said, ' it's so distressing that I could not talk of it till after dinner. And you're just in time. It's three o'clock ! '

" I was ushered into the dining-room, where there were five curates about a table : three on one side and two on the side near me. Before each of them was a turkey on a plate. ' Boy, another bird for Mr. Conlon,' his Reverence shouted."

" As if it were a snipe," gloomed Tim, greatly amused.

" Well, it showed fine instincts and considerate hospitality on the part of his host," said I.

" Go on with your story," said Tim.

" My friend goes on to say that when he had cut sufficiently through the turkey to see his companion on the opposite side of the table, the bird was removed by the boy. Apparently it was only a hors d'œuvre, or his delayed deglutition was taken for lack of relish. Then dinner began in earnest.

" ' Towards nine o'clock,' said Conlon, ' with my back teeth floating, I said : " Father, you promised to tell me of the outrages of the Black-and-Tans."

" ' His Reverence sighed, and took a sip of green Chartreuse, and said : " Mr. Conlon, I'm sorry you broached that subject. I was just getting over the shock. There are outrages in all parts of the country, but there are none of them as bad as those scoundrels perpetrated here last Saturday week back. I've hardly got over it yet." '

" He paused and looked round the table, but the chorus was too reminiscent for words. Finding an atmosphere charged with sympathy, he went on : ' Two lorries full of them came down the principal street, sitting back to back, covered over with wire, as if they were a lot of hens, to protect them from bombs which were never heard of in our village. When they got opposite the parochial house they thought fit to fire a salvo, and they bombarded the place and black-and-tanned it up, down, right, left and centre. Fortunately they hit nobody, but they killed Baldy Doody's pig. She had a litter of thirteen, and he was a family man himself. It was a terrible and irreparable loss.'

" A vision of the curtailment of the Harrogate cure crossed Conlon's mind, he confessed to me, when he heard of the outrage on the village livestock of the ' family man himself.' ' The times are bad,' said he, lamely enough. ' They couldn't be worse,' his Reverence replied, ' I don't know where they are leading, but you're forgetting to help yourself, Mr. Conlon. . . .' "

" You're an awful ruffian," said Tim to me.

" I told your Excellency it was not my story," said I. " I know too much about the Church, especially the Orders, to leave an unqualified impression that all clerics have easeful lives ; even the old men in some Orders are treated as if they never passed twenty-one. They are up early and they have every hour of the day taken up with duties. There is not a comfortable chair in any of the rooms I have seen. For too much secular ease, there are, as Lady Lavery told me, ' Retreats.' "

So I had some slight revenge for her ' command.'

Lest Sir John would carry away a wrong impression, Tim described some of the exercises of abstinence and the rigours of religious life.

" The jokes about the Church are reminiscent of Rabelais ? " Lord Lovat asked.

" Yes. Jokes show the healthy affection in which it is held."

" Very likely," said Tim, who had never heard of Rabelais. And, to use the amazing provisions of legal phraseology, would not have read him had he heard, or, having read him, would not have approved of him. To confirm his statements he welcomed the reference to a ' Retreat.'

" Tell us the story of the Retreat for Parish Priests . . ."

" Lord Lovat will be disedified," said Lady Lavery. " He is probably a Presbyterian, and so out of sympathy with the austerer forms of celibate life."

Tim smiled : " If it happened in Milltown, there cannot be much harm in it. Go on."

" Father Tim Fagan was giving a retreat for parish priests, and he warned them that the loneliness of their lives might

lead to indolence if they were not perpetually on their guard.
This is the kind of thing, I mean :

' Mary, get me my slippers.
' Mary, put the shawl on my back.
' Mary, is the pillow behind my head ?
' Mary, poke the fire.
' Mary, bring in the hot water, I'll attend to the rest
myself.'   ' Till in the end,' said Father Fagan, ' you wouldn't
know which of them was Mary.' "

"Your Ladyship is worse than the Senator," said the
Governor-General, who was not at all pleased.   He had been
caught out by Milltown.   Turning abruptly to his neighbour
he changed the subject : " You were in the House the other
night ? "

"Yes.   I heard Austen speaking.   After the debate
Asquith passed him a note saying that he heard him read
the last Will and Testament of the Liberal Party ; but that
for his part he intended to die intestate.   Austen's reply was
quite as witty but I did not see it."

" Ireland always got more from the Conservatives than
the Liberals, though she expected more from the Liberals.
Did that ever occur to you, Sir John ? "

" Possibly, if it be a fact, it may be accounted for by the
longer terms in service of the Conservatives."

" It's not the Way, but the Will," said Tim.

I gazed at the high intellectual brow and the pointed chin
of the man who sat opposite.   An Heloiseless Abelard, and
like Abelard, tall and comely : a dialectician of the first
degree, an intellect like a ray in its penetrability, capable, for
unbound, of taking either side : Nominalist or Realist it
mattered little, for his pleasure lay in the triumph of the
acuteness of his thought.

We were talking of the Pipe Cemetery at Salruck where
the strange custom survives of putting pipes on the graves
of those who lived on land but oars on the graves of those
who won their living from the sea.   A custom old as Time.
I tried to recall the name of the helmsman in Virgil who had
an oar erected on his tomb.

" Could it have been Palinurus ? " Sir John prompted
politely.

He has at his instant disposal everything he has read or
experienced.   A *lux perpetua* of a mind.   And I remembered
the impression the last act of *Hamlet* gave me of that other

intellect not inappropriately associated with Sir John's, pervading like the light of lights and rapidly destroying its creation by a clear irradiation of inexorable reason, terrible as electricity, inevitable as Fate.

It saddened me to think that he could never be popular. To be popular one must be somewhat pitiable: the British crowd is won by weaknesses; but who could purchase or persuade that inflexible intelligence as clear and as amiable as glass?

He quoted from three poets and a line or two of his own. The Governor-General said: "Here's a poem of Irish manufacture," and he quoted *Down by the Sally Gardens*.

Then Sir John gave an example of the shortest witticism he had heard. Two Cricklewood 'bus drivers, in the days of horse-drawn 'buses, were in the habit, in the negative English Blighty way, of hailing each other in a friendly manner by imprecations as they met. One morning a driver missed his friend, only, after weeks of sorrow and loneliness, to find him perched aloft driving a four-in-hand—a hearse. At the moment they were recovering from surprise a little child ran under the leaders' hoofs. The hearse driver reined in desperately just in time.

"Greedy!" said the 'busman.

Sir John knew Dublin. He had been over for the Compensation Claims Committee. The Royal Hibernian Academy had been burned, and the artists who had lost pictures at its exhibition were claiming for them. He did not know how the Artist Gray, a painter of Highland cattle, arrived at the estimate of his loss. Or, rather, he did discover it. Gray was a painter of Highland cattle and he claimed for the loss of a characteristic work. He could not make up his mind. It was a great picture. If it had not been burned in the Royal Hibernian Academy, it might have been in the Tate Gallery. He got great delight out of painting it.

"How much is it worth?"

"Worth? You can't talk like that to an artist!"

"Well, at how much do you assess your loss?"

"That u'd be hard to tell. It depends on the demand and on my patrons."

"Yes? Yes?"

But it was time to adjourn for lunch.

"I'll have to get expert advice."

"By all means."

During the lunch-hour the artist sat with a crony of his in the nearest pub. They exchanged drinks and resolved to get a reward in some proportion to the needs of the occasion, seeing that art is inestimable. On the Commission's sitting being resumed, Gray explained:

"There are twenty cattle on the hillside."

"Twenty?"

"And at fifteen pounds per head that would work out at three hundred pounds, besides those hidden in the mist. My friend here is an expert on values. He is the best known butcher in the town."

How can Reason, however pure and serene, prevail against an artist? Yet he made no claims for the mist!

"That is not absurd at all, but the finest thing I have yet heard about Dublin," Lady Lavery rebuked me. "It only means that an artist is found taking his creations for real, and Shelley calls artists' creations 'more real than living man.' It is splendid to realise that there is a man left in Dublin who values the creations of an artist's mind as solidly as his own cattle. Where is that splendid butcher? Or is he only a figment of your mind?"

"On your own showing, even if he were only a figment of my mind, he should be as substantial as if he were not . . . what I mean is, as if he were real. . . . Where am I getting? Your Ladyship is quite right. I remember now that somewhere in the Purgatorio, Dante provides local habitations for Antigone and Ismene 'si triste come fue,' and the daughter of Tiresias and Thetis, the mother of Achilles, and yet these are but the creations of poets, placed in a poet's purgatory: dreams within a dream. Had Sir John sent Gray to prison and impounded his cattle we would have comparable situations."

"I'd like to buy some of his Highland cattle," said Lord Lovat.

"Could you tell us," said Tim, "if they're liable to foot-and-mouth disease?"

"Beyond me, sir," said I.

Tim entered into a history of the Waterford Glass factories at Waterford and the factory for glass at Cork. I had heard it all before as well as the history of each piece. Celery filled four large Irish glass celery-bowls. I waved a stalk gently to attract the attention of Lady Fingall, since I was to jog her memory; and her story about Tim's celery was more amusing than the history of Tim's celery-bowls. But she was not to be drawn, so the tale must be left untold like that of old grouse in the gun-room which, however, I can guess: there were flint-locks in those days! But I dare not pirate Lady Fingall's story. That was the only piece of celery I took from her bowl.

"Ramsay MacDonald has a fine head," Lady Lavery was saying, "but he is totally devoid of humour, which, after all, is a blessing; for if a Prime Minister does not take himself seriously, who will?"

"How do you know that he has no humour?" Lord Lovat asked, standing up for his countryman.

"I told him how Bernard Shaw went to church the other day and, when they passed him the plate, moved aside murmuring 'Press'."

"He probably thought it was irreverent," said I, who had ground to make up.

"And he would be quite right," said Tim, who had suffered a good deal.

Lord Lovat, who presided over the Colonisation Committee, told how successful he had been when he got a whole village to emigrate from Scotland: "Parson, doctor, dentist and all. . . . No home sickness."

"And all what?" growled Tim.

"And all the scandals, of course," Lady Fingall interjected. "It is the absence of scandals that makes the heart grow fonder and long for home."

"Can the reason why the English are great colonists be that they make their own scandals wherever they go?"

But no one took any notice of that presumption.

Sir John was telling of a rebus in the Sonnets of Shakespeare which I wanted to hear. I often wondered why there should be such a search for lines that more than their meanings tell in the Elizabethan poets. In those days there were only seven Worthies, and anyone who wanted undeserved immortality had to put the come-hither on a poet as the chief journalist of the time, just as the Romans tried to bribe Tacitus for a chapter in his history; yet he gave from his admiration of him more space to Arbiter of the Elegances than to all the "prominent people." Nowadays, all are famous, because Fame itself has become ephemeral in order to escape from the makers of ramshackle immortalities. The men who "feature stars" and judge books by the sales and read " best-sellers." The *Rubaiyat* of Fitzgerald never sold at all.

In Shakespeare's days the poet was the photographer, reporter and, if he were the dramatist, the producer of notable men and events. Hollywood was now in Whitefriars and then in Southwark. And the actor in the Puritans' time was Public Enemy No. 1. But now Publicity is Enemy No. 1, because it has undermined fame and substituted itself for Good Report. Virtue and Nobility must yield to notoriety. Thus it happens that the directors of publicity can juggle with values and ideas, hide what is excellent and exalt what is mediocre and worthless. The advertisers become the advisers of public taste and the Arbiters, not of the Elegances, but of vulgarities. To the vulgar you must appeal through vulgarity.

Is it any wonder, then, that the aristocrats or those who wish to remain private and apart should come to have a horror of publicity and to hold all purveyors of " ideas," as well as ideas themselves, suspect, and to prefer life to literature ?

Only in the secret precincts of their own homes and among their intimates can they safely relax into genius. They must in public confront the over-informed and under-educated Public with " good form," their armour against " information." And they succeeded in appearing to believe that intelligence is the prerogative of the intellectual classes. And the intellectual classes are persuaded to believe that there are fools in high places. They fooled even that immortal School Inspector, Matthew Arnold, who found them polite and admirable: but they were impotent of ideas and had a " dangerous tendency to become studiously frivolous."

When we find ourselves confronted by " best-sellers," movie " stars " and fashions which are " put over," gilt edges, go-getters and magnates clothed with ephemeral fame, is it any wonder that a man of taste should shut himself in from such things, ' closit in his tower ' ? Not content with manipulating money, the Mesopotamian mongrels must dictate " ideas," make it virtuous for you to turn the other cheek while they pick your breast pocket. They put that " across." Now they seize on every thought of man and take it to their bazaars and sell it shop-soiled, spoilt or copied at second hand. The Public is deceived instead of being inspired by the thoughts of humanity's finest minds. Is it any wonder that the " landed Gentry " should hold all " ideas " suspect and fight shy of them and these dealers in the Virtues? They are, after all, from the "eminent" novelist to the share-pusher, but trammels to catch and to exploit the men who have won and inherited the land.

They know that in the past their ancestors got on very well without letters. Unable to read or write, each had his "latimer." It should not be necessary to be clever to retain one's property. They know that frequently they have lost their estates through the machinations of clever people from the steward to the pettifogging attorney. In a world of false notions and false "values" the aristocrat born can trust no man. He has come to place his trust in the horse: the totem of his conquering tribe! Hengist and Horsa! To comfort himself he has invented and built up a wonderful form of symbolism, Fox-hunting. Here, he who rides may read the meaning of the symbolic ritual—the cleverest animal hounded down by men upon horseback. Fox-hunting is the ritual of the aristocrat. In vain does the socially ambitious stockbroker strive to rise socially by falling off his hunter. His bandy legs may be more tribal than vocational, but they have not become bandy from horseback. In vain does he seek to emulate the "best people" by affecting concussion of the brain. He may implore the surgeon at the cottage hospital to add to the report of a broken collar-bone, "suffering from concussion." The hereditary Masters of Hounds are not to be fooled. They would not accept him were he to have his brain removed. Acquired concussion cannot open the doors of country houses. The better classes are born concussed, as my friend Aubrey Hammond informs me. It is a protective characteristic. (Pardon my stupidity!) According to the librarian, Lyster, "All we want is to be understood."

I remember realising this when I dined with an author among polo-players. It was at Wimborne House. Augustine Birrell, who had been spoiled by being taken for granted, bored me and the majority of the company. He looked like an old headmaster come out of retirement by (ordered) special request of some boys who had no choice in the matter. We had to wait on his words. So had he. This made us word-conscious, self-conscious, with no hope of becoming unconscious. Polo was opposed to pedantry. The horseman won. And then began a light raillery far wittier than any *obiter dicta* could be from the steady collection of a life-time. Give me sportsmen such as the great poet Pindar sought. And let the best-seller men sit silent staring at each other, each game-keeping his gaggle of words.

Suddenly I came to myself. Had I ever been in Scotland? Frequently. There is no country I enjoy so much: from " Auld Ayr " to the Outer Hebrides. Lord Lovat knew Islay well. What was I endeavouring to remember? Ah, this.

" Did you ever shoot on the Kildalton property ? "

" I did."

" And you swam a small loch after some duck ? "

" How did you come to hear that? It's rather inter-esting."

" Not so interesting to me. I suffered for you. I was the guest of Talbot Clifton, who owns Kildalton Castle and forest. The first day's sport took the form of a correctional lesson for his head keeper, who had described some birds as having been seen ' by Lord Lovat's loch.' "

" By my loch ? "

" Yes. It seems that you swam in after a wounded bird and so the deed was perpetuated by naming the loch after you. Now, the birds were as numerous as in an incubator, but it was not the birds that concerned my host but the fact that the keeper had forgotten to transfer his name to the loch you swam.

" My friend was six-foot-four in height, and when he jumped suddenly down a steep bank into a four-foot torrent holding his gun high above his head, I was amazed because I could see a hundred yards upstream a pine tree cut plank-wise for a bridge. He waded across and made secret beckon-ings to me to come on, putting his fingers to his lips. Thinking that he had found some prehistoric quarry awaken-ing from its pleiocene slumber, I took the plunge and drowned the gun and very nearly myself. When I retrieved both he helped me up the bank and said, ' Now Ramsay has to come on and he's not as tall as you; and this will teach him to talk about other people's lochs on my property.' "

Lord Lovat was amused. He knew Talbot and what a sportsman he was, and, like every hereditary landowner, jealous about property.

" It must be hard to get Highlanders to leave Scotland ? " Tim observed.

" It is much harder with Lowland miners. Segregation

on a flat Canadian ice-bound prairie has little attraction for them."

"They could not bring the mines with them, and if they did they would still be on the dole."

The gathering of the guests for the cinema show grew audible.

"I wonder if we are segregating ourselves too long," said Tim.

At this the ladies rose and curtsied to the half-risen Governor-General. He grunted, embarrassed somewhat; then turned to me at once when he had sat down.

"You were at the Senate to-day? Was there a debate on my Address?"

"There was a debate as to how to debate, and some confusion as to the procedure . . . it seems that there are no standing orders framed to deal with either the hearing of or receiving the Governor-General's Address. Glenavy suggested summoning a meeting of Senators and informing them in the Summons that the Address would be open to consideration.

"The Earl of Wicklow asked, 'What address? The Governor-General's speech is not an address.'

"Colonel Moore protested that an amendment which he handed in was objected to because there was to be no vote of thanks.

"Glenavy sat on him, 'Really, it's too bad if the Senator does not pay attention to what takes place in the Senate. I told the Senators that it was entirely a matter for them what their procedure would be. I suggested the best procedure until we had framed Standing Orders; and that recommendation of mine was adopted without the slightest dissent. I must say that I think it very unfortunate that any Senator should wish to go behind it, because it puts the rest of his colleagues in a very unpleasant position before the public and the country.'"

"You're lucky in one thing. You have got the best Chairman in Europe to preside over you in the Senate," said Tim.

I thought that very generous, for I remembered the well-known story how, when they were rival counsels, Mr. Campbell, as Lord Glenavy then was, wept at the close of an action for divorce in which he represented the plaintiff. Tim rose, and, to undo the effect on the jury, with awful solemnity began : 'Gentlemen, we have witnessed to-day the greatest miracle since Moses struck the rock : tears from my learned friend.'

He was about to rise when I hastened to inquire, " Sir, you know everyone in Cork, who is the Chieftain Harrington ? "

" Oh, that humbug ! Is he about again ? I'll tell you all about him. He is one of those Americans who want to make the impression on other people that they failed to make in their own country. He left New York some years ago and . . ."—the pause before the thunder—" his only recommendation was a kick in the rump. And now he's an Irish Chieftain. He picked up a rich Irish woman on the boat and married her."

" He must be descended from his wife."

" You'll see him any day walking, with white spats, beside a woman as fat as himself. Are you coming ? "

Before it was darkened for the screen, the lecture-room looked gay enough with the uniforms of the men who had fought to hasten the settlement with Great Britain which is known as the Treaty. Many have claimed since the truce which preceded the treaty credit for a share in the warfare in which they were not endangered or engaged. But most of the men present went out in arms against Great Britain, and by so doing placed a halter round their necks which failure would draw tight. It was possibly born of his hatred of humbug that Tim Healy sought about in his mind for a sly dig at the post-truce heroes. Every one of them had half died for Ireland if you would believe them, or were related to those who had died. To them alone Ireland owed its freedom. Taking my arm, Tim whispered, moaning gravely in his deep voice, while his eyes twinkled as he indicated the assembly of a free country, " Baldy Doody's pig has not died in vain."

Canada may be cold enough, I thought, as I watched the Tibetan mountaineers screened sleeping in their cloaks at 19,000 feet, on icy Everest, in an atmosphere so moistureless that one side of your face could be frostbitten while the other was sunburned. The climber told of how at 19,000 feet, birds cease to fly; how the air in the columned glaciers became so disintegrated that it acted like laughing gas on the carriers; and how, for a while, it was thought that these men were drunk. I saw the awful frostbitten fingers, swollen like pears, and the heroic rescue of the sun-blinded doctor of the expedition. But what brought the rigour of the ascent most to mind was the casual remark that dropped and rang, as casual remarks usually do, into my consciousness, which at the moment was as receptive as a gong:

" At this elevation (26,000 feet) the climbers were taking sixty gasping breaths to every step they took upwards."

As I went to thank the Governor-General for a most enjoyable evening, he said, " On Tuesday I have to open the Spring Show. I want you to come here to lunch and to take some of the ladies in your car. I am afraid that you have disedified Sir John Simon with your *contes drôlatiques*. Good-night!"

As I drove home I forgot the deep dissatisfaction and faction in the town, thinking of the possibilities of a lecture on *The Disedification of Sir John Simon*.

CHAPTER VIII

MR. CULLINAN WAS GROWING RESTLESS. I HAD ASKED HIM TO dine and to meet Sir Horace. Mr. Cullinan was the man who had subscribed the second largest sum towards the foundation of a paper for Sir Horace. Mr. Doherty had been the greatest sponsor. Mr. Cullinan is one of those Americans who are deprived by Nature of revealing their greatness in words. Had I not seen part of his fleet of bronze oil-tankers each as large as the liner to Holyhead, I should never have realised that I was in the presence of a man who could have bought an Irish county. I did realise that if Sir Horace was absent from dining much longer the charm which might well make such an experiment (in co-operation) possible would be broken, and Sir Horace might be judged on strictly business lines and found wanting in punctuality.

The servant called me to the telephone. There had been some firing audible as Mr. Cullinan left his hotel. Mr. Cullinan tried to glean some inkling of what the telephone message was from the man's countenance—a hopeless task; but I knew from the tension of a voice which I could judge that something serious was toward.

" Ah, my dear fellow, I am afraid that I will be late for dinner, so I just rang you up to ask you and your guests to have a little patience with me. . . . No! no! You must not wait. You see, I have been held up on my own drive and my car has been stolen by armed men. It will take me a little time to get another car. But I will come along."

The car of one of the most chivalrous, influential and patriotic Irishmen stolen on his own avenue! By " armed men "! I was sure that Sir Horace had not asked them for their " officer." I was not surprised; but how would Cullinan take it? What would he think of the wisdom of endowing a newspaper in the midst of a guerrilla war?

All I said was, " Sir Horace has just rung up to say that he will be along presently. We are not to wait."

" I hope nothing has happened to Sir Horace ? "

Regarded in one way, that was the trouble. Nothing had happened to Sir Horace during a life that was singularly thronged and ineffectual—about as ineffectual as Shelley's. . . . In the swirl of thought ideas followed—Sir Horace has a nephew Shelley-like but hardly ineffectual: Sir Horace, when he should have been a military man, is a reformer; so was Shelley, when he should have been a monogamist.

"Mr. Ryan, Mr. Cullinan, we are to dine without Sir Horace. He will be here presently."

No one should endeavour to entertain two American millionaires, at the same time, at the same table. They may be vegetarians, but they are not gregarious.

"That was during your Pittsburg period?"

"No, sir, I was never in Pittsburg for any period."

"I should have said?"

"I do not know, sir, what you should have said: but you should not have said that my town is Pittsburg."

"Mr. Ryan, surely you know Mr. Cullinan is the founder, we might say, of Houston, Texas. These succulent and delicious grape-fruits with their pink flesh are his gift. He travels about supplying his table, no matter where he stays, with the produce of his estates."

The background of my mind was disturbed by wondering, would Sir Horace, with his usual imperturbability, ignore the cause of his delay in meeting his American admirers and turn it aside with a murmur of polite phrases? A shot, rather close, judging by its noise; but possibly far off, allowing for the echo of Ely Place, rang out. This recalled old times in Texas not, unfortunately not to Mr. Cullinan of Texas, but to Mr. Ryan of Philadelphia. If he loves his brother man he will put Philadelphia "on the map"; but I want peace in mine inn until Sir Horace takes over.

"Mr. Ryan," I said, "you may not know that Sir Horace has devoted his life to his country."—Insincerely enough, I thought that Mr. Ryan deserved this kind of clap-trap.—"There is hardly any act of his which is not in some way bound up with the advancement of his plans. 'Advancement of his plans' should be one of those censored phrases." Then, more daringly, "We all know what those plans are?"

"Sure," Mr. Ryan replied.

Mr. Cullinan, who had contributed in cash to the advancement of some of Sir Horace's plans, felt that he should assume a proprietary air, at this juncture, over Sir Horace, and commenced to enumerate without elucidating the plans. I knew that he was a true disciple of Co-operation. Meanwhile, the mind of Mr. Ryan was losing the freshness of its insight and becoming sicklied over by the paleness of Mr. Cullinan's explanation.

" ' Everything for Ireland,' " I intoned pontifically, hoping that the emphasis of the asseveration would enable me to discover how Sir Horace's latest loss came under this category. For it was accepted by his disciples that everything he did, no matter how inexplicable, was bound up with Ireland. . . . But we heard his voice in the hall. It sounded full of little hard, crackling consonants, inarticulate and cultivated monosyllabic sounds, not at all unpleasing. These preceded him into the room.

"Ha! ah! Aah! I am so glad to see that. Ah! It might have been worse had I let the soup grow cold. . . . However, now that we are all together . . . there is . . . No ? . . . Ah, don't mind me, I never eat soup. . . . You have been at Battle Creek, Mr. Cullinan ? An excellent sanatorium. I am urging and making representations in the proper quarter, of course, for the necessity, the very urgent necessity, of having a sanatorium in Ireland run on the lines of Battle Creek. Diet has not been considered : that is to say, the importance of diet has been overlooked in the treatment of medical cases—internal medicine, as they call it there."

" Unless you ignore diet altogether, Sir Horace, do take a little food."

" Ah, my dear Cullinan, you should know that two kinds of proteins, those represented by the potato and those by the flesh of lamb, are opposed and should not be taken together. In fact, in the potato alone there is almost sufficient to rear a family, as indeed families were reared in Ireland before the famine. Water, if I may."

" We have progressed a long way since then, Sir Plunkett."

Sir Horace looked almost coy, as one embarrassed by praise. Surely he cannot hold himself responsible for the improved conditions since the famine ? He was " explaining " to Mr. Ryan. By the end of the explanation Mr. Ryan was confused, but vaguely conscious of Sir Horace in some *rôle* in which he was hardly distinguishable from Providence.

" We have only about one-third of our pre-famine population for whom to cater. The Home Brighteners have done exceeding well. They are devoted ladies who have helped enormously in the improvement of domestic conditions. They are associated with my I.A.O.S. They go into the cottages and make suggestions. The standards of living which are not wholly dependent in this country on wealth are considerably improved by their advice. What I mean is, that a farmer may be wealthy . . . I mean to say . . . suppose a poor farmer were to come into a considerable fortune, he would go on living as far as comfort and the raising of the standards were concerned, exactly as he had lived before and as his father had lived. The Home Brighteners . . ."

Crash! went a rifle in the street.

Mr. Ryan said, " I was talking to our friend here, Mr. Cullinan of Pittsburg, Sir Horace, before you arrived. He tells me . . ."

Mr. Cullinan rose with, " Sir, I tell you here and now and once and for all . . ."

" Houston Texas, Galena ! " I interjected.

" I can hear you, Cullinan, better if you remain seated," Sir Horace drawled.

There was what would have been elsewhere an awkward interval. But that would have been in company which did not know Sir Horace. He went on as if resuming a conversation held in New York but a moment ago.

" Your two visits to Ireland, Cullinan, have given you an intimate knowledge of the present political situation, which cannot be understood without getting, as you have done, into close touch with the chief actors in this extraordinary drama. This experience will enable you to explain the complex state of our public affairs to other leading American friends of Ireland. (Mr. Ryan had to come into this now or be for ever frozen out.) . . . But also to place before them the project of re-starting the *Irish Statesman*."

A bomb fell at the other side of St. Stephen's Green or just behind Ely House. " Echoes," I murmured. It might have been a cork popping for all the deflection it caused in Sir Horace's flow of speech.

" In cases where you have to present the proposal by letter, it may be helpful if I here summarise the reasons why you and I, after many conferences . . ."

" Count me in on this, Sir," Mr. Ryan exploded.

Sir Horace took no notice. His confidences were Mr. Cullinan's exclusive " option."

" . . . have come to the conclusion that a very real service may thus be rendered to those who are striving to bring order out of chaos"—another bomb—"' chaos,'" continued Sir Horace, " into which Ireland, with her proverbial ill-luck, has once more been plunged."

" She'll come right out," Mr. Ryan, reduced to the status of an acolyte, responded.

" As you know, Cullinan, the original journal had a brief career. The rapid rise in the cost of production . . ."

I waved the coffee aside.

". . . exhausted the available funds, after it completed its first year of publication."

How hard it would be to anticipate an end to one of Sir Horry's sentences! I found myself thinking.

" Competent observers are satisfied that the education it gave in Britain . . ."

Mr. Ryan nodded. " Competent observers." But he was losing his chance of becoming one of Great Britain's educators. Cullinan was about to be made *for Ireland* a ' Matthew Arnold ' under Sir Horace.

" The Dominions, and the United States (Ryan, how fallen!), were factors in enabling—some say compelling—the British Government to make to our country the largest political concession in the long history of the Anglo-Irish conflict."

' And to think that I only backed Mick Collins! ' thought Mr. Cullinan's rival.

" It had no small influence in persuading Irishmen that they can now enjoy in common . . ."

But the share in Ireland's greatness that Sir Horace was not inclined too readily to share, brought the business men, starved all their lives of imagination, to his feet. His perfect, cool rhythm made their eagerness to enter at the eleventh hour, as it were, the vineyard of Sir Horace seem indecorous.

" Freedom to develop the human and material resources of this country . . ."

Somebody broadcasting for the resources of civilisation threw another bomb nearer to my festive board.

". . . but even when peace is restored, the Government will need for this task a far clearer realisation than now prevails in Ireland of the scope and limitations of that representative and responsible Government. . . ."

His nephew, Lord Dunsany, is a poet in a far less hackneyed and constricted field than this in which Sir Horace's imagination towers. Who has the greater power of compelling dreams ?

Dunsany wrote : *The King of Elfland's Daughter*—our best modern example of romantic prose. Sir Horace wrote (helped by Æ) *Ireland at the Cross Roads*—(where it always has been, and shall be). Dunsany banished politics into Elfland: Sir Horace restored Elfland to politics.

"For the first time in seven hundred years," the crackling voice went on. What a response that 'Seven hundred years' is striking! "with this indication of the general end in view. . . ."

Dunsany's imagination appeals to imagination. But his uncle can create imagination even in millionaires. Judged by the fundamental brainwork . . . Oh, but he is marvellous! I must look upon him as a prose poet and a leader of the leaders of men. And he does it all by merely adumbrating, never expressing an idea.

"I will now set down the precise method by which it is to be attained . . ."

'Precise method' is good. 'Mobbled' is good! But how wrong I was! His next sentence refuted me.

"There will be registered in Dublin the Irish Statesman Publishing Company, Ltd."

I, who hate all business talks, plans, constructions, and syndicates, was casting about to escape, when one of his mesmerised millionaires inquired:

"Say, Sir Horace, may I call on you to-morrow?"

"I am afraid I shall be entertaining a British Cabinet Minister. But, let me see . . . I will get Longworth to telephone to you when we ascertain how our day is taken up. But why not come out and lunch with us at Kilteragh?—and meet Mr. Fisher?"

"Delighted."

If I am to prove a good host I must know my cue. Everyone could count on Sir Horace's being too tired to do more than to permit some rich American to distinguish himself by an exceeding-greatly-rewarding subscription to Ireland's illimitable future.

"Sir Horace is tired," I said. "If you will go upstairs you will find that some people have called who are anxious to meet you. I will run Sir Horace home."

Sir Horace groaned accordingly.

"Now that is very good of you indeed. One cannot do more than give rich men a chance of expressing themselves against the background of the Nation. Meanwhile, what is the least valuable car you have? Naturally, with all this highway robbery there are no taxis, and if I stay here for the night as you so very kindly suggest, Kilteragh may be burned."

As we passed in my Ford with its left-hand drive the church at Donnybrook, and the long walls were beginning, Sir Horace asked, " Have you a gun ? "

" Two."

" Let me take them. You cannot do two things at a time, and I have been in Texas. You must not mind if I shoot at sight. The important thing is to carry on."

" The safety-catch is on." I heard a click.

With the wind-screen raised as high as it would go, I drove rapidly through the dangerous darkness. With the corner of my eye I could see Sir Horace, wiry and alert, with a parabellum in one hand and a 430-Colt in the other, weaving them warily side to side in a small arc.

" They seized my car on the lower drive. They will hardly expect me to return the same way, therefore let us return by it."

" They have cleared off long ago, fearing reprisals," I asserted.

As the small, fearless figure sat beside me, I remembered the suit of armour in Dunsany Castle where Sir Horace was born. I thought that it was only a figure such as his that would fit into it. Back into the Past I rejected him—the beginnings of his family tree, a Norman knight repelling a raid against the bretesche which must have stood on the great mound or motte which guarded with wooden tower the road to Tara before the stone castle which stands beside the great dun was built.

The Norman-French crackled in my ears.

" Steady, men! Keep your horses on firm ground! Stop the pursuit there! Let them hide in the woods! " My mind flew back to the present, hardly to be distinguished from my dream.

" They have cleared off long ago, fearing reprisals," I asserted.

" I expect they have. By Gad! it's remarkable how history repeats itself. The indigenous Irish could never do more than raid and burn, because they resisted the discipline of their chiefs who might have kept them longer in the field. Once they found themselves confronted with asbestos block houses of stone which they could not burn, castles as they call them now, which protected for the Normans both serf and steer, they had no organisation to conduct a siege."

" They lacked co-operation," I ventured.

" Ah, spasmodic destruction was the only way in which their militarism could find expression; and you cannot found a civilisation on that. Now to-night they may take our car, your car, as mine has been taken, they may set fire to Kilteragh and I will lose my library : but are they any nearer to a civilised way of living ? "

" Don't let their pretensions excuse their performance. They are nothing but a lot of rogues and ruffians calling robbery Republicanism."

The locked-up houses were ominously still. The long demesne walls which flanked the road, with their belts of trees within them, were ideal for a snipers' ambush. When I am in danger I grow exalted, which is a form of excitement little different from hysteria. Probably my flood of talk was distracting Sir Horace. He interrupted me with a cackled, " Ha ! It has just occurred to me that, unless they want to collect every car on the road, they will not take this, for they cannot possibly know who are in it. We will only be identified by going into Kilteragh. I may relax a little. There is always a certain amount of strain in being on the *qui vive*."

He crossed the pistols in his lap.

" Every country goes through this kind of thing, raids and destruction, at some time or other. The remarkable thing is that Ireland has gone through it so often. It never appears to learn a lesson."

I thought of the Border forays and the relish of the balladist as he recounted the harrying :

> Now they have harried the dales of Tyne;
> And burned all Bamboroughshire;
> And Eskadale, they have brent it hale,
> And left it a' on fire.

The blaze through the night ! Ireland, too, all on fire !

" The side-lights should be sufficient about here. We turn to the right, then right again up the drive. You can go straight on through the other gate. I hardly think . . . Ah, my dear fellow, this is all right. I will jump out. Do not stop the engine. . . . No, on second thoughts, go right round the rockery and back by the way we came. It is too obvious that a driver in a hurry would carry on through the second gate. It is really extremely kind of you. Safe journey ! The guns are on the seat."

I had neither the courage nor the *sang froid* of Sir Horace. The night for me was peopled by surly men nursing an immemorial grievance or inventing one to justify outrage to their peculiar consciences. "Traditious obscurities." It was no use to drive off in a hurry. If one could not pull up when the highwaymen stood in the road, it meant a hail of bullets through the wind-screen. I thought of Sir Horace's drive in midday against a storm of British bullets. What a stormy petrel he is : I hope no adverse mascot. I wish I were driving home some stout fellow like Joe Magrath. It is half-past eleven. There are the lights of Kingstown and Black-rock. There is something encouraging in a light. The fighting Greeks hoped, if they had to die, for sunlight. Electric light would be better than this midnight darkness about Kilteragh. At Blackrock I became heroic retro-spectively. But soon I became indignant. Here am I, Irish of the Irish, to save my property, running away from Irishmen, and for no other fault than that I backed Arthur Griffith, who, as assuredly as Sir Horace Plunkett did, fell among thieves. They can hide in the woods. But Griffith is exposed to the howling storm of ingratitude, an Irish Lear, with Goneril and Regan, aye, and Cordelia too ; for Ireland has three characters, like the three ladies whom the hero of the old Dublin ballad " As I was going down Sackville Street " informs us that he " chanced to meet."

CHAPTER IX

KYLEMORE HOUSE, CONNEMARA, STANDS ON KYLEMORE LAKE, which lives clothed in purple and silver under windows lit by the southern sun. A blue-eyed giant of a man, with a golden goatee, is standing by the door giving orders to his spaniel, Judy, his chauffeur, Timmins, and his Scots terrier, Billy, at the same time. " In, Judy ! Keep the door open, can't you ? . . . Billy, come along ! " His silver Lanchester is simmering in front of the house, against the wall of which a salmon-rod is leaning with the fly stuck into the cork of the handle. He has tried a spell of fishing, but it was too bright. He cannot remain inactive. He is driving seven miles to look up his next-door neighbour. He is coming to see me.

My house, too, stands on a lake, but it stands also on the sea. Water-lilies meet the golden seaweed. It is as if, in the faery land of Connemara at the extreme end of Europe, the incongruous flowed together at last ; and the sweet and bitter blended. Behind me, islands and mountainous main-land share in a final reconciliation at this, the world's end. I am sitting on a little terrace overlooking the lake, watching the wider shimmer of the ocean beyond a thin line of green in the middle distance. It is good to let the eyes relax and to lose accommodation on wide prospects.

A butterfly, like a small, detached flame, is making excellent landings on the faintly pink blossoms of the thorn. Two bees disturb him alternately. But there is no harm done, and the morning is flowing on, filled with brightness and peace. No trout ring the lake with sudden ripples. It is too sunny for fishing : trout should pray for ' *mehr licht.*' The indolent sound of waves receding from the shelves of gravel on the beach near by, or the singing of some insect projectile, are all the ear can discern.

Behind me a wing of the long sea-grey house stretches for forty yards. In the evening the lake will send the westering sun dancing on the dining-room panels, the oak of which sun and age have reddened until it looks like the mahogany of a later day.

The sun is shining up at me from the lake and down on me from the sky. We have not long to live in the sun ; and here even the sunlight is not assured. Therefore let us enjoy it while we may.

'Work while ye have the light.' What an idea! As if one were an Italian navvy. It sounds like something from one of those Hebrew " Prophets " who prophesied nothing but uncomfortable things, or from that pre-Bolshevic, Leo Tolstoi. While the sun shines is the time to enjoy life.

O quid beatius solutis curis!

As the poet said whom mistresses and mortgages had never left carefree.

Galway is always inclined for peace. They called it a rest-cure for Black-and-Tans in the " Troubles." At any rate, it is fairer and more peaceful than Dublin is at the present moment. It is good for me to be here where no one comes to break in on my rich indolence.

Ah, but a warning horn is blown on the crest of the rising ground which flows in a semi-circle round the house. A great car dashes up the drive and grooves the gravel into brown lines as it is pulled up. My friend the Squire of Lytham, now residing at Kylemore House, has come to call. He is one of the mightiest sportsmen in the world. I, the introvert, am caught by the greatest extrovert I have ever known. What have I to say for myself? Convert him to loafing and inviting his soul? A hopeless hope! He has taken it for granted, since I was given no chance to deny it, that I share his passion for sport. And I have not the courage to protest now, and to lose caste, however undeservingly gained. Were I to disavow it now, I would die in his opinion and he would lose a friend.

He hailed me in a jerky, deep-sounding voice.

" Hell-el-lo! If you haven't been fishing, why aren't you out shooting seals ? "

I answered somewhat evasively, " It's too bright for fishing, and even if it were not, the bottom feeding is so good here that the big trout never rise in this lake. I once caught nine, all over two pounds, in ten minutes, during a hot wind from the west; but that was long ago. I haven't had a rise since."

This seemed to give him food for thought. Evidently, to him it was a matter of concern. I dared not say that I had never fished since that memorable day. It would have been honester than to let him go on puzzling his brains challenged by such an important problem, to give me good advice. After a while he jerked out cheerfully :

" I'll tell you what you must do. Drain the whole lake."

" The whole lake? But how ? "

"Oh, have it pumped out. Then, very, very carefully . . . sod it. Then let the water in again; and stock it with rainbow trout. You see? Rainbow." To him, with the wealth of Lytham, St. Anne's, and the half of Blackpool behind him, it was a simple and necessary proceeding.

"Already I have lost a hundred acres through the agitation of Canon McAlpine, who butted in to make mischief out of his own parish. If an additional hundred acres of good grazing land were to appear at the lake's bottom, I would have other people's black cattle up to the windows of my house."

"Why did you give the hundred acres up?"

"Oh, I did not want them. So long as the lake is not contaminated, and I am left with a certain amount of privacy, I don't care who grazes. But I did care when I lost my forty-acre wood of ash trees with its green arches carpeted by lawns. An ash wood is the cleanest wood there is. And the poor fools who felled it, felled it to use the wood for fuel while they sold the coal they got in relief during a shortage of turf. Now, like all ignorant peasants who hate trees, they have left themselves with no winter grazing or shelter for their cattle. And there is no milk in this district from November until May. . . . Their children are their victims, fed on stewed tea until they are old enough to enter the asylums, where their parents should have been.

"Damn it all," he said, not so much in commiseration as annoyance at the problem invincible ignorance presents. Then he bent down and played with his dog. Suddenly he rose, to his full height, and with, "Come along," moved towards his car. As he stood, I marvelled at the figure of the man. He was very tall and straight, but his hips had an un-English appearance. Something of the Arab, I wondered?

"What about a drink?" I asked.

"I never allow myself a drink until after six o'clock."

He looked out over the sea and made several suggestions.

"What you should do is to keep a motor-launch here. You should open up the outlet from that lake of yours so that the salmon and white trout may get up."

But there was something on his mind which he had not revealed.

"Also, you must put down some grouse. But have the vermin destroyed first."

"But where can I get the grouse?"

"Yorkshire. I will get you as many as you want."

" The Irish grouse is a bigger bird with more comb.   I don't wish to mix the breed."

" That's all very well, but if there are no Irish birds to shoot why not get hybrids that you can shoot ? "

" Thanks for the tip."

After a pause : " It looks a good day for having a pot at some seals ? "

" Last year I shot twelve, and only recovered one.   They sink."

" Then how did you get the one ? "

" I went overboard for it and caught it by the flipper. It dived between my knees, and I turned an under-water somersault."

" Very stupid thing to do.   Now let me tell you, when I was with the Esquimaux, the thing was to use a light harpoon. We'll get a harpoon with a very long shaft : then . . . ! " He transfixed a visionary seal.

" It's rather murderous shooting them at all.   They come out of curiosity quite close to the boat with their intelligent brown eyes, wondering what you are doing so far out at sea."

This was too much for the great hunter.

" Ho !   Don't forget that they are ruining the salmon-fishing in my lakes.   They take a piece out of the shoulder of the fish and then leave it to die.   They should be shot. The harpoon's the thing."

" I don't want to land them.   Nobody can cure hides properly here.   The few skins I have are like Zulu shields."

The treatment of the skins of the grey Atlantic seal did not interest him.   He was considering the ways and means of getting them.

" What kind of boat did you use ? "

" The ordinary curragh.   It is a most sea-worthy boat, though it is only made of canvas stretched on wicker."

" Hopeless !   We must get a launch. . . . By the way, how did you get back again into the curragh ? "

" Over the stern.   You wait for a wave and heave yourself in.   It is impossible to do it at the side."

" I should think so.   Now, lookey here . . ."

" Yes ? "

He walked over to his car.   As he walked he said, " Do you see that Lanchester ?   Now, the gears of that car are never out of mesh.   It has a continuous gear.   You can slip into reverse at seventy-five and come very slowly, very slowly to a standstill; and then, very slowly back." He illustrated the gentleness of the reversing movement by his hands, which he held parallel as if about to join them in reverence.

I knew where an implied disparagement was being aimed. I was not going to have my Rolls disparaged. I became brave, for I knew that at one time he had six Rolls-Royces to take his friends about his Scots shoots. "Who wants to slip into reverse at seventy-five? Has it no brakes? I should simply hate to find myself going backwards."

"Not the point, not the point. The point is in the gear-box—worm drive!"

"Leave the worm that turns; and come along into the house." I had a feeling that there was something on his mind which for once was not a problem concerning game.

In the library he produced a large golden fountain pen, which he laid on an inkstand, and, turning away from it abruptly, "I want you to have that," he said.

He cut short my expostulations with, "From me." Then he flung himself into an arm-chair and, with a change of voice, began: "Now lookey here! I came over to ask your opinion. I want to go over to see my cousin Lonsdale next week. . . ." He paused, as if embarrassed by having to take counsel with anyone but himself. Then solemnly, "Do you think if I leave Kylemore, my wife and children will be molested?"

"Surely not! Certainly not."

"You are living in a fool's paradise, my friend."

I could have answered, " I prefer to be in a fool's paradise than in the Board-room of a rationalist," or "Just at the present in Ireland, if one is to be loyal to the Government it is necessary to be a fool." But it was the wrong moment for facetiousness when such a man was struggling to confide in me. Instead, I exclaimed:

"Nobody molests women and children in Ireland."

"There is a lot of unrest, far more widespread than you seem to realise. You may be the first to suffer."

"I? But I have never done the people any harm."

"That's just it. You see, I have been in many uncivilised places where human life was of little consequence. I have met savages of every description. And the worst position you can place yourself in with them is to do them no harm."

I thought—' Anoint a villain, he will prick you: prick a villain, he will anoint you.' Then aloud: "Do you think you will be attacked?"

"Oh, ho! I do not think it. I told them what they may expect if they come sneaking about my place. But it's while the man is away that these kind of fellows gather courage and show it by intimidating the women and children. I thought you knew something about the people among whom you are living."

"Well, all I can say is, that I will be astounded if Irishmen attack women and children in a defenceless house."

He drew within himself. Suddenly the awful thought struck me—' Can he suspect that I am only lulling him into a false security ? Does he really believe that I am living in a fool's paradise and am not in collusion with *canaille* who would avenge themselves on women and children ?' I felt uncomfortable and embarrassed. I almost wished that I were attacked first, to exonerate me from all suspicion of duplicity to such a fine fellow. Nor was I relieved when he suddenly leaped up with, "Well, I'll be getting back."

I thought of his tall, dark, beautiful wife, his little daughters and his two sons, still children. As I pondered I began to have misgivings. How much "hang over" of hatred, centuries old, remained in the country to instigate "Revenge, be Jayshus! on the Sassenach"? True, the hatred had become more or less diverted into civil war, Irishmen hating Irishmen. Hatred's the thing! Perhaps the English would be overlooked. Then I remembered the louts who were playing at campaigning by stealing motor-cars : Sir Horace's, one of mine. Talbot Clifton had three cars at least at Kyle-more.

"If I thought as you do, I would not go."

"I have no intention of going just yet. I wanted to talk with you. That's all." He only waved his hand as he drove off. He did not look back. I was left feeling uncomfortable for the rest of the day.

Damn the vampire dead who have left us nothing but an heritage of hatred which operates equally against the "Foreigner" as against ourselves. In the Tenth and Eleventh Centuries the natives took sides with the foreigner. Against him now, and, a year later, allied to him, with the facility of the professional footballer for changing sides. Post-mortem hatred met by living suspicion of all our tribe makes a comely life impossible.

There was never a more attractive man than Talbot Clifton in many ways; but now I stood before him mottled by the corruption of a dead hate, whilst he was poisoned by living suspicion. Damn the Dead! When will they cease to infect both Irish and English with their mortality? Here am I, who never "let down" any man, a suspect and an accomplice against my will, and through no fault of mine, in every fatuous act and brainless brutality of the past, of the present, and of days to come. The "he who is not with us is against us" of the narrow sect! A curse on both their houses of hate. They stand between me and my friend. Is there no place in Ireland for a man of good will? There is in the monasteries, perhaps; but even monasteries provide no unbroken sanctuary in Erin.

There are many burnings besides the burning of the church of Cashel's rock to be remembered, before the English or the Foreigners could be accused of producing any excuse for such outrages. No; even the house of God is not safe when the tribal passions of Ireland are aroused. The object lesson of peace and aloofness from passion which they provide seems to have aroused vindictiveness all the more. And if this be so, what chance is there for me and for Talbot Clifton to be left to the enjoyment of neutrality? None. I should have pointed that out to him. But to make him believe it I should have to be victimised first. And I have not the least desire to be a martyr to "small-holders" even to show how right I am.

Leisure, and the accoutrements of leisure, lakes preserved, pictures, silver and motor-cars, these are as red rags to the congenital "Reds"—the under-dogs of all time. We shall be "taught a lesson." In other words, all we possess that is the outcome of the creative imagination of artists who had the leisure to dream and to give their dream a local habitation, all that took time and loving care to accomplish, be it the cover of the Book of Kells or a silver inkstand, by all that appertains to a household of continuance, aye, even the house itself must be destroyed. And not that anything may live but hate.

If this were told to me by anyone else, I would believe in it so much that I would at this moment follow Clifton and warn him to take himself and all he held dear to the safety of a country which has had only one or two civil wars. But in my case performance follows slowly on prevision. I know what will happen, but so great is the margin of the incalculable in Ireland that I wait to see. Should I have told him that fifteen pounds of mine was stolen from a post-bag in the name of the Republic which gathers public property? I only withheld the knowledge out of shame. Were he to hear it now, nothing would convince him but that I, through jealousy or some such motive entertained by " natives," was planning to have a rival expelled. In England he rivalled successfully the greatest sportsmen, from his cousin Lonsdale down. But he was no rival of mine. To become my rival he must needs loaf for weeks refraining himself from many things. He had the mind of a child in many ways. Some of his visits to me were due to his preference for the site of my house to that of his own. I had both lake and sea. He had only lakes. And the sea was seven miles from him. He had bought a derelict place, restored, equipped it, and now he was running it expensively. He considered me, humble as I was, a rival because Nature was my fairy godmother!

Petey, who was low-sized and broad-shouldered, because he was a hunchback, said : " There's an Englishman at Leenane helping the Republicans." He waited ready to interpret my comment later on, to my greatest disadvantage.

" How do you know ? "

" The Beach told me."

" And what did he say ? "

" Just that."

" But how did he know ? "

" He heard him drilling them, and giving them orders and telling them tactics." (Tactics : my fifteen pounds !)

Now, I knew this well. Mrs. Clifton took pity on him, and invited him to dinner. He must be so upset by his own tragedy that he must come over to upset this tragical country. But to discuss him with Petey would be, no matter what I said, twisted into an excuse for the conscientious ruffians who were by some cowardly euphuism called ' Irregulars ' to annex some more of my belongings. Petey threw the net again.

" They have taken—commandeered "— he corrected to a military word for robbery—" Mr. Clifton's big car."

For a moment I was shocked ; but soon that something " not altogether unpleasing in the misfortunes of our friends " came to me, or rather, anticipation of the misfortunes which would rapidly follow my non-friends who had stolen Clifton's car, consoled me. They were in for it now. The Lanchester was the apple of his eye. His fearless blue eyes would blaze.

On Sunday I came back from church to find my house had

been ransacked by armed men, " looking for Mr. Clifton."
On the breakfast-table was a red silk handkerchief, thrown
down carelessly. It contained a diamond tiara, a large pendant
and many more jewels. The frightened servants said that
Mrs. Clifton had been in.

" How did she come ? "

" In a pony trap."

So they had stolen all Clifton's motors, and he himself
was hunted. What could have happened ? He never would
have left his wife and family to the mercy of the ruffians who
stole his cars. Things must be bad at Kylemore when, in her
desperation, she tried to save her jewels by getting them over to
me. Mysteriously my one available car had ceased to be
available. I could not go over to make inquiries. The journey
might cost me my car, and cost her her jewels. I wondered
if the servants had seen the handkerchief full of diamonds on
the breakfast-table. I knew I was being watched. If I
buried them, I would be observed. The best thing to do was
to take them to Dublin as soon as the car could be put in order,
and then travel by night circuitously. Surely Clifton's three
cars would satisfy the rabble for the present.

I began to realise how the country victims of the French
Revolution felt, and how it came about that, in spite of their
numbers, they never organised themselves generally to resist.
They were lulled separately into a false security because each
family believed, until it was too late, that their relations with
the local tenantry would make their case exceptional. Even
if the local tenantry loved them, the new passions in the air
abolished loyalties and any affection that might have been
hereditary ; but what none of them realised was the fact that,
willy nilly, the local tenantry were themselves the victims of a
grim central gang who could order the outlying units to arrest
their own parents if need be. (In some cases this may have
been done unwittingly.) Thus it was, so gradually did the
civil war affect us, that we took but little notice of it locally
and ignored the extent to which it had spread. *Ucalagon
ardet!* But, though next door, it did not necessarily mean a
conflagration for me.

Presently the news came in, magnified by rumours. Petey
said that Mr. Clifton had ambushed his own car and had shot
one of the men who had stolen it. This had a great effect
upon the narrator. He was frightened.

" I take off my hat to him, Petey," I said. " You can tell

them that when you are making your report about me.   He has only given them a taste of what they have been giving to others."

Petey was frightened.   He began at once to agree with me, but tentatively.

" Oh, sir, indeed yes.   These are terrible times, anyway."

One would think that the times had put themselves out of joint.   I got rid of Petey and prepared to go to see Mrs. Clifton, to hear, if possible, what had happened.

But she had gone to the nearest secure place, Galway, fifty miles away, and had taken the children and some of her belongings with her.

This is what had taken place.   The day after his visit to me, Clifton's Lanchester had been seized in his absence by a gang of men, and used on journeys between Leenane and Clifden.   This brought it past his doors.   The thought of his farm-hands taking their girls to fairs and races in his car ! It was insufferable.   Having seen it pass to Letterfrack and knowing that it would return about midnight, he took his Star two-seater and his Ford, and barricaded the way at a cross-road some few furlongs to the east of his house where the ground rose high enough to cause a car to slow down.   He waited alone, with his Purdey in his hand ; alone, to hold up, how many armed men ?   He did not care.   After a while the great headlights could be seen searching out the invisible hills, sweeping up and down as the front springs gave to the bumpy road.   He could hear the hum of the engine at intervals. Nearer and nearer it came on.   At last the full blaze of the headlights met his obstructing cars.   He switched on his lamps and stepped out from the darkness.

" Hands up ! "

All threw up their hands.   One occupant of the stolen car could only obey partially.   He was a prisoner.   His arms were tied at the elbows, behind his back.   In the tension of the silence as the stately figure approached, one man's nerve went.   He leaped out of the car and started to run back, onwards to Leenane.   Thinking he was about to execute a flanking movement, Clifton let him get almost out of range, then discharged a barrel at him.   Mrs. Clifton suspecting what was toward now arrived on the scene, imploring for mercy :   " You can get many Lanchesters ; but you cannot bring back human life ! "   She hampered her husband's move-ments.   This gave the gang time to draw their revolvers and to threaten Clifton. Neither side would yield. Mrs. Clifton extracted a promise from the car-stealers that if they were allowed to keep the car they would not alarm her children nor molest her house. They promised accordingly. But later, armed men notified Clifton that if he did not leave Ireland that night they " would not be responsible " for his safety. Single-handed against a whole countryside, without telephone or any means of summoning aid, with the lives of a family which he could neither remove nor protect against a host, the only chance of saving them lay in falling in with their conditions.

In the dawn he drove across the island with his valet and a suitcase, knowing quite well how little Republican promises could be replied on to curb the itch for destruction.

This was the result of the promise not to molest his family :

> " *Oglaigh na H-Eireann*,
> *Headquarters*,
> 4*th Western Division*,
> *Castlebar*.
> 14/3/22

To Mrs. Clifton,
 Kylemore, Connemara.

On the night of April 12th, 1922, your husband, Talbot Clifton, with others who are known to me, lay in ambush at a point on the main road between Kylemore and Leenane, and fired at officers of this Division who were proceeding to Castlebar.

As a result of the shots fired, Captain Eugene Gilan of the Irish Republican Army is now hovering between life and death in Mr. McKeown's Hotel, Leenane. I am satisfied from information received, that you also participated in the ambush, and this is to notify you that an armed guard will be placed on your premises, and that you, Mrs. Clifton, are to leave Connemara before 12 noon, Monday, 27th. Otherwise other steps will be taken.

If you desire to make any statement, it will be necessary for you to come to Castlebar, and I promise you a safe conduct.

> (Signed) MICHAEL KILROY.
> G.O.C. 4th Western Division,
> I.R.A.

N.B.—The armed guard will remain on your premises pending the return of your husband."

As the outcome of this intimidation, Mrs. Clifton drove away with her jewels to Renvyle. We were out at the time, so she left them on the breakfast-table, and hastened back to Kylemore to prepare for the journey to Galway without delay. Her children were more precious than her gems, and if waylaid for the prize the precious stones offered, she could say that she had left them behind.

There was little time to be lost if we were not to be marooned. Roads were dyked, bridges broken, trains derailed. Yet before I set out for Dublin with her treasures I went to Leenane.

I could not find the teacher of tactics. But it gave me little comfort to reflect that, though they exonerated me from suspicion, this Englishman's tactics led directly to the theft of his host's car. It was not the Irish this time who were wholly responsible for Irish miscreancy, but one of this country's particular curses, the renegade Englishman who invariably inflicts, morally and materially, more damage on Ireland than he would be suffered to inflict at home. In spite of their adoption of Gaelic names there is hardly an " O " or a genuine " Mac " prominent in Irish rebellions. Since the days when Englishmen revolted in Boston against their King, they have been renegading in every country but their own.

I wonder, is the popularity of the Gaelic language due to the camouflage it provides for English names ?

The only worse thing than this intrusion of the English renegade is the female of the species. We have both.

I went into the bar, where men were hulking and drinking their melancholy from pint measures. I learnt nothing. They stood silently.

The jewels reached Dublin safely. West valued some of them for insurance. There were others he could not value, for they were unmatchable and irreplaceable. These were the brown diamonds her husband had given Mrs. Clifton because they matched her eyes. The insurance rates on the first consignment were so prohibitive, for even the post was not safe, that an employee of the Estate Office was sent from Lytham to bring the remainder to their owner.

Perhaps it is just as well to be back in Dublin, I thought. Not that anyone is safer against the Mafia if once it marks him down ; but it at least will not be a case of " Lonely unto the Lone I go," as it would be if I were to be kidnapped in the country. A gallery must make dying easy for the vain or the contemptuous. But to be done in seven to one in a cellar underground would be likely to make too great a demand on a man's courage, even though it equalled his fate with that of the Tsar. There were forces in the country not too widely to be differentiated from the forces and inflaming sentiments that led to the cowardly murder of the women and children of that unhappy king, forces that were bound to grow in the land if its prosperity was diminished, or if Justice became venal and relaxed.

As I left West's, I ran into Kevin. I told him of my errand and Clifton's ambush.

"Do you know that Kilteragh, Sir Horace Plunkett's house, is destroyed by fire from the revolving box on the roof, in which he used to sleep, to its cellars ? " he said. " Nothing was salvaged. The mentality that could ruin not only the frequent home but the repository of some of the best work of Irish artists is hard to analyse, and harder still is it to present the results of the analysis in a credible way."

"Don't think I don't know it," I answered. " The chief factor in the obscurities, traditious or spontaneous, of this mentality is Resentment. This resentment is not necessarily political at all, but is born of the under-dog's envy of the man who can build. Dull resentment against the cultivated and apparently idle and leisured figure is an attitude of mind not at all confined to Ireland, but found in almost every country where there is civilisation, for civilisation itself is the enemy of the under-dog. And its disappearance will not help him. Civilisation is a veneer on the unremitting forces that seek to drag down all that is elevated. It is a veneer on a quagmire that underlies all blossoming. The periods of what we call the efflorescence of the Arts or the great cultural periods hardly exceeded fifty years in the history of any country. And when we remember in this paradoxical country that its own period of artistry was contemporary with a time of raids and burnings, we can hardly look to the villain to respect the outcome of an ordered life so much as to spare specimens or examples of it. Even if it were possible to separate from the political the biological characteristics of civilisation, they are better omitted.

"The best pictures George Russell painted were those he painted for his friends, the men he loved. Thus Kilteragh held the finest examples of his art. It held books, all the first editions of the short-lived movement that placed Ireland amongst the nations whose citizens were awarded the largest international prize in history for eminence in the Arts. It held letters from every great contemporary, corner-stones of future history, if this country is to remain an historical country and not to become a fermentation that matures nothing, but merely sours all that brews."

" Hold on," he said, " you have not heard half the destruction nor half the humbug."

The Earl of Mayo lost his house. Sir Horace's family established themselves in Ireland in the Twelfth Century. The Earl of Mayo was a Burke, a de Burgo. No, they were not as Irish as the non-historical Irish or the Firbolg failures, or as those who came over thirty years ago from England to teach Ireland how to be Irish. That is the second ingredient in the mentality of destruction, a reserved belief or feeling that the native has a longer history, and therefore has more claim to a land he never honoured, ornamented or owned. The third arises from that frustration which makes him wish to remove all traces of what mocks his incompetence and points a finger at his failure. When these passions are aroused and justified by a national movement, by a fiery cross, you can imagine the result. But it is not, alas, left to the imagination.

It was saddening and maddening. What was there to do but to curse the half-breed who had split our country ? But what was the use ? Public representatives are the results, not causes, of popular behaviour. It is better to regard them as *les yeux du bouillon*, the grease-spots that floated to the surface in the cauldron in which Beatrice Cenci boiled her father. " And the eyes of the soup were the eyes of her father," as George Moore loved to quote from his friend Villiers de l'Isle Adam. They are the grease-spots in the Irish stew ; and as results they are not to be blamed for causes. But wait a moment !—I said to myself, thinking of the tendency that representative Government has to become static, *i.e.*, not immediately amenable to the national need or popular demand in an emergency ; and with its power of resisting a general election for years, maybe, combined with power to abrogate Parliament or to draw some red herring of a " war " across the trail when it should go honestly to the country ; the public man or, as he has become, the Party Leader, is to be held almost personally responsible for public defalcations and outrages. Never was there such an instance of the responsibility of one man within the country, and he not an Irishman, for the country's wrongs.   Our ruin is more one man's doing than ever before in Irish history since Cromwell.

"And freely to speak my thoughts, it argues a strange self-ove and great presumption to be so fond of one's own opinions, that a public peace must be overthrown to establish them, and to introduce so many inevitable mischiefs, and so dreadful a corruption of manners, as a civil war and the mutations of state consequent to it always bring in their train, and to introduce them in a thing of so high concern, into the bowels of one's own country."

Sir Bryan Mahon's house is burned.

Sir Thomas Esmonde's house is burned.   He had an ancestor hanged for fighting for Ireland in '98.

If the English proletariat, nine-tenths of whom are wage-earners, choose to elect a Government nine-tenths of whom are landowners or capitalists, they may expect but little relief from the employers and masters of men.   But England can trust its aristocracy;   and the system which it has spun voluntarily from its own vitals, to maintain and safeguard above all individual liberty.   Ireland cannot trust a system which has been taken over and retained and worked for the opportunity it affords of the most unworthy as a rule attaining office and an income they would not have a chance of obtaining in an open market.   The Irish people do not trust their Government.   They elect it, hoping to lead it when it comes into power.   That is why Ireland always outruns its " leaders." The leaders are well aware of this and stop short of few sub-terfuges to retain their leaders' jobs.   Thus it comes about that into the hands of one man in Ireland, and he not an Irishman, was placed the power to do Ireland more harm than any external " tyrant " in the last hundred years ever did : never did, if what she had to lose in the old days be compared with what she has lost in these our times.

And thus the Irish farmer has, by exercise of his vote, only succeeded in placing over him, instead of the old-fashioned landlord, a new inhuman and merciless vote-buying and tax-collecting syndicate.

The calibre of the men who tried to be superior to Arthur Griffith may be judged, if the documents and reports of the dispute regarding the Treaty (a dispute that should never have arisen) be hard to come by, from their behaviour against the majority of our countrymen after the Treaty was signed and partly repudiated by members of this group.   I go so far as to say that Irishmen, if left to themselves unfomented and uninstigated by alien foolishness or knavery, would soon settle into a give-and-take existence.   Little constructive, much *laissez-faire*.   The one man who could have given them an interesting and progressive policy was Sir Horace Plunkett. His house was the first to go.   He tried to co-operate with, and not to exploit, serfs that could only sulk and conspire when not exploited.

I said : " If Government could be so simplified that a cook could govern Russia, then a market gardener should govern Ireland.   Instead of this, it is governed by born blunderers and the banks.   And the only bank that failed was the Land Bank !—and this in a country that has less than half the population of London, which is governed by a few aldermen and a Lord Mayor.   Three Commissioners reduced Dublin's rates in a year.   Three Commissioners could run the whole country, which is not half so complicated as the City of Dublin. But it won't be worse before it is better ; it will be worse before it is worst.   Ireland is about to become a crannog in the Atlantic Ocean.   And the Government will act as eviction agents, not of the Sir Horaces and the Lord Mayos, but of the very men who backed them and nursed them into power. The Irish people, whatever layer that term applies to now, always outrun their leaders.   The present hosts and backers of the Government, the men who, believing in their promises, nursed them into power, are about to be betrayed—in fact, are betrayed already in favour of a still lower and more out-at-elbows order.   Thus the host is betrayed as Talbot Clifton was betrayed.   And they can be removed only by the methods that removed the landlord of old.   This is what the brother of the murdered Minister for Justice said not long ago :

" ' The Government has given a legal existence to the most unjust and harshest landlord that ever cursed the people of this country.   If Balfour with his battering-ram had sucked £21,000,000 a year out of the Irish agricultural industry and had in the same year used armoured cars to get the landlords' rent collected, landlordism would not even have lived so long as it has lived in this country.   The farmer of the country could not easily differentiate between a lie and a statement calculated to deceive.   The whole campaign of Fianna Fail had been to assure the country that if Fianna Fail got into office the farmers would not have to pay any annuities.'

" Government by deception cannot last long."

" How will he end ? " asked Kevin.

" Howling," I said.   " He will go out making a virtue of Frustration and probably get away with it, or he may give one of his endless interviews to Ceres' son-in-law."

" So long as we get him away, what does it matter ? "

" Before that gang relinquishes office they will give us what they gave us before."

" What ? "

" *Si monumentum requiris . . .*"

" Ah," said Kevin, with a grim yet pleasing smile, " ' Even in their ashes . . .! ' "

" But come with me, I am going to Switzer's."

" What for ? "

" To buy an egg cup."

" You can get one at Woolworth's."

" Switzer's egg cups are far more fashionable."

CHAPTER X

I LOOKED WITH A FRESH EYE AT THE SHABBY STREET THAT HAD once been fashionable and prosperous. It was timidly walked in now. Double rows of troops, dressed in "feldgrün," set back to back in great lorries, gave it an appearance of unhealthy robustness as they rolled by. They were looked at indifferently by the passers-by. But some, the shabbiest, glared at them furtively after they had passed.

It takes some courage to put up with this and to sustain the weight of despondency it engenders. Have I to carry the town's and country's melancholy on my back? "By the Light of God," I swore, "I'll not let the bagmen or the bogmen drag me down." Melancholy, indeed! All because a few thousand men have not the guts to protest and agitate against third-rate tyranny! The town and country seem to be in a state of melancholy unrelieved. Only I refuse to be *atrabilious*. Am I an Irishman at all?

Suddenly the thought struck me. Irishmen like to be melancholy. It is the national pastime to brood full of black bile. I remembered the dark figures in the Connemara pub. Even their drink is black! They chew on melancholy as a cow on the cud. Shane Leslie attributes it to "hushed hate." It is more than that. It is independent of external circumstances. They take pleasure in darkening with melancholia God's sweet air. They sin against the light. "Accidia!" Of course, the obsolete Deadly Sin. There were once eight Deadly Sins. They are now only seven. Why? Probably the whole country were sinning, and what everyone does cannot (or can it?) be a sin. Something wrong somewhere with my reasoning, I think. It may have been found that there was no remedy for accidia in Ireland and so they let it slide. But what an escape I had! I might have been living in the eighth Deadly Sin and taking it for a form of patriotism. What an escape! It's a pity it is not a better known sin so that I would have more merit in exemption from it—Accidia!

How pleasant it would be if all sins were things one did not wish to do! This is one of the few which can never tempt me. I refuse to be "sullen in the sweet air," or to be with those who wilfully live in sadness. No! I will not!

I steered for the Bailey.

McLoren was describing, over a whiskey-and-soda, the austerities of India. A copy of Pater's *Renaissance* lay on the counter beside him. Instead of seeing Shamus, and telling him how I enjoyed a letter that morning with its paragraphs flowing bravely as banners from a castle wall, I found Chich, whose name rhymes with " which " and denotes our Dublin etymologist. To his researches I owe the discovery of the meaning of pettifogging. To his more advanced researches I owe the amendment from ' *pettus* ' and ' *facere* ' to . . . Well, let him speak: " My dear fellow. . . . Just a moment. . . . Waiter! I find that . . . You see, curiosity prompted me to discover the real derivation of pettifogging."

" But I am quite satisfied with your original discovery. Leave it so. Many things are ruined by being traced to their derivations."

" It is ' petty ' and an obsolete word to ' fog,' to cheat or deliberately to blind to something or other, and, also, there is the old Dutch ' focker.' It is a pity that my little theory is incorrect."

" Let it be correct until I have done with it! ' After me the Truth! ' "

Undiverted, the scholar continued: " With regard to those old tenures, Langdale in Norfolk was held by one Baldwin *per saltum, sufflatum et pettum*. That is, he was to come every Christmas into Westminster Hall, there to take a leap, cry, ' Hem '; and . . . precisely! "

" When he got old and stiff and could no longer leap, he must have sent his subtle lawyer. So it comes to the same thing in the end. I would like to take one of those old tenures and to send my man of business to hold it and renew, claiming audience of his King. Now, if Sir Thomas Beecham . . ."

He had just come down from Henry the Third to Henry the Eighth with his Laureate, Skelton, when I excused myself and left, only to find Sir Plunkett Barton looking into the window of a fashionable hairdresser. He is a type that will not be long left to us. His gentle, scholarly mind has long ago been ruled out as extra-national. I spoke to him about his book ' Shakespeare and Ireland,' thinking of its erudition and pellucid style. He seemed embarrassed at hearing it acclaimed; or was it shyness? Perhaps it was neither, but that he sensed an impertinence on my part in posing as one qualified to pass an opinion.   I became infected by his indifference.   I felt that in some way or other an apology was needed.   I began to explain myself: Fatal!   I floundered somewhat.   It is hard to explain that you did not mean to praise a thing when you wish to be taken as appreciating it!   I looked into the hairdresser's window and saw myself as in a glass darkly.   That only made it worse.   It seemed now that I had come spying to see what he was looking at!   Had I a faint touch of epilepsy this morning?

Turning from the multitudinous bosoms of wax in the window, I gazed at Sir Plunkett with an aggrieved eye, and hurried round the corner.

Instead of the spear of de Burgoes I nearly ran into the sabres of Endymion, who was advancing up the street.

" What are you doing this morning, Endymion? "   A relief to meet a better fool than myself.

" Verifying, verifying."

I noticed that his speech was not so thick as before.   He was more coherent.   He had replaced his cuffs by leggings.

" Verifying what? "

" I would have you know, if you would know," he said, " that the Professor of Gaelic Astronomy in the National University announced in a lecture that the sun rose in the East."

" Well, so it does.   It is universally accepted."

" Wait a while.   I had to verify it."

" Well? "

" It did rise in the East.   And that shows . . . and that shows that a thing may be an universally accepted fact, and yet be true."

" Of course it's true."

" Wait, wait!   Can't you hold on?   Is not New York our West? "

" Yes."

" And the sun rises for the people living in San Francisco in our West? "

" But it is east of San Francisco."

" Our West is their East? "

He threw an arm out, fixing me with his little merry eye. Rumbling with laughter, he asked: " But where does it rise at the North Pole?   The eternal verities, the eternal verities! "

He grumbled and laughed in his throat, and went his way.

There surely cannot be a Professor of Gaelic Astronomy? Astronomy is an universal science. More of Endymion's imagination, I hope. Otherwise this " nationality " rampage will narrow the very heavens if it goes on.

On the left-hand side of Kildare Street I met Father Paddy, possessor of one of the greatest brains and the best memory of any Irishman. His broad face was smiling broadly. " You'll be glad to hear that Mallow Viaduct is blown up. Cork is cut off and a Republic has been declared." To my amazement he seemed in earnest.

" We shall soon be all cork when we are cut off from the Commonwealth."

" The sooner the better! "

" A cork won't be much use without a bottle ? "

" The British Empire will go flat."

I did not wish to be short with a priest even when his politics were preposterous and dangerously charged with disaster to his Church. I said : " The British Empire has a knack of effervescing when necessary. The only thing that will kill it is suicide. And it had attempted that, without success. *Deo gratias !* "

" They have bled this country white for the last hundred years. They have taken millions out of it. They have blighted every colony they touched."

" You talk like a babu barrister," I said. " An Indian who, seeing British Civil Servants lolling through his country in their Rolls-Royces, forgets that they have brought it to the law and organisation which enable it to produce wealth. Let the natives have a try and it would quickly return to the Juggernaut and the Suttee, not to mention child-marriage and inter-tribal atrocities. But who is bleeding it white now ? England ? Ireland had a trade balance of fifty-two million pounds a year when enslaved. What has it now under its Republicans ? "

" Freedom, anyway," he said.

" ' He who is in a state of Rebellion cannot receive Grace,' " I quoted. " There's no use talking to you." Then suggested cheerfully, " Ireland's a free country, shoot whomever you please. We have too much liberty."

He withdrew his mind from his face.

" The same could have been said in Athens long ago, when Persia threatened Greece. There were faint hearts and merchants who were ready to drop the struggle for freedom."

" Of course it could be and, as a fact, was said with a
variation. But with our case there is a parallel only in the
respective sizes of the countries. Otherwise the positions
are reversed."

" How!   Reversed ? "

" There is more potential tyranny of opinion and tyranny
in the name of liberty in this would-be bully of a country,
and less culture, than in all ancient Persia. Athens fought
for freedom. Ireland has to be anchored to it in the Commonwealth, or we couldn't call our soul our own. Suppose
Ireland conquered England ! . . ."

" That would be just the same as if Athens conquered
Persia ? Of course ! Can you imagine an Ireland fed on
hatred of Imperialism conquering anything ? Think of the
activities of the English fleet once it had become Hiberni-
cised : ' The Rathmines broke off action ; on the Brian
O'Lynn the firing died away.' "

He roared with laughter at ' Brian O'Lynn.' The name
recalled something. Soon he quoted :

> " Brian O'Lynn had a house, to be shure,
>   With the stars for a roof and the bog for a flure ;
>   A way to go out and a way to go in :
> ' Shure, it's mighty convenient,' said Brian O'Lynn."

" Yes," I said, " we of the O'Lynn family have the stars
above us and the untrammelled air, but we have neither the
desire of nor the capacity for building—empires least of all."

But there is no use talking to a clergyman gone political.
It means that he has gone polemical too.

" I saw you talking to the fellow who fell into a vat. I
saw you," he said, with a show-me-your-company innuendo.

" Endymion ? Yes. He is our *vates*."

He " laughed " uproariously, with a laughter that was as
annoyingly out of proportion as the laughter by which some
people deluge a *lapsus linguæ*. But it was a joke or a pun
which was forming in his own mind at which he was laughing.

" Don't let him fall into the vat again," he said.

But he must be getting back. Driven in a Ford, he
would pass through the Sphinx-surmounted gates of Maynooth's old manor house and the porter would salute—the
same porter who, when asked what the Sphinxes were, not to
appear ignorant though they had no connection with Maynooth,
told him, " Them is for strength." And what a symbol of
political Ireland is provided by a Sphinx ! In front, a

beautiful face and bosom to allure, and wild beast's claws behind, to tear and to disembowel those who are mad enough to throw themselves on her breast.

"I have been wondering what's come over you," he added. "You must have a bad conscience. You are walking about as disgruntled as if you were Timon of Athens."

"'By him who drank the hemlock 'tis not true,' but Timon had an Athens behind him."

"There you go again! What's come over you? You must be suffering from Accidia. You are gloomy in God's day. You used to be merry, hopeful, sprightly."

"Sprightly?"

Again he laughed uproariously, because of the recollection the adjective brought to his mind. "*That sprightly girl who was trodden by a bird,*" he quoted from Yeats. Yeats, anyway, is quoted in his own town. He repeated the quotation, *Sprightly girl who was trodden by a bird*, with mock professorial emphasis and seriousness, to make it all the more ridiculous. A sly glance at Yeats's pontifical paganism. I caught a glimpse of the mind of the man I loved. A mind full of imagination, with all the charm of all the Muses at its call . . . . a mind to which myth and metamorphosis were as present as if he were a denizen of the translunary world.

But the Untouchables had touched him and claimed him politically for their own. He walked away still smiling, glad that he had got over a meeting and the awkwardness of conveying to me that he regarded me as a foe.

I saw his long, slightly curved legs, walking as if they lacked an ash-plant, carry him away for ever.

"Accidia," I said to myself. "Accidia: I suffer from it? Well, dammit, that is very strange! It was what I thought that a great part of the country had. And now I am said to have it myself, by one who is, after all, more or less of an authority on the Deadly Sins."

I wonder, can it be that we attribute to others our own diseases? It would account for so many paradoxes if it were true. Gangs in power moulding their countries in their own images, infecting the masses with the sourness of their souls. And I imagining that everyone was queer but myself.

How would it be, were a doctor to dispense diseases instead of healing them? Specialists . . . but the train of thought faded, and I turned towards the Green.

It was disheartening to think that such an intellect could be so purblind when " patriotism " put its finger in his eye. He was able to hide from himself the fact that a minority was devastating the country and murdering fellow-countrymen. He no doubt compromised with his conscience by condemning the majority as having been " bought " by England and as traitors. But the logical conclusion, that if this were always the case then it was a natural national condition, never was allowed a moment's hearing.

A lorry, a great heavy lorry with its driver ensconced on high, pulled up beside me on its wrong side. A short, wiry figure, growing stout in the early fifties, descended.

" How are you, Gussie ? " I held out my hand. He took it, and stretching it downwards, pressed it hard. I looked at the genial, good-natured snout for the smile that always surrounded it. It was gone. Turning sideways, still holding my hand, he said solemnly :

" They're after you."

" As my red-setter is when I walk out."

" Watch out, now. And, coddin' apart, don't say I didn't warn ye."

But I should have been more grateful. He had taken a grave risk in giving me warning. He climbed up to his seat and, as he sat, he produced an imaginary revolver from a hip-pocket, fired from his knee and jerked it away. With a slam of the gears he moved off. A good friend ! I have known him for twenty-five years. We raced together, reckless on the track. That was his tip to me to carry a revolver. But I had carried one until my back was sore and I could not sit anywhere in comfort. I carried one until I realised that it must appear that I was suffering from *spina bifida* if anyone noticed the bulge in my back-pocket. I carried one until I realised that the crew I had to deal with would take care to arrange the odds. Their idea of duelling had lost all sense of proportion. Besides, to be a good gunman you have to take your gun to bed, and who can suffer Republicans to appoint his bedfellows ? I carried one until the detective who used to take me under his wing whenever I crossed to Holyhead advised me to get a permit for it in England, or to hand it in to Scotland Yard. This I did, because I was curious to see the inside of Scotland Yard innocently. My " gun " is in a desk high up in a storey, with a view of the river, of the County Council Buildings and of St. Thomas's

Hospital, where the Inspector's son was a house surgeon when I handed it in. It was better than having it taken from me in the Irish Mail. I carried a gun until I had to put it away for safety's sake. I was glad to be rid of it: " He who lives by the sword . . ." And one cannot go through life always thinking of death. It is a great bore. It requires too much concentration and tends to make one self-conscious. Besides, Death is like a woman, in that it largely depends for existence on the interest taken in it. We have to a great extent invented Death.

CHAPTER XI

" SAVE MY BOS ANOA."

It was a wire from Talbot Clifton.

Good heavens ! does he expect me to return to that destroyed area for the sake of a stuffed head ? The *bos anoa* is an animal said to be a cross between an ox and a stag. It is found only in Celebes. It is so rare that when the special expedition which Talbot led had reached Celebes, the only specimen he could get was brought in wounded by his snapshot by the natives. All the precious things he had left in Kylemore faded in his mind before the importance he attached to this head. If I have to go back . . . but Mrs. Clifton had left it in my Dublin house. I could look after it now until a messenger arrived, or safer still, put it in the bank. The idea of lodging a cross-bred calf's head in the house of those who worship the golden calf had the attraction of novelty. I could say that it was more important than ivory and gold. Not being sportsmen, they would not believe me. Then when they found out, they would realise what they had missed : possibly Talbot Clifton's account. There was a time that *pecunia* meant heads of oxen . . . no use expecting them to go back to that standard now, even though in Ireland of old seven oxen would buy a handmaid. I will myself preserve the *bos anoa* with its budding horns, its bee nose and its little black calf's head.

I was expecting to hear his cheery knock at any moment now. Five or six taps, and we knew that it was George Russell the mystic, the poet and the economist (economics being more fanciful still than poetry) who is called Æ. Had not Sir Horace, his chief, wired to a friend—I am quoting Hone—" We men of affairs keep a poet in our office " ? His pen-name came about when he was devoted to Theosophy, and Æ was the short for Aeon. Anyone who heard his knock in my house could have told that it was Friday evening. He never failed us. I felt that he would not fail us now, though it was not safe to be out after nine when the firing began at the fall of night.

In he came, the Angelic Anarchist, his great Johnsonian body clothed in a brown tweed, his flowing tie half seen beneath the rich brown beard, his kind eyes shining more than the lenses of his glasses shone. He crossed the room amazingly light-footed and took up his accustomed place to the left of the hearth in the corner of a short sofa. As he sank in with a sigh of contentment, he said, " Ah, well ! "

Some small talk was necessary as an overture before he could get going and hold the room in an harmony of sound.

" You were very good to come, Æ. There is a lot of firing in the streets and it gets worse as night falls. My street is particularly unhealthy between nine and eleven." He waived the implications aside. Luckily Monty appeared. An audience was gathering.

" Oliver, I thought you were ordered into the Government Buildings ? "

" So I was, Æ, when it was reported that the corner boys who kidnapped me and let me escape had condemned one another to death if I were not recaptured within a fortnight. But I could not stand life in the Government Buildings. The members of the Government have very little conversation. They are charged with so much statesmanship that silence is the only form of expression, between elections, by which their significance may be conveyed. That is why they play cards."

" Do they put their cards on the table ? " Monty asked.

" If they did, it might put an end to the most persistent heritage of the illiterate Middle Ages, cards. I like the King and Queen and the Knave, but the pips ! "

" The pips represent the proletariat."

" I would rather be taken ' for a ride ' again than live with people who play cards."

" He has guards instead of cards now ! " Monty, of course.

" I have," I acknowledged. " And they are causing me the greatest anxiety. They fall asleep during the night : one night they were all disarmed by their own sergeant— and I have to lie awake to guard them from my enemies. In the day-time they are in danger of shooting my household or themselves. Last week one of them shot the hand of a companion and two legs : his own leg, and the leg of a Chippendale chair. Words could not express my alarm and concern : it was the only leg by Chippendale, the one from which Hicks had reconstructed the whole chair by help of Sir Thornley Stoker's Chinese ' museum piece ' as one reconstructs some wonderful thing from a limb in the Gobi Desert. The house is not safe with all these guards."

" They give employment," Monty observed, " to the other side, whose activities in turn provide them with the job of guarding you."

" I cannot see why I should have a guard. It is like shutting the stable door when the steed is stolen. I had no guards when I was kidnapped. Now that no one wants me, I have seven guards who draw the Republicans' fire and the Free State Government's pay. My personality is diluted. Seven spirits have entered in. My guards are more important than I."

Æ was growing restless. The problem Monty raised was more or less an heterodox form of political economy.

" I hardly like to ask Yeats out this night, though he lives very near," I remarked.

" Better not," said Æ. They blended badly, Yeats and Æ.

" Would it not be better if Mr. Russell were to pull that settee away from the bay window ? " Monty asked.

" Perhaps it would. There is a machine gun which sweeps the street and protects me at intervals of fifteen minutes."

" That's the worst of bay windows. If you sit in one, you may find yourself in ' the Waveless Bay.' "

A small piece of moulding became detached and fluttered to the carpet. We pretended not to notice it. Æ was served with a cup of tea and the piece of cake which he never exceeded. An odd shot only now. The peace that just preceded nine o'clock fell on the street.

" They are breaking up the old moulds," Æ began. " You see, when empires have been cast into the melting-pot and crowned heads deposed, one naturally expects that the small nations will strive to change their polity and to alter their regime." He sighed contentedly. His words were finding their ranks now.

De Valera, as Jeffries said, was marching on Dublin at the head of 20,000 words. But Æ was there to defend it with an inexhaustible arsenal. His words were filing past.

" Senator Phelan of San Francisco, Sir ! "

Two young American ladies, who had letters of introduction, and copies of the *Renaissance* by Walter Pater presented by Captain McLoren, came in at the same time. The great beard awed them a little : Tolstoi ? They were placed near Æ. Senator Phelan, who had spent most of the afternoon in Plunkett House, already knew Æ. He

must have benefited by his experience, because, " Don't let me
interrupt you, Mr. Russell," came quite naturally the moment
Æ sat down. With a little purr in his beard, Æ went on :

" I was just explaining to our friends here that it is quite
natural that there should be some disturbance at first at the
birth of a new state or polity. ' One must have chaos within
them to give birth to a dancing star,' and the chaos is but the
prelude to a newer loyalty, to a newer system that will come
sooner or later to be devised."

Good Lord! Is he excusing the Republicans ?

" The signature of the Irish mind is not apparent anywhere in this new machinery for self-government. No one
has taken the trouble to ask if the adaptation of the British
Parliamentary system will suit our people, or if it is adaptable
at all. The obvious failure of representative government
taught our politicians nothing, though its shortcomings must
have been obvious to them."

A spatter of bullets splashed the street.

" We obtain our political freedom under the old rules. I
do not criticise those who devised the new machinery of
self-government ; but those who did not devise it and damped
down and discouraged the exercise of political imagination in
Ireland . . ."

" Political imagination. Sure ! " said Senator Phelan.

The acrid smell of cordite from the rifles of my guards
who were " replying " from upper windows after allowing a
decent interval to the fire of their trade-unionists on ' the
other side,' drifted down into the room.

" Imagination . . ." Æ continued.

" This is a real thrill," said one of the girls.

" Say," said the Senator, " someone will be shot."

" The only thing that will be shot is a bullet," Monty
said. " Yes, Mr. Russell ? "

I looked unobserved at the letters of introduction.—Bryn
Mawr ! At once the ladies came to life and were clothed
with personality in my mind. They were pupils of an old
friend of mine. And no one in Europe who has not been
to America is safe in judging an American girl or an American
scholar by limiting their excellence to the cover.

" Æ will be impatient in a minute if people prefer to
listen to his military hecklers than to him. You were just
talking of the discouragement of political imagination. Go
on, Æ," I requested.

" Visitors to our country should know that revolution is De Valera's idea of evolution."

" His ideas of constitutional representation must be falling short," the Senator said.

" I hope his leaden ideas will keep falling short "— Monty.

I thought I heard a knock, but it was hard to tell at the moment with the noise.   Windows of the opposite houses could be heard going up, hopeless hopefulness as to casualties urging their languid occupants to look out.

" There was an artist once," Æ continued, with his gaze on the ladies, " whose fantasy it was first to paint his ideal of womanly beauty, and, when this was done, to approximate it, touch by touch."

" Cell by cell," I whispered mischievously into a coral ear, recalling to her Walter Pater.   She brushed down her skirt.

" General Collins ! "

He marched into the room in front of his name.   Everyone stood up.   The delight on Æ's face glowed.   He had been longing to meet him for years.   He extended his delicate hand, and instead of withdrawing, tried to lead him to the sofa.   But Collins had to be introduced and refreshed.

He was a burly man, whose burliness hid his height.   He was a smooth, burly man.   You could see it in the unlined face and the beautiful, womanly hands.   His skin was like undiscoloured ivory.   His body had the unroughened strength that a woman's limbs might have or the body of those wrestlers who are bred to incredible feats in Japan.   I have seen such athletic limbs in a Spanish swimmer whose arms, when extended, were hardly dimpled at the elbows.

Low forehead, but what was seen over the clear-cut brow was straight.   The hair grew down and his head tilted forward as if his chin sought repose on his chest.   Napoleonic ! But a bigger and a more comely specimen of manhood than Napoleon.   In his newly acquired position, he kept his distance by an aggressive but good-natured abruptness.   The finest and most life-like portrait is that of his head in white bronze by Doyle Jones.   It gives the countenance in all its swiftness of the quickest intellect and nerve that Ireland bred, of the kinsman by antithesis of the author of the " Ode to Evening."

I took him to a side table and poured out a full measure as if for myself.   " My nerves are on edge," I said jokingly.

" If they want all that to soothe them they must be in the hell of a state. If it's for me put half of it back." Then, as the babble hid our talk, " You're a bloody fine host," he whispered. " You had me nearly killed on your doorstep. I knocked three times and I could not get in."

I was astonished. Everyone else had got in at once from the darkened and dangerous street. Why was Collins's admission delayed ? I could trust the servants.

" I can't imagine why they did not open the door. If I had heard you I would have opened it myself. What happened ? "

" I was stalked by three."

" Gunmen ? "

" I think that they were only spotters trying to find out where I sleep. I went for them. Two ran off. The fellow I caught was not armed."

" You will never be delayed on my doorstep again," I said. " Here's the latchkey."

He took it with, " Right! . . . How's the President ? " he asked. " Look after him," and he turned his back to the room.

A few weeks later Emmet Dalton sent that key back from the blood-stained tunic of a murdered man.

Just like Collins to walk about unaccompanied by a guard after nightfall. Just like Collins unhesitating to attack regardless of odds. Just like Collins to send his enemies flying before the terrible exhibition of his courage. One of the constituents of courage is contempt. Collins's contempt for the men who turned on him after his battle against the glorious Greenwood's criminal militia was terrific.

However silent Senator Phelan had been trained to remain in the presence of Æ, silence, now that he was in the presence of the man who had taken on and successfully defied that part of the British Army which was held to be too scoundrelly to associate with soldiers and so was sent over here by a Canadian to prepare us for Dominion status, could no longer be sustained.

Senator Phelan took the fireplace.

" Say, General, to-morrow night I am giving a little party to some very particular friends who have done what in them lay in their different vocations to promote the cause of Irish Freedom. As its chief promoter—and I feel honoured by the opportunity now presented to me by our good friend here to hail you as its achiever—I hope you will join us at the Shelbourne. Sir Horace Plunkett, Æ there, our host, and half a score of other devoted . . ."

Collins smiled, shook his head and laughed good-naturedly. His laugh conveyed his " I'm afraid I don't dine out much these nights," inoffensively as a refusal. A shot outside sounded convincingly.

I saw in my mind's eye what awaited us on the night of the morrow. The festoons of smilax on the rich dining-table ; the festoons of oratory before and behind each guest as he was introduced to speak to those who already knew him perhaps far better than his senatorial host ; and the festoons with which he would be draped when he concluded. After-dinner speaking is the national pastime of the United States. Only for alcohol it would go on for ever. The people of the well-chosen words are even more numerous in New York than the Chosen People. And there would be no escape. I had to see President Griffith before midnight at latest in the nursing home where he was lying ; for the rest, they would have to listen until " Time " was recorded ; and with Senator Phelan living in the hotel, the ordinary licensing hours might be extended.

I did not want to go. Apparently the Senator's call on me had been made with the intention of inviting me personally. He had done so much for Ireland in California and he was a man of such outstanding good-will that I would not have, in ordinary circumstances, thought of refusing him. But as Collins had a bedroom and a bathroom set apart for him in my house, so that he could come and go and put those who believed that he returned nightly to the heavily guarded Government Buildings off their ambush I felt that I should stay at home. The Government Buildings were not four hundred yards down from me on the same side of the street. They made the third block on my side and the last. They were flanked by Leinster House, and the great space of Merrion Square faced them.

Members of the Government who could not endure being as it were confined to barracks during the civil war, took the risk of leaving the Buildings and visiting me after dark, for I also refused to be confined. Thus they could communicate with the outer world and with those who could not be expected to face the grille of steel and sentries' scrutiny.

Collins had heard so much of Æ's wisdom that he was

filled with curiosity and glad to meet him undisturbed and at his ease.

"The English mistrust genius in high places," Æ announced. "They choose forceful average men as leaders. Intensely individual themselves, they fear the aristocratic character in politics. They desire that general principles should be asserted to encircle and keep safe their own national eccentricity. They have gradually infected us with something of their ways, and as they were not truly our ways, we have never made a success of them."

"What do you propose doing, Mr. Russell?"

"Well, General, we must fall back. . . ."

Fall back? I silenced myself.

"We must fall back on what is natural with us, on what is innate in character, what was visible amongst us in the earliest times, and what, I still believe, persists amongst us— a respect for the aristocratic intellect, for freedom of thought, ideals, poetry and imagination as the qualities to be looked for in leaders; a bias for democracy in our economic life."

How well the Plunkett House provides these contradictions! I mused. The General's glass was held somewhat sideways now. He could gesticulate without spilling it. A reflection on his host. I hastened to replenish it.

"We were more truly Irish in the Heroic Ages. We would not then have taken, as we do to-day, the huckster and the publican and make them our representative men, and allow them to corrupt the national soul, as if Irish Nationality was impossible unless it floated on a sea of liquor. The image of Kathleen Na Houlihan anciently was beauty in the hearts of poets and dreamers. We often thought her unwise, but never did we think her ignoble; never was she without the flame of idealism, until this ignoble crew declared alcohol to be the only possible basis of Irish nationality . . ."

Senator Phelan confided to me in an audible aside his reasons for being a life-long abstainer. In vain I quoted Yeats:

> "'And one who found in the redness of wine
> The incorruptible rose.'"

To encourage the others I pressed a syphon. Our Oracle went on: "We are losing the Ideal of Being for the satisfaction, or rather the blunting of the senses. We are putting out the eye of light.

" I have never had the high vision of those who have gone into the deeps of being and returned rapture-blinded by the glory and cried out in a divine intoxication to the Light of lights :

'Spread thy rays and gather them. The Light which is thy fairest form. . . . I am what he is.'

I do not think that many have brooded long enough on that distinction of soul and spirit which St. Paul made when writing to his friends at Corinth. He speaks of many unexplained things : of a third heaven, of a soul and spirit, of psychic bodies and spiritual bodies, of a mysterious power which seems to be the fountain of all powers, which enables one to discern spirits, and gives to another eloquence—poetry in fact—and to another magical and healing power. Some of these powers I tried to wake, but I will not speak here of them, for I am trying to supplicate the flame which gives wisdom rather than that which gives power.

" While I could comprehend a little about the nature of the *psyche*, I could not apprehend at all the spirit which transcends the soul ; for, as the seers said of it, it is eternal, invisible and universal. Yet because it is universal we are haunted by it in every motion of the mind. It is at the end of every way. It is present in the sunlight."

Suddenly Collins sought his pocket, revealing as he did so, a large revolver strapped to his thigh. He produced a stubby pencil and a little book.

" As we pursue it," the much-encouraged golden voice went on, " it ever eludes us, but it becomes more and more present until all that we see or are swims in a divine ether :

' It will meet thee everywhere, and be seen of thee plain and easy when thou dost not expect or look for it. It will meet thee waking, sleeping, sailing, travelling, by night, by day, when thou speakest or keepest silence. For there . . .' "

Sharply Collins said : " Your point, Mr. Russell ? "

Consternation seized me. I had overlooked the fact that Collins could not have been expected to share with me the little mysticism of which I am capable, by which I hear a voice from out the Golden Age speak, whenever Æ indulges in a monologue which is all music and half poetry. There is no other Golden Age but that which we bring about ourselves. Æ's voice and ideas shed the light of an endless day about me. No one questions a choral organ in the dim religious light when it unrolls the banners of Heaven. ' Your point,' indeed! The quotation did sound alarming, I admit; but the proper mood for Æ is one in which his waves of sound are allowed to undulate over your mind. Any or all of the three waves of Eire. ' The wave of Toth, the wave of Rury and the long slow-heaving wave of Cleena.'

Had Collins said, " Your Tangent," or even " Your Co-sine," he would have been slightly nearer to the third heaven. As things were now, we were all ' earthed.' The Senator was " one up on " the General in that he paid the tribute of silence while the spell was being woven. Eager for facts though they all are, the American girls were entranced beyond the exactitudes of everyday existence.

But why had I allowed my attention to be distracted while Æ was getting off the subject? If there were only a fusillade now or even a little bombing to relieve the tension, it would be welcome. ' Your point,' indeed! But no. The only time when such sounds would be welcome they were not to be heard.

Boldly I myself plunged into the gulf.

" Will you kindly tell these ladies, Æ, the promise of God to the Thrice Great Hermes, if he followed the straight way? "

Now, I always admired that title, Trismegistus, Thrice Great. I even forbore to ask myself what constituted his first greatness, or even his second, just as I never would think of asking what were the Faculties of both of which Paracelsus was doctor: " Doctor of Both Faculties." The name, not the meaning!

" Perhaps, the General? " Æ asked tentatively.

" Blaze away! Don't mind me! "

I pulled Senator Phelan into the breach. With a whisper to Collins that Phelan was a big noise in San Francisco and should not be ignored, I made a ' contact.' Collins was not trained for a room. He would not move. The Senator had to lean over him. I heard him saying, " Imagine my position." While attention was taken up in this way the ladies pleaded to hear the promise of the God. Thus the golden chord that Collins broke was repaired.

An intermediate thought occurred to me, it would: are not all we who look back to the Golden Age traitors to the present?

Æ glowed on, and repeated the interrupted oracle:
" It was not a promise of beauty in a heaven world but
an illumination in this world:

> ' It will meet thee everywhere and be seen of thee plain and easy
> when thou dost not expect or look for it.   It will meet thee waking,
> sleeping, sailing, travelling, by night, by day, when thou speakest or
> keepest silence.   For there is nothing which is not the image of
> God.' "

The faultless memory that was an illumination in this world
ceased to recite.

There was a difficulty ahead of me.   Collins could not
leave.   It might meet him anywhere!   He would have to
outstay the rest.   But would the Senator go before him?
I could not let it be known that he was sleeping in the house.
To Æ—" Friend, take Phelan with you when you are
leaving.   Important.   I can't explain now."   He nodded.
Well he guessed.   For all his unearthliness, he was as practical as Collins himself.   But Collins, who had driven up
from the Curragh, was tired.   He solved the difficulty, and
with a sudden " Good-night now! " he bade us good-bye
and left the room.   As to where he slept no one was any
the wiser.

The ladies woke to life.   They learnt more about the
General whose tenacity, capacity and courage had saved
the movement for independence when it was about to go the
way that every other effort went.   I did not allude to the
danger his fellow-countrymen had been incited to provide.
His heartbroken disappointment could only be exceeded by
President Griffith's broken heart.

They were over here to study Oliver Goldsmith, who was
to be the subject of a thesis for their Ph.D.   They were
going down to Athlone to visit the Deserted Village.

" Dublin is a far better example," I urged.   " It has been
deserted by nearly everything that makes a town worth living
in.   You know that line of Oliver—

> ' Ill fares the land to hastening ills a prey
> Where louts accumulate and lords decay.' "

They had never heard of it.   Suddenly I remembered how
taboo irony in any form is in the United States.   They
looked incredulous and puzzled.   Incredible must have
seemed my gratuitous rudeness.   It was as if I went out of
my way to misdirect strangers on a journey through my

country. I hastened to laugh it off. One asked Æ if he knew Mr. Yeats. Yes, Æ knew Willie 'Yeets'—so he always pronounced the name. The girls said Mr. Yeats had lectured twice at Bryn Mawr. The first time it was not so good. But the second time, after he had gotten tortoise-shell glasses, it was a great success. What the subject of the lecture was was not quite clear, but he looked every inch of a poet, and he had a most beautiful voice, like Mr. Æ's voice, more so in some ways, but it was not so rich in sounds. They had no poets like him in the United States, no poets at all.

"What about Witter Bynner, the author of ' Rain '? " I asked. "And what about Robertson Jeffers, that lone eagle on his granite tower by the green Pacific, who looks towards the illimitable West ? Of our own Ossian he wrote:

> ' This is the proper fame to have, not cornered in a poem :
> Fabulous, a name in the North.'

How I would like to have written that ! And what about your Robert Frost, with his Wordsworthian feeling for American landscape ? And what about Vachel Lindsay, who galvanised the English language, every word of it, when it was becoming about as empty as urns in a graveyard ! "

It fills me with a moon-cold fury when I hear American poetry decried. No, no. I mistook their meaning. They did not mean that they had no poets in the United States, but none who looked so good as Mr. Yeats.

Æ, who, once he had risen, used to hurry down to the hall to put on a thin overcoat in winter or to take up his broad hat in summer, turned round to the ladies and said:

" 17 Rathgar Avenue. Sunday night."

They were invited to his Sunday gathering of friends. They had made an impression. Æ had been too often in the United States not to know the mental capacity of American girls that conversation quite often insufficiently reveals. Read their letters and you will find an infinite variety of ways of seeing the facets Life can present on its surface. Superficial, of course. But is there any Life which, if it is to be tolerable, must not be superficial ? Try to probe or dive beneath its glittering surface, and it is as if the sliding beetle ruffled the well and broke the smoothness of the bright, still lymph.

Language is living and growing in the United States.

There is a vivid eye and a courage in the use of adjective or metaphor that we do not hold in our " Outworn hearts in a time outworn." I have a line or two that one of these girls wrote after she had visited Connemara, that illustrates very well what I am endeavouring to say.

> There is a garden by a lake
> That greener grows for Nature's sake,
> Than any garden ever planned
> By squinted eye or craftsman's hand.

Our wild natural gardens, compared with the formal ones of England or Versailles, where the engineer looked along a line or squinted into his theolodite. Women in the United States are not only amorous but artistic :—

> There is no lust like poetry !

I went with the ladies as far as the hall. Senator Phelan would see them to the Shelbourne. I would walk with them to the turn from which it could be seen.

" But is there not danger ? "

" Not at this hour."

" Wasn't he just marvellous, your Mr. Æ ? "

" Of course he was."

" I thought him wonderful. I never heard his equal."

" No one can hear his equal. He has no equal."

" If he would only lecture in the States, the halls would be booked out."

" But on what would you have him lecture ? "

She was somewhat hesitant for a moment, then she said :

" On just what he's been talking about upstairs."

" Now, just what has he been talking about upstairs ? "

She was taken aback. She looked at her companion puzzled, then reproachfully at me. It seemed so disloyal to suggest that Æ's talk had no meaning or that no one could tell what he was talking about. It would take some time to explain and to absolve myself from a suspicion of insincerity to my friend. I felt that they would think even worse of me were I to recount, by way of explanation, excellent example though it was, how O'Leary Curtis lost his Faith one night through listening to Æ, only to find it again next morning when he tried to explain to Father Paddy exactly what he had heard.

" Aureoles for the outcasts ; and all kinds of problems solved."

" Your problem at the moment," said Father Paddy, " is ' Who is going to stand ? ' "

Father Paddy was thinking of Seumas's joke:

> "I met O'Leary Curtis, and he took me by the hand,
> Saying, 'How is poor Old Ireland? And who is going to stand?'"

No. It would never do to explain away Æ that way. Instead:

"Girls," I said, "you are as bad as General Collins, who you remember made us all to feel so uncomfortable when he took out his little book and pencil with, 'Your point, Mr. Russell?' And just at the moment when the wave of Toth was about to break into the room."

"The wave of what?"

"Oh, forgive me! It is only a way I have of recording the different stages of Æ's influence upon my mind."

"But there must have been some point?" And they looked at me more puzzled and reproachful than before.

"To explain my meaning, I want you to think of this house of mine as a house for artists, and not for lecturers, readers, preachers, teachers or people with points. It has been said of Æ that he is one of those rare spirits who bring to us a realisation of our own divinity and intensify it. He enlarges the joy that is hidden in the heroic heart. He is a magnifier of the moods of the soul; and he communicates them more naturally by music and murmuring sound than by messages or points. Don't forget what Robert Louis Stevenson said about geniuses like Æ. 'Such are the best teachers. A spirit communicated is a perpetual possession. These best teachers climb beyond teaching to the plane of art. It is themselves, and, what is more, the best in themselves, that they communicate.' That is the secret of Æ. He is an artist. He teaches nothing. He communicates himself, and the best in himself, which consists of poetry, loving kindness and a passion for beauty more than for anything else. So you see he is far more like Plato than like the Tolstoi whom I saw that his appearance suggested to you at first sight."

They blushed, looked at one another betrayed by my penetration.

"It sure did," was all the bemused girl could say.

"You have forgotten your *Renaissance*. What will the Captain say? A moment, while I run up to bring the books to you."

When I returned, Senator Phelan would not hear of me leaving, as he knew the way to the hotel.

CHAPTER XII

THERE WAS SMILAX IN THE SHELBOURNE AS IT HAD BEEN GIVEN me to behold in vision. The dinner-table was beautifully decorated, and Senator Phelan received his guests in a well-appointed room; but the sight of an ebony piano in one corner caused me grave misgivings. The speeches would be familiar. I could write a formula for them all. Given so much declared achievement and self-satisfaction on the one side, hospitality and generous self-assertion on the other, the resultant would be National Aspirations and tributes to our host. But the piano brought in another note.

Some men have music forced upon them at public dinners, others pretend to like it. I am in the first category. The piano I like is not a black ebony one by Bechstein with a kind of jib-boom to hold up its lid, but one of those little ones that harmonise symmetrically with the wooden " art " coal scuttle on the other side of the fireplace which you can plug in as a counterblast to the song of the vacuum-cleaner, while you leave the room on pointed feet, your face Saharaed in a smile.

The dinner, which made a table-cloth a platform for orations, had lasted some hours. It was nearing midnight, and still the Senator's unhastenable drawl groaned on. Æ had just sat down. He had spoken for forty minutes, using only two gesticulations, which consisted of short downright choppings of both hands at once.

" Having introduced Mr. George Russell " (to me, and even to closer friends), " it is now my privilege, before reintroducing Sir Horace Plunkett, whom I may truly and justly describe as his chief, to make a few appreciatory remarks about the oration to which you have just listened. He has, as you are well aware, opened to us a heaven of his own imagination. Sir Horace has laid the foundation stone of many Irish ' Movements.' Æ edits the *Homestead* and lends his inspiration to the lowliest cotter, cottager—that is to say, farmer.

" Sir Horace will now reply. Sir Horace has very obligingly, earlier this evening inaugurated this little dinner, to which he came at very great personal inconvenience and risk to his health. No more auspicious auspices could hearten any host. Sir Horace has brought Battle Creek Sanatorium to your notice.   Sir Horace himself has been an inmate . . . that is to say, a visitor, guest, or, rather, patient at the Sanatorium at Battle Creek; he hopes, if his life be spared, to set up a Battle Creek in your green and pleasant land where cases which are not as yet registered as pathological may be diagnosed and treated accordingly.   Only by institutions such as this will lives as useful as Sir Horace's be prolonged and the age of retirement from active public service be indefinitely delayed.

" I call on Sir Horace Plunkett . . .

" Sir Horace."

Sir Horace rose and inclined his head.

It was 11.45.   But coyly Sir Horace began:

" I cannot detain you, Gentlemen, as the night grows late, but there are a few remarks of Senator Phelan's which I feel bound to deprecate, flattering though they be.   Perhaps a short revision of what my work has meant would not be out of place.   My work, as you may know, Gentlemen, lies in the spheres of voluntary effort, especially organised voluntary effort, and not in that of legislation or public administration. It is true that when much younger I represented an Irish Constituency for eight years in the British Parliament.   I presided over the Irish Convention—its ivory gavel is one of my treasured possessions—I worked for the Dominion Settlement, without the Partition. . . . And now I come to the actual work of the I.A.O.S., and must explain why its services are needed, although, as I have told you, it calls upon us all to do all these things for ourselves.   When bodies of farmers in any parish have made up their minds that they have got to join together for any of the purposes I have described, the first question they naturally ask is—How are we to set about it?

" Of course, it is essential that they should learn to trust each other, and take my word for it, before they have gone very far in the practice of co-operation, they will find that mutual confidence pays. . . ."

Sir Horace was getting thoroughly warmed to his task of revising his life-work when, most unexpectedly, as I was slipping, unnoticed as I thought, from the room, our host the Senator joined me at the door.

" You are going to see President Griffith?" he said.

" I have to see him before twelve o'clock; it is close on that hour now."

" Bring me with you," he requested, " as I am leaving

early in the morning . . ." and then hesitated, realising that he could not leave the room while Sir Horace was speaking.

"Well, it is your only chance of seeing him," I said, "because if you are leaving early in the morning I could not bring you in."

He looked doubtfully at Sir Horace.

"Sir Horace is good for half-an-hour or more," I assured him, "and I will tell you all that Sir Horace will be saying while we walk along the Green."

As we turned the corner into Leeson Street I saw a little barefooted urchin on the steps of No. 97 deliberately fire a pistol in the air. I charged upon him, but he ran down the lane, dropping the pistol as he fled. This was part of the nightly fusillade provided to keep Griffith awake and to add to the torture of his mind, which was seriously disturbed.

He must have heard our voices, because, as I pushed in his door, he sat up in bed challengingly and irascibly : " Who's that ? Who's that ? " he said, pointing to the door through which the Senator had not yet appeared.

"An important American Senator—Senator Phelan, from San Francisco."

" I'll see no Americans," said Griffith in a voice which could easily be heard by the Senator, whom it was too late to withdraw.

A very short and constrained interview took place which, however, Griffith's natural courtesy did much to relieve. The Senator must have been satisfied with his " contact," because, on our way back to hear Sir Horace's peroration he thanked me effusively and was genuinely grateful. We were in good time.

The guests departed after a rather sleepy discussion on general principles.

Senator Phelan left early in the morning. I never saw that good-hearted man again.

§

By the quay-side we waited : midnight and as yet no ship. All communications with Cork had been destroyed. Only by sea was there a way to Dublin. The corpse of Collins, the vital, the mighty, was being borne by a boat long overdue. I stood for hours at the North Wall. Drizzling rain added to our gloom. I stood by the river-side hour after hour with the officers in their uniforms blackened by rain—officers of an Irish National Army that Griffith created by a stroke of his courageous pen.

At last in the silence of the dark a moving light appeared, coming slowly up an invisible stream. The death-ship carrying the mortal remains of the most rapid and bright soul that alien envy in Ireland ever quenched. Troops formed up. A gun-carriage received the coffin. It was bound for the City Hall.

I reached home in the early hours. I had to make provision for embalming the body.

Never in our life cycle shall we see the like of Mick Collins. He dwelt among us as our equal. Now that he is dead, we find that we were the familiars of a Napoleon who knew no Waterloo.

No matter how it may be diminished, the fact is that Michael Collins beat the English in the guise they chose to adopt at a time of great stress: England's extremity was his opportunity. He kicked it hard. Opportunity brings more than opportunists to the front. Ireland's struggle was old and long sustained tenaciously through the years, opportunities or no opportunities. Hundreds of Irishmen in every age were glad to put their necks in risk of England's halter and quick-lime. Collins alone pulled his generation out.

My guest was coming home to me to be embalmed. Not England, but his fellow-countrymen murdered him.

What an unlucky shake-hands De Valera gives! He shakes hands to speed Collins and Griffith to London. They are dead within a year.

I had to be up betimes if the embalming was to be completed before noon. Hardly had I slept when a loud knocking summoned me. Desmond Fitzgerald, Minister for Defence, to keep me company. It was 4.30 a.m. As he knew little of such processes as embalming, he was anxious that no time should be lost. In my bedroom slippers, I walked him round through the empty streets to awaken the porter of the College of Surgeons. No answer. We went round to the great gate at the back of the dissecting-room. Loudly we knocked, hammering with the flat of our hands to make the greater noise. A bullet embedded itself above our hands. Hastily I kicked the door. Oh, my slippers! I had forgotten. But the invisible sniper guessed what we were about. Another plunge of lead in pine. We must get out of this.

" Leave it to me," I assured the Minister. " The job is not a lengthy one. I will come back at six o'clock. Meanwhile, I will try the Anatomy School of Trinity College."

Arthur Griffith lay on a small mattress in a room off the Ministry for Justice high up in the Government Buildings, as the place intended for a College of Science in the days of the British Administration was now called. He was besieged by a large part of the " Irish People " in whom he believed. He could not leave the building without risking his life. His guards were troops drawn from as distant places as possible. They spoke like Scotsmen. If you wished to see him as a medical attendant, you had to put your face into a large letterbox-like grille and hold it against the revolver of the sentry on duty, before the door was opened. When you were admitted into the Hall you found yourself in a small chamber, walled by bullet-proof sheets of steel. Search and interrogation preceded your admittance. The lift was not working, neither were the charwomen. Through dirty marble halls and up dirty staircases of a building never designed for dwellings, at last you reached the fourth storey. A long corridor led to the Ministry. Past both, you reached the small closet where Arthur Griffith lay. At a glance you recognised a man who was very ill. He had a solicitor administering to him. The hour was nine o'clock of a morning. My mind was made up at once. Out of this he must be taken. But before removing him permission had to be got from G.H.Q. Generals Mulcahy and O'Sullivan were the higher command. I drove without loss of time to Portobello Barracks. There was no nonsense, no red or, what is worse, green tape about these men.

" Griffith is ill and I want him to have adequate nursing and attention, which is impossible in a building designed for offices, not for homes."

" Certainly. But we must know where you intend to take him so that we can provide the necessary guard."

Griffith has to be guarded from the Irish People ! I suppressed the chain of thought for my patient's sake. No. 96 Lower Leeson Street recommended itself to me because, being as it was the private hospital of the Mercy nuns, I hoped that their sacred character would prove a bulwark against the assassination of the man who believed in his fellow-countrymen.

With military formalities complete and adequate guards, the Father of the Free State was taken secretly from the Government Building and as far as possible from De Valera and his besieging Irregulars.   I could never countenance this euphemism " Irregulars."   They were mostly town riff-raff misled, or country dupes and discontents whom De Valera aroused when he found that his methods had landed him in a minority.

" I see you have Arthur in the front drawing-room of 96," one of the hard political women said to me with a knowing smirk, an hour later.   She had seen Griffith from the top of a tram as he moved restlessly to and fro in front of his windows.

Knowing that there was not a moment to be lost before she would spread the news amongst the gang that aimed at breaking his heart, I ordered that Griffith be removed from the first to the fourth floor.

" There is the fireplace and there is your armchair, Arthur, and don't expect a single visitor until I come again this afternoon."

Arthur grunted.   " What's wrong with me ? "

" You've had a hard life for fifty years and you think ease is a disease.   But you have got to resign yourself to rest, and even to comfort, for the first time in your life, and to obey your doctor when you would resist a friend."

That he did not " stay put " in his armchair was only too evident.   I was returning with shaving tackle and pyjamas for the suddenly removed President, when I found him sitting crosswise from the fire with a chair on each side, on which he placed the daily papers as he read them.   He could read print as easily upside down as upright, for he was at one time a compositor.

I moved and turned his chair with him in it to the fire, saying, " No Irishman ever sits across his hearth.   For God's sake, Ireland's sake, and all our sakes, give yourself a little relaxation and behave as if you had escaped from 17, Crow Street for a day or two."

" What do you mean ? "

" I mean . . ."

" I'm all right ! "

" I'm not ; for I have to look after the worst and most fatal kind of patient—the health snob who will not look after himself."

" There's nothing wrong with me."

" That's one of your symptoms.   But I am carrying your complaint.   It's up to me to get myself right with you."

" Ugh ! "

" All the newspapers!   No visitors.   No telephoning. Me thrice daily.   And all the Cabinet stuff can wait.   You are going to be decorated for the first time in your life with carpet slippers."

" I must keep on the telephone."

" No.   Unless it is laid on to this room."

He took his pince-nez off and polished them resentfully. I knew that so much depended on his complete removal from affairs that I was anxious to remove myself before he could formulate objections to his isolation.   You are handicapped as a medical man when it comes to making an invalid believe in his illness.   An Englishman likes to be invalided with his back to the wall so that he may summon to his aid his *vis medicatrix*.   He fights best in a tight corner.   A man like Arthur Griffith looks upon disease or illness as a nuisance and something to be shaken off as we shake off an importunate bore.   He cannot react to that which he will not recognise.

" Try to think you are taking a holiday."

" I never had a holiday in my life, and I don't want an artificial one.   I'll go back to the Building.   Kindly send for my clothes."

" Do you really imagine or think that I am keeping you here in order to provide myself with a patient ?   I want to provide you with regular meals and rest.   Consider yourself a ' nudist ' meanwhile.   If in three weeks . . ."

A nurse brought in a large envelope containing reports from the Cabinet.   Knowing that these would make him restless and increase the irascibility which was manifest of late, I said that I would permit his secretary to see him or allow him one or two of his colleagues in.

Not for a moment did he refer to the report.   He kept his troubles to himself and his responsibilities unshared.

Next morning nurse telephoned: " You are wanted at once, Mr. Griffith is very bad."   He is fighting hard against my orders, I thought.   But I went round without hurry, thinking that he had become enraged at my restrictions on the visits of his secretaries and friends.   Sir Thomas Myles lays it down that a doctor should never hurry.   No Athenian gentleman did.   If the condition be fatal, what can you do ? If it be not, the probabilities are that a minute or two will make no difference.   But what you can do in the first instance is to avoid arriving at the critical moment.   Callous philosophy, were it meant to be taken seriously!

I was at the nursing home within four minutes.   This absolved me.   At the stairs' head President Griffith, the man who believed in the Irish People, lay on his back.   His left arm was outstretched and bloody.   A long incision of four inches gaped where his pulse was.   It was not bleeding, though the artery had been severed by Mr. Meade, who was on the spot, the only attempt that could be made to counteract cerebral hæmorrhage.   Nurses and porters were fussing about asking each other if it were not terrible.   Did they think he was really dead?

"Take up that corpse at once," I said, letting something of the bitterness of my spirit escape into that harsh word.   A moment after, I regretted it.   "Take the President's body into the bedroom."

"I perish by this people which I made"—KING ARTHUR.

Rumours take the place of prodigies in Ireland.   Instead of risen corpses in the Forum and chickens with three legs which would have satisfied ancient Rome's superstition, it was given out that poison slew Arthur Griffith.   Much as I hate the Republicans and their spurious pretensions, I will affirm that the only poison about them is turned against themselves.   They are poisoned by false doctrines.   But they do not poison their enemies, only themselves.   It would have been a simple thing for me to order an inquest and to have viscera examined for poison.   But the poison that slew Griffith was envy and jealousy and calumny, which can be deadlier than prussic acid, and, what is more mortal to a martyr, ingratitude.   He had not the armour with which I, for one, was invested, be it irony or motley.   His sincerity was a bow and his belief an arrow which, if deflected, slew his faith.   His limitations allowed neither for torrents nor for lakes.   Precipitation was as intolerable to him as delay. From the ideal of Louis Kossuth, from the idea of a Dual Monarchy for Ireland, he never advanced or retreated. Therefore it is absurd to write of his parley with English Ministers, Churchill, George, Birkenhead and that ilk, as an "ordeal."   It has been presented lately to the Irish public as if it were a campaign in which Griffith fought a rearguard action. A battle wherein Griffith was on the retreat. What is the truth? When I think of what Griffith set out to acquire and the character of the man, which was indeflectible, his achievement of the " Treaty " is a conquest which excelled all that he set himself to accomplish twenty years before. His " concessions " were conquests. His camp followers may have expected more loot, but the General's plan of campaign cannot be decided by the avarice of the hangers-on or the *vivandières*. A Dual Monarchy was Griffith's ambition. His triumph went beyond it.

CHAPTER XIII

THE LONG, LONE
house in the ultimate land of the undiscovered West. Why
should they burn my house? Because I am not an Irishman?
Because I do not flatter fools? If the only Irishman who is
to be allowed to live in Ireland must be a bog-trotter, then
I am not an Irishman. And I object to the bog-trotter
being the ideal exemplar of all Irishmen. I refuse to
conform to that type.

So Renvyle House, with its irreplaceable oaken panelling,
is burned down. They say that it took a week to burn.
Blue china fused like solder.

How few pictures make up one's memory of a place
continuously dwelt in!

I see the long, nervous hands of Augustus John tearing
at the ivy which threatened a window of that ancient house
—Lu, the Long-Handed, the Gælic Apollo, god of all the
arts!—Also, I remember the giant fuchsia bush spreading
like a banyan tree and the garden paths blinded by its growth.
The walls six feet thick which left little rooms between their
doors, doors which opened and closed of their own accord
unnoticed, until Yeats, the poet and mystic, visited us on his
honeymoon and saw sights invisible to mine unenchanted eyes.

The Blake family who held the place before me, having
taken it over from a member of the Clan O'Flaherty, Princes
of Iar Connaught, left a ghost behind them to resent newcomers. It resented Yeats of the second sight even more.
At least it could make its displeasure manifest to him by
more than the sounds and strange happenings, which by me
might have been attributed to the noise and movements of
Atlantic gales.

It is true that there were unaccountable happenings noticed
before the coming of Yeats. The door of a north room, the
only second-storey room with barred windows, could not be
opened one evening. Men were sent up by a ladder to remove
the bars. They entered the room to find that a chest, heavy
with linen, had been moved a few inches so that its edge
overlapped the door.

Alone in the house one winter's night, lying in a room at
the end of the corridor which passed the haunted room, I had
heard unprogressing footsteps in the passage. It was about

1 a.m. I was so frightened that I knew I could have no rest that night unless I brought the affair to an issue. I opened the door as the footsteps increased in loudness, strange steps that seemed to approach without ever coming immediately outside. But so suddenly did I open the door that its draught extinguished my candle and I was left in darkness; for the matches could not be found. Silence ensued.

On another night, when the main seas were disturbed, I heard the sounding of a siren far off shore: no hope for any ship on that shark-toothed coast. Nearer the sounds came, until I imagined that there was a motor car feeling its way along the back drive to the yard by the beach. And, finally, drowsily I put the noise down to the drumming of some night insect that had entered the room. To me there were no further manifestations, or they were forgotten. Not so to Yeats.

"Willie," said his wife one evening, "do not leave me to dress alone. I do not want to see that face again looking out from the glass."

Doors had been opening quietly and shutting quietly as we sat in the library before dinner. I never paid much attention to them, attributing their opening and shutting to the opening and shutting of doors in the passage side of the very thick walls.

"What face?" I asked.

But I was not answered. Yeats and his wife left the room. I was resigned to being treated as uninitiated, but my friends looked at one another. Evan Morgan, a Cymric Celt, from immemorial Wales, felt the supernatural at once.

"You never told me about this," he complained, all alert.

Now, you cannot ask a man to meet a ghost, because ghosts are not to be counted on.

"I did not care to talk about it," I said. "I thought that Yeats . . ."

I could not say—'If you met Yeats you met enough of færy, as much as I am ever likely to meet.' I implied that it was far more in Yeats' province than mine, and, that being so, the omission was not mine wholly. But he was not quite satisfied. My hospitality fell short of the necromantic.

After dinner there were very few in the library—in fact only Seymour Leslie and one or two. Evidently something was going on. Seymour could not be left out when anything exciting was taking place. He left the room to investigate. I lolled in front of the fire, hoping that something, no matter what provided it was exciting, might occur. A maid brought me a note.

"Take your friend Leslie away from us. He is a regular vortex of evil spirits." It was in unmistakable and distinguished calligraphy. Good Lord! What is this? There must be a séance in full blast going on somewhere and Seymour has butted in: "A regular vortex"! If Seymour is a vortex I must be a regular maelstrom. I drown evil spirits. Seymour, it seems, circulates them. But, crestfallen, Leslie returned.

"What's up?"

"They are all at it. Lord Conyngham, Yeats, Mrs. Yeats and a fourth. They are getting after the ghost."

"But how?"

"I just looked in to one of the rooms. Lord Conyngham was at the Ouija board. When I appeared, everyone stopped. Yeats said significantly, 'We cannot go on until we hear what Mr. Leslie wants.' That meant that I was politely asked to go. I am to see you."

"To see me?"

I am determined not to trespass. I want the poet and his party to be left alone. But I must be on my guard if I am not to be used by the very inquisitive and masterful Seymour as a stalking horse. If he goes back it will break up the séance. I know Yeats.

"I for one shall not butt in," I said. "I don't hold with séances. I am not sensitive enough." Winds moaned reprovingly in the chimney. "I was kicked out of the Hermetic Society on the only evening I went with George Moore to see what it was all about. Let us have a smoke."

"I don't smoke." (Oh, don't you?)

"Have a drink and we'll 'hit the hay.'"

"It's far too early."

"Séances," I said, with the authority of one who makes a premise suit his needs, "usually last many hours. There are people in the next room. Would you care to make a fourth at bridge?"

I knew that Evan Morgan was in the drawing-room with half-a-dozen friends, who saw Shelley plain in him with his long, white open neck, high forehead, chestnut hair, and aquamarine eyes. I hoped that their company would prevent Seymour from spoiling what, if left to itself, would prove to be one of the most interesting psychological experiments in our country. A ghost which had been felt first hand by me and many others. None of your ' I-heard-for-a-fact-from-a-friend' ghosts, but one I had heard myself, and two of us had *seen*.

As the folding doors closed behind the reluctant Seymour, " Evan is psychic," I called after him. A moment later, I was left alone. . . .

How this one memory furnished the lost house for me!

I believe in ghosts : that is, I know that there are times, given the place which is capable of suggesting a phantasy, when those who are sufficiently impressionable may perceive a dream projected as if external to the dreamy mind : a waking dream due both to the dreamer and the spot.

The book I read was becoming a crystal because I was merely using its pages as a screen for the subconscious.

Smoke from the fire we light on summer evenings in Ireland for the sake of homeliness, puffed down. A puffing chimney was unusual. But there it was. It proved that I was not asleep, for smoke is hardly a soporific. But I did notice suddenly, as if awakened, that the folding doors were opened and that there was no one in the room beyond.

If it was too early to go to bed some time ago, perhaps it was not now. Where had they gone ? What was the restless ' Regular Vortex ' doing ? Not interrupting Yeats, I hoped. But it would interrupt him were I to search him out in mid séance. This ramshackle house has many chambers. If the guests are not gone to bed they may have gone to the kitchens to listen to the fiddlers at the dancing, or gone somewhere else to play ping-pong.

My lamp is making little noises. The room is gloomy. I will go into the next one, which is brighter and is not filled with smoke.

Ah, well! There is a lot to be said for rooms furnished by a woman's hand. They are devoid of design. They elude and defy calculation. They have so many fancies and knick-knacks. What is that famous paper *Vogue* but the ' Woman's hand ' in journalism! Thick crowding fancies, notions! I remember promising to give Sir Thomas Esmonde that cameo of his long-nosed grandfather which is on the mantel-piece. Beside it is a Chinese mandarin with a short nose. Was this the fact that justified their juxtaposition ? Below, the Venetian mirror, for all I knew, may have suggested Marco Polo to counterbalance the Chinese porcelain. Vague, *Vogue* and the exotic chintzes!

Suddenly! Was that a scream? There, it shrieks out again! Now what the devil? It must be a very loud scream, or very near, to reach this part of the house. With the thick walls we never hear the fiddles and the dancing in the kitchen. Lights are moving on the stairs of the west wing. Frightened friends in their nighties peer out, but someone is running towards me.

"Quick! Evan is dying!"

"Where is he?"

"In that room there!"

Evan was being supported on a chair by two ladies. His face was deathly pale and his head had fallen forwards. Seymour was hopping in front of him saying, "Don't take it so seriously, old man!" A table had fallen on its side, presenting a cool shield of green baize.

"What's all this about?" I demanded.

"Evan suddenly became hysterical."

His pulse was racing. He was but semi-conscious.

"What on earth were you doing?"

"We were holding our own little séance, and just as we were getting results Evan got the jigs or something rather like them."

Relying on me, the lady supporters released their hold. I was barely in time to catch him as he fell sideways.

"Leave him to me and run to get some brandy."

I carried him into a dressing-room and laid him on the bed. Presently three returned with brandy. Seymour expostulating "He shouldn't have taken it so seriously."

I put them all out of the room. No audience.

His body was smooth as marble: heart firm: no aspirin about. I could not understand the collapse. Presently he broke out in a cold perspiration. Slower pulse, breathing audible.

"What did they do to you, Evan?"

"The ghost!" he gasped, and tore at his open collar.

"The ghost? What ghost?"

"Seymour sent me into the haunted room to raise the ghost, but when it came it transferred into me all the thoughts by which he was obsessed before he went mad."

"Now really, Morgan, you know very well that there is no ghost; no ghost anyway here who is insane."

"It was Seymour's séance. Yeats was having one . . ."

"I know. Quite." A rival séance! Wait until I catch

that 'Vortex.' " Try to sleep, old man.   I will sit here until I can get someone to take my place—unless you would care to come down with me."

" Seymour heard that Yeats spent hours in the haunted room. ' Now it's up to you,' he said. I went in about 12.30, and after they had locked the door . . ."

" Locked the door ? "

" Yes. Locked me in . . . I felt a strange sensation. A sensation that I was all keyed up just like the tension in a nightmare, with the terror added that nightmares have. Presently I saw a boy, stiffly upright, in brown velvet with some sort of shirt showing at his waist.   He was about twelve. Behind the chair he stood, all white-faced, hardly touching the floor.   It seemed that if he came nearer some awful calamity would happen to me.   I was just as tensed up as he was : nightmare terrors ; twingling air ; but what made it awful was my being quite awake.   The figure in brown velvet only looked at me, but the atmosphere in the room vibrated. I don't know what else happened.   I saw his large eyes.   I saw the ruffles on his wrists.   He stood vibrating just as I was vibrating.   His luminous brown eyes reproved me. He looked deeply into my eyes.   Then, oh then ! . . . Oh, my God ! . . ."

" Old fellow, you know I am solid enough and all damned spirits steer clear of me.   Don't talk about it any more. What about a large one and a spot of soda ? "

" I must, I simply can't go on until I tell you."

" Yes, but don't weep because Seymour sent you into the worst-furnished room in the house."

" Yes, but let me tell you.   The apparition lifted his hands to his neck, and then, all of a sudden, his body was violently seized as if by invisible fiends and twisted into horrible contortions in mid air.   He was mad !   I sympathised for a moment with his madness and I felt myself at once in the electric tension of Hell.   Suicide !   Suicide !   Oh, my God ! He committed suicide in this very house."

I'll " commit " Seymour when I go downstairs, I determined.

" But what about your yellow dressing-gown and a few of your black-and-yellow Chinese sleeve-birds in it ? Just to show the girls that you are your own man again ? "

He seemed to consider it.   But again he wept in pity for the ghost.

"How did you get out?" I asked foolishly; yet thinking to relieve him by the story of his relief.

"Seymour let me out. 'It seems to be a poltergeist, Evan,' he said, 'from all the row you are making'—and I was not making any row. But, oh, that . . .!"

"Your Moroccan slippers are here. Here's your dressing-gown. The birds are in the next room. Don't you think you can do your bit in the drawing-room now? I'll just peep into the haunted room. I don't believe the Yeats party have started for it yet."

"Oh, you mustn't! Don't leave me. Don't risk that room! I'll go down with you. Promise me that you will never go near that room again."

"Well, all right. As a matter of nerve-training I used to look into and grope around it for half a minute whenever I was left alone of winter nights in the house. Not a thing! Nothing but my own fears, with which I refused to people the room. I'm afraid I'll never make a gigolo for ghosts; nor allow myself to be terrorised by the cellars of my own imagination."

Perhaps it was curiosity for the results of the prolonged séance which was still sitting in the opposite side of the house that decided the skiaphobe and obsessed youth to follow me. He put aside his delirium as suddenly as it came. I did the decanter drill once more.

It must be awful, I reflected, to get the horrors before the excesses. Delirium without a drink! The shock before the shell! That would do very well for a definition of madness. I recalled the words of my well-loved friend and mentor Dr. Tyrrell of Trinity—"My dear boy, believe me, there is nothing more disconcerting than an illness one has *not* brought on oneself!"

How true! We can cure the results of excess by excelling. But a visitation of uninvited disease! The effect without the cause!

Downstairs Freddy Conyngham was asking for perfume and flowers. Presently Sabean odours filled the room. There were many contributions. Flowers were taken from bowls here and there. Yeats's ghost had asked for flowers.

At 2 a.m. Yeats appeared.

"She should be down any moment now," he said casually. "Yes, she should be here presently if all goes well."

But where was she, Mrs. Yeats?

It transpired that the ghost had communicated with Yeats through automatic writing. He objected to the presence of strangers in the house. But he was in for a course of adjuration he little expected from the Archimandrite Yeats.

1. You must desist from frightening the children in their early sleep.
2. You must cease to moan about the chimneys.
3. You must walk the house no more.
4. You must not move furniture or horrify those who sleep near by.
5. You must name yourself to me.

Now, Yeats could never have guessed that it was the custom of the Blake family to call their sons after the Heptarchy. And yet he found it out and the ghost's particular name. I had never gleaned it from the local people, though I lived for years among them.

The troubled spirit promised to appear in the ghost room to Mrs. Yeats, as he was before he went mad sixty years ago.

" She should be here any moment," Yeats repeated. " We must wait. We must wait. He has promised to appear to my wife as he was before he went mad." He waved his beautiful hand up and down, on which a ring as large as a wrist watch gleamed on the side of the armchair.

Far up behind the great flue round whose hearth we were gathered was the gaunt, deserted room, in which Mrs. Yeats was keeping solitary vigil. I felt a strange fear, a fear that nothing could combat. What courage she had! But we attribute courage to those whose professions to us are unfamiliar : to the soldier, sailor, aviator, none of whom claims credit for it for himself. So, too, the psychic researchers are unfamiliar with fear in their vocation.

Presently Mrs. Yeats appeared, carrying a lighted candle. She extinguished it and nodded curtly to her husband. " Yes. It is just as you said."

What was ? we all wondered.

After a whispered consultation Yeats announced :

" My wife saw a pale-faced, red-haired boy of about fourteen years of age standing in the middle of the north room. She was by the fireside when he first took shape. He had the solemn pallor of a tragedy beyond the endurance of a child. He resents the presence of strangers in the home of his ancestors. He is Athelstone Blake. He is to be placated with incense and flowers. Lord Conyngham ! "

With grace, and saving presence of mind, Lord Conyngham presented flowers and his collection of scent bottles to Mrs. Yeats.

Memories, nothing left now but memories. In that house was lost my mother's self-portrait, painted when she was a girl of sixteen. Her first attempt in oils. And her sampler of the big parrot, made with thousands of beads, outcome of patience and peaceful days half a hundred years ago, under the tuition of the nuns of Taylor's Hill. One of the many Irish convents which, as an Irish-American kinsman truly said, "train girls to be ladies." Books, pictures, all consumed: for what? Nothing left but a charred oak beam quenched in the well beneath the house. And ten tall square towers, chimneys, stand bare on Europe's extreme verge.

CHAPTER XIV

THERE MUST BE "SOMETHING OF THE SEA" ALL SIB TO MY spirit. I go down to it as if there existed an understanding between us; as if the "pathetic fallacy" of external nature's indifference were not fallacious but true. I trust myself to the sea with the abandon of a confidence I never feel on land. It may be because I was born with a caul. The fact remains and is always to be relied upon : I can rest on the sea as I can never rest on land. So when I lay in my bed on the British and Irish boat to Liverpool, I felt an inexplicable peace flow up from the depths. The very marrow of my bones softened ; and I was filled with honey heavy peace, a peace that comes but once in a lustrum.

Could it have been that I was under a strain for years without realising it? Or is this peace due to the lulling movement of our prime mother, the world-enfolding sea? Relaxation is not of the will. It comes from a release from care ; and it cannot be turned on as those who begin noonday entertainments in America with an order to "relax" imagine it can be. America rings to that pitiable appeal 'Relax.' Into what will they dis-relax at 1.1 p.m. . . . ?

I am fondled by the sea in which I trust. Strange it is : never through the many thousand miles I have sailed has there been dangerous weather. And I have sailed in my time far into the blue deep. But what is more unnatural than a voyage without undulations? All noises of the ship's mechanism without motion obtrude. A calm passage is unnatural. I do not ask for a storm to leave me suspended three inches above my falling berth, or to tear my pyjamas as I correct the sidelong roll. Up and down three feet, up and down above a mile depth of element more viscid and visible than the air. Charged with terror is the unplumbed deep. Horror and horror float and dart in the saline vat which, bottled, is our blood. And even in our blood, on the battle goes. Invisible fishes drift and multiply ; and we are no more masters of that stream than of the outer sea. I must be a go-between, a liaison officer of sea and circulation. Else, why do I feel more at home and freer from care at sea than on land ? Panics on deck move me not. I never shall be drowned. All who sail with me are safe—'Back! One by one to your boat stations ! Women and children first. Call that gynæcologist back! This ship will keep afloat. I am here!'—I should be endowed by steamship companies to sail on special voyages assuring calm and halcyon weather. I have fancied myself in many *rôles*, but never before as that symbol of azure days, the halcyon or Kingfisher. "By Jove, a bird!"

And now I am sailing to Liverpool in one of the well-equipped cabins of the "B and I," the best way to sail to England. If the electric light were only behind and not in front of my eyes, I would recognise a sympathiser and not a cynic in the marine architect. He did not believe that any of those likely to travel by his boats ever concerned themselves with a book. So the light is midway to help the stewards with the drinks. But a bookworm, no! They are not supposed to sail with the "B and I." If he read at night he may be blinded by the dazzle that sheds light upon the navel and the eyes. Two feet towards the bed-head . . . but this is asking for intelligence and imagination where maximum illumination is provided.

The sun is getting behind me, but I know all about Dublin in the evening glow. I have not the least desire to look upon it. It is too typical. *Der Untergang!* The Sugar Loaf, called the Golden Spears, will be visible on the south. Howth. . . .

Hoved, the Head. . . . Well, what about it? Men from Norway named it and took a "great prey of women from Howth." For all their sailing these are still in Moore Street, sturdy, snub-nosed, hawser-haired "Danes." But no one in Ireland knows Irish history. So we are suffering from a nightmare culture of imaginary Gaels.

I will not have my peace disturbed by thoughts of my town house in the hands of guards, of my visitors subjected to searchings, hatred mistaken for patriotism.

I was astounded at how little I regretted leaving my native land, where patriotism consists in going native, or where usury enjoys an extra two per cent.

> Confound their politics;
> Frustrate their knavish tricks;
> Shut off their 606.
> God save the King!

I will lie *solutis curis*. The last time that phrase entered my head, my peace was magnificently disturbed by Talbot Clifton, who came bearing a gift of gold. He is endowing me this time with a goldener gift—the gift of peace. What is

the cause of this peace? " My Native Land, Good Night " or
the fact that I am on the sea?   The sea whereon all can sail
and become brotherly by so doing.   Why is it that I don't
accuse myself of lack of patriotism?   Or why—and is not this
a further dereliction?—do I look upon patriotism as paranoia
and a kind of restricting curse?   The sea has neither confines,
prejudices nor politics.

Against the light I read his invitation—" And stay here with
all your family as long as you like."

I have experienced much hospitality in the United States,
which seems to be its home.   But this man's hospitality is
illimitable.   The salvation of his *bos anoa* could not account
for it.

How wonderful was his Lancashire welcome!   The Clifton
gold plate was out in our honour.   We feasted long and
sumptuously.   Our host wore a scarlet tail-coat faced with
lapels of light blue silk.   It was a uniform he had designed for
the President of the Lytham Golf Club, over which he presided.

I gazed at him as he sat in scarlet at the head of his table in
the great dining-hall hung with old-rose velvet and gold.
Golden candelabra expanded all around.   He sat magnificent
and munificent.   And for all its arbitrariness, the uniform in
which he was attired was not bizarre.   It well became the
scene.   I watched his long, bony hands, golden from many
suns.   I thought of that Emperor, a great gift-giver, who had
golden fists.

> Voire, ou soit de Constantinobles
> L'emperieres au poing dorez.

I had been sailing to Byzantium: but I am in it now!

But he was taking great trouble to entertain us.   After
dinner he would deliver a lecture on his adventure in Celebes,
and as he hated speaking in public it was a compliment indeed.

He imagined that he had an impediment in his speech, but
it was not a stutter, only a little halt now and again which gave
it emphasis and the charm of distinction.

Nevertheless he was ill-at-ease when the tenants began to
file into the Long Gallery.

He beckoned me aside.

" Lookey here, this kind of public lecturing always upsets
me.   Not that I am nervous.   No, of course not.   But there
are so many things to be synchronised.   The lantern fellow,
and the last man in.   I hate the noise of boots after the lights

have gone out.   However ! "—cheerfully— " I have arranged
to allow myself a drink for every minute that lantern fellow
delays me."

He held a long billiard cue like a lance over his right shoulder.

" When lecturing, the thing is to seize the attention of your
audience.   You see !   Now, these locals know nothing of
Celebes.   Nothing !   If that damned lantern fellow is late
bang goes this whiskey—Here's, ' happy days.'   What more
can one wish for ?   Happy days !   Damn it.   It's nearly
9.56.   The lecture is at 9.45.   Well, it's not my fault :
oxy-acetylene or something of that sort. . . . Have another
with me.   Well, then !   Do you think they'll like it ?   I only
lecture now and then as a duty, you see.   When I was President of the Orchid Club of Great Britain I chartered a rather
large yacht and just succeeded in capturing that rare orchid
after which I called one of my daughters.   But this is a more
serious affair—addressing one's own people.   Have I time for
another ?   I never allow myself . . ."

Cheering and " barracking " drew his attention to his
tenants.   The oxy-acetylene lantern evidently had projected
its beam and proved itself.   " Squire !   Squire ! "

" By Gad ! "

He rose magnificently against the screen.

" First picture ! "

A map appeared.

" You see here Borneo and Celebes.   Borneo is to the East,
West . . . and . . . It is upside down !   What are you
doing ?   Oh, well ! that's better.   Borneo and Celebes.   You
may ignore Borneo.   This is Celebes, and the blackened marks
are our tracks for five hundred miles by sea, swamp and forest.
Next picture ! "

A group of natives and thin-legged native children with
enlarged spleens was projected.

" Now !   Well !   Yes.   That's it !   Now you see here a
group of natives.   These little cads are very camera-shy.   It
is very hard to take their photographs.   They thought that
they were going to be shot.   They were quite right.   Next
picture ! . . .

" Here there are no little cads.   They have been exterminated since the last picture."

The tenants moaned in " Oh ! "

" Not at all !   They have been exterminated by the Dutch
Government—quite rightly, because they resisted civilisation.

Next picture ! " The house acquiesced in some finer shade of justice.

A bleak landscape appeared. Natives by a beach with what looked like a dug-out canoe.

" Now this is our boat. We have two hundred and fifty miles yet to paddle. Next picture ! "

Sun-stricken desert. Four posts holding up a roof of palm thatch. Desolation.

" Our hotel."

The oxy-acetylene hissed like a snake. But the lantern, after much blank light, at last projected a Chinaman.

" This is our host. He came from that shack to welcome us at the beach which you see here with ' Good-bye ! Good-bye ! ' as he led us towards his house. Next picture."

Surely the greatness of the Englishman may be deduced from that depth of character wherein even the ludicrous becomes invested with a kind of grandeur and significance.

The long itinerary, as Thomas Cook would call a journey, was displayed and described. Mrs. Clifton, festooned with leeches, had followed her lord and master through tropical swamps for miles and miles. Aigrettes it seems were sighted. So were humming-birds—in coveys, packs, broods, ascensions, or what ?

The journey charmed me because its purpose was so un-apparent. " It is better to travel hopefully than to arrive." Besides, he did not arrive. He was exploring. No explorer arrives. If he were to have a goal he would be merely a traveller, and not an explorer, whose chief claim to distinction is that he does not know where he is going. He is finding out.

On the whole the lecture was a success. The lecturer was concerned for his audience, and his audience were concerned for their lecturer.

A reciprocal success ! That is as it should be. The lecturer had demonstrated what some governments do to their nationals. But the lecturer's tenants went away with a dim, instinctive feeling that one who had visited so many lands for no apparent reason must be a good landlord and the last man to exploit his own retainers. A most successful lecture ! Their Squire had to go for hardships to Celebes because hardships were far from home.

The next lecture—if any—was to be " On my explorations in the Arctic." This, if told from the Esquimaux's point of view, would have told of a jam he got them into, into which they would never have got themselves and of how, when the ice was cracking, they turned to him and asked ' What do we do now ? ' They believed that he had taken over the administration of the North Pole.

One day while speeding along his thirty miles of highroad by the discoloured sea, he said :

" You must have lost considerably by the upset to your work."

" Of course," I acknowledged.

" Now, lookey here. You can have one of my Lanchesters, a short wheel-based one, for a mere song. You see, with a short wheel-base you get a little, just a little more speed. And it corners better."

" I couldn't raise wind enough just at present to inflate one of its tyres."

" Oh, in that case, just drop in and name some little sum to Elwes, who has it at present in Brick Street, Park Lane. He will let you have it. A man cannot be without a car."

I heartily agreed. Life would be endurable—that is, one might retire and trust to Life if one had the means of unrestricted movement, wheels and wings. Rest, even peace—immobility of any sort—is a form of death. But for all that I could not take his property, though offered with a tact and consideration which only those who took the trouble to know him and to put up with his sudden passions and impulses, could realise were deep at heart in the man. He had a golden heart as well as golden hands.

But the kind days among magnanimous Lancashire men could not go on for ever. My host was growing restless. One night towards the end of dinner he said suddenly :

" Let's look up Lonsdale."

" Lonsdale ? "

" Yes. He's my cousin."

My hostess intervened mildly, without astonishment.

" But he's in Scotland just now."

" Of course he is ! Everyone must be there in a day or so—that is," looking at our group, " if these good people will come along. . . . But I can run up to Lonsdale's this evening in the Lanchester."

The progress proposed was clogged perhaps by our presence ; perhaps by something that diverted his attention.

" A little speeding will take us up there. He'll be surprised to see us." Is an invitation for life to Lytham as short as a life sentence for some political outrage in an Irish gaol?

That I could believe. But we were bound for Scotland with no escape.

Kildalton Castle is not antique. It is modern, comfortable and desirable. Its 17,000 acres of deer forest, moors and covers constituted my only misgiving, together with the Thorburns which walled the dining-hall with water colours of every kind of game birds.

I am in for it now—' Sport!' I said to myself.

But off my bedroom was a bathroom. Books were at my bed's head. Mine host had printed "Private" in his own hand on a card—I have it yet—which he hung on the library door, so that I should not be disturbed. Kindness could go no further, nor his toleration of a literary lout. But still there was 'sport' staring me in the face during the daylight hours.

He broke it gently.

"To-day is a *dies non*. To-morrow, when you are rested, we might look about us for a bird."

My father had an estate in his time on the banks of the Nore. He looked about him for a bird, but my memory of his sporting activity consisted of a newspaper opened under a bough and shot at from sixty, seventy and eighty yards when it was too dark to walk the moors any longer. My share in this " shoot " was to count how many pellets had hit the papers at the different ranges, and to record in my childish calligraphy whether they were No. 6 or Swan shot. What ensued next day at dawn was worse. My father threw saucers, cups, the breakfast set— many sets, up from behind a haystack. Unless I hit them, breakfast was omitted.

My eye improved with inanition.

" What about the teapot? " I inquired after an exceptionally destructive morning.

" Don't be impertinent," he said.

Though grouse were easier than sidelong saucers, I could not even now dissociate them from alarming repercussions and a bruised collar-bone.

" I am quite content here," I said. " I am under no misgivings about being a shot. Long ago I have hit enough to last a lifetime."

" Nonsense! No one sets a limit beforehand to a bag. Just you see."

I who had blamed Yeats for forgetting his bathing-suit while being driven seaward, now said:

"I have forgotten my gun."

He roared with laughter.

"Ho! ho! There are Purdeys in the gun-room for every kind of man. Take your choice. Get one with a balance to suit you!"

Condemned to heavy Trulocks thirty years ago, I am now promoted to Purdeys.

"You very kindly set your library apart for me. I think, if you don't mind, that I'll stay in and look round it."

"Now, lookey here. We must think about our boys. We cannot set them a bad example. What will my son Harry think if his friends' father does not turn out? If you are not in form, the Chaplain here, who has very bad sight, will save your face. Come along!"

The line advanced, spreading out for about 120 yards. Mine host's son, my son, myself, my son, the Chaplain, and mine host. The setters were perfectly trained.

Bang! from the left. Tawny feathers floated in the air. A dead bulk thumped vertically downwards to the ground. Dermot had scored first shot. He awaited recognition.

"Now, what the devil do you mean? You have murdered a grey hen, the potential mother of eighteen black cock, which are getting rarer in Scotland every season. Fall out of the line, Dermot!" Stricken, the child retired.

Rather unfair, I thought, on a lad who was concentrating on not missing anything that broke cover and who had not been warned about grey hens, much less had he seen one.

"Now let us walk on."

I watch with admiration the well-trained dogs and the way our host picks birds instantaneously out of the sky by his magic wand of a gun. They are setting again. Careful now.

A brown pack of whirring wings radiates out from the heather. Bang, and then bang!

His heir has stopped one with his left barrel as accurately as his father. Grouse falls from the air. His right only wings and wounds. Unforgivable in a Clifton.

"Out of the line, Harry!" Though Harry was shooting with a 20-bore.

Two sportsmen in disgrace. O Lord, what am I to do? Miss? But then it will put my mentor in an embarrassing position. He can hardly kick his senior guest off the grouse moor. Twenty minutes elapse. My left wing supports me no longer. They are somewhere in the rear. I alone am in command on the left. Hah! Under my feet a pack breaks. Not yet! No, by no means. I am too old a hand to shoot at radiating birds. They are not twenty yards away and flying fast, low and slanting. Forty yards. Yes! That's one. The middle member of the brood swings high to the right almost in front of the Chaplain. I give him the second barrel. He has twenty yards yet through which to fall. Suddenly he blows back towards me again, a mass of scattering feathers. He is bandied like a shuttlecock. My host has given him his left barrel as he falls. His Reverence solemnly fires a salvo over the grave. However, I am still in line. What will my remaining son, who by this time must be rather nervous, do? But his sight is superb and his aim accurate.

The moor falls to a burn. A rowan or mountain ash is the only tree to be seen. It stands branchless save above some distance to our right. A quarter of an hour. The birds do not like reeds. On we go. The dogs stand still again right ahead.

I am sure that I shall fall into one of these bog-holes two feet deep. I cannot watch my step. I cannot even " see what flowers are at my feet " and keep an eye on the setters. If you fall into a little bog-hole I can hear the command, " You stay there! "

I thank God I am to the left. It is up to my son now or mine host, or to his Reverence, who intervenes.

More birds! Left! That's one; but another diverges far to the right: eighty yards at least. Will Noll ever get it? Ah! It topples just in front of the mountain ash. But our host is rushing on in front to reach the tree before all the shot-shent leaves have fallen. What does the tree conceal? Why is he in such a hurry? He stands beneath it and points to the leaves which are still coming down over his head.

" You damned well might have shot me! Out of the line, Noll! Harry and Dermot back to stations again."

" Don't worry, old chap! " I said to my retiring son, who was bruised in his heart by this, his first experience of injustice.

" Harry and Dermot back! No grey hens! Now, Father Chaplain, you must get a chance! "

Uphill! There was a pink glow towards the east, a reflection surely from a fine sunset behind me, but I dare not turn my head.   These setters and the concentrated alertness they demanded!

" Turn back ! "

O, thanks be to all the gods of harbours and homesteads! We opened out as we met the gamekeeper with his two thin boards between which the necks of the game were held.

" You see, Father Chaplain, one must be always alert. Perhaps your gun is just a trifle, a very little trifle, too slow in coming up.   Now, if a gun is unbalanced you can never hope to shoot, that is, instinctively at sight ; and after all what else is . . ."   Bang !

" Ah, that was just so that I might illustrate the excellent balance of my Purdey.—Makenzie ? "

" A grey hen, Sir."

" Damn !   Well, all right !   Add it to the bag, for who can be expected to see against a level sun ?   Home all ! "

Home we brought the grey hen dead, trying to break our steps lest anything funereal should appear to creep into our march.

(I wish I could hire a wild ass to " Stamp o'er my head " to-night so that I may be " fast asleep.")

In the game-book I traced lightly and almost invisibly in lead pencil after the list of birds " and 36 black cock."   Because the death of the two grey hens, as we had been informed, added to a potential bag 36 black cock.

I am feeling somewhat Homeric this morning : like a man who strove with gods.   But to be the guest of a god entails strife of a sort.   Had Clifton, that great hunter, lived in the Stone Age, he would have been feared for miles and miles around in all game reservations.   The skulls of his wives would have borne the biggest bumps and presented with pride the bluest wooing bruises.

" No morning tea !   Take it away : who the devil invented this degeneration ?   I will not have my bath turned on either to cool or to overflow.   That will do.   You may go."

A quiet shave while soaking in hot water !   Like Julia in her bath.   I

> Lay at length like an immortal soul
> At endless rest in blest Elysium.

Certainly Clifton has turned Kildalton Castle into an Elysium were it not for the agonising recreations he pursues.   I must look into his library to-day.   He has marked it " Private " to protect me from interruption when I am reading, but I haven't succeeded in getting within its sanctuary yet.

He never took breakfast. He sat at the breakfast-table like a warder waiting until I had finished masticating. I knew that the moment my jaws stopped chewing he would deliver sentence for the day's diversion—I was quite right. I laid down my cup.

" Deer-stalking ! Be ready at ten ! "

To this, like Pantagruel, I ' replied nothing.' But inwardly I was self-possessed and I met the challenge bravely. I met it, as a matter of fact, half-way. The reason was that I had provided myself with such a good deer-stalking suit by such a good tailor that it reduced the grassing of a deer to the least of things that followed my investiture. It had all the colours of brown heath and shaggy wood, though woods were not necessarily included in a deer forest. It had hints of bracken, gorse, heather and heath so well blent that I said to my tailor :

" What does one want more than the sentiment of the Highlands ? Here it is ! You have done me very well ! This felt on the shoulders lest the rifle should saw through my collar-bone shows admirable consideration. Such forethought ! And my cap crowns all the moors as the high place of Edinburgh crowns Scotland, or Branksome's lofty towers its banks and braes. No need to go to Scotland, now that I am invested in it."

" If Ah wiz you, Sir, A'd think twice before turning down an invite for deer-stalking. Many of our clients pays around £1000 a head when all comes to all. That is considering entertainments and friends."

I appealed to my host. " May I have a minute to jump into another suit ? "

" A minute, yes. No more ! "

I reappeared looking like a moving bog or one of those mountains which could " skip like rams." The general effect was greenish, although heather, streams, rocks, tartan and the counterpane of Mary Queen of Scots' bed had been suggested in the woof.

As he realised what Savile Row thought of Scotland, the imperial on his chin shut up against a smile. He thought—the poor devil has done his best. His heart's in the Highlands !

As we drove to the forest, " The great thing is not to be seen," he said, and, " This is your spy-glass. Put it on ! "

I strapped a shoulder.

When the road ended a Ford met us. We went on until it could go no farther.

" Out ! "

We walked or stalked for twenty yards.

" The first thing is to learn how to spy."

" My sight, that is one eye, is pretty keen. I don't need a telescope."

" It's not a telescope. It's a spy-glass. Who ever used a telescope stalking deer ? "

If this goes on, I thought, I will find myself Victor of Trafalgar or the Nile. We are going backwards at such a rate.

" Now ! "

He plopped down on a dry tussock and extended himself backwards until he lay flat. He crossed his legs and slowly brought his head upwards. Between his knees his balanced spy-glass rested.

" Now we spy. Fallow ! " he jerked out. " Take no notice ! Spy ! And—don't stand up. Lie down just where you are ! "

" I am in a puddle ! "

" We are stalking ! "

Poole is in a pool, thought I. I opened the unnecessary telescope, spy-glass, or whatever the yard-long sections of tubing were. Water oozed through my symbolic knicker-bockers. I jerked my hips towards higher ground.

" Stay still, can't you ? Or you'll never spy a stag ! "

There is a " One-day Valeting Co." in Dublin. Perhaps they may be able to do something with my ruined breeks, I hoped.

" What do you spy ? "

The coast of Antrim was distinct. Ireland my home! " Oh, to be in Antrim now Craigavon's there ! " Out of focus ! I shot a section or two into my only eye. What is this ? A moving barn with black spots ? No. A ladybird !

" There's five on the brae side," the voice of the keeper was heard whispering cautiously in my ear. What a Christian the man was ! But what and where was the brae ?

" Now you see why we have to begin at the beginning. Spying is of paramount importance. You see nothing ? "

" There's five on the brae," I echoed.

He was far from convinced.

" Oh, are there ? Then count the tines."

I worked the telescope in and out like the pipes of a trombone. At last far off, what is it ? Distinctly deer. The leader is a great dark grey stag with eleven tines . . . I shall have lumbago. . . .

I hope they are in Scotland and not reindeer, I thought, as I announced :

" Eleven tines."

" Eleven tines ? "

He jerked himself into action on his back from his bed of dry heather. Apparently I had discovered a rare species or a sport. Under the circumstances he could hardly ask his pupil " where ? "

During the long delay I managed to slide landwards from my nine-inch pool. I waited until he had, having handicapped himself as much as possible for the ritual of sport, at last seen what were quite plain to a naked eye, five royal heads with the leader who had eleven tines. The deer ignored us.

" Oh, it's not eleven tines, but the velvet hanging down from a brow antler."

" They are coming our way," I ventured.

" Nonsense ! Get up ! After spying, stalking begins ! Now ! "

He threw some thistledown into the air and watched it as it floated past.

" Wind's in the right direction. Watch me ! "

My tall and forthright friend suddenly became furtive. He stooped down and made little unaccountable forward rushes. Now he lay *ventre à terre* and wriggled on. Then he stopped behind a rock. He looked back to find me standing gazing in admiration.

" Do I do it now ? " I asked.

" Dammit, of course you do ! Lie down."

" You told me to watch."

" Dammit ! We're stalking."

I lay down.

" Now crawl along and take cover."

I should have covered myself in an older suit.

" Never, never let yourself be seen ! "

" They are miles away."

Luckily he did not hear me. He was advancing crouched along a ditch.

Where is his gun ? The keeper, invisible but slightly

audible on account of his laboured breathing, followed. He probably bears the gun.

" Does this go on for long ? " I whispered.

He put his finger to his lips, then pointed ahead. He trailed a gun in a green canvas bag. I could see a dagger in his belt. Kit Marlowe had one. So had Willie Shakespeare. Tradition ! He looks frightened. Maybe we are in for an attack. I distinctly saw the deer moving in our direction. It may be soft with the velvet, I opined, but I am absolutely unarmed. If I had only kept the Browning (not the writer) that I carried in Dublin, I now might have a chance. It is five to three. And of course Clifton will demand the only gun. I remembered hearing somewhere that stags or bulls cannot gore you if you lie down. But I am lying down. I am getting miserably damp—thanks to that puddle—and nervous. I elbow myself into a rounded hollow thick with grass and little ferns. This would be a good place to hide—no, ' to take up my position.' I crawl head on into a large pair of hobnailed shoes. A long finger comes back and waves at me like the barrel of a revolver.

" Have we far to go ? "

" Shut up ! Who can teach you stalking if you talk ? "

I am putting him in a bad temper ; but, dammit, he is putting me in a most uncomfortable position, into a series of uncomfortable positions. When will this entertainment stop ?

We reach a smooth open space. I can see the Paps of Jura. Above them long drawn strato-cumulus clouds streak across a watery blue sky. It must be lovely and pleasant to be over there on a fine day like this.

Now, how had he got himself half across this tennis-court or putting-green ? Of course, it could not be one or the other, but it were just as flat as if it were. He was moving by inches, crawling forward like a tortoise on his elbows and the sides of his shoes.

I go next. I think I will make the passage a trifle slower to register zeal and compensate for my mistakes. He disappeared. But presently I caught his eye glaring at me from behind a rock.

With his free hand he beat slow time like the conductor of a soundless orchestra. He crooked a finger and beckoned me to advance. I rubbed my face well into the fragrant sward and by a mixture of the movements of a *danse du ventre* and my toes, I moved as if the place were being re-sodded.

" Very good ! " without words.

He raised his wrist-watch and pointed to the sun.   His meaning was beyond me, but I nodded.   I could not be cross-examined just then.   The head keeper made the passage. And, in answer to an inquiring look from his master, inclined his head in some sort of understanding.

Now what was going on ?   This is collusion between them. They must have the stags under observation all the time. Look at me !   I am not allowed to raise an eyelid !

We caterpillared up a slope fringed with a natural wall or bank breast high.   He stopped here.   Now he rolls on his back.   The keeper crouches at his feet.

What a relaxation !   I could see the sky and a wide prospect. I who had been prospecting and nosing roots of ferns.   I hoped my face was dirty.   It would show what a sterling stalker his pupil was.   We lay for twenty minutes on the restful bank. But he was moving one foot.   The keeper slid the rifle up towards him.   He is going to shoot something soon, I thought. Soon I hope ; this mountain sickness makes me very hungry. It is long past time for lunch.   Quietly he undid the cover and disclosed a little rifle with a barrel of dark blue.

" Two forty," he whispered.   " Flat trajectory, full bead up to two hundred yards."

" Yes ? " I said.   " Quite."

" Take it, can't you ? "

Good Lord !   So it is I who am to shoot.   I had never imagined that.

What was it the fellow said ?   " Some gents pays up to £1000 a head when they takes a deer forest in Scotland, all said and done."   And here was my good friend handing me £1000 and I not even grateful !

I pulled myself together.   I must make whatever slight repayment the gratitude and enthusiasm of a guest may mean to him.   I must shoot a stag and revel in the griolloching.   I must cast away apathy—Accidia ?   My God, of course it's Accidia !   My besetting sin !   If only I were Sir Horace, then even this act would be altruistic.   This blood would be shed for Ireland ; or to make room for reindeer whose milk is tubercle-free.

" Give me that gun ! "

" It is not a gun.   It's a rifle."

" Sorry !   Rifle."

" Hold on now.   Just a moment.   Let me tell you one

thing. No good sportsman wounds a stag. One of your singing friends rented a forest and sent his beast skipping across Scotland tripping in its own entrails. That kind of thing is simply not done."

" What do I do ? Kill it ? "

" No ! "

Good gracious ! Does he mean me to catch it alive single-handed ?

" You grass it."

Well, I suppose if it stays on the grass it will be pretty well dead, I reflected. Suddenly, he remarked :

" They'll be getting up now. They usually get up about four, but the flies may be annoying them. See what you can spy."

Forgetting the unwieldy spy-glass I peeped through the blades of a grassy tuft. To my amazement I saw the whole opprobrious hillside moving. There were from fifteen to twenty or more stags. I withdrew my head cautiously in awe. Never had I been so near to such large animals in the wild.

I signalled on my fingers—twenty. Instantly he became alert. He verified my observation in a second. Tapping the lock and whispering " full bead two hundred yards," he passed me the little rifle.

Very cautiously I pushed it through the blades of grass. A great dark grey stag was leading the rest slantwise down the side of the opposite hill. He was about two hundred yards away, judging the little I knew of distance by the space between targets in the Royal Toxophilite grounds where shooting begins at a hundred yards.

Thank heaven for the " full bead two hundred yards." If I had to juggle with the little metal bootjack on the hither end of the barrel, all would be lost. I did not forget the safety-catch. Maybe he thought I would.

I could see the leader better now as he felt his way down the steep slope. I was afraid to look at the others. I waited until the royal beast should reach level ground. A small spray crossed the sights. But a gust removed it. Three points were in line : The great stag's shoulder and my near and fore sights. I pressed the trigger. Again the leaves ! Too late. Thunder in the hills. What a sudden rush of windy hooves ! Not one left now !—But, ah, I had seen a lordly beast crumple when my view was cleared from the gusty ferns.

The stag sank down backwards but did not subside. His

forelegs, placed apart, balanced his splendid erect antlers. His paralysed hind quarters slanted to the ground. He looked like an heraldic figure. What had I destroyed? Grace and speed and an untameable heart! I felt disconsolate. But for the first time a cheery note sounded from my host.

" Just four inches too high! Too full a bead. You would not believe that the trajectory is flat for two hundred yards. You have not done too badly, though. His spine is blown to bits. Come along! "

The keeper who had lain at his feet now appeared fifty yards in front of us. Respectfully he waited until the Laird inspected the stag.

Antler high, crouched with back sloping from the shoulders, the terror-stricken, immovable beast regarded us with reproachful eyes. Men had never come so close to him before. His instinct was true, no good comes from man's proximity. But he could only rear his antlers. The swift haunches lay sideways inertly on the ground.

" Now! "

The keeper went towards the noble head. He seized the right antler and forced the left to the ground. On this he stood with one foot, and while the great beast was nailed sideways but yet fully conscious, he unsheathed his long blade and plunged it into the root of the neck. He was digging for the aorta. Presently his knife work was rewarded by pints of hissing blood. The stag slumped down. It rolled on its back, dead. The moist knife cut out, first the genitals, then the great white-bluish sack of stomach, full of grass and moss.

I looked on bemused, thinking how like to the inside of an oyster shell is the colour of a stag's full stomach. Mine host was stooping down. He appeared to be dabbling or looking for something amid the bloody guts.

I was no longer concerned about his attitude towards me. Surely I, his pupil, had justified his teaching. A dead shot, first time, at two hundred yards. Suddenly he straightened up. He slapped me smartly across the face. Red dew splashed my eyes. Cheerily he exclaimed :

" You are blooded now! "

No novice can afford to be angry when he is learning a game. I tried to make my face assume a " We are seven " innocence through its five-fingered streaks of blood.

Signals may have summoned them or the sound of the shot ; but it seemed as if the Highland pony and his keeper appeared

out of the hillside. The stag was tied dangling across the
sturdy back of the little steed. We made for home.

"Were there not at least thirty stags when you spied them
first?" he inquired, solicitous for his forest.

"To make an honest confession, I got such a surprise when
I saw your hillside, braeside, alive with moving game that I
could not count. But they were some lengths apart from
each other and they extended sideways about as far as they
were from me. How many stags go to two hundred yards?"

"Nonsense! That would mean fifty or sixty."

"Well, you saw the stampede. They had nothing to do
with our five of this morning's spying."

"Yes; but you may have counted the hinds."

("Don't show your ignorance," I warned myself.)

"Anyway, home we go! You were just six inches too
high. I said full bead."

"You gave me a tip which made it possible for me to bring
off that amazing fluke."

"Just a trifle high; but you grassed him in spite of a bad
shot."

I remain modest.

"And for a first shot a record stag is not so bad, considering
the way you stalked."

Now to show my humility.

"But, Laird, I deserve no credit. The deer are more or
less tame. My friend, Inderwick, champion bowman of
England, could kill them with an arrow. So could I, and my
score for a York round rarely tops two hundred."

(Which of you can kill a buck? And who can kill a doe?)

"That's because you are not musical," he said, and he
laughed in sudden mockery. "And you did not gut him.
Fluke. Ho? If you were a singer you might have only
knocked off his horns."

It was ordained that the guests in Kildalton Castle should sit
two-some at little tables in the dining-hall. The principal
guest sat with his hostess, while the host sat with the wife
of his guest.

There was feasting in Kildalton and toasts in my honour.
I felt dishonest. I had never shot anything save an arrow
more than a hundred yards.

"And no *nouveau riche* shot!" he exclaimed, raising his
glass. He is still obsessed by that shot, thought I. What
am I to do? Here I find myself, through no merit of my

own, in the most delightful place I have ever seen or ever shall see—if I know my destiny. How am I to reply? How am I ever to convince him that I am grateful?

The refrigerating larder held three deer when I looked in. One he had given to my son to grass; one probably was his own; and now a third which was mine. Not his cousin Lonsdale with all his lands and sportsmanship could extend more generosity and largesse (*Au poing dorez!*) to what, as at best, I must have appeared to him—'a little Dublin doctor.' The immediate tribute I must pay is humility. No boasting! I must not accept congratulations for a fluke!

I lolled and revelled in his library. "Private." Now be very fair, I said to myself, and differentiate hospitality from domination. If my father had not died when I was twelve, what would have happened to me? I might have been (no, for I never exceeded high grade mediocrity at anything), for the sake of argument, a second-rate shot and a first-class ignoramus.

The radio on the tower of his Castle is out of order for the moment, but the receptiveness of his wife and his sensitive son to sentiments and ideas is not. Poetry is sacrificed to the poultry we call " game."

What a tragedy! His eldest son ordered out of the line for no fault. His wife never allowed any prominence for her excellence. I think of Lady Lavery, who was an admirable painter, but, for her husband's sake, she suppressed her talent. Stags instead of stanzas, and grouse instead of verses. How many birds and deer fall annually, and have been falling for the last hundred years, and of all who shot them,

> How many lie forgot,
>   In vaults beneath,
> And piecemeal rot
>   Without a fame in death?

Well I know the difficulty—forgo sport altogether and become a prey to pretenders and poetasters: is there no middle way between Helicon and the heather? Men like Lord Dunsany prove that there is.

Why do I allow my mind to dwell on the normal or the unexceptional? Here am I who always pretended that I would like to meet the mighty and the unsurpassable. The moment I do, I find myself endeavouring to reduce them to the ordinary and to make them amenable and comprehensible. Why?

Talbot Clifton is, as his wife divined, only to be judged by rules made for himself and changeable to suit circumstances—like cricket at Dunsany.   He is to be judged, but not by us—so why judge him at all ?

An unique and dominating personality which cannot or will not express itself within the measures of mediocrity is reduced to the survey of us who can never be his equal.   Why this straining for the Overman when we can neither recognise nor bear with him when he appears ?

Talbot Clifton was metaphorically the last bachelor, though he was of the sons of William Rufus, and the first of that great race whom modern Nietzsche called : The Ubermensch, the Blond Beast, the Uncompanionable, the Fearless and Lonely One.

Of what use were all his expensive and spasmodic excursions ? What did he achieve ?   Nothing.   Nothing in the huckster's view or the view of the solicitor's clerk.   He was noble, aimless, irascible, bullying, dauntless, extravagant, generous, scorning craftiness or thrift, golden-hearted, golden-fisted, fast to his friend, sadistical and successful—a figure unhorsed into our humdrum days from Roncesvalles or Fontarrabia.

Let us give up the pretence of wishing for the times of Charlemagne again if we cannot admire in our own time Talbot Clifton.

What does he see in me to make me his guest-friend ?   I know not.   But I do know that the first time he does anything that can be construed in our safety-vault box age as " helpful " or " practical," I will disbelieve in Homer and Mallory and spare " no lord for his piscence."

My greatest tribute to him is that he is incredible in these our times.

It is no use cavilling, ' His Life—What was it all about ? ' I can answer.   He is the figure of an ideal predominant in the mind of the yeomen of England.   A friend of the people, a Robin Hood.   A man they choose to represent.   A man they hail, acclaim and depend on.   Because he is to be trusted to obtain and maintain for them that indomitable freedom he impersonates and represents.

The piper who had played a merry skirl three times round the dining-room had just retired.   The sounds of the pipes faded, sobbing in their bag.   He had worn the Royal Tartan of the House of Stewart.   The Laird sat at his table, also wearing the Royal kilt.   He and his wife were descended from the Merry Monarch through the Duke of St. Albans.   But the Stewart tartan in a Campbell stronghold !   Well, I have had enough of politics.   In Scotland such things may no longer provoke.

But we spoke in whispers, maybe because we were tired from, or thoughtful of, the afternoon's sport.

Suddenly the Laird's voice rang out :

" Harry !   Second picture from the top corner on the left ? "

" Canvas-back duck, Father."

" Right, go on with your dinner. . . ."

" Dermot !   The one in the corner ? "

" Sheldrake, Sir ! "

" Correct ! "

During the ensuing lull my voice was audible.   I was merely remarking without any suggestion in it of relief that darkness put an end to a day's sport.

But I had been overheard.

" Nonsense !   Flighting begins at eleven.   The duck will just be coming in as you will see, or hear ! "

Why had I spoken ?   Flighting.   Now what is that ?   I was to have a night sport just to refute what he took as an implied slight on his property : that it could not produce sport at any hour.

After much clambering down through tunnels over-arched with shrubs, we reached a little cove.   I resolved to explore these paths by day.   Beside the sea, in the cliff face, they must be very beautiful.   There was hardly enough light in the night to show the cove's watery floor.   You could feel that the rocks were well covered in seaweed.   I was given the best upholstered one.   I tried to find something drier.   I trod on one of the retrievers.   Blunders are concatenated. We shall have no luck, or rather it is I who shall have no luck, to-night.   I tried to comfort the dog.

" Hush !   not a sound ! "

Nor a sight.

" What is the idea ?   Who can see to shoot in the dark ? "

" That's just it.   When the eye fails the hunter's ear comes in.   We may be able to hear them swimming about ! "

In the sultry dark we waited for over an hour.   The unfamiliar sounds of the night brought many surprises : a lapping wave that made a noise as if some animal were lifting itself shorewards; the seaweed crackling and sighing, tinkling sounds behind me on the sand. These were not immediately audible. There was no sound of them for the first ten minutes after we had sat down. Did the ear become accustomed, or were they really made by unseen living things that had grown bold?

An hour passed. The air hung limp in the stillness. Invisible woods were reversing their process of exhaling fresh air. The damp on which I was stationed was unevenly distributed. This means a cold, I thought.

"Would it be any harm if I just took off my things and slipped into the little bay for a swim? If I cannot see the land I will whistle and you can call."

"Good God! And the duck waiting to come in! Have you any knowledge of wild life at all?" And this to me who had been with him in Ireland.

I gazed crestfallen at the dim brown watery plane. Perhaps he is right, but I never heard of duck flighting, or anything flighting except owls, bats and mosquitoes in the dark. I must wait and see. I had to, whether I liked it or not. The next thing he would have to be angry with would not be me, I resolved. He could take it out of the weather, or the stillness of the night. I will not make another remark for fear I might blurt out the word "Dawn." And that might suggest to him an all-night sitting; for he knew that he would not sleep well during the heat wave.

A moth or some insect was trying to land on my ear. I brushed it off. He heard the sound, "Hist!"

Ah well! I thought, it is better to be here by the quiet, the very quiet sea, than in Dublin with my guards who shoot each other and the furniture. But is it? If he heard my slightest movement, what will happen when he is shooting by ear? And though sideways, I am between him and the sea. It would be ironical if I were to escape from enemies in Dublin to be peacefully shot by a sporting friend. If my guards shoot each other it might be just my luck that my host should shoot his guest in the dark. If I could keep still it might not be so alarming. But I simply cannot sit still, wait for people, or stay still. I attribute this disease to being deprived for hours, when I was but a tiny boy, of freedom of movement, which in children is an additional appetite. Perched high up beside my father in his "mail phaeton," I was driven round while he visited patients.

And forbidden to clamber down, I had to sit still when the coachman took his place to walk the horses.

It must have been nearly two o'clock, when :

" No flighting ! They are waiting for a moon. Come along ! " There is not the least good in writing to George about this, I thought. My avenger must be Dunsany who will throng the air with feathers if I can get him invited for a shoot.

" In those days, Harry, the world was reclining on its elbow." I hastened to explain to the puzzled Harry that it was a figure of speech intended to call up the image of a patrician at a banquet or a statue of one of those river gods who lean on an urn from which water pours its beneficent gifts. I was reclining in an armchair in his father's excellent library. " Civilisation had reached the most distant lands to which the Peace of Rome had spread. There are very few periods in history wherein the peoples are aware of their good fortune. Augustan Rome was the Golden Age of the world as it was then. Slaves there were, and hostages, injustice and persecutions, forests were felled and roads were made and simple tribes conscribed ; but for the lords of creation prosperity was at its height. Augustus the Emperor, the Divine, the descendant of Venus through Aeneas (that is what the little dolphin means that follows in that statue at his heel, the Sea-born's son), was a mixture of Kitchener and the Archbishop of York, soldierly and sententious. He patronised the Arts. He listened patiently to deputations, addresses and the hexameters of his civil servants until he was rendered immune from insomnia for life. But there was one who made hexameters in a way that no one realised was possible in the Roman tongue. You would need to read Lucretius, who was his elder by years, to see with what easy grace and silver light Virgil had flooded his page when compared to that didactic atheist who preceded him. I cannot tell you whether Virgil was a great poet because it was a great period, or whether it was a great period because Virgil was a great poet. There are questions which do not admit of an answer because the fallacy lies in their being put at all.

" Virgil was a great poet because of his style, his lofty outlook and nobility of soul, and because of the Tiber-like flow and volume of his verse which reflected cultivated hills and stately towers.

" ' *Fluminaque antiquos subterlabentia muros.*'

" He came from the north of Italy where beech trees slope to a little stream that had as gentle a course as the Evenlode or the Windrush near Oxford.   I think it is better to imagine it as the Windrush, for it was ' crowned with vocal reeds.' And it must have flowed as gently as sweet Afton flows gently by its silver birches, for the very sound of the poet's name is gentle, not a rod to battle down the proud, but a wand to lean to all the winds and spread its leaves to airs it turned to sound.

" A man from the north meant something very different to Rome than it means to us.   From Scotland many poets have come.   Very few have come from Ulster to Dublin, because they have sold their souls for common-sense.   Facts are not the stuff out of which dreams or poems are made. There must be something far off and strange, ' fine translunary things,' as Ben Jonson has it, for the fabric of good verse. Something unworldly and even a little foolish.   Virgil was a dreamy man.   I think he had a little asthma and that he suffered from sinusitis.   He suffered from headaches and he preferred to live in the neighbourhood of Naples than in the skyscrapers of crowded Rome.   I can see him so distinctly ; tall, stooping a little like Shelley, but walking by no means so fast.   Shelley had a squeaky voice and his verse at best is somewhat strident.   Virgil's voice is always smooth, therefore he never hurried, and his utterance was low and soft."

" Won't you read me a few lines of the Eclogues ? "

" It is not necessary, my dear Harry, we should only bore each other, and a feeling of affectation would result.   We should never read poetry, we should make it.   I was put off from ever becoming a Latin scholar by having to read Latin.   Had someone told me about hexameters and the way their long lines went I would have read for myself. Now I know nothing of Latin, but I can talk of Virgil and so can you, provided you do not read him.   Parsers killed his poetry just as mediæval logicians killed the Logos, the Divine world of Reason with their mnemonic ' limericks,' Barbara, Celarunt, Darii !   The world forgot the Muses for eight hundred years. . . .

" Your father, by the way—where is he now ? "

" He will be back any minute.   He went to look after some eggs."

"Those paths by the sea, Harry, where do they go?"

"For miles along the coast."

"Will you show me them? I would like to go at once, if you don't mind. Bring a book along. . . .

"Can you bring it to your mind's eye? It was the greatest tragedy from which Humanity ever suffered. It was paralleled perhaps by the ruin in Russia; but in the darkness that fell on the world Virgil was not forgotten. He was given the only tribute ignorance and superstition can pay genius. He was regarded as a wizard. He became a kindly fiend. It was as if Shakespeare or Tennyson were forgotten and their pages turned to amulets or charms.

"Think of the greatest and most silenced betrayal in history: Rome's dereliction of British Romans. For four hundred years England had the privilege of being a greater Rome than Romulus's town. Her climate was better. The stature of her men was better. 'Sed Angeli' and she had the blending of many Northern races to fortify the South. In a day the legions are recalled. Girls engaged to noble Romans find their betrothals nullified. Hairy and horrible the Greater Scots burst in over Hadrian's Wall. They helped their kinsmen to ravage and to destroy. Never to rebuild or to replace. Mark that! Gardens were weeded over. The hypocausts or central heating systems which went under the floors came into light and were, later, taken to be, to your knees bared, 'journeys to Jerusalem.' Was there ever such a collapse? I stood with my friend Boni on the Palatine Hill on the floor of Nero's Golden House, and he showed me how in the Middle Ages pilgrimages to Jerusalem could be curtailed at Rome by shuffling on bare knees round an ancient central heater. Plumbing had caught the pilgrims.

"When our Heroic period consists of the destruction of the world's greatest civilisation, who can blame the attenuated resentment of our tribes?"

If I am not careful, I said to myself, I will end by making Harry regard literature as he must by this regard the stern discipline of sport. Let me leave at least one young person to forage for himself. "Where Helicon breaks down In cliffs to the sea."

We reached without interruption the resinous woods. To the right the upshot light of a silver sea. Harry led the way. He did not speak. He had been taught to be so

" observant " that the wide prospect and the revel of light and shade were to him blotted out.

" This is the kind of thing that gave Virgil his pensive, preoccupied and almost melancholy note. The necromancers put it down to a mood of prophecy. Prophecy of what ? Rome's ruin, nothing else. You might as well see in Tennyson a prophetic welcome for Lenin as in the fourth Eclogue an advance publicity notice for St. Paul."

Harry said : " Are you bored by stalking ? "

I reassured him. I had set aside Accidia. I had resolved to be full of gratitude.

" I just wanted to know how you will like a much bigger stalk to-morrow."

" Virgil," I said, giving myself time to pull myself together, " got that peculiar pensiveness of his from a realisation of the unintermittent war between civilisation and culture. Fell the woods, and what becomes of Pan, Sylvan and the Sister Nymphs ? Leave the woods and the barbarian threatens Rome. Simplicity against civilisation : civilisation a safeguard from contagious terror and taboo. ' Sunt lacrimæ rerum ' balanced by ' Tantum religio.' "

If one year's seniority at the University is unbridgeable, what must twenty-five years between pupil and tutor be ? And when the tutor is himself a pupil of the youth's father, authority goes for nothing. That is the way it should be. But how am I to get an inkling of the thoughts of youth ?

" It's one hundred yards from the last tunnel," Harry said, and Harry had been taught to be observant.

" If you must be observant, note how a grey cloud shadow becomes purple on the sea. And feel no deprivation because you are not in Sicily when you read about the ' Green and purple glow of Syracusan waters.' Only the blind, not the observant, count their steps."

Who tunnelled this solid rock to make a riviera ? Who planted the estate with magnificent forest trees ? Nobody observes them. I am aware of the many shades of green which make up to me in exquisite delight for the neglect and want of development of music within me. Is it not a sign of some sort of depravity to be moved overmuch by the shades of green ? Maybe, but the harmonies of the tones by which Spring astonishes my eyes are more to me, though transient, than all the vocable glories of everlasting noise.

If I sit by a little brook, Harry will not think that I am thinking of its significance in terms of trout.

" Let us sit here for a while and wait and see. There is nothing to see but that four-feet waterfall, and nothing to wait for but the thoughtlessness it brings."

If I in my youth resented rest, naturally this youth did too. How few are there who take their pleasure in looking for hours into the amber depths of a mountain torrent! But it brings me moods of mysticism—the transparent becoming visible, or serves as a reminder of the harnessed torrent of Pindaric verse.

" Why wouldn't you let me read Virgil ? " Harry asked after a pause.

" Because if you read other people's poetry you will write about it instead of making your own. It is not poetical to write about poetry. You become second-hand and easily dated. Europe has not as yet recovered from the Renaissance, nor has English poetry recovered from Alexander Pope.

" We might go hunting in the village for living words, words such as those with which the tramp in Kylemore hailed your mother's house. ' It's a fine still place you have here, Ma'am, surely.' Remember it was near one of these Isles that *Aiken Drum* was written, and that poem contains more live poetry than any pastoral verse I have read. The goblin Aiken Drum promises to ' Ba the bairns wi' an unkenned tune.' Now, that's what poetry is, ' an unkenned tune,' not a repeated air. And listen : ' Last night I dreamed a dreary dream beyond the Isle of Skye.' That is beyond what was Ultima Thule to the Scots poet, beyond the edge of the known world where the Land of Dream begins. We are nearer Ultima Thule here than we ever were before. Magnificence amid mountains islanded and for the pettiness of Life no care. Your father stalks like Achilles on the island of his translation. And I feel just about as much at ease as if I were spending a week-end in his tent."

Next morning I was reclining on both elbows in the library which was marked " Private " but not sound-proof, and I heard the loud command,

" Stalking ! "

I read no more that day in the book.

Three hours later, after almost subterranean creeping

through the deepest and narrowest dykes, we emerged into sun and dryness on a hill. A little hill fifty feet or so high and separated from its fellow by a valley eighty yards in width. The position lacked humour and was even too heavy for sport. I was under a cloud, and I had to wait until it burst. What had I done ? Whatever I did, must have been done before the morning of the present day, for the stalk began under penalising rules. The deer were evidently wilder and more alert than ever in their career. We lay without talking for half an hour on the hill. Mine host's flask, which he had invented so that its covers, becoming separate, made two drinking-vessels instead of one, was almost empty. The air was full of midges, which were spiteful and had constantly to be repulsed. Under a rock-roofed ledge half-way up on the opposite hill ' royals ' were lying down. The head and antlers of the first were plainly visible, which meant that he could see us if we showed. The second and third had only antlers visible. In a corner where the rock sloped so that it was hard to rise if startled, lay a fourth stag with a very poor head, a " switch." He lay back in the dark recess of the rock. His companions were full in daylight but out of the sun.

" Surely," I asked as I smacked a midge, " they will get up if the flies keep on pestering them ? "

" Put in your cuffs and turn up your collar, or you will frighten the hinds which are over there about a mile away."

I obeyed.

" If you give me the gun—rifle, I can get a close-up if I slip ten feet down the valley so that the first stag cannot see me. I then can walk straight over the rest of the way."

" There are no valleys in a deer forest."

He drained his flask, and ten minutes later added :

" Only corries." Later, after an equal interval :

" And no ' close-ups.' "

" Sorry," I said, " I am totally ignorant."

" Only too evident."

Perhaps this was a part of the training of a hunter, to irritate him so that he should be able to shoot even with his temper frayed. It may be a means of obtaining the equivalent of the fatigue of a long vigil. If I have to slap another fly my cuff will appear. The hinds will be startled, and then good-bye to the stags. It must be worse, I brooded, in the swamps of Africa where they temper the Cyprian extravaganzas of their chieftains by exposure to mosquito bites. But any hunting megalomania that may have threatened me is already anticipated and cured in advance. I am humbled in the presence of the Laird. If I lie on my face and bury it in the grass I can cover my ears with my hands and so avoid the pests.

I could not have fallen asleep; but I evidently had not heard some whispered command. He kicked the rifle towards me: " Have your close-up."

Head-first I slid at an imperceptible pace, not daring to look up until I had descended twenty feet. I marked the dark rock and its two tufts of heather. Then, rising, I walked briskly towards the ledge and began to climb. It was at an awkward height, with a shelf about the height of a mantel-piece beneath. As I was wondering how to mount it unheard, a loud voice just behind me said, " Remember your beast is lying down." There was not a moment to be lost. With one hand I grasped the rock above the mantel-shelf, and with rifle under my arm, made a leap. But the stags were startled, all but the one hampered by the rocky roof. He stuck against it as he scrambled to his knees just as I got a moment's equilibrium in which to pull the trigger of the rifle that touched his charging breast. It must have seemed as if a shot had gone off accidentally in the air, to anyone who saw me rolling down the corrie after the stags, who were already two hundred yards away.

My host was exultant. " Ho! Ho! Ho! So you thought they were tame, did you? You see where they are now."

I sat where I was and wiped the grass-stained stock. The cloud was bursting. I had called them *tame*!

" Let me tell you something. You thought it was all beer and skittles, deer-stalking. Now perhaps you realise that it is the sport which requires more skill than many outdoor sports. It is a very difficult science. Every one misses a stag now and then. King Edward missed his beast and had his stags driven, thereby ruining his forest. My very good friend the Duke of Leeds missed six and he actually wept."

" Am I supposed to break into tears ? "

" Certainly not, but you are supposed to acknowledge that you thought it was too easy. You should have said,

' Clifton, I am very sorry, but I got buck fever and consequently missed.' "

" Buck fever ? "

" Yes, over-excitement in the presence of the quarry which makes a fellow lose his head."

" But I assure you that I killed the stag. Not any of the ' royals,' but one you could well spare."

" Lie number one."

" I am not in the habit of lying gratuitously, as I will say to fit in with the estimate you seem to have of me. I have nothing to gain or to lose."

" Lie number two. You have your lack of moral courage to conceal."

" Dammit! I only did what you told me to do—have a close-up. If I had missed, it would have been worse, for you would have thought that your teaching was wasted on a ham-handed ass."

" Lie number three. I never told you to shoot from your hip like a German shock trooper."

I could feel the slow anger rising which floods the brain until reason is drowned and the irrational instincts are set free. Thus it appeared to me that I had been deliberately taken out to be made to miss, to be shown up—that it had been taken for granted that I was a vain coxcomb, proud and presumptuous at another man's expense.

But it is all very easy and sometimes self-indulgent to yield to anger. How will I appear to my wife and family if I return no longer on speaking terms with my host?

And how am I to stand on my dignity and borrow at the same time the means of transport? There is not a car to be hired on the island, and it is seven miles to the nearest port.

While I was about to cast decency to the winds in spite of the fact that my host was breathing heavily in anger and to let resentment loose at what seemed an abuse of hospitality as a trap, an *ex machina* gillie appeared.

" Me Laird, the stag is dead ! "

" How ? Where ? What ? "

" Aboon your head."

He looked up. The tawny throat lay limply upside down from the shelf of rock.

" Oh ! "

A sudden thought.

" Go and see how long it is dead."

" Ye can see the blood oozing the noo ! "

I pitied the spoilt man-child now. He stood flabbergasted.

" Ho," he said to himself and " Ho ! " again. I could not be separated from the slaughter. Lie number one was no lie. And those arising from the assumption no lies.

I hate being witness to anyone's embarrassment. I tried to walk away. I handed in my " gun " slowly to the gillie. I walked, as I had told Harry I thought Virgil must have walked, with the natural sorrow that is at the heart of all things on his shoulders.

Buck fever, indeed ! What had Clifton now ? Increased irritation with me for putting him in the wrong.

" At any rate you'll acknowledge that it is the sport of kings," at length he said.

" No," I said, " I will not. King Edward ruined his forest according to you."

On reaching the Castle he yelled for my wife. She failed to appear. He shouted for his own. She appeared immediately. Mine appeared soon after to inquire what it was all about.

Round the circular plot in front of the hall we went, careful not to overtake each other. I tried to explain. I could see by his back that he was denouncing my duplicity and unworthiness.

" And could you not have humoured him, you who know him so well ? "

" Yes. But what would he think of his teaching if his pupil bungled ? "

" You say that he wanted you to bungle so that he might demonstrate to you the results of over-confidence."

" He certainly did."

" I have no patience with you ! "

" I am leaving to-morrow."

The dressing-bell relieved our restrained stalking.

Again, the munificence in the dining-hall. But we spoke in whispers, overshadowed by the guilt of my success.

" Imperial Tokay since the war is unobtainable," I ventured to remark.

" Makenzie ! The cellar keys, a tumbler, and a torch." Me, he summoned with : " Come along."

The Castle must have been built on an old foundation. The cellars extended far underground. At last through tunnels we reached an over-arched shelf. Ten or twelve squat flasks—Imperial Tokay!

"My cousin Esterhazy kept some for me. Here's your very good health."

He looped his finger round the neck of another bottle and swung it as he moved along. It was broached in the dining-room.

"My mother," he announced, "never realised that a child was born to her who had the making of a most excellent flautist. She discouraged my music, and my flute-playing never got a chance. And I could have been a rather out-standing. . . . Ho! I bet you don't even know the word for one who is proficient on the flute?"

Although he had just said it, I said, "No. I don't." (Lie number one!)

"Well, then! Let me tell you, and you boys remember this—it's 'Flautist.'"

To the butler he said, "Bring me my golden flute."

A case, like one of those which contain fish slicers, was presented. It opened and disclosed two golden tubes. These he screwed together and began to play.

"Will you play upon this pipe?"

I determined that I would be the most perfect failure he had ever triumphed over, even if I were to be drawn like Marysias from my sheath of skin. I put one end to my mouth. Luckily, not a sound. "My Laird, I cannot."

"I pray you."

"Believe me, I cannot. I know no touch of it."

"It's not a tin whistle. See here! 'Tis as easy as lying. Govern these ventings with your finger and give it breath with your mouth and it will discourse most excellent music. Lookey, here are the stops." He set it sideways and fluted a few notes. "Now try."

I tried, making sure that not a note would escape.

"Why are you sticking your tongue into the stop?"

"To get out some of the Imperial Tokay you blew into it just now."

He was on his feet instantly, with the flask and an apology as he brimmed my glass. After all, I was his guest.

"My friend, I am very, very sorry."

Surely I took my "fill of deep and liquid rest forgetful of all ill."

He expanded imperially and told us how he discovered

the Yukon gold before the money-grabbers, and inestimable wealth in iron on an Hebridean property his men of business would not allow him to buy.

I have met some of the world's greatest men.   If I dared to interfere with the march of death, I would like to petition that fell sergeant for leave for a hunt again with Talbot Clifton.

With what a problem would we not be presented were it given to us to bring back one or two of the dead!   Would we choose from the throng of the world's great shadows or of our relatives and friends?   It would depend very much on how recent was our sorrow.   Immediately on the death of a relative or friend, or some great personage, we might be tempted to exercise our gift of recall.   But given time to recover from grief and to think, we would not be so hasty, having philosophised.   It comes to this then, that Time justifies everything, even its own outrages.

What would it avail to recall Julius Cæsar from the dead? His work was done and Time's procreant waters rose and made it fruitful.   How could he, who hardly knew the direction in which he set its sources, deal with the majestic river's emerging deltas?   If those who were to be redeemed from beyond the irremediable river were to be, not only aware of all they caused to grow, but to be held responsible for two thousand years of Time's trend and magnification, would the recall even of Pontius Pilate from the dead to-day be fair or just to Pontius Pilate?

This means that only our contemporaries or friends still unforgotten might be given the benefit of our gift of resurrection.   But would an heir recall his father to his own disinheriting, and to the double death of his parent?   Would Lloyd George recall Haig, or the British Navy, Nelson?

The only recall I can think of without hesitation as desirable has been imagined 2300 years ago.   The recall to her orphaned children of the young mother, Alcestis.   It is not quite so safe to recall an infant dedicated to death.   A foot-bound child exposed whom a shepherd found, came to but little good from his rescuing.   But the younger mother whose breast grows cold to her infant's fingers, appears to present the tragedy of tragedies to me who am loth to tamper with Time or teach the prophetic world its business.

I can only pray that Time will match its step to its funeral march and teach its striplings slowly.

It was no use. I am not born to the purple. Like the girl in Bobbie Burns' lyric who

> " Wadna hae a laird,
> Wadna be a leddy
> But she would hae a collier
> The colour of her daddy,"

I could not be a laird or stalk beyond my walk in life contentedly.

CHAPTER XV

I RECONCILED MYSELF TO FALL BACK ON MYSELF, SO I PRACTISED my profession for a while in London.

Often I stood aside and looked at its ordered greatness. A city is the face wherein a nation's character may be read. Disciplined might and millions organised! " Make no mistake," Tom Kettle used to say, " the English have organisation! " Here was Freedom visibly being founded, apportioned and assured. The queues outside each theatre witnessed to this order, as their humour and their patience witnessed to their goodwill.

London is a university with ten million graduates qualified to live and let live. And the use of the English language makes all nations undergraduates to this Freedom. " At a great price purchased! " . . . But I was born free.

There is no poll tax on newcomers to this town, this navel stone of civilisation. No charge for protection against molestation or robbery. The *Pax Britannica* safeguards all. How many " nationals " who had sought to overthrow her order were glad to seek Great Britain's sanctuary in the end ?

And here was I, an Irish Nationalist all my life, " on my keeping " not in the Glens of Wicklow or Connemara but in the neighbourhood of Mayfair.

When working to restore Ireland to nationhood, I should have ascertained first what a restored Ireland's idea of a nation was likely to be. Would it give leave to live to all its nationals ? Would its idea of freedom be universal or restricted to a gang ? When working to release Kathleen, the daughter of Houlihan, so long imprisoned by the Sassenach, I should have asked myself what sort of soured harridan was likely to emerge. Would her long incarceration not have perverted her and made warders and turnkeys and worse warders the fancy men of her free choice ? Had Freedom dazed her?

Too late! Kathleen was out, and she was quickly picked up by those men who knew her for a jail-bird, being themselves so apt for prison service.

Thank God none knew me for a patriot here in London! I could walk without a guard. But walking without a guard did away with a Senator's identity. It was as if a barrister had lost his umbrella. I found this out when I called on Lord Granard at Forbes House. He wanted to hear my news. So I walked round to Halkin Street, but the dark iron gates were closed, and it took a long time for his detectives to believe that I was I. Lord Granard was a Senator too, and it was a Senator's privilege to be escorted! Unescorted, so much the less Senator he!

I had no news, only that *The Field* had an account of what had happened to me and a stag in the Isle of Islay.

" You know my Galway house is burned ? "

" They have exploded a bomb in the hall of Castle Forbes. I do not yet know how much damage has been done."

We were partners in affliction. Our country was afflicting itself into a republic of ruin where all that is outstanding is levelled to the ground.

Next to the Percy and the Douglas families, I would like to be one of the Forbës' Clan, for they are mentioned in the Border Ballads. And I cannot even as yet bring myself to believe that anyone can be any good who is not mentioned in Song. The poetic predilection in me is more ineradicable than the poetic licence.

The best families of England and Scotland and even of Ireland are ballad Worthies. " Colonel Hugh O'Grady is now lying dead and low "—gone with the Wild Geese!

But listen first to the record of the great swordsman of Lord Granard's family, the family of Forbës :

> The first ae stroke MacDonald struk
> He gart the Forbës reel;
> The first ae stroke that Forbës struk
> The great MacDonald fell.

The measure of the man is not felt until his loss! He is great because his fall has great consequences: Leaving Forbës greater still.

Yes, the place mentioned in the ballad is still in the possession of the Forbës family. They could not become families, nor retain their hold, had they not had the physique and prowess of the sword. Greater the Forbës proved themselves than the Lords of the Isles—Halkin Street houses a branch of the family whose chief was victorious because he was the first to recover from a blow.

As for England, I can see the plumes swinging in the press of the verse as the knights swayed in the battle riot.

Suffolk his axe did ply;
Beaumont and Willoughby
Bare them right doughtily
Ferrers and Fanhope.

" By the way, would you care to see the dining-room ?
His Majesty is dining here to-night."

I pulled myself up sharply.   There I had been off again
with my babble about great verse; and my addiction to
monologuing the conversation without ascertaining whether
my listeners cared for verse, or rather for my gratuitous
recitations and sound-intoxications.

" Yes.   Of course!   I would very much.   Sorry for so
much talking."

We entered the great dining-room.   Sixty places; golden
plate again, fit for a king !

And then I thought of a lonely kingly man, striding about
a far Northern island companionless, who had spread his
plate of gold for me.   Gladly, if he wished it, would I give
a few years of life to revive Talbot Clifton at the expense of
my own expectation of life.   The measure of a man is not
felt until his loss.

CHAPTER XVI

JOSEPH CHAMBERLAIN MAY NEVER HAVE STOOD "STIFF IN stour" like a Forbës or a "campion" in the battle dust; but he dealt in steel and founded a fortune which gave him respite to found an Empire. I was dining with his son.

Of all the men I have met no one stands more clearly and simply to my mind than Austen Chamberlain. Because his simplicity needs no conjuring from the memory's shadows, there is nothing dim about him. He is the finest and most forthright spirit I have ever had the luck to meet. Upright, blond, with an odd sweeping gesture of his arm, he says his say with assurance. His father's greatness was his prerogative but not his privilege. He is great in his own right and in his own way. And that is the grandest way ever a man had. Right and simple and unswerving. His honesty is contagious. We talked of anything but Irish politics. In the middle of dinner someone who directed the *Times* came in. He was scolded in a way that elsewhere might be turned to party advantage, but no one could betray his host's sheer faith in the common honesty of men. He made what statements he had to make subject to no conditions. In any other country they might have been made the subject of a "Stop Press" and the fodder for the curious upsetting indiscretions. The grandeur of the man lifted all about him above pettiness. No need for Wellingtonian "Publish and be damned." You were damned in your own estimation if you ever entertained the thought of taking an advantage of his expression of opinion.

He told me of his early years, of the time he spent in Germany and in France. I saw his father's ambition for him justified as largely as his own life had justified and fulfilled that lofty patriotism.

The story of Arthur Griffith self-consumed by his indomitable and unswerving purpose, of his abject want and his refusals of wealth and notoriety, astonished him. Later he paid him the tribute which is now historical. "He was the most courageous man I ever met." He said it with solemn assurance. He who had met the most outstanding persons of our generation said Arthur Griffith was the most courageous. I have met not a few in my day. But one of the grandest human beings I ever have met is Sir Austen Chamberlain.

In the cool of the night dominated by Westminster Cathedral, I said to myself: Now what have I done? I have dined with a ruler of England, therefore I have become a traitor of course, a spy consequently, and a betrayer of what?— A betrayer of the Bog of Allen. The residence attributed to Brian O'Lynn. I will go down to history as the man who betrayed Brian O'Lynn and the O'Lynn idea of Ireland! But will there be any history for that? Will the pigmies ever forgive me when they hear that I have met a man? I cannot pretend that I am greatly concerned. But is it not sad to think that even if they had their dreams, such as they are, and their ambitions, such as they are, fulfilled an hundredfold, never could they imagine a man in all their Utopias equal to, or even to be compared with, Austen Chamberlain. What's wrong with us? There's something rotten in Rathangan.

I walked secure through the silent city as if I were in a pleasant park, released from alertness, thinking of the magnanimity of governing souls such as Austen Chamberlain's, whose material expression is strong and established peace.

Never had I kept an engagement book, for the simple reason that I had no engagements which I could not hold in my head. But now many names and unfamiliar addresses needed tablets for my memory.

Once a traitor always a traitor, so I might as well dine with Lady Lavery and take the risk of the fact being distorted in my country. Everyone who dines in London is a traitor in Dublin nowadays. This will go on for a few years until the traitor-setters themselves become entertained and so traitors in their turn and a new set of unfeasted appears. It is like the " orgy " which I have defined before.

I sat on the left of Lord Birkenhead. He was commiserating gently with himself for the ten years he had been a Don at Oxford. He had worked hard. I said, " And you walked hard." He held the record for the walk from Oxford to London. A great athletic figure. One of those natural athletes who require no training—in fact, who seem to thrive in spite of indulgence. He had risen to great prominence against all the rules. Turmoil helped him, but he was there to seize " glittering prizes " and not to suffer. He was an example of what happens only once in a century, the Rake becoming a success. Caius Julius Cæsar and Pitt were his antecedents. When a rake succeeds why is it that most of us are secretly gladdened? It does me good to think of its ingredients. And why? Because we feel that his humanity is not sacrificed to success. It is like the award of the Garter or a prize in the Irish Sweep. That is one reason why Galloper Smith, Lord Birkenhead, High Steward of Oxford University, Lord Chancellor of England, endeared himself to his friends. He was not the first to make Ulster a springboard to the Woolsack. The art of politics is to get some sort of prejudice in your favour; and for prejudice what place was ever more exploitable than Ulster?

I admired the way he kept his figure without exercise. I loved the way he filled and emptied his glass: no half measures about it. He laughed heartily at Dr. Tyrrell's remark when the unnecessarily inquisitive waiter who, instead of bringing " whiskey drinks for two " forthwith, stayed, ruining business, to ask and to make a guest self-conscious, " Large or small? "

" Get this into your head. There is no such thing as a *large* whiskey."

" You have had a pretty strenuous time? "

" In Scotland, yes. In Ireland it lacked humour."

" Like the lady on your left."

The 'lady on my left' was the wife of a Continental Ambassador who had been insistently cross-examining his Lordship.

" Don't you think Winchester is the best school in England? "

" I do not."

He rotated his 'balloon' glass, which held half a pint of brandy, leaving no room for the aroma. He raised it to his lips. His left elbow nudged me as the lady again put him to the question. " Horrible," he said.

" After all, you must admit that the best men in England were at school there."

" Name one."

" Mr. Asquith."

" Who happens not to have been there."

" Perhaps it was someone else."

" I should not be at all surprised."

" But don't you think I ought to send my son there? "

In judgment: " If you wish to stereotype mediocrity, I do." And there an end.

" There's not much use in drinking sherry at this time of night," he remarked.

That puzzled me. Could he be under the impression that his brandy was sherry, or had the butler been under orders to replace the lighter for the stronger drink?

Napoleonic brandy! There is some at every well-regulated board, so much indeed that it is easy to see why Napoleon had such a victorious career—half Europe must have been making brandy. There is no Napoleonic vodka. As soon as he clashed with countries who were not absorbed in labelling his name for posterity, he met with reverses. Who ever heard of Wellingtonian brandy? Beer was his Waterloo.

His pallor increased as he drank, as if it were an outward sign of the cold clarity of his mind.

He was a sentence-maker, not an epigrammatist or even a *diseur*: Isocrates!

"So you chose Wuggins when you went to Oxford probably because they acted *Comus* in its gardens. It is what I would expect you to do."

"I only went to Oxford because I was not clever enough for Trinity, Dublin, as Mahaffy said of Oscar Wilde."

"What's that about Mahaffy?"

"He said, ' My dear Oscar, you are not clever enough for us in Dublin. You had better run over to Oxford.' "

He smiled as if thinking of some severe remark.

"Mahaffy! Do you tell me so?"

From the way he said ' Mahaffy ' it dawned on me that he was at least as familiar with him as with Jowett, whom he did not revere. Mahaffy is better known in Oxford than in College Green. Again his glass was filled! No wine could o'er-crow his reason.

"Why he stayed on in Dublin is a mystery," he remarked. "Why? Can you enlighten me?"

I suggested that a Fellowship in T.C.D. brought more immediate emolument and promised more in the end without chopping and changing than any comparable post in Oxford.

"But Mahaffy?" he objected.

"He is Provost. He has been knighted. What Fellow in Oxford can be knighted without being benighted first?"

Again the Foreign Ambassador's wife leant across me and tried to catch his attention. He was not to be diverted.

"There is a lot to be said for Dublin according to Mahaffy, as a step-ladder to social success. He may have been ironical, but he used to say to Oscar Wilde, ' Now you have been to Greece, go over to London and tell them all about it.' "

" And he did, too literally, perhaps," mused Lord Birkenhead.

He contemplated his glass, thinking of God knows what. His mind was leaving the room. I remembered his quotation of Lloyd George earlier in the evening.

" There is no slump of Dukes in this house. Their two ' Graces ' Sutherland and Argyll at the head of the table."

" The third, of course, being our hostess ? "

" Yes. That is what I meant to say."

But the question about a slump in Dukes brought Lloyd George into the conversation again.

" Have you met him ? "

" No."

" You should meet him, he . . ."

" I would rather not," I said, " I am over here convalescing from Celts."

" What are you convalescing from ? " asked the central Grace, our hostess.

" Celts of all denominations."

Their Graces were silent as the Dreadnoughts to which the Welsh solicitor had compared them, who had begun by disparaging England's foundations and then rushing, when self-advertised and successful, to the maintenance of all for which England stood. It would sicken me had I not had experience of the " codology," as we call it in Dublin, of politicians ; and a conviction of the soundness of that Romulan system which can enlist with impunity all sorts and conditions to its preservation.

" He did a great deal for the Empire," said Birkenhead.

" It is for what he didn't do that I don't want to meet him."

" What was that ? "

" Let one of your own countrymen answer." I quoted from a friend's great verse :

> " Chiefly to-day in *this*
> Your mastery towers—that you forbear to stir
> A finger, while your missions fierce and fell
> Shatter doomed Ireland's homes and build in her
> A suburb of the great metropolis
> Of evil and woe, whose name on earth is Hell."

He listened, greatly impressed. At last cross-examining :
" An Englishman ? "

" Yes, one of the greatest left, Sir William Watson."

" Are there any Englishmen in England ? "

" I am one," said Birkenhead.

" Yes, but let us examine that.   Cuchulainn, the Hero of Ulster, its Achilles, came from the Mersai tribe who dwelt on the banks of the Mersey about Liverpool.   He was called the Hound of the Smith, and the Smiths were honoured in the Ireland of those days, that is 1500 years ago.   And you cannot deny that it was in Ulster recently that you made your name."

Dinner at the Laverys' brought you into the company of persons of incalculable importance.   An house which was welcomed as an unofficial meeting-place for rebel and ruler was of inestimable use and service to both sides—Ireland and England.   Without it what is the picture?   Mr. Collins makes his statement to the powers that be, and is answered with all the stiffness which such statements must have for the followers who put each side into power by utterances.   Formal, public, inelastic, irrevocable.   But at 5, Cromwell Place men could meet as human beings beyond the scent of herded wolves, and exchange views and reveal difficulties.   Arthur Griffith was grateful for this accommodation, as once under less important circumstances he was grateful to me.   The Laverys did more to bring about a settlement than all the weary official and overlooked weeks at Hans Place.

No one can call me a spy to-night even though I have dined with two Dukes, an Earl, Knights, and a few Excellencies.   No!   A useful clearing-house for " obscurities."   Griffith was grateful and so was Collins.   And they were not spies.   Well, that's that!   But what is this I heard O'Higgins said: " I laid my guns at Lavery's only to find that the targets were shifted."

When a guest is not a spy, the hostess must be, to satisfy the inordinate suspicion of a primitive tribe.   Lady Lavery as a spy!   O'Higgins was as suspicious as that famous member of the police force he helped to create, who when a puny little Frenchman inquired during the war (when every foreigner was a spy) the way to Westland Row, took his pronunciation of English for French ; but as nothing should be beyond the purview of a Dublin Metropolitan policeman, he answered him in a set of three wonderful enigmas which concealed ignorance of everything but of the fact that a question was being asked.

"You don't know?"

"You could never tell?"

"And what would you be after doing if you did?"

And thinking of spies, I thought of how different a spy had been sent in the old days of Dublin Castle's detectives' rule to trap Arthur Griffith. We had been in the Bailey one night, where Griffith met Hubert Murphy with:

"Hello, Hubert! Where have you come from?"

"I was on holidays in a country where there was no income tax."

"There should be none here!" said Griffith, reaching for his hat. It was eleven o'clock.

Boyd-Barrett, Griffith and I had got as far as the Provost's Wall, when a well-spoken young woman accosted us: "Good-night, Mr. Griffith!" Evidently she did not know him, for it was to Boyd-Barrett she made the remark. Griffith jerked himself forward with "Come on, boys! Take no notice! Dublin Castle is on to me!"

We walked in silence, pondering the infamy of Dublin Castle that could employ forgers like Pigott and an unknown prostitute indiscriminately. A prostitution in face of the rule of Queen Victoria. Suddenly as we crossed Earl Street at the foot of the great Pillar from the top of which the admiral took the midnight watch, the silence was broken by a woman with a broad Cockney accent.

"Oh, Alliver, that waistcoat of yours saved me and the choild!"

It was somewhat embarrassing. Quickly I pulled myself together and got rid of the encumbrance.

"Take no notice, boys. Scotland Yard is after me!"

"Good-night!" said Griffith gruffly, and left us standing.

"Dammit!" I said to Joe Boyd-Barrett. "Am I to have no political significance at all?"

"So that's what became of your gold-buttoned waist-coat?"

CHAPTER XVII

I SAID TO MY HEART: DON'T YOU REMEMBER WHEN YOU promised to compensate yourself for a self-centred and sensuous talk with Tim Healy's lady guests by an intellectual discussion with Yeats, only to find that he was concentrated still more on the self-same theme, you resolved never to fall from the frying-pan—and so on? And yet you fell. By that disappointment, resolve never more to have to do with Dukes or Earls or grandees, so much the less traitor you shall be. The notice in my appointments book gave promise of respite. "Call at 5 p.m." It was near the top of Park Lane.

I called at five o'clock.

Mine hostess said hastily: "They arrived rather early. They don't usually come until everybody is going away. They are two Crown Princesses. Don't speak until they speak to you: no politics, no local topics, no cosmetic themes and so on. Blond and buxom. Very attractive."

"I am. Yes! Quite so. Only three months. Even in spite of autumn fogs. Not so bad! Hospitable. I agree."

I was getting on famously, even though my best-laid scheme for not meeting any more notable people was going somewhat agley.

"His Royal Highness, the Duke of Connaught!"

"Bow lower than ordinarily and only call him ' Sir.' "

A tall, spare, active, blue-eyed, soldierly figure entered the room. His presence, instead of embarrassing, put everyone at their ease. He nodded then, and took a seat. "Who is this?"

I was introduced. I bowed low and named myself.

"You are from Dublin. When I was in command in the Curragh, Nanetti was Lord Mayor." Faultless memory summoned instantaneously.

"What do you say? Eighteen holes of golf to-day and three hours in the saddle. What do you say?"

"You are threatened with immortality, Sir!" No restraint. Days later at lunch, the genius of the Duke revealed itself. How can such things be translated to those who have lost, or have never known the grammar of greatness? Something better than ourselves!

There must be something if not of the courtier, then at

243

least of the flunkey, in my composition. I like to have people better than myself about me. They radiate on me a security similar to that Julius must have felt when he had men about him of his own liking. Every Irishman loves an aristocrat. In all the sagas of Erin there is not the name of a commoner mentioned. Even the charioteers were noblemen. Let my critics digest that. Anyway, I dearly love a Lord, and I think I can analyse the reason : he stands for an established order of things, for an household of continuance with the obligations its traditions confer. " The men who dare not be afraid," for there is no spot on earth that can hide a disgraced member of a noble English family. There is the knowledge that they, like kings, seldom have any selfish or personal interest in mundane affairs. Their axes were ground long ago. They can be trusted not to lower others in order to gain height themselves. Long ago they " bare them right doughtily " ; and, stock-raisers as we are, we Irish, believe in good blood.

Not only do my countrymen believe as I do that there is something innate in noble beings that may not be achieved fortuitously—Pindar had a faith much like it—but it is borne out by the fact that they cannot do themselves justice if far removed from the inspirers of their chivalry. They must not be separated far from their springs of valour, which are in their case the aristocrats, their superior officers. Blame me not at all or as much as you like when I honestly betray what may not be called a weakness in me, but a yearning towards the better than myself, to the " Beyond Man."

If Irishmen cannot fight but fail the further they are removed from their aristocrats, how should I be blamed who appraise and honour this ideal of great men ? When you find Irishmen taking up arms for " Labour," look to some outside instigator. You will not find the warriors who loved to follow the inspiration and example of their breed's best, casting all to the winds for an increase of wages.

The nearer they are to their own superiors the better is their battle. The cause matters not so much as the Captain. And is not this as it should be ? When you review the world's long wars, the motive, the reason for them, even the justice of them, succumb before the personality of the leaders. The victorious Captain makes his own political good and evil. Victory engenders Justice.

These thoughts increased my admiration all the more for

the soldierly, indomitable figure, which was upheld so upright by the unbreakable spirit of the Uncle of the King.

"Threatened with immortality?" he said a few days later as if nothing and nobody in his crowded hours had, meanwhile, intervened. "That could be such a threat!" In a few words he left me to consider the philosophical implications of my spontaneous remark.

What a kill-joy is a scientific training! What is called "observance" becomes a form of observation shortly removed from spying. I was taught to observe. And I cannot lose that lowly second sight. To me the gestures of the Duke as he sat at the table bespoke more than even his terse and considered words. He had what beauty seldom companions, and that is Grace. Even the movement of raising his glass seemed more like a dispensation than a personal movement. Every gesture suggests largesse. I was shocked and stilled by the realisation that his intimates about him were as blind to these things as he himself was unaware of them. How far I am removed from intimacy with greatness may well be guessed. Else how could I have sat observing?

But how uplifted I am now that I am near to that which I recognise as better than myself! Far be it from me to suggest that my reason for leaving Dublin was that I could not find anyone better than myself, but who in Dublin could make me feel as exalted as I am now? A Republic will make me feel about as lively as a recital of its Soldier's Song. I must have "a kingdom for a stage, princes to act"! Here is a soldier who can make a nation sing, 'God save our gracious King!'

But too much hero-worship is bad for the worshipper. It makes him lean his weight upon the hero at the cost of his own responsibility and power of initiative. Wait a moment, I assured myself, and I shall recover and contradict myself.

If the Irish warriors saw something of themselves in their chieftains, if like seeks like, what have I in common with two princesses whom it is not permissible to address? And they, poor creatures, are losing the best gossip in the town. Out upon it! I will call upon my friend Augustus John. There's a name for you like a fiat of creation. Something accomplished, something pat, something John. "John" suggests the last stroke of a hammer dulled on a malleable metal; a foundation stone laid, the blow of a mace.

Through the "long slum" of Ebury Street, "where I

live "—so George Moore described it to annoy Lady Ebury —I walked and passed Moore's house, 121. I knew that he was in its warm old rose room, but the hour was too early. The last time I called about this hour he kept me waiting ten minutes. "I had to keep you waiting until the strain of composition had faded from my face." I will visit him, I resolved, on my way back—that is, if I ever come back from calling on Augustus John.

I found the bell of the flat oaken door. "Yes, Sir, he is in." I descended to the great studio. In an alcove he sat brooding, great-headed, golden-bearded—Leonardo da Vinci!

The aura of the man! The mental amplitude! He raised his hand in welcome. In silence I sat down. I must wait for him to speak. . . . Now what kind of majesty is that I have "escaped" into, I wondered, if, even in Chelsea, I am not allowed to talk? It is the majesty of genius. I could feel its force and the force of him in the room. And never since the athletes of Olympia has there been a man of such beautiful stature. Tisdall, the Wicklow athlete, is as well built, but John has grace concealing strength. I thought of that great lyrist, the lover of athletes:

"Yet, withal, we have somewhat in us like unto the Immortals, bodily shape or mighty mind." Augustus John has both.

"Have a drink!"

So the jury within him had reported favourably on my case and he had decided. I felt somehow that it would have been just as appropriate had he said:

"Get out!"

The pleasant business of the glasses—sweet bells jingled into tune for minds that are not harsh—and the gay gurgling! I revived. I was about to break, not exactly into song, but into speech, when he forestalled me with:

"Over here for long?"

"I don't know. I cannot make up my mind. London with its law and order sometimes chokes me. There are three or four people too many in it. It takes an hour to drive to the edge of it, and then I find that the countryside is almost as much built on."

"Come to Alderney and stay with me."

"Now, that is an idea. I will drive you down any day," I said. "I hate inhaling exhaust fumes and seeing everyone getting yellower and yellower. Besides, I don't like the hard water over here."

" Neither do I."

He pushed the bottles in my direction and suddenly his cheeks islanded themselves in an exceedingly genial smile. The smile of Augustus John can only be compared to that of the All-Father on Ida's summit when Love and Sleep conspired.

In mid studio the great portrait of Madame Suggia stood. Her rounded right arm slanted across the canvas to her cello. What an advantage the painter has over the poet! He can make his dreams visible! They are there for all to see. He who has an eye to see will see more. Like a rain-maker he can manifest the power of his soul, the power of his creative imagination, independent of languages and the abuse of words. But the poet needs happy moments, leisure and sophistication amongst his readers. Second sight compared to the Vision Splendid!

And yet I feel that, master without compare though he is of his medium, his medium cannot carry away the torrent of his imagination. He needs another outlet for the swollen streams from the mountains of his thought. Poetry? He has written poems. But only one poem in the world is fit to be attributed to the fire within his mighty heart. And no one knows who wrote it—The Red Haired Man's Wife

> But the Day of Doom shall come
> The earth and the harbours be rent . . .

Augustus John's inexhaustible force!

It was very pleasant, this bathing in the glory of Augustus. I felt myself growing so witty that I was able to laugh at my own jokes. To think that they spelt Sherry with an ' X ' in Spain. " Xeres." Absurd! Just as absurd as the people in Dublin who persist in calling Guinness's Double X Guy-niss Twenty! I was thinking of the Tommy Atkins I heard in the railway restaurant at Crewe who ordered " A Guy-niss Twenty, Miss."

" Why do you call it a ' Guy-niss Twenty ' ? "

" Aw, Oi don't call it. They calls it that, I suppose, because it supports you twenty times longer than any other beer."

" In Dublin we call it Guinness's Double X."

" Just loike you Irish! "

How magnificently I was turning the tables on Reality by making it wax and wane to suit my ebb and flow of consciousness! My philosophy was quite a success. Quite!

" Be careful. Two steps! "

Two flights led down from a kind of platform in front of John's hall door. It would make an excellent rostrum from which to address the men hidden in the mighty motor sweeping brushes which whisk behind each other up Mallord Street long after midnight.

" Let us put a stop to the brunettising of Europe! Keep England fair. Blue-eyed! Sweep out the brown, bring in the blue! "

" Are you? "

" Yes. Yes! Quite all right, thanks! There are all these taxis, you know! "

" Good-night, old man."

" Good-night, sweet Prince! "

Days and days after, I called on George Moore. He sat in the ground-floor room with his back to its deep red curtains beside the fireplace, over which a Muse leant on the dial of a clock. French Empire. Rather " Ompire," as a Great Lady corrected a friend of mine. " Ours is the Empire."

Two rooms were thrown into one. He liked space. So too at No. 4, Upper Ely Place, Dublin, he opened the folding doors.

He rose, subsided, and said with an expiring sigh, as if exhausted by my presence :

" It is good of you to come! "

He thinks I travelled over specially to call on him since his illness. How shall I gently disavow my merit in his eyes? He gave me no chance.

" Let me see. Ah! Why did you not warn me that the young novelist whom you sent to consult me was quite pretty? "

" Was she? "

He affected an air of the deepest disgust at my attempted hypocrisy.

" Oh, my dear friend! That will do! "

The maid came in with the broken Sèvres tea-pot and set, and quietly withdrew. He swept his hand about to indicate side tables and flower-loaded shelves.

" To-day she sent me flowers! "

" In America it is the other way about."

He resented what seemed to him an implication. He could " register " impatience either by a shrug or grimace, or a suppressed ejaculation, better than any man I know.

" Surely you didn't come to Ebury Street to wrangle about American customs ? "

Moore was the most potentially cantankerous man one could meet. An explosion was always imminent. Petulant should be the word. He had all the petulance of a spoiled child. And he was spoiled. A spoiled soldier, a spoiled painter, a spoiled boon-companion, and a spoiled Parisian Bohemian. Light-footed as a woman on the rough *pavé* of Life, he sheltered himself from its robust jostlings. His epicene genius gave him a double advantage. He could describe all his experiences, and all his acquaintances, from a detached standpoint, and include himself in the pageant. It was impossible to be a friend of his, because he was incapable of gratitude ; and we all know that friendship lives only on interchange of companionship, confidence, understanding and affectionate loyalty, one to another. With him you could never count on " auld acquaintance." You could never be sure of George Moore. This must be qualified by the out-standing fact that he never betrayed you ; but you had to find that out by experience. You could never count on him beforehand. Even though this sense of uncertainty may have been unfounded, he lost a lot of human fellowship and confidence through this withholding of intimacy and his inability to be man to man.

" So she sent you flowers ? "

He did not answer. Perhaps he was thinking that I was laughing secretly at the reversal of the order of things. I tried again.

" I know her well. She is writing a novel. I told her that no novel could be written unless it was in a form that might pass muster with you. If it appeared without your being consulted—well, then too late ! " I waved my hand as over the abyss of despair that might open if anyone were to write without his sanction.

" How often have I told you that no woman can write a novel ? No woman ! They can if they will only realise their *métier* is to inspire . . ."

I thought an interruption would be fruitful :

" No woman. What about Pearl Craigie ? "

"Pearl Craigie?" His eyes were upturned at the thought, and he threw up his arms, delighted to surrender to the delicious impeachment it implied.

"Ah! My very dear Friend!"

We were all supposed to suspect that Pearl Craigie was his Mistress and his Heloise-like pupil.

> Pour qui fut chastré et puis moyne
> Pierre Estaillart à Saint Denis.

"Too apt a comparison!" I can hear Yeats saying.

But if you were not shocked by the enormity of the suspicion, he would proceed to betray her in the indicative mood for fear that scandal might be missed.

CHAPTER XVIII

ISLAND ENGLAND, THIS ISLE—SILVER SEA AND SO ON, HAS NO strands, only watering-places. Water-carts wet the seaside cement while children and adults put pennies in the slots. Brighton—cement, shingle and companionate Semitics. Drive desperately off—Selsey Bill : shallows and tide races. Weston-super-Mare ! Even the water in the syphons is salt : and Frinton-by-the-Sea depends on tennis-rackets. Ilfracombe is an arena for competing restaurant-keepers. Scarborough is in Yorkshire, but Blackpool is Yorkshire's Elysium. It comes to this, all England has only one watering-place from which the sea may be seen and bracing airs inhaled : but Blackpool has to recuperate all England.

Now, if the long sands of Tramore, the great strand, or silver Portmarnock whence Transatlantic planes take off, or the unimaginable West coast of Ireland where " twice-washed " Renvyle is, were known, what an invasion there would be ! But trippers do not expect sea at an English seaside resort. They look for girls in Thetis-thin habiliments, and they are there. I can imagine bathing-dresses being worn years hence as far inland as Winchelsea is now. And no one to dig up old customs ! The tradition of land and sea !

But such holiday-makers would hate Ireland with its 3000 miles of open ocean and nothing to do save swim or sun-bathe, *sans* suits, *sans* slots or listenings-in. Can it be that England owes its greatness to its " watering-places " because they drove men in desperation to go down to the sea in ships to look for water, and thus they came to rule the waves that knew no shore ?

" Nevertheless," said General Macready, " Dublin has also produced the greatest poltroon of our time. You have often heard that So-and-So went on his knees to this or that magnate, but it was my embarrassing experience to see one of your townees approach me actually on his knees. When he was ushered in he knelt down and waddled up to me, saying, ' Surely it is not the policy of the Great British Empire to have anyone killed as a set off against the murder, or death of O'Callaghan, the Mayor of Limerick ? '

" ' Get up, damn you ! ' I said."

" All I asked you, General, was to agree with me when I

said that Dublin, in Bernard Shaw, produced the greatest genius of our time. You cross my track with an exemplary coward."

But the poltroonery of one of our citizens depressed me. I was more or less a refugee. How then could I pose as more courageous than some citizen who was possibly too paralysed by terror to move?

" I have a great deal of Irish blood in me," the General said, " and it made me rather sick to see an Irishman on his knees crawling to me for mercy, as he called it. Had he told me to go to Hell and shoot, I might have asked him to lunch. But what are you to do when confronted by the negation of all manhood ? "

" I know. I know," I said. But I myself had already lost caste through the irrefutable fact that I was a townsman of " the greatest Poltroon of our time."

" Forget the crawling seeker for sanctuary, and answer me, General, or deny it—you who are the grandson of a great actor : what country has produced a greater genius than our friend, Bernard Shaw ? "

Long fingers swept my hair. The tall American triumphs over the awkwardness of great height. The insufficiently interested in George Moore, Lady Ebury, intervened :

" Leave him alone, General ; he never crawled. Would he be here if he did ? "

Both of us expostulated. The General rose and held back the tapestried division. The ladies sought the dining-room.

" A magnificent curtain ! " said Seymour Leslie.

I cannot bear unmitigated facts for long. And the matter-of-factness of the downright honest Londoners, their surprise at a mind that had to fly if Reality was becoming too rigid—in other words, my inability to stand boredom—together with a warning that was daily growing more insistent, made me long for a change. The warning came from a remembered saying of the greatest poseur Dublin ever produced, Oscar Wilde : a genius, a poseur, but no poltroon. " You may have one season's success in London, but not two."

Now, it had never occurred to me that people's hospitable kindness could not go on for ever. I, for my part, could not go on for ever accepting it. I could part with friends whom I would never see again. Mr. Asquith, who was equal in years and almost in wit to my friend Dr. Tyrrell. With him I should never lunch again, or hear his remark whispered to me, at the young Countess Odescalchi's exuberance, " Youth would be all very well if it only came on later in life ! "

The town where somebody knew me in every street was drawing me from the town where I only knew those who were somebodies. The people whom I could please and shock as they shocked and amused me.

A dinner with Larkey Waldron booming at the head of the table would be more amusing : when the ice-pudding, served half-way through it, transformed your stomach into hemispheres, and the dinner began again for a conquest of a New World : the butler sent in mid repast to the library to verify a quotation which was forgotten with the next mouthful. . . . I would like to see St. Stephen's Green again with Father Sherwin, young and silver-haired, as Cardinal Newman must have walked to his lych-gate at Littlemore. Father Sherwin, who had the photograph of a ghost, a photograph which would mysteriously disappear. Father Dwyer, keen and scholarly, who takes an interest in politics and knows everyone for miles about the Green. I will listen to the angelic anarchist Æ again, and see Endymion's cricket trousers that are whiter than the whitewash on London taxis' wheels.

What is wrong here, I thought, is the absence of the metaphysical man. It is nearly as bad as the town of Buffalo, where fast-driven human automatons are engaged in " gogetting " all day long, " relaxing " for a minute and looking at their watches. Nobody has leisure for speculation. But it is not quite as bad, because here those engaged in speculation of another kind at least compose Limericks, the only poetry that London produces now. We want more village idiots over here. A country without village idiots is not worth living in. Without them there is no way of knowing who are sane. True, they may have all been voted into Westminster, as Al. Smith suggested, when he told me that America's village idiots had all gone to Washington.

I want to go back to the town where we are all so poor that we can dabble in ideas without being imposed on or robbed.

Society in London goes in circles and tight compartments : you cannot flit from one to another without letting your hosts down. There are no Fannings here. If there were, it " would not do."

They are all watching one another ; they are all gossiping about one another. Gossip is the national pastime of the

English. What constitutes the Englishman's silent strength? He is loth to say or waste words on an outsider. He wants to keep them all for his club. He won't let a foreigner in on it. Is it any wonder that I was forbidden to talk to the two Crown Princesses! Gossip is the national vice. It is worse in the country villages. England extends freedom to everyone but its own citizens. They are all watching, watching! Commenting and criticising among themselves. Let me get out before I go back on all my ideas of the freedom of English-men. Before I appear ungrateful. The visitor never realises this. Unlike us, they keep all their drawbacks to them-selves.

A taxi rolled by with its tyres newly whitewashed. This has to be done by the driver every morning, I thought. He probably likes doing it, though the tyres will be covered in dirt by the end of the day. It is a labour of love, or rather a duty he has invented and imposed on himself. " England expects ! " every man to invent a " duty." The best is just about good enough for the Rulers of the World. But I am not a ruler of the world. I am an ordinary medical man, and if I don't return soon, I will lose whatever little knowledge I may have of medicine. Here the doctors are so kind and professional conduct is so nice that they never contradict each other. To maintain this harmony it is taboo to make a diagnosis. In Dublin, where the conspiracy is unfriendly, it is necessary to keep the wits keen if one has to live on his professional brethrens' repairs.

I went to do a little flying with my friend Uwins. My visit to Bristol was all that was needed to make my nostalgia irresistible. I saw the masts of ships at the end of a street! It might as well be the Custom House docks with George's lighters by the river wall, and the sunny gulls on the water!

" You may waken me as early as you like," I said to the steward. I must drive through the streets before the lame men come out. The clerks are in their offices by 9.30. But between 10 and 11 the streets are full of lame men : whether their lameness keeps them late or no is not the point. What I complain about is that there are so many : men with stirrups under their boots, men with thick boots, men with crutches, and agitated men who spring along as if they were shearing invisible sheep with their knees. At eleven o'clock their places will be taken by housewives with magnificent manners to impress irreverent greengrocers : but the impression goes with the cabbage, and it has to be imposed all over again next day.

Had I thought of it some years ago I should have sent a wire to Dublin Castle " advising " them that a new Chief Secretary was coming. Nobody would have known what he was like or what to expect. And in return I could have pretended not to know Sir Henry Robinson. He would be at the pier with his well-kept automobile, and before I had time to look about he would whisk me off to his favourite hotel in Recess, Connemara. With a wave of his hand he would point to that lovely desert full of peace, comparatively. This would save the Chief Secretary, who, in any event, could only hold office until his Government went out, from a boring visit to Dublin Castle and possibly many " deputations " and other vexations, particularly the idea that Ireland was not peaceful and content. But for Ian McPherson to be with Sir Henry in Connemara! What a change after London! And how well the Irish Constabulary in Co. Galway had been trained to salute men in positions of such responsibility or in the company of Sir Henry, which was much the same thing.

I like to think about Dr. Bodkin's story of the Chinese mandarin who sat for his portrait looking at a landscape through a window with his back to the artist. His choice of landscape was a better clue than his face to his true self. With my back to England I am looking at Dublin with its central river and its roiling quays light on its spires lifted in the West.

How I love the old town where every man is a potential idler, poet or friend! I love the old town where sock-suspenders are less important than poems! And directions depend on inns. " Up past the yellow house, where Robert Emmet hid, to the Lamb Doyles."

What, I asked myself, has Dublin to offer me in place of the town I have just left? It has neither dignity, majesty, rank nor fashion. Where are its aristocrats? Then I wondered if the autochthones ever envisaged majesty as we know it; if they ever wanted dignity as we know it; or indeed if they would tolerate it if it were presented to them now. What, then, is the native idea of an aristocrat? Obviously he is not a landlord: even 800 years' residence will not commend a landlord to the Gaelic heart. And yet they had their chieftains, their aristocrats. If I could ascertain what the native idea of an aristocrat is, I would know one when I

met him. Long descent is so taken for granted that the
tribes never thought of recording their antiquity in any
Register of Gotham. Long descent is tribal, not personal.
The name of the person, if it be a well-known Irish name,
secures him his quarterings. But what personal qualities
and characteristics must the hero have if he is to be accepted
as a hero? First of all he must be physically great, big-
bodied, burly, the full of a door. His personal courage must
be outstanding and unquestionable, he must be rosy, generous
and chivalrous. He must have some noble, endearing fault
which is easily forgiven, extravagance for choice. But, outside
battle, he must be gentle and courteous and capable of com-
radery. Such a one was Goll MacMorna, and Finn and
Conn the Hundred Fighter. To-day such a one is Sean
McKeon. He took on a hundred and fought them to a
standstill. In an unchanging people it is evident that there
must be repetitions and reincarnations of type. Conn is
now McKeon. Who would Dan Breen have been in the
old days which are now elevated into an Heroic period?
Cuchulainn, I think. Cuchulainn was more his type, which is
not as big-bodied as McKeon's. Goll McMorna or Conn
for McKeon: Cuchulainn to-day is personified in Dan Breen.

Deep in the heart of the Gael these heroes are enthroned.
Long they lie hidden under the hills or in the lakes like that
great Earl who waits beneath Lough Gur but at times is seen
to ride in armour by moonlight on its surface. We have
not reached him yet. We are deriving from a remoter past,
but his time shall come.

I gazed up Sackville Street. The grandest thing we have
in Dublin, the great Doric column that upheld the Admiral, was
darkened by flying mists, intermittent as battle smoke; but
aloft in light, silvery as the moonshine of legend, the statue in
whiter stone gazed for ever southwards towards Trafalgar and
the Nile. That pillar marks the end of a civilisation, the
culmination of the great period of Eighteenth-century Dublin,
just as the pillar at Brindisi marks the end of the Roman road.
The men who first founded this city set up their pillar where
Brunswick Street is now. How long, I thought, would it be
before the Gael if left to himself would have set a pillar up?
A long time, and a longer before he would have crowned it with
Griffith, Collins or McKeon. It took a hundred years to
set Michael Dwyer up in Gorey. More likely a pillar would
be set over his heroes as it is set over Parnell.

We are not pillar-builders, nor do we erect trophies, and we shall never erect anything so long as we keep up the pose of setting our faces against Empire and Conquerors and soldiers of trophies. Would this pose ever have permitted a people to be anything else but shirkers? Would it ever have countenanced the British Empire or the Empire of Rome? Yet all we have and most of what we are proceed from these strong sources.

"Excuse me, Senator," a sailor said, as he wound a cable round a mushroom-like protuberance on the quay, "there's a few stanzas in my pocket that I would like you to look over if you have time." A patron of Martin Brennan's, I believe! "I'll have time enough now that I am home."

§

Father Paddy met me one morning.

"Home again?" said he.

"I was never away."

"Oh, weren't you?"

"No. I only thought I was. You know that Ireland is a place or state of repose where souls suffer from the hope that the time will come when they may go abroad. I was only in London."

He slapped his leg with an invisible ash-plant and passed on.

CHAPTER XIX

IT WAS THE 13TH OF DECEMBER, 1921, SO IN A WAY ONE OF
the omens, the unlucky 13, was already set. The Dail was
to meet on the morrow to decide whether it would approve
the " Treaty " that Arthur Griffith had signed in London with
Lloyd George. If Griffith was of Welsh descent (ap Gruffydd),
Lloyd George was a contemporary Welshman, and we had
misgivings about anything to which he set his mind. But
none of us had misgivings about Griffith ; any misgivings we
felt were centred on the man who lurked in the background
and sent Griffith and Collins—" Plenipotentiaries "—to bear
the brunt of responsibility while his watch-dog, Childers,
never lost touch.

Would the Dail accept the Treaty ? It was a measure
surpassing by far any dreams of Home Rule our country
had imagined for many years. But the Irish public always
outruns its leaders. Griffith had been a leader of a party for
twenty years. There had been an armed rising in 1916.
How far had he been outrun ? He had founded his whole
movement on Kossuth's in Hungary. The foundation here
of a Dual Monarchy was the farthest point he had reached or
desired to reach. He never altered and never trimmed.
Probably, with his deep instinct for realities in politics, he
knew just how much " freedom" the Irish people could sustain,
or possibly his character admitted neither change nor evolution.
So far as he was concerned, the Treaty supplied all that his life-
long devotion to his country had desired, and even more
through the *vis a tergo* of the Republican movement. Therefore, those who represent Griffith as making concessions to
Lloyd George may have inside knowledge of the proceedings
during the many interviews, but they do not know Arthur
Griffith, nor do they take account of the scope of his demands.
They have probably not taken the trouble to acquaint themselves with his teaching.

To some extent, then, Griffith found himself in a false
position when he set out for London as the delegate (plenipo-
tentiary ?) of a Republic. Yet he brought back more than he
had ever envisaged, only to be repudiated and condemned for
not bringing back a Republic for which its chief advocate
preferred to make Griffith a scapegoat, than go fearlessly and
face Great Britain as Griffith did, who at least secured his

demands. This treachery is so characteristic of members of the sub-races and so utterly unfair to honest Arthur that the contemplation of it and of Griffith's betrayer has a physiological effect on me. I cannot proceed.

But we are assembled in 15, Ely Place, on the eve of the Dail decision. We sought to satisfy our anxiety for the future by invoking omens. Happily, men with a knowledge of the classics and the traditions of the classics happened to be present. Father Dwyer, Professor Alton, J. M. N. Jeffries and one or two more. Mrs. Bentwick, Talbot Clifton's sister-in-law, was among the ladies and can witness to the experiment. But there is an excellent account of it in *Blackwood's Magazine* for March 1922.

We decided to put the *Sortes Virgilianæ* to the proof. Virgil through the Dark Ages was regarded as a necromancer. Some dim memory of his magical mouth flickered in the Central Darkness. And his book was used to foretell the future, for had he not foretold the Golden Age that Christianity was about to bring in his Fourth Eclogue?

There are two ways in which a great poet may foretell the future. One by his aloofness from mundane affairs, which gives that distance which makes stars so fixed that they may be used as guides. Something afar from the question is necessary, why else should not a *sors* with a newspaper or a volume of Ella Wheeler Wilcox suffice? And the farther it be the vaguer and more mysterious is the atmosphere conjured up for prophesying. If a bridegroom as vacillating as was Panurge were to put his key into a volume of Shakespeare and to find that it rested on the first two lines of the first sonnet, need he "take counsel" any more? And the second way which helps the first is the exultation which the muttering of great verse alone can give, an exultation which in those attuned can produce a magnification of soul which makes everything possible and the future pliable.

But you cannot initiate a ritual suddenly and without seriousness. Professor Alton called for the book and for a key. I produced my folio and a large key. That is what is done. The book is placed on the table and cut by inserting a key between the leaves. The prophecy shall be read down from the line which the tip of the key shall indicate.

" Right ! " I said.

" Wait a moment ! The key can only be inserted by a chaste person, a child or a priest."

There were no children present, so I retired in favour of His Reverence.

Yeats, I said to myself, would propose that I should send across the street for George Moore.

Now we must be unanimous as to the question we want answered. What was disturbing my mind at the moment was what would happen to Arthur Griffith, who had seized what he could for Ireland before all chance was lost in a slough of debate. What happens to all who sacrifice themselves for her? Well I knew; she sacrifices them.

This anxiety may have imparted itself or have been already shared by others. I found them setting down the question, and then Father Dwyer advanced to the Book. He inserted the key and carried the key and book to Alton, who, holding the key in position, opened the book. He paused as if he had difficulty with the translation, gazing over his glasses at the page. We knew that it was not difficulty but shock that made him pause. At last he read, translating as he read:

> ". . . spretæ Ciconum quo munere matres
> Inter sacra deum nocturnique orgia Bacchi,
> Discerptum latos juvenem sparsere per agros."

"What will become of Arthur Griffith?" '*Spretæ quo munere*'—spurned by which gifts—repudiated by the Treaty; *matres Ciconum*—the Mænads—the mad women in the celebration of the Gods' ritual amid the orgies of night-wandering will tear the young men to pieces and scatter them over the wide plains."

It was a passage referring to that "enchanting son" who spied on his frenzied mother. But who could have seen Griffith lying dead, tracked by one of the Mænads to the holy place of a nursing home owned by nuns with his left arm sliced open?

Solemnly the Professor laid down the book. No one spoke. A mysterious and strong fear enveloped me. I felt all the terror of the fabulous darkness when such prophecies were fulfilled with import for those whose minds were credulous and necromantic.

Instead of being deterred by the gloomy oracle, we were fascinated and drawn, as it were, to test again the Virgilian lottery.

"What will De Valera do? Are we all agreed that is the question we want answered?"

Again Father Dwyer inserted the key.   Again the Professor gazed over his glasses at the magical hexameters :

> " Quaere age et armari pubem portisque moveri
>   Laetus in arma jube et Phrygio, qui flumine pulchro
>   Consedere, duces pictosque exure carinas,
>   Coelestum vis magna jubet."

But lest I be thought to have forced the translation let me quote from the account of a disinterested commentator and his rendering of the Latin.

> Rouse thee now, and with joyful heart bid thy young men arm themselves and move to the fray and destroy the leaders of the foreign oppressors who have settled on our beautiful river, and burn their painted ships.   The might of Heaven orders this to be done.

And even as the Professor continued reading there flashed to my mind a sinister remark made by this same De Valera to one of the Southern Unionists in the days when he was still bandying words over Mr. Lloyd George's initial offer of peace.   ' If the fighting starts again,' he is reported to have said, ' the Southern Unionists will not be treated as neutrals. And many unpleasant things will happen.'

And now, with De Valera's challenge to the Treaty already thrown down, and the possibility of his overthrowing the Free State, either in Dail Eireann or in spite of it, looming like a dark cloud on the horizon of Irish peace, not I alone but all present were thinking of the unpleasant things that might happen—if the Sortes told sooth.   I am, as I have said, no scholar, but as a schoolboy I often laboured long and woundily at the *Æneid* after my more prehensile fellows had gone forth to play.   And now the story of that weak and egotistical young man, Turnus the Rutilian—another De Valera if ever there was one—came back to me : how Juno, ever harassing the Trojans, even as some malign fate seems to sow perpetual discord among the Irish peoples, sent Alecto disguised as Madame Markiewicz, or rather as Calybe the priestess, to urge Turnus to attack the Trojans.   What the others were thinking about I do not know, for our host, with unerring instinct, was already urging us to replenish our glasses, and setting the frozen stream of conversation flowing again.   And so we continued to talk, mostly about Ireland and what the morrow's meeting would bring forth, until it was time to go home.   But nobody suggested that a third attempt should be made to consult the oracle.

Endymion's landlady wished to see me. Her lodger had barricaded his door for two days. He had eaten nothing. If I could persuade him. I went at once to Pleasants Street. After some persuasion I heard his chairs and tables being removed. He let me in. It seemed he had composed some music for his violin. He was afraid that the score would be stolen.

" But can't you copy it out and give me a copy to keep for you ? "

" I could if I had a copy."

" But where is the score ? "

" In my head."

" Thieves never come through doors. They use windows. Let me secure the window, and come out for some lunch."

But as we went away my work was nearly undone by the landlady allowing her relief to express itself in " *Pax vobiscum* to the pair of ye ! "

Indignantly Endymion turned and shouted :

" *Nux vomica!* my good woman. *Nux vomica !* . . ."

" I never allow the common people to outquote me in the classics," he explained.

§

I must go down to Dunsany and see how the playwright is getting on. Dunsany Castle is about twenty-five miles from Dublin, and the journey takes about three-quarters of an hour in a useful car. The great gates are seldom opened, so you go through a short drive through a gateless Gothic ruin, a " reproduction " as Sir Thornley Stoker, the connoisseur, would say. Sheer up from the dark gravel rises the grey pile. The square tower beyond the door is half covered with ivy. The hall is filled with armour and trophies of the chase.

" His Lordship is not at home, sir."

I well knew the difference between not being at home and not being in.

" Are you sure that he is not on the top of the tower composing ? If you just say . . ."

" He is not in, sir."

" Then, where is he ? "

" He has been arrested, sir, by the Black-and-Tans."

It was Maunder, the major domo, speaking. He could be

relied on, with such a master, carefully to frame his sentences and to choose his words.

By the Black-and-Tans! Well, of all the countries! But what the devil was Dunsany doing to be arrested by the Black-and-Tans? Was he after all a rebel at heart, following in the footsteps of his ancestor, the Blessed Oliver Plunket, who was condemned on a trumped-up charge and hanged, drawn and quartered in 1681? If so, it is a surprise to me. I thought I knew a good deal about his points of view in literature, criticism and politics.

I have it! He has been comforting Ledwidge, the Bard of Slane. That he had been supporting and educating him I knew. And now the master is arrested for the man. And there was in my mind the memory of a poem which Ledwidge broke off, dissatisfied. " I got weary," he said, " as it was no good."

Let me see how it went. I can never remember prose, but I cannot forget verse if it be smooth :

> What rumours filled the Atlantic sky,
>   And turned the wild geese back again ;
> When Plunkett lifted Balor's eye,
>   And broke Andromeda's strong chain ?
> Or did they hear that Starkie, James,
>   Among the gallipots was seen,
> And he who called her sweetest names,
>   Was talking to another queen ?
>
> Now all the wise in quicklime burn,
>   And all the strong have crossed the sea ;
> But down the pale roads of Ashbourne,
>   Are heard the voices of the free.
> And Jemmy Quigley is the boy,
>   Could say how queenly was her walk,
> When Sackville Street went down like Troy,
>   And peelers fell in far Dundalk.

They probably found a copy of that when raiding Dunsany Castle and so were sure that Lord Dunsany was the Plunkett who lifted something. So they lifted the Plunkett. They had to lift something. But it was the wrong Plunkett. The Plunket who died in 1681 had but one " t " in his name. Norman Plunkett, corruption of " le blanche jenette," may not have been his ancestral line. His name had lost a " t."

But what am I to do? Here I am undoubtedly under surveillance coming from the great stronghold of Dunsany. It was a stronghold in 1181. It is a stronghold still. But a

" rebel " stronghold now.   At last the Dunsanys have become
Irish !   No longer can it be said of them, or of the Irish,
that they refuse to blend.   Magnificent !   With a leader
like Dunsany this rebellious movement will be lifted out from
the rut of the commonplace.   All that Ireland wants is a lead
from its gentry.   Now Dunsany is striking a blow for the
country of his ancestors conquered over 800 years ago !
What though his life gives Ireland another martyr ?   Where
he leads, I follow !

    " Geordie, give me my lance ! "
But Maunder had heard nothing.   General Hammond,
the nearest neighbour, might supply particular news.
    Coming from this rebel, bretesche, peel tower, castle
or stronghold, I will be suspected of connivance with its
chief.   I begin to grow nervous.   What persuaded me to come ?
    " Maunder, when the Black-and-Tans came, what did they
do ? "
    " Searched the house, sir."
    " Did they arrest his Lordship ? "
    " His Lordship was not at home."
    " Not at home ? "
    " Not at home, sir."
    Lady Conyngham told me the whole story.   It seemed
that Dunsany had been raided by Hamar Greenwood's
Black-and-Tans.   They could not find its lord, simply because
he was out in the bogs shooting snipe.   But everyone in
Ireland was forbidden the use of guns under a penalty of
death—more or less—death in Cork for Nationalists, a repri-
mand in Ulster for its conditional loyalists.
    Snipe sent to " friendly " members of the Kildare Street
Club (where has a poet a friend ?) rather got on the nerves
of those who had sacrificed their snipe-shooting to the Empire.
And here was Dunsany sending them snipe when their
loyalty forbade them to shoot.   Couple after couple appeared.
None of your " jack " snipe, but Meath snipe from the Red
Bog, with breasts on them like wood-pigeons.   They were
nestled and nourished in the succulent bogs of the perennial
and abounding Boyne.   Great birds, great herds, great eels
and a great river—Royal Meath !
    But Dunsany was betrayed by his club mates, not by a
poem.   Nevertheless his Lordship was captured.
    Through his tenants he was driven in a motor tumbril
to a Dublin prison, to be tried in Kilmainham !   Dunsany,

who had been shot for wearing His Majesty's uniform in 1916 by the men the Black-and-Tans identified him with now. Seemingly he had backed Ireland both ways!

But Maunder never lost his poise because, as the lorries drove away, he asked:

" Who shall I say called ? "

How England loves to show how impartial her Justice is at the expense of her noblest and most loyal sons! Dukes in prison give a sense of distinction to the house-breaker. But if a Corkman is hanged in whose house an obsolete revolver is found, and a Carsonite in Belfast merely admonished for possession of remnants of the rebellious but super-loyal Galloper Smith gun-running of 1914, the obvious impartial path lies midway between Cork and Belfast—Meath.

A peer may claim the privilege of a silk rope. But a silk rope has its drawbacks—that is, it draws you back; and you may be jerked up and down like the game called yo-yo, until you are dead. There was a sack of clay in my garden. This would stiffen the rope if the rope were wetted, and if the sack were left in suspension overnight it would be as abrupt as a hempen collar.

I tried to cheer his Lordship with this idea, but he said, " There are some subjects which are not jokes, and one of them is my hanging." This was disconcerting. I had imagined myself a cloud-dispeller. Now look at the gloom I had evoked!

" From a medical point of view a broken neck is more merciful than slow suffocation, and less indecent."

" My solicitor thinks that on the whole it would be better for you not to bail me out."

" But who else will come forward ? "

" You are identified too much with the Sinn Feiners! "

But, utterly mystified, I exclaimed: " Is it not you the Black-and-Tans have arrested—not me ? "

I did not like to obtrude my goodwill further. But here he was arrested for bagging snipe, when those with whom he was identifying me, who derailed and bagged trains, were at large. Later I learned that all the Sinn Feiners around his Castle were marching on Dublin to bail him out. He was a good landlord.

" Would you say that eight hundred rounds of ammunition will look a lot to the Court Martial ? "

" Oh, my God! "

Dunsany used to sing of his Uncle, Sir Horace, in his relation to Æ.

> " My Uncle has a poet, and he keeps him on a string,
>   And what do you think he keeps him for ?
>   He keeps him for to sing."

And he took to himself a poet with the result . . . " on a string " ! It was too horrible !

And now the gloom began to invest me. No more golden evenings in Dunsany in the mellow lamp-light before the great fire, listening to the latest lyric recited or read in that vivid and pleasant accent of his. Exquisite language, excellent verse ! Shall I see never again the well-formed knuckles holding the leaves of manuscript, and the long limbs out-stretched ? The only living man who could write romantic prose, the architect of Pegana, the meadow of Pegasus, peopled with, not heroes, but gods, as Homer peopled his *Iliad*, the playwright of the *Gods of the Mountain*, *The Flight of the Queen* and thirty other works, including the *Sword of Welleran*, arrested for being in possession of a gun !

If I could only send him some of that ale in a Saxon rumkin which " bids valour burgeon in tall men," or play him a " spring " such as McPherson played when

> Sae rantingly, sae wantonly,
>   Sae dauntingly gaed he ;
> He played a spring and danced it round
>   Below the gallows tree.

But meanwhile, would it not be a good idea if I hid my revolver under a tree-root, just in case, just in case I am searched on my way home ? It is not in falling between two stools that the tragedy consists, but in falling off each stool in turn.

You can see along a straight road for a mile and more on the way between Dunsany and Clonee. I saw a heavy car that looked like a lorry well ahead. But it must be going very slowly. I am catching up on it rapidly. It is going very slowly. It is glinting strangely in the sun. I am nearer now. Gun barrels ! rifle barrels ! It's a lorry load of Black-and-Tans ! I don't want to catch up on that. But I have been sighted. It is going at a walking pace. I have no chance of turning. I must go on. They are waving to me to approach. I notice that the lorry is not full. There are two of its number scouting in the fields behind the hedges on either side of the road. They fear an ambush; another ambush, it would seem. They look as if they had been already ambushed. There is blood on one of their bandoliers and one of them seems to have lost a finger. His hand is bound over the stump.

" Get out ! "

I put on the brake and, leaving the engine running, stepped out on the road. Two of them advanced white with nerves and pushed their revolvers into my stomach.

The smaller, a pasty-faced little fellow, asked :

" Wot are you doing alone 'ere ? "

" Driving home."

The second, who spoke more correctly and quietly, said : " Let me see your permit."

I produced a chit of pink paper which gave me permission to drive " within a radius of twenty miles from the place of issue."

" Where have you been ? "

" You can see it there," I said, ignoring the direct question.

They both examined the paper, which was issued, the last time I was held up, from Chapelizod. They knew no local geography.

" Was you at Chapelizod ? " the little cad in khaki, who looked like someone who was dismissed for dishonesty with a gas-meter, asked, regardless of grammar.

" No. I was . . ." I said, adding, " If you don't stop trembling that gun will go off."

" It can be loaded again." But the reference to the state of his nerves galled him. He smiled wryly. I thought of that old Irish triad : Three things to fear : the horns of a bull, the heels of a stallion, the smile of an Englishman. He tore off my hat and ripped the lining out. " Nothing 'ere ! Hands up ! 'Ere, search him, lads." He slammed my hat down on my head.

A tall figure of a man in a black uniform, with a black tam-o'-shanter worn rakishly, approached. He rapidly ran his hands over me and searched my pockets. His fingers slipped in before and behind a cigarette case which he neither opened nor even removed for examination. It contained a collection of rather biased cuttings enumerating the atrocities of the Black-and-Tans.

My first surmise was correct; they had lost a comrade in an ambush. I was ordered into my ransacked car to lead the way to Dublin. Two of them sat behind me with rifles. " Thirty miles an hour all the way ! "

If the " Boys " knew we were coming, I thought, it would be well worth taking a sporting risk and running the whole gang right into them. They have the wind up badly and will scatter like deer.

I take my hat off—well, a better hat than this—to Dan Breen, who, single-handed, shot up a lorry load of ruffians such as these, and then, wounded with his arm hanging useless, came back for more. And to Sean McKeon, who beat eighteen first-class soldiers with eighteen untrained men, and then beat eighty-four Auxiliaries the same evening.

Flames! I said. That was a great fight. It does not matter who was right or wrong. The brave man is always right!

My brand new hat! " Nothing 'ere in the lining." Indeed! And I used to think I had something in the lining of my hat. There was this reflection for one : the best thing that happened for Ireland was that the Germans invaded Belgium. Whether Great Britain first broke the guarantee of neutrality by fortifying Belgium, as the Germans claim, matters not to the argument ; but the self-righteous blather and skite about the rights of small nations which followed had bound more or less the upholders of the rights of small nations to practise what they preached. Great Britain hates to have her preachings cast in her teeth. She is loth to loosen her grip until her hand trembles. Well, her hands were trembling already in the persons of her representatives in Ireland for the rights of small nations, her Black-and-Tans. Her financiers were trembling about the terms of the American Loan, and her sailors were trembling at the prospect of having to race the proposed naval expansion of the United States. Therefore it was of paramount importance to placate the feelings of the Greater Ireland which exists overseas in mighty America. And you do not placate popular feelings among nationals by turning loose the offscourings of English ergastula on Irish fathers and mothers and sisters and brothers. Thus Greenwood was manufacturing rebels at the rate of thousands a day. I was the latest and enthusiastic recruit.

Grimly I quoted that great and magnanimous Englishman Sir William Watson, great verse sent by him to me after the outrage :

> To Sir Hamar Greenwood.
> No thin, pale fame, no brief and poor renown,
> Were thy just due of thee shall wise Time say :
> " Chartered for havoc, 'neath his rule were they
> Whose chastisement of guilt was to burn down
> The house of innocence in fear-crazed town
> And trembling hamlet, while he had his way,
> Converts untold did this man make each day
> To savage hate of Law and King and Crown.
>
> Great propagandist of the rebel creed !
> Proselytiser without living peer !
> If thou stand fast—if thou but persevere—
> 'Twill be thy glory to complete indeed
> Valera's work, that doth even now so need
> Thy mellow art's last touches, large and clear ! "

So three fears freed Ireland—Fear of charges of Hypocrisy, Fear of High Interest, Fear of an Invincible U.S.A. Fleet.

We dawdled back to Dublin. In the Phœnix Park they called a halt by the Wellington Monument to send me on my way. Why not have Clonee incised at the base of that obelisk to Wellington ? It would be a famous victory where England had fought, for the first time without allies, and defeated me unarmed, by eleven to one. Or it could be cut in letters of gold under the beautifully engraved " Copen-hagen " on Nelson's Pillar, for that was a victory also with overwhelming odds on.

" You ought to go to the Abbey Theatre to-night. There's a play there called ' A Serious Thing.' It will make you laugh. I wrote it myself," I said as a parting shot.

I drove along the quays revolving many thoughts. The background of all of them was angry. I recalled another passage in a pamphlet sent to me " Across the by no means estranging sea " by the poet to whom England in its junker ignorance prefers Kipling, who never rose from the Sergeants' Mess.

Referring to the cross British want of understanding Sir William Watson wrote :

I do not know whether it testified to our curious English unaware-ness of the typical and very natural, or to a callous determination to insult and outrage that pride to the limit of endurance and to trail it wantonly in the mire. As to the statesmanship that dictated or sanctioned the whole hideous proceeding (the rounding up of unarmed boys), it should be borne in mind that many individual members of that village throng, or rather that human drove, were no more than boys in their teens. All those boys when they grow up to be men will carry within them to their grave a blazing hatred of the very name of England. For my part I should despise them if they did not.

But my spirits improved as I passed along Brunswick Street. A crowd had collected outside the jail. A merry crowd. What had happened? A crowd seldom laughs at the discomfiture of one of its members. Presently, fuming with indignation, Endymion emerged. He was set free. But he was not satisfied. He was indignant still. " I paid for it this morning and I hold the receipt. I am arrested for illegal possession in the afternoon." Another pistol? What had he bought?

At ten o'clock, when there were few people about, he had demonstrated with a cutlass before a ham which hung with twenty others on a rail outside one of those shops which are called Italian Warehouses in Dublin. They would be called grocers' shops elsewhere. He chose the last one on the line. He paid for it. " No, no! Leave it there! I will call for it this evening. Give me my receipt." Whether or not there was a change of staff when Endymion returned at five in the afternoon to sabre, transfix and run off with his ham, is not known. Probably the police did not wait to inquire. All they saw was a fugitive shouldering a sworded ham. After some chase they overtook and apprehended Endymion. He was now being set free. But this freedom brought him little satisfaction. " Arrested for claiming my own property."

But so much depends on the way the claim is made.

CHAPTER XX

cousin, Robert Barton, made him sense a contempt for them among the Representatives of Great Britain at the Treaty debate.

> They had nothing but contempt for Barton because they saw in him a renegade to his own class. But they accepted Collins and myself at our own valuation.

He told me about his manœuvres to prolong the debate until a Friday, for he knew that the week-end is the English Sabbath, from observances of which no Englishman exempts himself. If he could only get the debate spun out until Friday, he might count on a respite and time for consideration until the following Tuesday. He began an historical explanation which spun out the time. Again and again Birkenhead or Lloyd George would either anticipate or ask whither it was leading. He held on until Friday called the Ministers away.

" Chamberlain was the best of the whole lot. A clean and honest man." He withheld his admiration from Birkenhead. Like to like: Griffith to Chamberlain; Collins to Birkenhead. He had nothing but distrust for Lloyd George.

> He said something in Welsh to his secretary, Jones, when we were discussing the occupation of Haulbowline, and Jones went out to return with a map stippled with red crosses off the south-west coast of Ireland; each cross marked the watery grave of a British victim of a German submarine. The Germans sank two a day. There was nothing to be said.

He might have asked how would the continued possession of Haulbowline and the other ports make the British Navy more efficient. But this might have altered the humour of his opponents.

" There was nothing to be said."

Had we, who have not a ship to catch a herring a hundred miles off Kerry, undertaken the naval defences of Ireland, the awful drain for the upkeep of a navy equal to such a purpose would have been almost as ruinous as the loss of half or three-quarters of our trade.

" There was nothing to be said."

There was one thing to be said to the Five Plenipotentiaries in the room on the fateful evening when they were discussing the terms proposed by the British Government. " I will not break on the question of the Crown." Gavan Duffy, who was making balls for Barton to throw, sat silent while Edmund Duggan broke down Barton's resistance to the British offer.

> I sat in a cell in Kilmainham during two days while my best friends were taken out and shot. I was inside. They were outside dying for their country. I was in Mountjoy in a cell that overlooked the execution shed. Nine times I saw the English hangman go in and out. There are often times I wish I had been hanged. This is one of them now. I, and not they, ought to have been hanged, for they merely followed the course we laid down. And I, who am not hanged for my country, will not spit in the face of those dead men whose sacrifice brought us the terms that we are offered now.

Barton left the room to consult somebody, presumably Childers. Apparently Duggan's eloquence held. He voted for a Treaty crowning the sacrifices of Ireland's innumerable dead, and he prevented, for a while at least, the life-work of Arthur Griffith from being directed by an Englishman. Barton was the first to repudiate his signature.

But those who resent the Englishman, Childers' influence on even one of the Plenipotentiaries have refused to consider him in one decisive moment. What sent Barton back to vote ? When a weak man leaves a room to consult a dominating character, is it to be supposed that the stronger has no influence ? Childers may have sent Barton back to vote for the Treaty. Let me crave for him the benefit of this doubt, for he was as gallant a man as ever died in Ireland.

Since I was defeated by the Black-and-Tans at the battle of Clonee, I have grown rather particular. I don't like soldiers or pseudo-soldiers, especially when they are dressed as soldier chauffeurs. Therefore, on returning rather late one evening, the sight of several of them in a large limousine at my hall-door made me meditative. It would be a good idea before my latch-key identifies me to retreat to some place and to ring up my house. It was all right. Mrs. Clifton, who had been dining with Lord French at the Vice-regal Lodge, had dropped in for an after-dinner chat. I wonder ! But I hasten home.

They do not send ladies from the Lodge with warrants for arrests. The soldiers are merely escorts for Lord French's car.

Like a young man's dream of Andromache, she stood tall and darkly lovely by the fireplace. She had important news for me. At dinner that night the Provost of Trinity had warned Lord French that I was the most dangerous intellect unapprehended in Ireland. Did not this mean that I was likely to be arrested any minute ?

"I have been frequently arrested, but only for a few minutes, and I don't expect that Lord French will listen to a sneak. Intellect indeed! And the Provost is now trying to intellectualise himself into the Kingdom of Heaven, having resigned the Archbishopric of Dublin. It is not done, this resigning an Archbishopric to take up a better job. But Dean Bernard, Dean of St. Patrick's, as Dean Swift was, Dean Bernard, whilom Archbishop of Dublin and now Provost of Trinity, has a strange way of dealing with its alumnus which is I. Probably someone told him that when he took up the Provostship, I commented on the translation by remarking that he had exchanged the Thirty-Nine Articles for the Thirty Pieces of Silver, which, if anything, brought him closer to his Biblical archetype. We must not blame him if the only truth in him is that he is true to form. Probably he blames me for the showers of pennies which the Undergraduates throw at him whenever he appears."

"He was certainly most vindictive."

"Lord French is a soldier, and with him a renegade archbishop won't cut ice."

"What can have made him hate you so ?" Mrs. Clifton asked anxiously.

"Cardiac cases are often unaccountably irascible."

"Has he heart disease ?"

"Did you not hear that the Lord punished him by substituting angina pectoris for his pectoral cross ?"

Gratitude and contempt! Gratitude to the lady who took the trouble to obtain a car from her host to warn me, an acquaintance of a few years' standing, against the Provost, the Head Master of my College. She has repaid now any discomfort I suffered from the suspicious peasants through my association with her husband : to these such as he was a "spy"! And contempt for the pusillanimous breed that he represented, a breed that rightly incurred the hatred and contempt of all Irish Nationalists, old or new. The mim-mouthed crew that Bobbie Burns fought against without means or backing. The gang that denies the Splendour of God and would turn His grace into a narrow monopoly. The parson caricatured, penurious and opportunist. I cannot imagine Dr. Fogarty of Killaloe selling out and doffing his pectoral cross to manage a technical school or to become Chairman of the Electricity Supply Board for the Shannon Scheme. But here is Dr. Bernard " going one better " than an archbishopric to take over the well-paid Provostship of Trinity College. There was a time when its soul could bear Molyneux and Berkeley and Burke and Davis. . . . But it remained for Bernard to cash it in.

" How did French take it ? " I asked.

" ' He's operating on me to-morrow,' " was all he said. " Are you ? "

" I am more concerned for Trinity," I said, without answering, " than for Lord French. The fate of a patient of mine is within my control, as Epictetus has it, but the Provost is beyond me ; and he will make the College as narrow as himself. You cannot expect to turn an University into a gangsters' conspiracy to get a rake-off the ' wise-cracks ' of the classical world and at the same time raise its alumni above narrowness and pusillanimity."

" He never forgives himself for his *faux-pas* with the Provost . . ." remarked someone, laughing at me.

" Maybe you are right."

" When and where was it made ? " Mrs. Clifton inquired. " And what was your *faux-pas* ? "

" I don't want to elaborate it," I said, " but I was staying at Castle Forbes and, because some people like to show their catholicism by entertaining the narrow-minded, Lord Granard included the Archbishop, as he was then, in his house-party. It was dark when we got into the brake from the train. Everyone going to a house-party dislikes and disapproves of the other guests, as is the way of guests before they, all amiable, unavoidably meet at dinner. I could see the silhouette of the Archbishop like one of those old *Freeman's Journal* cartoons of a rival newspaper, where the sheaf is humanised by an angular nose and a pair of thin legs. The Archbishop's nose left his high, flat forehead like a gnomon at an angle of inhuman rectitude and, as he walked, he walked in perspicaciously.

" Things were growing dull at dinner while we waited for some enlivening or even an interesting remark ; but the Archbishop remained in his purple clothes as silent as a statue in a Catholic church on Good Friday.

" Just to cheer myself I told the story of Dr. Tyrrell's dinner at the Deanery of St. Patrick's. It never occurred to me to ask myself who was the Dean at the time of the story.

"' Once,' said Dr. Tyrrell, mildly cynical with the mellowness of his pleasant seventy years—' once I received an invitation to dine with the Dean of St. Patrick's. Well, you know, I could not give it to that old curmudgeon to say that I got drunk in his house.' I found myself wondering how and when my friend, Silenus-like in his wisdom, had found grace to refrain. I was not left wondering long. ' Oh, no ! I took the obvious precaution of coming drunk.'

" I laughed at my own story of the delightful old man. A few of the guests simpered, but the Archbishop's nose registered disapprobation and disdain. After an awful pause, he said, shooting a sharp momentary glint in my direction, ' That actually happened at my house.'

" And I had spoken of him as ' that old curmudgeon ' ! "

" That might explain some of his disapproval of you, but hardly all," Mrs. Clifton said.

" Then there were my bad manners in not waiting for him to speak. But what assurance had I that the Holy Ghost wanted such a mouthpiece ? I tried to dissipate the effect of my *faux-pas* by defending the Germans from charges of torturing their enemies.—' Woe to Great Britain's foes, they get a bad Press. . . . After all, the Chinese torture people, and they represent an old civilisation.'

" ' The Chinese tortures are a little more austere,' the Archbishop, very much to my surprise, remarked ; but with such an emphasis on *austere* that I felt myself somehow rebuked. But then my conscience automatically becomes bad when I meet an archbishop."

Be that as it may. He himself is the explanation of my disapproval, but nevertheless, if positions were reversed, I would never felon-set him or act the informer to have him imprisoned or hanged.

CHAPTER XXI

ARTHUR GRIFFITH HAD SOMETHING ON HIS MIND. WE WALKED IN silence along Duke Street. He had been telling me that he modelled his style on that of Dean Swift. And I had recorded how Dr. Tyrrell asked Carlyle whom he considered the greatest writer of English Prose. " Swaft! for his parfaict lucidity." Arthur rolled in his gait ' like a dove,' the Kaffirs said when he went to the mines in South Africa. " Cugaun " they called him. He used it for a *nom-de-plume*.

Suddenly : " I want you to do something for me."

" Consider it done."

" It is this. I have got word that Smuts is on his way from London. He will arrive at Kingstown early in the morning. I want to catch him before he reaches Dublin Castle. Can you have your Rolls-Royce ready at 4.30 in the morning ? Meet me at the church in Lower Merrion Street. Not a word to your man. I want you to drive me yourself. Barton and the Lord Mayor will be with us."

" I will be there punctually."

" Right ! " He gave himself a jerk, straightened his shoulders and marched on. We entered the Bailey. He made no further reference to the arrangement for the morning. It seemed as if he were relieved from a burden—the burden of having to ask anyone to assist him in his plans.

When much depends on a car starting, it is all you can do to prevent yourself lessening its chance of starting by over-attention or tinkering with it. I kept a bottle of ether ready in case. But it never gives me trouble, I reflected, yet at that hour of the morning, without a chauffeur, even the car may be asleep.

But all was well. Griffith and Barton were met, but where was Larry O'Neill, Lord Mayor ? We did not like to cruise about too noticeably, but Griffith was getting anxious. The Lord Mayor's presence will make it harder for General Smuts to escape from us and to consult the Castle first. Round the Square, then round by Westland Row. Will we just make one turn before giving him up ?

In the stillness of the empty streets a car was heard approaching. Soon we sighted Larry in his black clothes, sitting at the back. He changed into our car. Off. We must be at the pier by five, or our bird may have flown.

Along the Merrion Road we hummed. Black smoke far down on the horizon to the east far out where the Kish Lightship rocked.

"Plenty of time!" I said.

We stood on the pier while the boat was being made fast.

Larry was the first up the gangway. "Tell General Smuts the Lord Mayor of Dublin wishes to greet him."

Griffith grunted. That was spoiling our plans. We were to surprise the General, and now Larry had damped the effect with his 'Lord Mayor of Dublin.'

The steward said—he had learnt his lesson well—"General Smuts is not on board."

"Stand by and let me know if he slips ashore. I want to see the passenger list."

Griffith examined the list many times, looking for any South African name that Smuts would have been likely to adopt. To all our repeated inquiries the crew persisted in knowing nothing.

"We can only wait until they are all out of their cabins. Everyone has to be ashore by eight."

A pleasant prospect for me, who detest waiting! But there is one advantage which food has: it helps to pass the time.

All four of us breakfasted. Still no sign of Smuts. We dawdled about after breakfast until "all ashore!" rang out. We had our journey for nothing.

"Where to now?" I asked.

But Griffith never answered. He appeared not to have heard me. He was deep in thought. On whatever information he had he could implicitly rely, and yet there was no Smuts.

Let Larry rouse him.

"Where do you want to go now, Mr. Griffith?"

"Five Merrion Square."

That is Dr. Farnan's house. So Farnan is in the movement. We were not long in reaching 5, Merrion Square.

"I'll be back in ten minutes," I said. "I don't want to have this car seen outside the house. It would give the show away. I'll put it out of the way. It might lead to an arrest."

De Valera was breakfasting with Dr. Farnan. I was not present when Griffith arrived. I do not know how he explained missing Smuts. De Valera was supposed to be in hiding. We were supposed to be in the secret, but of course not to divulge it under pain of death.

Presently the telephone bell rang. I think I took the call. It is not important; but what was memorable was the consternation of both Farnan and De Valera when blandly came the voice, " May I speak to Mr. De Valera ? "

" Who is it ? "

" Alfred Cope, speaking from Dublin Castle ! "

And De Valera's hiding-places were such a secret ! This knowledge of where he was to be found meant that Dublin Castle could lay hands on him at any moment, if it wished. It rather lessened his importance. Collins could not be found. But De Valera was " on the 'phone."

" Is your car at the door ? " he asked me testily, thinking that its presence might be associated with a meeting of the group and so I might be blamed for giving his whereabouts away.

" I am not quite such a fool," said I.

Cope, it seemed, had telephoned to say that General Smuts had arrived at Dublin Castle and would like to confer with the Irish Leaders. Would eleven o'clock at the Mansion House be suitable ?

At the Mansion House I learned afterwards that Smuts advised them not to insist on a Republic.

" I tried a Republic, and it was a failure," he said.

Afterwards, too, I learned that he had purposely eluded us and avoided meeting Griffith, by hiding on the lifeboat deck, until he should first have reached Dublin Castle.

CHAPTER XXII

AS A RULE I GO TO THE ABBEY THEATRE TO LOOK AT THE AUDIENCE.
One can derive much interest from observing them, especially
if they are looking at a play by the observer. Lennox Robinson attributes so much importance to the audience that sometimes I begin to ask myself : Is it the audience or the play that
is the thing ?

But the house had two rows filled with Black-and-Tans.
They were much amused by ' A Serious Thing.' A play
which showed Judaea occupied by troops in khaki in the days
when Pontius Pilate was Procurator. Two were on guard on
a wall beside the tomb of Lazarus. Judaea was under curfew,
permits to move were necessary ; notes, mental and written,
were made by Rome's constabulary, of every speech. Great
exception was taken to moral apophthegms because it was suspected that under them lay incitement to disorder. There
had been a swine drive of sorts at Gadara.

Lazarus came forth and walked out without a permit,
disobeying the sergeant, who ordered him to halt. When
court-martialled subsequently and asked why he had not
killed Lazarus, the sergeant answered simply enough, " Because he was already dead." Of course Rome could make
little headway against a nation of resurrections.

It did me good to see the Black-and-Tans laughing, unaware that their legs were being pulled. Nevertheless, the
Author did not respond when the call for " Author ! " came.

Edward Martyn asked me to let him read the text. I never
saw him at the Abbey. Like every Irishman who can afford
to be an individual, he ran an opposition show, a theatre of his
own in Hardwicke Street. I went round to his rooms in
Nassau Street beside the Kildare Street Club. He was living
with monkish austerity—plain oaken chairs and table ; church-
warden pipes galore because they were so brittle. His
austerity appertained to everything except his appetite. He
read on in his short-sighted way while I looked at the deep
pink cheeks which festooned his collar. His pince-nez
made his nose and eyes appear even narrower than they were ;
and so belied the promise of his broad head and brow.

This is the man whom George Moore calls " Dear Edward." This is he who entertained Yeats and Moore in his
Castle of Tulira, hoping to win their approbation of his play.

I wish he could read faster. I hate being kept waiting, particularly in a kind of cell in a low-ceilinged mezzanine between the first and second floors. But soon it will be eight o'clock and he will scent the beef in the Kildare Street Club. He will seize his stick and his man will help his protein-crippled limbs to the carnivorous festival of rheumatism and gout. Strange last survivor of an ancient Galway family, the Martyns. For their liberality and humanity in the bad Seventeenth Century one of them was exempted from the confiscations which robbed the contemporary chieftains. Jaspar, James and Nimble Dick! Nimble Dick, who challenged the O'Flaherty, Prince of Iar Connaught, to single combat for an insult levelled at his mother, and who carried the combat, unattended by seconds, alone to the Castle of Auchnanure, only to be treacherously stabbed in the back by a retainer : then Humanity Dick, the originator of prevention of cruelty to animals. Yes, the Martyns were a noble clan, I heard myself saying. But suddenly a fat shout from the plain oaken chair.

" The Divine Voice ! "

" Yes ? "

" You have brought the Divine Voice on to the stage ! "

His gills cardinalised into crimson.

" But—well—what harm ? There has to be a miracle to get Lazarus to arise."

" Ugh, ugh ! But the Divine Voice ! "

" Well, if you can devise a means to get Lazarus up, I will omit it. The play, if we can call it a play, is symbolic. The Resurrection of Lazarus symbolises the nationhood of Ireland re-arisen from the grave wherein it lay dead—dead from the dilution of its individuality by identification with that of every Tom, Dick and Harry nation on earth, as a result of the system of ' Intermediate Education ' and regulated ways. Lazarus has found his soul. He is alive ; he is risen. He defies Imperial Rome and its Black-and-Tans. The nation's call has roused him. Is not *vox populi, vox Dei* ? And what is that but the Divine Voice ? "

But the thought of horse-radish and succulent rump steak attenuated any little interest he had in me or my play. Therefore all the more he wreaked on me his " advice " about the Divine Voice, especially since he had not an idea to offer as to why Lazarus could arise without a miraculous mandate.

I suggested that he should come behind the scenes and call

out reverently from his chair, " Lazarus come forth ! " I knew that his voice would sound so soft and soothing that the danger was it might deepen the sleep of Lazarus ; but I wanted his co-operation to protect me from spiteful little mandrakes who would concentrate on irreverence in the play and nothing else.

Everything was ready to bear him to dinner. He was the only man who took a motor-car to cover fifty yards.

I saw the trousers striped grey and black and the short black coat disappear gradually into the motor. To-morrow he will read an account of my play in the papers. He will wonder why I should have waited to seek his advice after the thing was staged. What will he think of me then ? I cannot say, but I know what he is thinking of now that the gong has gone, and that is about as far as I shall ever see into his mind. His branch of the Martyns cannot be descended from Nimble Dick !

I sat in the Abbey thinking of the gang who occupied the front rows. How many of them had been offered the alternative of service in Ireland to a long term in gaol ? English magistrates, it was said, were giving criminals that choice. They had killed priests, shot a pregnant woman and tortured prisoners ; yet they called the half-armed, totally untrained men who opposed their machine-guns and whippet tanks, cowards.

I remembered the account of one ambush—the only one, I think, that happened in County Galway. The local sergeant was acting unwillingly as guide to a lorry-load of Black-and-Tans. Very probably he was forced to act, for the Royal Irish Constabulary refused to co-operate with such ruffians. Along a lonely road in the bare West country, in sight of the mountain called the ' Devil's Mother,' the lorry came. The sergeant sat in the front seat beside the driver, who pulled up whenever he approached a spinney or rough ground to let his crew jump down and investigate, on guard against ambushes. The boys knew this, and they lay a hundred yards in front of a wood in a moor where there was hardly enough cover for a wild goose. They hoped it would be the spot where the lorry would come to a halt and a few of the Black-and-Tans would go ahead to search the spinney.

Lying flat on his chest, the captain would feel through it the rumble of the approaching lorry as it shook the light bog road.

How many were there? He dare not raise his head to look. It was anxious work holding down, not knowing whether his party had been observed or not, uncertain whether he would be shot in the back without having fired a shot.

"Just look at that there wood, Jerry!"

He could hear the foreign accent ten feet away. It was harder on the half-a-dozen lads under his command: but his responsibility gave him courage. And they had their rosary beads. He counted thirty, forty, fifty paces as the advance guard separated. He gave them another fifty until he could hear them no more. A hissing whisper "Soldiers, let them have it!" There were four men on each side of the lorry sitting back to back. Two were shot point blank. The driver got a bullet through his forehead. The two who had gone forward to the wood opened fire from the road. The sergeant jumped down and ran off unarmed.

"I did not like to quench him," said the Captain.

Something like that was coming surely to some of my audience in the Abbey Theatre. And the devil mend them!

I had no programme. I was only interested in my own play. It was not necessary to have a programme for that. And as for foretelling what would follow, you could tell that without any programme. It would surely be something by Lady Gregory. I must get out before her namby-pamby humour deadens my spirits.

How much of her plays did she write? Yeats had spent many months annually in collaboration with her in Coole Park, and I knew how generously Yeats presented me, for one, with golden lines or ideas. I was wrestling catch-as-catch-can with a sonnet. I wished to get a simile for joy reigning in the dark places of a hospital. I had failed to grasp " The happy hand of Chance." Yeats murmured for a minute sonorously to himself and said, with a sudden emphasis on the 'leap':

"' The blackbird *leap* from his dark hedge and sing.'"

The Divine Voice! It made whatever was worth making in the sonnet. How much more would he not do for Lady Gregory? I almost got him to acknowledge his authorship of 'The Rising of the Moon.' I think he said that it was understood between himself and Lady Gregory that a play might be attributed to the one who had the idea!

Possibly Lady Gregory thought of the title, which was that of a well-known ballad. But the perpetual presentation of

Lady Gregory's plays nearly ruined the Abbey. They were put on as curtain-raisers, comic reliefs, or they took the whole stage.

One who had contributed many hundreds of pounds to the Abbey, only to have a play of his cast unworthily, used to chaunt:

> " I heard the pit and circle say :
>   ' Gregory bores us,
> And one by one we slip away.' "

How different was the first play written and in part acted by an Irishman in Dublin! It was put on in some hired hall near Clarendon Street, George Russell's (Æ's) " Deirdre." The poetic mind had been awakened and inspired by Standish O'Grady's heroic fragment of Irish History. Æ was profoundly roused. He read theosophy into the tales of ancient gods and heroes, and compared them with the trilogy of deities he saw in every religion.

In his " Deirdre " the lovers are being drowned by the uprising of invisible waves. They are supposed to be friendly and, in some mysterious way, beneficent waves, for Æ could not sustain the thought of anyone being injured. At the moment they were overwhelmed, the dark purple curtain which backed the stage opened in the middle. The golden-brown beard and full, fresh-cheeked face appeared. A sonorous voice chanted one long name:

" Mananann Mac Lir."

It was the author, Æ! Shakespeare is said to have played the ghost in ' Hamlet ' because he had a fine voice. Æ's only appearance on the stage was a partial appearance, the head of the God of the Waves of Erin, Mananann, the Son of Lir.

Then, farther up the town in Camden Street, Synge would be sitting watching his rehearsals. He sat silent, holding his stick between his knees, his chin resting on his hands. He spoke seldom. When he did, the voice came in a short rush, as if he wished to get the talk over as soon as possible. A dour, but not a forbidding man. Had he been less competent it might have been said of him on account of his self-absorption that he " stood aloof from other minds. In impotence of fancied power." He never relaxed his mind from its burden.

I asked him if he did not intend his " Playboy " for a satire to show up, for one thing, how lifeless and inert was the country where a man could be hailed as a hero for doing something kinetic even though it were a murder, and how ineffectual, for,

as the event showed, even that had not been committed.   He
gave me a short glance and looked straight in front of himself,
weighing me up and thinking how hard it would be to get the
public to appreciate his play as a work of art, when one who
should know better was reading analogies and satire into it
already.   He shook my question off with a shake of his head.

We were nearer to poetic drama than we shall ever be again.
Intellectual life was astir.   Joyce and I used to go to see
how the actors were getting on with John Elwood, a medical
student, who enjoyed the licence allowed to medical students
by the tolerant goodwill of a people to whom Medicine with
its traffic in Life and Death had something of the mysterious
and magical about it.   To be a medical student's pal by virtue
of the glamour that surrounded a student of medicine was
almost a profession in itself.   Joyce was the best example of
a medical student's pal Dublin produced, or rather the best
example of the type, extinct since the Middle Ages, of a
Goliard, a wandering scholar.   The theatre off Camden
Street was approached through a narrow passage.   John
Elwood got so drunk one night that he lamented that he could
not even see the ladies stepping over him as they came out.

" Synge looks like a fellow who would sip a pint."

" John," I said, " if you had done more sipping and less
swallowing you would not have got us all kicked out."

Joyce knew far better than I what was in the air, and what
was likely to be the future of the theatre in Ireland.

Who can measure how great was its loss when Lady Gregory
gave him the cold shoulder ?   Maybe her much-announced
search for talent did not contemplate the talent latent in
medical students' pals or wandering minstrels.   After an un-
successful interview he met us in a " snug," where, very
solemnly, with his high, well-stocked forehead bulging over his
nose, he recited solemnly, waving his finger slowly :

> " ' There was a kind Lady called Gregory,
>   Said, " Come to me poets in beggary."
>   But found her imprudence
>   When thousands of students
>   Cried, " All we are in that catégory " ! ' "

The elision of " who " before the " Said " in the second
line is a parody on the synthetic folk speech in Synge's " Playboy."   And the strained " catégory " the beginning of his
experiment with words.   She had no room for playboys except
on the stage. . . . So Ulysses had to strike out for himself.

Dublin's Dante had to find a way out of his own Inferno.   But he had lost the key.   James Augustine Joyce slipped politely from the snug with an " Excuse me ! "

" Whist !   He's gone to put it all down ! "

" Put what down ? "

" Put *us* down.   A chiel's among us takin' notes.   And, faith, he'll print it."

Now, that was a new aspect of James Augustine.   I was too unsophisticated to know that even outside Lady Gregory's presence, notes made of those contemporary with the growing " Movement " would have a sale later on, and even an historical interest.

" He's discovered a wonderful poem in 4, Faithful Place, which he sent to Father Delaney."

" Surely it is not

> ' There was a kind priest called Delaney
> Who said to the girls, Nota bene ' ?

Because I have heard that ' not once or twice in our rough island's story.' "

Twitching and elusive, John did not reply.   He was one of those countrymen to whom a direct question suggests that the answer should be withheld.

He kept his eye glued against a point in the window from which the muffling of the glass had been worn.

Excitedly, " There's three auld ones," he said.

I was trying to recall what spark had been struck or what " folk phrase " Joyce had culled from Elwood or me that sent him out to make his secret record.

Secrecy of any kind corrupts sincere relations.   I don't mind being reported, but to be an unwilling contributor to one of his " Epiphanies " is irritating.

Probably Father Darlington had taught him, as an aside in his Latin class—for Joyce knew no Greek—that ' Epiphany ' meant ' a showing forth.'   So he recorded under ' Epiphany ' any showing forth of the mind by which he considered one gave oneself away.

Which of us had endowed him with an " Epiphany " and sent him to the lavatory to take it down ?

" John," I said, seeking an ally, " he's codding the pair of us."

But John could not be enlisted to resent.

" A great artist ! " he exclaimed, using " artist " in the

sense it has in Dublin of a quaint fellow or a great cod : a pleasant and unhypocritical poseur, one who sacrifices his own dignity for his friends' diversion.

" A great artist ! He may be codding the two of us, but he's codding himself ! "

" Codding apart, John, why is he taking notes ? "

" We're all on the stage—Jayshus, we're all on the stage since the old lady threw him out, Yeats, Roberts, Vincent, me and you—you're in for it worst, for you stood him a pint— Colum, Magee—we're all in a poem—' hat unfix.' " John jerked a word or two out, trying with his intermittent mind to recall Joyce's poem probably confided to him but once. Hopeless !

" Gargle that and have another. I want that poem from Faithful Place."

" Ask him for it when he comes back."

He'll hardly give it me, I surmised, but long afterwards he did. . . . The door of the snug was pushed in ; the three " auld ones " appeared. " Excuse us." We made room. One of them wore her bonnet, toque or hat on the ridge of her left eye. Her friend's face was obscured. James Augustine reappeared. He evinced no surprise. Beside Elwood, the " auld ones " intervening, he took his seat. As if nothing unusual had happened, he adjured them dictatorially with lines from his favourite Ben Jonson :

> " ' Still to be neat, still to be dressed,
>   As you were going to a feast.' "

" Well, now isn't your friend the queer body—and we're only recovering from a wake this morning ! "

> " ' Still to be powdered, still perfumed.' "

James Augustine continued uninterruptedly :

> " ' Ladies, it is to be presumed . . .' "

John looked at me with dancing eyes the lids of which were as defined as a warrior's of the Fifth Century B.C. and something of an archaic smile hovered always on his well-cut mouth.

" Isn't he a real artist ? "

Well-charged with diary of an evening's dissipation in Dublin, Ulysses could relax from listening to his companions' talk. But he sat on any resentment he bore by assuring himself that he would crucify us all in due course. Meanwhile, over-politely, he invited the old women to "join him in a drink."

" I know that yer laughin' at me," she said recklessly, " but, coddin' apart, I've reared five children and ye wouldn't believe that me father was a boat-builder beyond at Ringsend."

" He must have been an artist," yelled John.

Joyce rebuked John Elwood. John was as unaccountable as a faun.

" Madam, my friend is using artist in the Augustinian sense. St. Augustine, you may remember, uses ' art ' to express the third manifestation of the power of the Soul— practical life or ' art ' which comprehends all our activities from boat-building to poetry."

She flung herself into a spate of words which held Joyce by their sound—sense yielding to sincerity.

" Eight children and the girls married and himself dead and me sons' father, and here am I in The Bleeding Horse and only one gentleman among the lot of yez ! Not that I'm saying a word against the other two."

Solemnly James recorded,

" ' Love still has something of the sea.' "

Then, as if relenting from that detachment : " Madam, another pint will do us good, though over there with the actors it only makes them talk unnaturally."

" May God bless your lovely blue eyes, and hold His hand from your queer friends. Here's luck ! "

" A boat-builder ? " I inquired.

" Yes. In Ringsend, the town that thrun back Strongbow and sent him on to Dublin ! "

Elwood nudged me.

" Every old one loves him and leaves us on our . . ."

" John ! "

" You're as bad as them."

" That poem. If you misquote it, maybe he'll give it to us."

But James kept quoting Jonson still adjuring the three old trots :

" ' Lady, it is to be presumed.' "

So James Augustine mesmerised the old women. How much the name equalled him in experience with the Saint will never be recorded. It was far pleasanter and simpler than the ritual of Yeats or Æ. I attended a lecture by Æ in Camden Street and when, in answer to Yeats's invitation to comment, a man in the audience asked : " How many gods does your friend disbelieve in ? " majestically Yeats remarked : " My interrupter has asked an interesting question. Æ will reply."

" He's solemn enough now to be linked home ! Have I time to sing ? " Elwood asked.

" Don't ! John ! Take a pull at yourself ! "

" I'll recite then ! " Who can resist an audience ?

" This is what Joyce unearthed from No. 4. And he won't give anyone a copy. It's paved by the cobblestones of the Eighteenth Century, and in it a braver Dublin rings than we'll ever see again ! Where can we find men now who are not too cowardly to speak of ' bloody fine whores ' ? No bloody where ! You're all a pack of hypocritical funks ! " And he broke into :

> " ' As I was going down Sackville Street.' "

" Steady, John ! " I adjured.

> " ' Hey, Ho ! me Randy O,
> Three bloody fine——' "

" Who were they ? " I asked.

" They're symbolical of course. Everything with him is. They may be Patriotism, Politics and the Great Pox for all I know."

" Present company always excepted and double exceptions for Jimmy Joyce. The ' auld ones ' took up the chorus and were singing now. Whisht ! "

Released from cark and care, James had the old char-women singing, and at the same time reverencing him as if he were an evangelist. America would have been his happy remunerative exploiting ground if only he had been dishonest ! He was gifted with a seriousness that was unremitting and could resist even his own jokes.

" How does it go, Anna ? "

> " ' I chose the one with the curly locks !
> Hey Ho !——' "

" That would be the Muse of Politics, John," I remarked.

" Time—Gentlemen, Time ! Now then—Please ! "

" Good-night to you now, Master ! You've a lovely pair of blue eyes ; but I don't like the company yer keeping."

" You," said John.

" You ! " said I.

" What about going to a shebeen in the kips to cleanse our-selves from Synge ? "

" Apart from your quest for natural speech, I have my own reasons for going," said I.   " For everyone has business and desires ! "

" Yer a great pair of artists ! " John shouted as we went into the night.   And then as if thinking of the romantic bullies of Dublin's golden age he sang a stave :

> "' Whom did I meet but Tiger Roche ? ' "

" Great, John ! " I shouted.   " How does it go on ? "

But the swift eyes eluded me, and he ceased to sing.

One of the first meetings of the Irish Theatre, or rather of those who were about to produce Irish drama, took place in the Nassau Hotel.   Maud Gonne sat on the opposite side of the table.   Synge was at one end by Lady Gregory.   Patrick Colum sat next to me.   Suddenly Yeats exclaimed in admiration of a scene he was reading :

" Æschylus ! "

" Who does he mean ? " Colum whispered, amazed.

" Synge, who is like Æschylus."

" But who is Æschylus ? "

" The man who is like Synge ! "

We talked while Yeats was reading.   I was surprised at Maud Gonne's small voice.   For one so tall and striking you would have expected a voice full and contralto : but no, hers was a small voice.   And like the man in Douglas Hyde's song, she had a large heart—

> I'd rather have if I got my choice,
> A large heart and a small voice.

A tall and tawny woman, the daughter of a Colonel in the English Army, greatly she inspired Yeats.

" It is hardly possible for anybody in Ireland to write any-thing at all without becoming a genius.   I am off "—to Colum.

But Colum, who was fast becoming one, refused to discuss it disrespectfully.

The Abbey Players have now a theatre all their own.   And the plays of the least inspired of that old group of nascent geniuses are played the most frequently.

Happy and wholesome days with genius in the bud and the status of a medical student's pal recognised as a profession!

" Medicals " were immune from molestation even in the most lawless purlieus of the town.

" Mebbe they're on midwifery duty, helping a poor woman. Ye never know."

They were safe in every shebeen from the Gloucester Diamond to Hell's Gates when the " kips " were in full blast. This side of the Yoshiwara there was never such a street as Tyrone Street for squalor with wildest orgies mixed. Here reigned the Shakespearean London of Jack Greene. Here nothing but the English language was undefiled.

The names of its brothel-keepers, bullies, and frequenters were typical of a city which, like Vienna, had forged for itself a distinct identity. There were certainly not Irish nor wholly English names. Dublin names, euphonious and romantic!

Now that the Abbey Players are world-renowned, I begin to realise that with such an audience and such actors an author is hardly needed. Good acting covers a multitude of defects. It explains the success of Lady Gregory's plays. It explains the favouritism enjoyed by the Fays. This is no place for me! I am off. But if I could father ' A Serious Thing ' on the Old Lady, it would never stop running.

CHAPTER XXIII

ELY PLACE, DUBLIN. LIKE ITS NAMESAKE IN LONDON, IT IS
a *cul-de-sac*. From St. Stephen's Green, Hume Street runs
into it at right angles, and Ely House, the residence of the
long-dead Marquis, looks down Hume Street to the west.
The prevailing wind, which is western, blows the dust of
Hume Street against the great house, seven windows wide,
and makes it unsafe to keep them open. Ely House is one
of the few remaining palaces of the spacious Eighteenth
Century which exist in Dublin without having fallen long ago
into decay: old houses which were dedicated to mythological
persons. Belvedere House to Venus, Ely House to Hercules.
The Farnese Hercules stands like a pillar at the foot of the
great stairs, which are balustraded by representations in gilt
bronze of the wild beasts such as the Nemean Lion, which fell
to his club and whose hide he holds for ever on his left arm.

Sir Thornley Stoker, the famous surgeon, lives in Ely
Place, and in the Eighteenth Century, which he never really
leaves; hence the house is filled with period furniture, of
which he is a collector and a connoisseur. Chippendale,
Adams, and old silver candelabra, match the silver jambs of
the doors, and are contemporary with the silver linings of the
great fireplaces, under their mantels of Siena and statuary
marble.

A figure with hair silver as a dandelion in summer, pink
porcelain face, sloping shoulders and peg-topped trousers in a
suit of navy blue, came strolling down Ely Place from its
garden end. He carried a Malacca cane with an ivory top
shaped like an egg; he strolled leisurely, as became a novelist,
a personage and a man of independent means. When he
reached the long railings of Ely House he drew his stick
across them as he went, causing a noise which he calculated
would reach and irritate the somewhat strange and irascible
owner. He passed on.

" Be sure you come punctually," said Sir Thornley to me,
" it's a sign of bad manners to be late for dinner. Augustine
Birrell is dining with us; but it's not for that reason that I
ask you to be punctual, but for the general principle."

The great dining-room was lit with candles, which of
course were waxen.

" Nobody ever heard of paraffin candles at the time that

this house was built; you see how much better the stucco designs appear on the blank walls in this mellow light. This is Mr. Birrell; now I think we can all be seated. There is no use waiting any longer, and one has to consider the soup more than a tardy guest. Take your places, gentlemen."

We had just finished the soup when the door of Domingo mahogany swung silently, reflecting the light. The butler said, " Mr. George Moore."

Sir Thornley Stoker only half rose and turned sideways, holding his napkin like an apron in his lap.

" Sit down, Moore," he said testily, " sit down. We couldn't wait for you any longer."

Moore went over to his empty chair, balanced it on its hind legs, admired what Sir Thornley would call " the excellent skin " of its glossy Chippendale wood, and turning from his scrutiny, with a look of inquiry towards his host, asked: " A cancer, Sir Thornley, or a gallstone ? " referring to Sir Thornley's habit of buying after a big operation 'a museum piece.'

Moore resented the presence of Birrell. He had decided for the evening not to have read *Obiter Dicta* or, at the worst, if anyone mentioned it, to be unaware of its relation to Mr. Birrell, or of Mr. Birrell's relation to it.

Sir Thornley asked: " The shoulder or the belly of this salmon, Moore ? I'm chining the salmon. I killed this fish in the Slaney—King Harmon's water—and I think we'll find it a palatable fish. Shall I help you to the shoulder ? "

" No, I think the fin, Sir Thornley."

" Now, Moore, don't be peevish. You are the last that should pretend to be careless about your food. I've just been reading your long letter in the *Irish Times* on the grey mullet. Nobody ever heard of a fin."

" On the contrary, the Chineses—as my friend here insists on calling them—find sharks' fins delicious."

These antics fail to draw Birrell, so Moore addresses his remarks to me. Then Birrell says, " How is your brother Bram, Sir Thornley ? "

" Haven't seen him for some time."

" Is he living in Herbert Street, or is he in London at all these days ? "

" He is engaged on scientific research somewhere," said Sir Thornley.

" Not on the habits of Dracula ? " said Birrell, with a laugh.

At this stage the mahogany door burst open, and a nude and elderly lady came in with a cry, " I like a little intelligent conversation ! " She ran round the table. We all stood up. She was followed by two female attendants, who seized whatever napery was available, and sheltering her with this and their own bodies, led her forth, screaming, from the room.

Our consternation held us in the positions we had suddenly taken. Birrell looked like a popular figure in Madame Tussaud's, Sir Thornley, with his knuckles on the table, inclined his head as if saying a silent grace. At last he broke silence with : " Gentlemen, pray sit down."

Nobody liked to begin a conversation, because the farther it was off the subject, the more purposefully self-conscious it would seem. Sir Thornley recovered himself and spoke :

" Gentlemen, under my mahogany, I hope you will keep this incident, mortifying as it is to me, from any rumour of scandal in this most gossipy town. And now, Moore, I conjure you most particularly, as you are the only one who causes me grave misgivings."

" But it was charming, Sir Thornley. I demand an encore."

Sir Thornley rose, went over to Moore's chair, and pointing his beard into Moore's ear, hissed something. Then, taking the novelist by the shoulder, he pushed him to the door and into the hall, and out into the street. We heard the door banging and the yapping of her Ladyship's Pomeranian dog.

Sir Thornley insisted on his guests drinking more wine. The dinner dragged on, Sir Thornley asking questions without waiting for answers, from each of us in turn. I was counting the minutes towards the end of this melancholy feast. After some minutes the butler leant over and said something to Sir Thornley.

" Did you admit that scoundrel ? " said Sir Thornley harshly.

" He says, sir, it's a matter of life and death."

" Will you, pray, excuse me, gentlemen ? I have to leave the room for a moment."

We could hear the inarticulate sound of voices, and suddenly two loud screams. It transpired that George, on his way home, had been bitten by a mad dog and was in danger of hydrophobia. Sir Thornley had enlarged the two slight scratches on Moore's right calf and was screwing caustic into the wound. The yells increased, and through the door, which

Sir Thornley had forgotten to close, we could hear him saying, " I don't care whether you're in a dinner-jacket or not. You'll have to send to your house for my honorarium, which is five guineas, before you leave this hall." Moore produced a wallet of flexible green leather and handed Sir Thornley a five-pound note, with " I'll send the silver in the morning by my cook." The butler opened the door, to let out George Moore, and to let in a little Pomeranian dog. . . .

George Moore returned up Ely Place, still straying his stick against the railings of No. 8. Sir Thornley Stoker, far back in his dining-room, placed the *Graphic* on the *original* red leather of one of his chairs, stood up on it, so as not to be observed, and satisfied himself that the source of the corrugated irritations was the novelist whom some weeks ago he had saved from Pasteur.

I bought my house because of its Florentine knocker. This rattled loudly at a quarter to ten.

" I know where he is," said Thornley, entering, " I'll find my way up."

I met him on the stairs.

" Where can we talk ? " said he.

I took him into a little room that looked out on George Moore's garden—which was a glory of apple-blossoms and the deep hue of lilac beginning to unfold.

" As a Fellow of the Royal College of Surgeons, you've taken the oath of Hippocrates," said Sir Thornley.

" I have," said I.

" Well, I bind you by that oath," he said, " not to lift a finger in aid of that ruffian who lives opposite you up the street. He'll come over here, cadging for free medical advice. Remember, you are not a physician. I loathe the word ' specialist,' but your activities are on the surgical side. . . ."

" What's wrong with him now ? " said I, wondering how the oath of Hippocrates, who had forbidden men to accept any emolument for medical services, could prevent them extending a helping hand to an invalid who sought it. Then suddenly I had it—Artaxerxes! Moore was to be refused aid as Hippocrates had refused to help the Persian enemy of his country.

" I've noticed this morning," said Sir Thornley, " that that fellow who lives opposite to you up the street is about to have an attack of weeping eczema where it will hurt his vanity most.

Already there are three little vesicles on that shiny forehead of his, and in a day or two they will be confluent or generally distributed.   It will lay him up for two or three weeks, but remember, you are forbidden to interfere.   He will come over to you, because I have refused to let him in, and he will try to pick your brains.   Let him seek for aid anywhere but in Ely Place."

I affected to be greatly concerned, hoping that Moore would not appear while Sir Thornley was shutting off aid, no matter how inadequate, from the nearest member of the profession.   We spoke on other subjects.   He corrected me in matters of good taste in furnishing ; he said, as he got off the chair : "Hepplewhite, not Chippendale.   I hope you haven't been taken in."

I was about to admit how little I cared, when I suddenly realised what an admission of vulgarity this could not but appear to Sir Thornley, who had made myself and most of the doctors in Dublin gentlemen by persuading us to buy a Chippendale table, with a lion's mask or shell, for our halls or waiting-rooms.   I said I found them at home, and that I got them " restored."

" Good God ! " said Sir Thornley ; " ' restored ' !   You are incorrigible.   I suppose you had that mirror re-gilt."

" I don't know," I murmured, " I'm not sure whether it's old or new."

" Well, you should know," he said, " for these things make all the difference between ignorance and culture."   Then, going down the stairs, out of that great human heart of his— " But, by the way, if that poor devil gets too bad, you may give him this . . . where can I write it ? "

I provided pen and paper ; and in the kindness of that troubled heart of his he wrote out a prescription.   In the evening I saw George Moore ambling from the second last house on the left where he lived, but he still remained on the brown granite slabs of the walk on his own side.   He passed Sir Thornley's, but made no attempt to transform the railings into a harp of low tone.   He was endeavouring to placate Hippocrates.

After dinner I was beckoned from the room.

" A gentleman wants to see you, but he won't come upstairs. I think it's that gentleman from the other side of the street."

" Ah, my dear friend," said George Moore, " I want a

word with you. Where can we go? Bring me to a private room with a good light."

I switched on a lamp. He pointed solemnly to his forehead, leaning his finger, like the rod of Moses, and asked in an awestruck whisper, slowly elongating the adjective, " What are these loathsome things ? "

I scrutinised his brow with a steady stare for as long a space as the solemnity of the occasion demanded, then, breathing a sigh, I diagnosed, " Memoirs of your Dead Life."

" Good Lord ! " said he. " Can it be possible ? It must be thirty years ago."

" Even unto the third and fourth generation . . ." I said.

To my astonishment he recovered quickly. In fact, he assumed an arch air and waved his stick, saying, " Oh, well, that kind of thing can be cured."

" But not by me," said I. " Very sorry ! But with all these oaths of fellowship going about, and Sir Thornley watching, I can't touch you, until it gets into one of my departments. Your ear, or up your nose . . ."

" You don't mean to say I'm to be vivisected and tortured alive, till the disease gets into my ear ? Do you think it will spread so far ? "

" You may have absolute confidence in me. It will be in your ear in a few days."

He went out expostulating, but I did not hear him threaten to consult anyone else. Perhaps he thought he could buy Sir Thornley, by the silence of his railings.

But I was wrong. Next day I saw the brougham of a well-known dermatologist in the street ; two days later another physician was called in. They had accepted Moore's version of his Dead Life, and greatly increased the outbreak by applying an actual remedy to an imaginary disease because the second physician doubled the dose of the first. Moore came over to see me.

" I want to see you as a friend," said he, " even though your conduct is most unfriendly and inhumane. Perhaps you are satisfied now. The beastly thing is in my ear."

I searched for the remedy of Sir Thornley. Luckily, I found it, committed it to memory.

" Have you dismissed your physicians, by the way ? "

" Don't speak of them," he answered, with a sigh.

" Well, if this cures your ear, you may apply it to the rest of your face, on condition that you do it at your own risk."

" My face fell off this morning, in the bed," said George.

" But there's a much more important condition," said I.

" What is that ? " he demanded.   " I'd do anything under the sun."

" Well, you will do this out of the sun ; for you must promise to remain for fully a week in your house.   You must not go for one moment out-of-doors till this day week, which is Monday."

" But, my dear friend, how can I go out-of-doors with this leprosy ?   I would want a leper's rattle. . . ."

" You could rattle the railings, but don't do it in my part of the street. . . ."

" Well, my good friend, I will remain indoors.   I promise you that."

" The promise will probably hold out until Sunday, for that's your cook's day out, and you used to dine with Sir Thornley, Lord O'Brien, or with me.   You can't even come over to me ; nor can I go over to see you.   I don't visit patients in their homes."

George Moore had refused my mother's request to exclude my name from *The Lake*.

" But, Madam, if you can supply a name with two such joyous dactyls, I will change it."

It caused her much pain.   And I came in for a lecture on the company I was keeping.   " Show me your company, and I'll tell you who you are ! "

" But I am not George Moore ! "

However, I was his keeper for a week.   And now for revenge.

The one regret he often expressed was for his thoughtless attack on Mahaffy, made when he was full of enthusiasm for the Gaelic language.   Socially, intellectually—in many ways, it recoiled on him.   Now, if an invitation to meet Mahaffy and to make up the quarrel at dinner in the College Hall were to reach Moore on the first day of his isolation, it would exasperate him.   And he could not break prison owing to the state of his face.   Yes.   And another for Tuesday from Bailey.   Bailey he knows so well and has dined with him so often that it will appear quite natural that he should invite his old friend.   The bathos of this familiar dinner compared to the exaltation of a dinner with Mahaffy in Dublin's seat of learning will test his temper.   It was not hard to get Bailey to comply. Let me see—for Wednesday Lord O'Brien. But Lord O'Brien said,

"Why should I ask that fellow to dinner?"

"Because he can't come," I said.

Now I had put my foot in it!

"Can't come? What do you mean?" said the old Chief Justice, sitting up.

He had been called Peter the Packer because in order to get a conviction in the Land League days he packed the juries with twelve complacent men. He and I were not on very friendly terms since I had offered in answer to his advertisement for a shooting brake to hold twelve, a seven-seater limousine.

"But——" said the agent.

"If Peter the Packer can't get twelve into it, who can?"

I tried to explain the predicament. But this made it worse, for it only elicited sympathy for George Moore. I had to do a little jerry-mandering. And Moore received what looked an invitation. That would be three. Now for a fourth. What a pity Sir Thornley's present mood admitted of no reconciliation! Also he knew the condition of the patient, and even if he did not, he took his dinner-parties so seriously that he would never have made a meal the subject of a joke.

Would Rolleston invite George? The difficulty, I could see, would arise from the proximity in which they dwelt. Rolleston might take it into his head to call with an invitation. Invitations had to be written. They had to come from acquaintances close enough to excuse their short notice. A difficult problem. Rolleston might not be inclined to see George Moore so soon again. I remembered, before the "leprosy" broke out in 4, Upper Ely Place, a long argumentative wrangle over the date and the excellence of Angus O'Gillan. Rolleston had produced a superb poem "From the Irish of Angus O'Gillan." Its metre alone would distinguish it from any elegy. The theme was Clonmacnoise, an ecclesiastical town on the left bank of the Shannon below Athlone, which in the early centuries of Christianity became a Westminster Abbey of sorts wherein all the famous in the land were interred.

What a glorification of Death! Rolleston's poem is well known, but it cannot be known enough. In any case, it is well for me to recite it to myself, for it is one of those poems which I always wish to have at call in my memory.

CLONMACNOISE.

In a quiet watered land, a land of roses,
  Stands St. Kieran's City fair;
And the warriors of Erin in their famous generations
  Slumber there.

There beneath the dewy hillside sleep the noblest
  Of the Clan of Conn,
Each beneath his Stone with his name in branching Ogham,
  And the Sacred Knot thereon.

*   *   *   *

Many and many a son of Conn, The Hundred-Fighter,
  In the red earth lies at rest :
Many a blue eye of Clan Colman the turf covers,
  Many a swan-white breast.

In the red earth! And the lovely women too!

Was it any wonder that Rolleston dressed like Alfred Lord Tennyson? His height justified it, his poem, and his trim beard; but he was a better-looking man than Lord Tennyson, and Lord Tennyson, though laureate of England, had done nothing better than "The Dead at Clonmacnoise," whose heroism and beauty endow Death and make it partake of their glory.

But I am forgetting my hospitality to George Moore. There is no dinner for him on Friday. Let me see.

Ah! Sir Horace, of course! I thought of Kilteragh, with its perpetual house-parties, which invariably contained some American reporter of outstanding ability and a British Cabinet Minister.

"Don't you think, Sir Horace, that Mr. McPherson should meet George Moore?"

"Hah, my dear fellow! Can you bring him to dine to-night?"

"If you give me a note, Sir Horace."

George will be summoned forth on Friday. Meanwhile I will take a look at his windows across the garden from my back room.

Beauty for Saturday. There must be a beautiful woman pining in the Shelbourne to meet the famous novelist. Now who shall it be? If I choose Isodora Duncan, he may read in the papers that she is in the South of France. An actress of course, of course! Better still, a ballerina; and Anna Pavlova is appearing in the Gaiety and Count Markiewicz knows her well. Not so long ago my friend, another 'George,' was telling Joe and myself about the Count's cocker spaniel and Anna Pavlova, and of his own chivalrous exploit.

About eleven o'clock the other evening the Count invited this other George to go to the Gaiety to see Anna Pavlova when she should come off the stage. They found her in her dressing-room. The Count spoke Russian, and George was introduced. He did not know what they were saying, but she looked at him and then questioned the Count. She was about to take off her costume.

" Do you mind if I change ? "

" Oh, not at all."

" But your friend ? "

" George won't mind ! Oh, my God, no ! " the Count assured her.

" She stripped herself stark naked. She had a lovely body," George said. " The lines rippled down to the beautiful hips. Her breasts were firm and out-pointing."

" Was she dark ? "

" No, her hair was a sort of brown. But when the Count was having a whiskey—she kept a bottle on her dressing-table—I noticed his dog mouching about. Presently he went off through the partly open door. Pavlova went on dressing. Suddenly she came to a halt and made an exclamation in Russian, pointing to a deficiency in her clothes. She missed her knickers. At once I realised what had happened."

" Splendid fellow ! "

" I went after the dog, which had escaped into the street with Pavlova's undies in his mouth."

" Did you get them ? " I asked breathlessly.

" I did," said George solidly. " And I brought them back."

" I have not eyes like those enchanted eyes," I quoted to myself, looking enviously at George, who had gazed on Nature's naked loveliness.

" Was she a Jewess ? " Joe inquired.

" No, she was the loveliest figure I ever saw," George admitted. " She was a Slav."

" A Slav to your passions," Joe remarked.

Count Markiewicz would be charmed to pull Moore's leg, or anyone's leg. His six-feet-five made him kinsman of the gods. An invitation to George Moore to her suite for a light supper after the show. Exactly !

" And, by the way, Count," when I had explained the limitations of the novelist, " what about Sunday ? "

" Oh, ho, ho, ho ! "   He roared at his idea before expound-
ing it.   His wife was dressing to go to the Vice-regal Lodge
that night.   He had to be there too.   Leave it to him !
" The notepaper, and a soldier !   It will be all right.   Ho !
ho ! "

The scheme was to obtain the notepaper, write an invitation
to George to dine with their Excellencies on Sunday night,
and despatch it by a lancer.

" The lancer with pennon will look very well and the chain
reins will jingle outside his windows.   Very pleasant indeed !
A martial memory ! "

Now, it costs twenty shillings to detach a private of the
Lancers from duty for even ten minutes.   All he had to do
was to ride up Ely Place and attract attention.   If necessary a
little boy would be sent on to knock at the door.

" Leave it to me," said the Count.

Later we watched the horse curvetting in front of No. 4.
We could see the red dressing-gown flashing and the white
hair appearing and reappearing behind now one window and
then the other.   The Count deserved his bottle of whiskey.

" It's very pleasant to sit here dispensing Vice-regal
hospitality ! "

" Very pleasant. . . . Not too much soda ! . . . Very pleasant
indeed ! "

But a maid was leaving Moore's house.   Presently I heard
a knock.   A message from Mr. Moore.

" Say I am not at home ! "

" None of us is at home," the Count added.

Before evening a letter was handed in.   After assuring me
of his complete recovery and his total lack of appreciation of
what a few hours' extra detention could be expected to do, it
continued :

". . . I would have you to know that this is not an
invitation.   It is a command ! "

" A relapse is utterly incurable," I wrote.   " You
promised to give the cure a chance by remaining indoors
until to-morrow."

As for commands, I said to myself, I hope I shall persuade
the postman that three or four letters addressed to the addresses
I have listed must be referred to me.

George Moore never knew the cause of his transient hebdomadal popularity. On recovering, he explained its sudden cessation to himself by his having had such a loathsome disease.

The lady friend of his to whom I told it in London, hoping that it would reach his ears, misunderstood the whole thing. She thought that the idea was to give him a lift into Vice-regal society which he never needed. " And had he not every right to go ? "

CHAPTER XXIV

" HAH ! MY DEAR FELLOW. WILL YOU COME WITH ME TO THE Front ? Just you and I ? I am thinking of going out next week."

Sir Horace gnarled on over the hard vowel sounds of the next sentence he intended to utter. I guessed that it was to explain some reason for going out other than mere curiosity, something really of constraining and national importance.

Not wishing to appear hesitant, I replied before he could say more, " Of course ! Delighted. Splendid ! "

But he hastened to assure me of the enormity of the undertaking.

" It's not a holiday. It is far more important than you seem to realise. I have written to Haig to expect us both at Headquarters. I mentioned your name. I have no doubt that I can work you in. I wrote to Haig about a fortnight ago that I should be ready to go to France by the 24th. The reason I am postponing your inclusion until the last minute is that I may any day get an excellent excuse for bringing you with me."

I wonder for what great cause I shall be travelling. It is a first principle with Sir Horace that whatever he does must have a transcendental purpose. Sir Horace has so many national and international reasons for doing exactly what he pleases that I wonder how I shall fare when enlisted under " an excellent excuse."

I imagined us at the railway station amid the sadness of farewells—reassuring brave " co-workers " with a handshake firm enough to be too expressive for words—everything packed, and at the last moment having to leave the train because we had forgotten to put in " a national purpose ! " Then Sir Horace remembers it, and we steam off determined come what may to co-operate with Haig.

We are not bringing Æ, was the first misgiving which flashed across my brain. Why are we going ? It cannot be to fight, for I am not much of a fighter. I am given more to prolonging life than cutting it off in its bloom.

" Haig on the 24th ! " he emphasised challengingly.

Does he think I am funking it ? I am somewhat, but my nerve is within reason's control ; and I can soon bring myself to the sticking place. Fearing that he might think what he had every right to opine, I hurriedly said—realising with the assurance it lent that it was to G.H.Q. we were bound:

"You have only to ring me up. I am at your service."

But all the time the question kept asking for an answer, What is Sir Horace up to? Lay the foundations of a gun emplacement? Declare a barrage open? Start a co-operative movement among the Allies? Their buying power is enormous! But their explanation was beyond me. Meanwhile I interposed:

"I am at present attached to three military hospitals. I suppose I shall have to give them some notice."

"Hah, you know nurses!" He pondered. At last: "You must not mention this, but there is on foot a project for getting Irishwomen to work in the American hospitals— a service, I am inclined to think, which might be willingly rendered if the matter were properly put after ecclesiastical sanction had been obtained. . . . Let me know your movements."

"Forwards!" I cried.

Isn't Sir Horace wonderful! Here was our international purpose, our excellent excuse—Irish women, American wounded! But when, on his departure, the double mesmerism of Sir Horace's effect on me and my effect on myself by wishing to appear nonchalant in mid battle had worn off, things began to take a less assured form.

There were first of all submarines in the water which had to be sailed. True, Sir Horace said something about a destroyer which I did not clearly hear, nor did I, had I heard it, wish to make it seem that I counted on it. The word 'destroyer' is disturbing anyway. Then those aeroplanes which kept over Boulogne trying to drop things on the T.N.T. freighters, even a brick or a spanner, or one of the 'planes itself if shot down and the wreckage were to fall on the ammunition ship . . . shells too, even though we were only off to G.H.Q. No use assuring oneself that the one casualty that never occurs is that of a Commander-in-Chief. Killing a Commander-in-Chief simply is not done. Otherwise the war might stop, and what would those who are engaged in waging it do? It is not professional etiquette to bomb, shell, shoot or bury a Commander-in-Chief. Sir Horace knew everybody. I narrowly escaped the Dardanelles, after saying glibly one night that even Homer knew that they

were only to be commanded from the Asiatic side. Sir
Horace had been at school with Admiral de Robeck. "Hah!
That's a good idea. One worthy of reviving, I mean. Longworth, make a note of that. I may send it to de Robeck
by our friend here. Or I may go with him myself."

But a watery grave was preferable to a land one only in
that it would have been over by this. "*Nunc habet pro
tumulo toto*—what would Dardanelles be ?—*ponto*." But France
'*The kind strange land, Whereon we stand*" is not our
country's clay. No, it would be somewhat *outré* to be buried
in France. To rise for ever in an endless officers' mess. And
there would be little use adding a proviso to my will that my
remains were to be brought home, if all that were left of me
were the heels of a boot. Boots? If the soles of my boots
were to be painted white they would act as flags of truce and
signals of peace in case I fell back on my second line. But
these are thoughts unworthy of me.

How does one dress going perhaps officiously, but certainly
unofficially, to the Front with Sir Horace Plunkett on a
visit to his friend Haig? If I wear a tall hat it may attract
the notice of the enemy, if any. A dentist whose hand
had acquired such a tremor when at the Front that he could
no longer draw teeth, still could draw, as he complained,
the enemy's fire. He had not joined up for that! A tall
hat would attract snipers. Plus-fours would be out of the
question except in the base hospitals. If I ask too many
questions before we are actually *en route* it may imperil my
invitation. Meanwhile, I must make myself war-minded.
G.H.Q. is safe enough to cover a great deal of military diffi-
dence. Discipline's the thing!

I took a turn down Merrion Street.

"In the name of God, what's wrong wid ye?" Jimmy
speaking. A sturdy, short, reddish man in a bowler hat.
"I thought you were spavined or doing the goose-step."

Coldly I replied: "I am merely walking down the
street."

"I thought I'd seen a drill sergeant. What's come over
you lately? I'll go a bit out of the way with you if I can
keep in step." And he suited his action to his words and
walked along.

But any ambitions I may have had to fall like a soldier
were dashed. I got a letter from Sir Horace complaining
that because I did not keep his intention secret he could not

go. It seemed that Lord Granard asked him in the Club,
" Where are your tabs ? " suggesting that he was already a
General.   He hated anyone who tried to pull his leg.   Instead
of going to the Front, he fell back on Kilteragh, and I never
met Haig.

CHAPTER XXV

DR. TYRRELL!

" Is it the benign doctor?" He came in a little breathless.

"Oh, oh! Yes, ah, my delightful friend, I nearly missed the train. We are staying out at Greystones. I am not familiar with the lanes. I was directed to a short-cut, but I had no time for a short-cut this morning. Ah!"

He relapsed mellowly into an armchair, concealing a smile at his satire on directions for short-cuts. He looked like one of the clean-shaved Cæsars. His beautiful profile and *embonpoint* adding to the resemblance. I filled a tumbler one-third full of whiskey, adding soda. He took it and remarked after a lengthy pull, as he sighed contentedly:

" There is nothing more disconcerting than an illness one has *not* brought on oneself.

" Happy is he who discerns first causes; he can disregard the clamours of hungering Hell.

"Oh, yes. How quick you are! '*Felix qui potuit*,' of course. Now I can set about curing myself with a tranquil mind. What happened was this. I was walking to the Club with Willie Atkinson, when that little bandy-legged solicitor with the chattering teeth met us and invited us in. I thought it was into the University Club—the steps are about the same—but the surroundings were unfamiliar. The ceiling of the dining-room was blue and prankt with stars—Orpen, they say, painted the ceiling and added the stars. What superb genius he has! A lesser man might have painted them on the floor. ' Welcome to the Friendly Brothers' Club,' the little fellow said. ' Here's luck, Perfessor.' He called me ' per ' instead of ' pro,' possibly with the idea of choosing a stronger prefix.

"Well, of all the places I have drifted into! It was a discovery in a way, for I often wondered where the descendants of those who of old escaped death by duelling as the natural result of their bad manners had managed to conceal themselves.

" Friendly Brothers!

"Now had they called it ' The Sick and Indigent Roomkeepers' Society,' it would at least have had the advantage of a magnificent if somewhat pretentious title. After a while we managed to escape, only to find that in the University Club drinks are no longer served in the Hall. And after we had scaled those steps!"

He took a sip and continued:

"No. They are to be served upstairs on the topmost flight—Bernard, of course, that old curmudgeon, instigated the Committee to make the rule. He thought we would be deterred by the climb. Would you believe it, as I sat resting in a window-seat, I saw him coming up the stairs? As cheerfully as I could, in answer to his very curt nod, I said:

"'They shall be afraid of that which is high.'

"Parsons hate laymen to take their words out of their mouths. He frowned and went up to the Library. Had he been present at the wedding feast of Cana he would have soured the wine. Thereby weakening our faith. And this morning, owing to the vigilance of the village, I had no opportunity to undergo a cure."

He paused and leant his face into his tumbler which I had replenished because I had to break what might be unpleasant news.

"Hearing that you had been to the Friendly Brothers with the little chatterer, I invited him to the picnic this afternoon. And now I am afraid he'll turn up. 'The worst thing about him,' as Yeats said of a colleague, "is that when he is not drunk, he is sober.' However the absence of Mahaffy may compensate you for the inclusion of the moron."

He asked with a show of interest why the Provost was not coming. I said that I feared he blamed me for including Æ in a lunch.

"The Provost had a bottle and more of claret, and was just seeking a windless corner of the garden to smoke a satisfactory cigar, when Æ rushed after him and said: 'Why won't you use your great influence, Provost, to have these scandals in Russia stopped? It makes my blood boil to think of the way they are being knouted and sent to Siberia!'

"Sir John Pentland Mahaffy, the only cleric who obtained a title in recent years, turned, displeased by the disturbance, and asked icily: 'Let us get this right, my good man. Who is knouting whom?'

"'Oh, the Czar is knouting the Russians and sending them to Siberia in thousands and thousands. It makes . . .'

" ' Well, all I can say is,' Mahaffy said genially, ' that if the Czar does not knout them, they'll knout themselves.'

" But his afternoon siesta was spoiled; and now *nec mihi Apollo respicit.*"

Dr. Tyrrell raised his glass as if toasting the relief he felt at the absence of the critical supervision which might be his lot if Mahaffy were to accompany us. There was little love lost between them. He murmured:

" I never quite forgave Mahaffy for getting himself suspended from preaching in the College Chapel. Ever since his sermons were discontinued, I suffer from insomnia in church."

" Why was he forbidden to preach ? "

" It's a long time ago now, but when he had overstayed his leave in Greece with Oscar Wilde by about a month, he made matters worse by preaching about the Unknown God. He told the congregation that the Athenian altar was erected to the unknown gods for the sake of foreign visitors who might use that altar for the worship of outlandish gods. And when St. Paul claimed it for his particular God it was quite improper —' Think of the impertinence of this impudent little Hebrew talking to the Sages of the Ancient World in that manner.' He added, ' I can never quite forgive St. Paul. There was an excellent University at Antioch, but he seems never to have availed himself of it. Never ! ' "

" So he was in Greece with Oscar Wilde ? "

" Oh, yes. Are you not aware of that ? Wilde got most of his superciliousness from trying to imitate Mahaffy. Mahaffy of course would call his attitude εὐτραπελιά well-bred arrogance; but the evidence for good breeding in great measure is absent."

The doctor's snuff-box was beginning to behave eccentrically. He murmured to himself on a high-pitched note. He captured it just as it had disguised itself as a butterfly pulverised with brown.

" Wilde was the grandson of a Yorkshire land agent. But the Provost's well-bred arrogance is susceptible to good breeding. When an undergraduate called Birde caught him by the gown at a dinner in College and said, ' Sit down, Mahouf ! ' he was yclept Mahouf by those of heavenly birth, but plain Mahaffy by the race of Earth.

" When his friends awakened him next day, he realised the enormity of his rudeness. Birde, sober, realised that nothing could save him from rustication. So he resolved to play the man and gentleman by calling to make his apology to the Provost before being sent down.

" ' Come in ! '

" ' I came, sir, to . . .'

" ' Now, who are you ? '

" ' Birde, sir.'

" ' What bird ? '

" ' I am an undergraduate, sir.'

" ' Of what College ? '

" ' This College.'

" ' And what do you want ? '

" ' I want to apologise, sir, for my inexcusable conduct at dinner last night.'

" ' What dinner ? '

" ' Dinner with you, sir.'

" Realising astutely that he was dealing with a gentleman because he had the good grace to apologise, Mahouf said : ' Sit down, Birde. And mark this : a gentleman never takes the least notice of what another gentleman says when he is in his cups.' "

The doctor commented after a pause, and sourly : " He was only ' in his cups ' because he was dining with Mahaffy. Had it been me or you we would have been ' disgwacefully dwunk.' "

Later, after a dream with himself, he remarked :

" If you take the trouble to inquire, you are certain to find that Birde's father owned an excellent shoot."

" The picnic party will be coming in on us," I suggested. " If we go ahead now, they can follow. Otherwise we shall be in the procession of motor-cars."

The party had been arranged. The meeting-place by a lake in the Wicklow Highlands had been named.

The doctor found it hard to interrupt the progress of his cure.

At last we got into the motor. We had not gone three miles when, in passing Stillorgan, he remarked : " It's amazing how motoring blows the alcohol out of one."

I ignored the innuendo.

Nodding, he said : " ' οὐκ ' forbids and ' μη ' denies, but seemingly Dublin has a more negative asseveration. It is at its best in an example. ' Picnic ' reminds me :

' Are you coming to the picnic, Mrs. Murphy ? '
' Picnic, me neck ! Look at Mary's belly since the last picnic.' "

" An excellent example," I acknowledged.   " It reminds
me of the invitation to a whist drive presumably held by that
same lady, whereat the favours of the hostess were assessed
only as second to the first prize, which was a bottle of stout ! "

The presence of this third enclitic " me neck ! " proves
that Dublin still uses the English language as emphatically
as the Elizabethans could.   And they could say more in it
than we in spite of our increased vocabulary, rendered, as it is,
anæmic by the abuse of words.

A greenish sea lay to our left.   Howth shone incredibly,
save to our greatest painter, Nathaniel Hone's retina, amethystine across the Bay.   No whitecaps marked the footsteps of
the wind overnight.

The three tips of Bray Head, purple like the Paps of
Jura, appeared.   The doctor opened his eye, and putting the
onus on me, said :

" If you are quite sure that this is the tower and town
of Bray, I am reminded that I am still a member of its Country
Club."

Resigning myself to the imposition as I thought of an
unwanted drink, I stopped, and we entered the Club.

" Two whiskey drinks for my friend and me."

He drank one, and, leaving the empty glass on the table,
disappeared with the one that was full.   Later, when he
returned with the second glass empty in his hand, he looked
at the first and asked, " Been entertaining a friend ? "

The plateau, rimmed far off by clear hills, is high.   It is
called the Calary Bog.   The air was thin and fine and the
far-flung light increased distances to the eye.

" Surely God in His infinite justice, and that rather contra-
dictory quality of His, mercy, never intended to lead us
into a wilderness such as this without punctuating it pleasantly
with a public-house ? "

I looked at the buff-coloured waste.   A deserted church
with a clump of sycamores over-topped by its grey pinnacled
tower.   One of those churches built to plan in the Eighteenth
Century when the abbeys were left to fall into ruin was all
that was to be seen.   On the right, the watershed of the
Roundwood lakes rose gradually.

" We have come to the utmost end of the earth," he quoted,
moaning to rebuke me, his guide.

" But, Sir, I see a mile or so off, on a gable, that blessed
word ' Hotel.' "

At once he became vivacious and vociferous like Friar John of the Funnels in that marvellous psychological study the *Discourse of the Drinkers*.

' Do you know Father Claude of the High Kilderkins ? '— How I wish I did! We have but few of them here. One or two, but by no means enough. And they that remain and those who admire are now subjects of suspicion of our obsessing Jansenists.

" Hotel ! " he said. " Now you know that though an absurd word—a French word, and not to be compared to ' Inn '—is very promising at this moment. I found an excellent hotel in Durham. When I entered, mine host appeared with a pint of port on a round salver.

" ' An old custom, sir,' he said.

" And only when I had imbibed it by the fire, did he ask me : ' How long are you going to stay ? '

" That was in Durham, an University town. . . ."

Nearer we drew to the gable on the left. ' Hotel,' it read certainly. But, to my horror, when we drew alongside— ' Powerscourt Temperance Hotel ' !

The doctor, even without his eyeglass, which I think he used for reading only, could not have failed to see the sign. He hardly glanced at it before his disapprobation found words :

" That's this country all over ! Not content with a contradiction in terms, it must go on to an antithesis in ideas. ' Temperance Hotel ' ! You might as well speak of a celibate kip ! "

I laughed so cheerfully and so long that the doctor's disappointment was appeased. He even smiled to himself. To distract him I said, " That reminds me, the kips need either to be rebuilt, ' moulded nearer to the heart's desire,' or abolished. Their condition is awful—as awful, almost, as that of the banks. In the world of good taste the architecture of the Dublin banks is just as deserving of censure as the brothels are in the sphere of morals. The banks have disfigured with their immodesty the quiet features of what was once a stately and dignified town. Guinness and Mahon's is the only exception. Pretentious display and meretricious design, medley of style and periods, vulgar mass supported by exotic pillars, all tend to confuse and to debauch the taste of the beholder, while dishonestly suggesting that solidarity in architecture is equivalent to financial security.

This exhibitionism in architecture is to my mind more indecent and less excusable than a display of lingerie. Lingerie is at least necessary : Aberdeen granite in Dublin is both far-fetched and dear-bought. And it is libellous for the banks to go for their substance to Aberdeen. I have found Aberdeen a most hospitable, humorous and generous town ; but defamatory legend makes all Scotland, especially Aberdeen, close-fisted and canny ; that is why, even if we accept this calumny, it is so unnecessary for the banks to import their symbols of thrift from Aberdeen. I have a plan to reduce the enormity of both these outrages on good taste and good living : banks and brothels."

"It will be interesting to hear it. They seem beyond redemption," the doctor said. "I cannot imagine how they can be remedied. What is your plan ?"

"To turn the banks into brothels and the brothels into banks."

"You don't mean to remove them all to the kips ?"

"No. Just exchange the staffs of brothels and banks for the present. All future banks I would place in that street which is straight—but who dare call it so ?—(from Lower Gardiner's Street to Buckingham Street), each next door to a kip in the following order : Bank of Ireland, Mrs. Mack's ; Teasey Ward's, Belfast Bank ; Munster and Leinster, Liverpool Kate's ; Piano Mary's, Provincial Bank ; Mrs. Hayes's next to the Royal and May Oblong's next to the Northern Bank.

"Most improvisators in policy must be prepared to accept a medley and to countenance compromise . . . forgive me if I am already using somewhat artificial language—a compromise might be reached wherein the over-rigid and formal lives of bankers would be gently offset by the more flexible manners of their next-door neighbours. Thus that 'certain neighbourliness' would be achieved. The braced and the relaxed, the formal and informal would meet and merge into the mellow mediocrity which is Dublin life. The de-humanised prose of the genial bank manager would lose the power which it has, when directed to women who are beyond reproach—that is, any reproach but his, 'on behalf of my Authorities '—of creating suffering and insomnia once it arrived 'By hand' in emancipated Mrs. Mack's. Just think of Mrs. Mack receiving the following composition and her reactions thereto : 'Madam,

While I do not want to press you unduly . . .' 'Jaysus, girls! Excuse me, ladies, I meant to say " oh, dearie me "!'"

The doctor, who rarely laughed, laughed now. He raised his head and the sunlight made for a moment translucent his wholesome teeth.

" Already I notice an improvement in manners, doubtless due to the compensatory recoil from the outrageous architecture of the banks, but, go on! What does the bank Manager say?"

" ' I must request you to put me in a position to report to my Authorities that, as far as in you lies, you have done your best to discharge your liability. . . .'"

" Liability," the doctor warbled, smiling. " And have you considered how the lady would reply?"

" I see her waving the letter before her love-learned sisters with: 'Here! Will none of yez tell this fellow where he gets off?'"

The doctor agreed, opining that those who had intelligence in Love would know how to soften the harshness of the mechanical money machine and to humanise him.

" Later then, in default of an answer by return, ' Madam, a writ is now issued. Will you accept service at the law offices of this bank or at your present address?' Fresh Nellie might volunteer," I said, " ' Tell him none of us would be seen dead in his kip.' Thus would he be ' told off.'"

The doctor, who seldom punned, but he said, as if to himself, " Telling a teller off?" Then he considered the subject as a whole.

" Yes; it is time something were done for the poor bankers. As it is they are condemned to lives as austere as the clergy's, but reaching, not as theirs does, to sanctity, but Sadism. Your idea of this neighbourliness is a good one, because we must in turn consider the effect the spacious and pretentious housing would have on the amorous inmates. Confronted by stucco pilasters, mosaic pavements and plaster ceilings, a projection into architecture as it were of their cosmetic paint and powder, they would gradually recoil from the meretricious gaudiness of their surroundings and come to yearn for something genuine and honest in their lives. Thus the vulgarity of the banks would be a salutary lesson to the late inhabitants of the brothels. Meanwhile the bankers, huddled and confined in the kips next door, would learn at first hand how the poor unfortunates had to

live.   They would have time to ask themselves how many
families had their inhumanity reduced to status of bankruptcy :
how many daughters of good families had their compound
interest condemned to live in such ' compounds.'   Piano
Mary may once have shown, among her loving family, skill
as a pianist.   To help an embarrassed father she may have
' gone as a governess ' and slowly reached the level at which
she is, or rather was, until lately to be found.   How can a
banker be expected to measure the iniquity of his usury without
going to the kips ?   The kips would Christianise the bankers—
that is, a certain proportion of them—just as the indecent
display and exhibitionism of the banks would make all women
who dwell in them revolt from any thought of flamboyant
living.

" And when tired of keeping their money under a pillow
or paliasse or in a vase on the mantelpiece, the bankers began
building extensions, strong rooms and managers' offices
in their respective kip, think how the rateable value of the
whole city would be improved !   Instead of having the most
squalid, fœtid and miserable stews in Europe, Dublin would
find itself without a kip of any kind except those ' in process
of alteration ' by the bankers.   Baths would be introduced ;
and with the sentiment of the Georgian period preserved,
as in Guinness and Mahon's, the kips would be exemplary
specimens of good and careful enterprise, while the banks
would be efficient houses of correction for pretentiousness and
display."

" I saw you coming out of Mrs. Hayes's ! "

The doctor thought it over, smiling to himself ;   then
facing me on a higher note, " Or was it Mrs. Mack's ? "
he asked, testing humorously my scheme.

" No ! " I said indignantly.   " That was the Royal Bank ! "

I will admit that until each had proved itself there might
be bad times in store for bawdy houses and borrowing houses,
but once merged, the morals of the bankers would be improved.

After all, it was not the Magdalen that the Lord scourged
from the Temple.

Clanging the gears we jerked forwards.   " It is only
ten minutes to Roundwood."   There was no time to be lost.

" This is worse than the lunch we had with Boss Croker
when he produced the gold medals won by his bulldog and

showed us the record elephant's ivory with 'Them's the biggest tusks outside Africa. . . .'"

"Ah, had they only been drinking-horns!" the doctor moaned. "Neither ivory nor gold amazed me more than his use of ' them ' as an adjectival pronoun."

Soon we found sanctuary.

"What a wonderful escape we had from dying of inanition on the desert crossing!"

"Yes," I agreed.

"The monks of St. Bernard would be well occupied if they built a monastery on the site of that 'Temperance Hotel.' The desolation reminds me of a Sunday I spent with Sergeant Dodd. Every minute I expected a neat-handed Phyllis to appear, but no! At lunch I would have died, only for the Christian negligence of the butler, who forgot to remove a heavy Waterford glass decanter of sherry from my side. As it was I nearly sprained my wrist. Days later my ' host ' had the audacity to ask me what I thought of a young subaltern who, incredible as it seems to me, got drunk in his house. 'It shows marvellous industry,' I said."

We turned to the right to begin the long ascent. The great car moaned high into the hills.

"This mountain is Kippure, a celebate kip in its way, for there is not a licensed house among all its water-springs. The other picnickers are to meet us at two o'clock by Lough Bray."

"But which of them has a car equal to this? And what time is it now, my dear friend?"

It was only one-thirty.

"Orpen will attend to you, sir, while I round up the guests. For losing us you would be left astray. The well-stocked hampers will be unloaded before long. And we will have an appetiser together."

> La concreata e perpetua sete
> Del deiforme reguo cen portava
> Veloci, quasi come il ciel vedete.

Light cumuli floated smoothly, sun-smitten, like nautili on the edge of the blue.

"Is the picnic on the top of yonder peak?"

"It is by the highest lake in the sunny highlands."

"Don't forget, dear boy, that this altitude evaporates one's drinks." He looked anxiously at the empty steeps.

" I have provided for that. There never were such hampers on these mountain-tops before. Even Æ's blood would boil at a lower temperature up here, and Mahaffy could afford to be sympathetic so high above the world."

" Who are coming ? " he asked, as if anxious for the supplies.

We entered a cloud of midges where the hills were thronged with streams. The wind-screen reflected the light behind my back directly into my eyes. The doctor took out his red silk handkerchief.

" When we are out of this ! "

Again we turned to the right at the topmost crossroads.

Four-and-a-half miles now.

" They have approached by another road," I said. " We took a round course so as not to travel with them all the way."

" How long will you take to do four miles ? "

" Six or seven minutes on this track."

" I can hold out that long," he said.

The little solicitor had not come. He was sitting in his office twittering and shuffling pens and pencils in the inkstand before him. He could hear his head clerk, whose high blood-pressure and well-held alcohol gave him not a moment's rest, brow-beating with profuse expatiation a confused and intimidated client. His syringe had broken. He was left diddering alone until his messenger should return, in his lunatic asylum of an office, disapproving all the while of Dr. Tyrrell, who unexpectedly had accepted a drink from him in the Friendly Brothers' Club, at one quarter-of-an-hour before lunch.

He would not, could not be a party to further frivolity. He mixed the tabloids with a little water. The injection reassured him. He was glad that he had the moral strength to resist the temptation of a unedifying picnic on the summit of Kippure !

" Orpen will be there, and Vera Hone and McGurk, the Master of Those Who Know, with Endymion, whom he found wading in St. Patrick's Well. My friend, the rare Alabaster, has been invited : and Major McLoren who fought with love even to the end in the person of Sylvia Langrishe, who is back from India now ; my wife and her sister, without whom there would be no entertainment ; a young American girl who has found peace through divorce, and our old friend McCabe."

" The good McCabe ! "

" Yes. He follows you for the language movement. He loves good style."

" That is the upper lake. The larger one is just down there. I can see the cars assembled."

He lifted an eyelid, but continued with his reflection :

" That egregious ass, George Moore, used to snigger and annoy Douglas Hyde by suggesting that Joseph of Arimathea followed the Disciples for the sake of the language movement."

" He held the Grail," I said.

A hundred yards from the road by a path that borders a rivulet the edge of the lake is reached. An ancient crater makes three-quarters of an amphitheatre which opens to the south and east. The lake lies deep within. Beyond, the semi-circular cup is dark green like the colour that invests Eternity. Pine-woods lie in a level to the right and hem a crescent of white sand.

By the granite outcrops the feast was spread. One of the rocks made a natural table with its flat top. Hampers were unpacked. Hard by, a cottage provided hot water for those who cared for tea. The sun shone on the lead-bright water.

" Who will bathe before food ? "

Luckily, before undressing I thought of the doctor. Where had he gone ? I gave him to Orpen so that he might be looked after while I collected the guests, but, like little Musgrave in the ballad, Orpen " had more thought of the fine women," so he left the doctor stranded by a rill. I ran across the heather. The six minutes for which he could hold out had been exceeded long ago. I led him to the feast. He rebuked me gently with : " It's amazing how many qualities of a drink water has ! " I protested my regret for his being deserted beside the little rill when he should have been seated by a syphon. Soon his spirits revived.

" I see we have with us the Master of Those Who Know, our most excellent colleague, the Professor of Moral Philosophy, the divine McGurk. But who are the other men ? "

" One is Alabaster, a friend of Orpen, the other is Endymion, whom McGurk brought, because though a little odd he is such a fine musician. McLoren is a Major retired from India, and the ladies are his friends—and mine. . . ."

" Friend," he said, subsiding, " it is good for us to be here. Alabaster ? A strange name."

" Yes. It is a derivative of Arquebuster—Herrick mentions it."

" Come along," they were calling to each other when we signalled that the feast was spread.

McGurk sat beside a Primus stove. Dr. Tyrrell sat with his back to a large stone on the top of which fruit salads were displayed. The ladies fussed about with the dishes; all but Sylvia, who sat in front of McGurk, her dainty shoes almost touching his soles. We were on a high and pleasant shelf. To see the valley it would be necessary to walk a hundred yards to the road : whence to the south-east stood the peaks of the Golden Spears, the Head of Bray, and beyond, a floor of shining sea. Some miles behind, a point might be reached from which Dublin could be seen smoke-veiled in its plain : St. Patrick's Cathedral seemingly still its highest and greyest mass beneath a pall of smoke, though Christ Church is higher. The dear and fog-crowned Athens of my youth !

Not far from where we sat the Liffey sprang to birth from the streamy mosses of Kippure—gathering water from that many-fountained hill before it could risk a long journey without being foiled by the flatness of its moors. For sixty miles it would wind through the loveliest valleys in the world to Brittas by Kilbride, where the Shankill river rushes to meet it through a gorge of rhododendrons and oaks, then, meandering, it will fall at Poulaphouca down to the level plain of Kildare, and to shine black and bright by Newbridge, and so on with many a winding to the Strawberry Beds for the first taste, at Island Bridge, of its salt and spacious home, Howth-guarded to the north beyond the Bull of sand and the old Green Plain, held southward by green Killiney and the shore that curves to Bray, to find rest at length beyond the Bay in the recreating sea.

The lake by which we lolled was a crater once. Our very table, tricked out with mica, was of igneous rock that told of old incredible cataclysms before man narrowed Time to be a measure of his years and superimposed his squabbles on the silver-shining granite that had reached eternal rest.

" If I merely say ' tricked ' in the doctor's hearing, later on," I said to the Master of Those Who Know, " we shall have a dissertation on ' Lycidas,' together with a recital of its last half-dozen lines."

He jerked his inco-ordinated six-foot-four. " You filthy

brute!" he exclaimed lovingly. "And why should you fool the dear old man? Cannot you leave the beloved doctor alone?"

"Oh, well, I want to add to the enjoyment of the company."

"By 'clanging' the poor old man with 'tricks his beams and with new spangled ore flames,' etc. It's poor and cheap and reflects more on your intellectual limitations than on his."

"I'll 'clang' you on 'you dirty brute!' and the other terms of endearment you have for me, before very long."

"What exactly is your vocation, Mr. Alabaster?" the lady with the beautiful name, Vera Hone, inquired.

Orpen interposed: "We brought Ally along so that he might try out his patents for filling in lulls in conversations. Ally has a lot of patents.

"His job was in the Oriental department of the National Museum; but when he took to jumping out from a replica of an Assyrian tomb in the Egyptian section on little girls, the Authorities superannuated him. Is not that so, Ally?"

"By a lake like this, as he tied a fly, Mahaffy said to me: 'I have had sixty-five love affairs in my life. And I have never regretted one of them! Not one! But, of course, they were all before I was ordained.'"

The doctor's high-pitched voice could be heard as he quoted aloud for our edification:

"'The King of Assyria was drinking himself drunk in his tent with the six and twenty kings who were with him and helping him.'" Then, as a commentary, "You know Mahaffy would not have refused a little light refreshment in that society."

"That was a marvellous dinner you gave us at Jammets," Orpen said.

Alabaster whinnied at the recollection.

He referred to Alabaster's answer to what he considered was an insulting "bonus" when he resigned from the Museum. He gave a dinner in Jammet's to five people at £8 a head.

"Wall-paper like this, Jammet, with lobster sauce, unthinkable!"

Bill-posters appeared during the meal and plastered up new wall-paper. A carpet of a different colour was provided with the game.

"Let Ally answer for himself."

But Ally preferred to tell how the landscape might be altered in the valley, if the farmers would pay more attention to the colour than to the character of their crops.

How self-effacing women can be! They can sacrifice themselves for the pleasure of others, reckless of the worth of their work or fame.

" This is cold punch, Professor ! " my wife said.

" Oh, indeed ? "

" Now, it is not a thing to be despised ! The proportion of boiling water to fifteen-years-old Jameson was, before it cooled, in exact ratio to the amount of Falstaff's expenditure on bread as compared with sack."

" I cannot refuse ! "

" And a little more chicken ? "

" The point is," Professor McGurk interjected, " whether we have improved on it since then."

" Improved on what ? " Sylvia asked.

" Life ! " McGurk answered.

" I was talking about Homer—beautiful, beautiful that banquet of the gods where they stretched forth their hands upon the sacred fare ! How delightful ! But the point is, have we improved on it since then ? Three thousand years have gone ! The question I ask is, ' Have we anything better to do than the gods did ? '—' They stretched forth their hands upon the sacred fare ! ' "

He reached to his glass and threw back his head.

" Did they do nothing but eat and drink ? Surely you have forgotten Love, Professor ? " Sylvia asked.

" Love ! My goodness ! " He raised his face and quoted ecstatically : " ' But for us twain, come, let us take our joy couched together in love ; for never yet did desire for goddess or mortal woman so shed itself about me and overmaster the heart within my breast.' " He struck himself dramatically.

Sylvia looked embarrassed, wondering whether it was a genuine quotation, or a proposal, or both. But her doubt was solved when the Professor continued declaiming :

" ' Nay ! not when I was seized with love of the wife of Ixion who bore Pirithous, nor of Danæ of the trim ankles who bore—— "

Sylvia withdrew her foot.

" ' If thou art fain to be couched on the peaks of Ida where all is clear to view.' "

" In this world of appearances," I said, interrupting, " it is well that things should look their best when all is clear to view, else let us wrap ourselves in a cloud of gold."

" Sylvia, what about a stroll in the wood ? " McLoren asked, by way of relief.

" ' It is as easy for a thing to be as not to be,' " I quoted, to draw the Professor.

Indignantly he turned : " How dare you, you dirty brute ! You have an impish mind with no respect for anything in this world of phenomena, not even for the great Hegel himself ! For you, Reality simply waxes and wanes ! "

By this time the word " tricks " had germinated in the benign doctor's mind. With a little moaning overture pitching his voice high, he began :

" ' So sinks the daystar in the ocean bed,
And yet anon repairs his drooping head.' "

He nodded.

" ' And tricks his beams with new spangled ore
Flames in the forehead of the morning sky ! ' "

His voice rose to a high treble so that he almost crowed when he repeated ' Flames.'

But the moral philosopher was annoyed with me.

" Scandalous ! You dirty brute ! " he grunted. " Could you not leave even our dear old friend alone ? "

A fiddle sounded from above us on a rock.

" Your friend Endymion, whom you found wading the other night in St. Patrick's Well when you neglected to close the gate in the wall at the foot of Dawson Street."

" And why shouldn't he wade if he wishes ? He played Chopin's Sonata, the scherzo of it in B Minor on my piano ; and that's a thing you could never do ! "

They had spent the night in the Professor's room improvising until dawn.

" I observe that he has laid down the sword for the violin. What is he playing ? " the doctor asked.

" Our national anthem."

" It's not the national anthem," McGurk thundered. " It's ' Johnny, I hardly knew you ' ! "

" I have always held that that ballad should be Ireland's national anthem. It is full of a kind of steadfast courage that can revel in disaster. It is as if the very spirit of Ireland mocked and revelled in vicissitude, deriding Death. The wife, Kathleen Na Houlihan, of course, of the war-broken veteran who hardly recognises her husband repeats :

> 'Ye haven't an arm and ye haven't a leg,
>   Huroo! Huroo!
> Ye haven't an arm and ye haven't a leg,
>   Huroo!
> Ye haven't an arm and ye haven't a leg,
> Ye eyeless, noseless, chickenless egg;
> Ye'll have to be put in a bowl to beg,
>   Johnny, I hardly knew ye.'"

But the doctor was recalling it, greatly amused.

"True," I said sententiously to tease the Professor, "recognition is hard to come by, particularly for minds which are not devout."

But the benign doctor took up the theme:

"You spoke of steadfast courage, but that was all that was steadfast in Johnny.   It goes on:

> 'Where are the legs with which you run?
>   Huroo! Huroo!
> Where are the legs with which you run?
>   Huroo!
> Where are the legs with which you run
> When you went to shoulder the gun?
> Begob, yer dancing days are done.
>   Johnny, I hardly knew ye.
>
> Where are the eyes which were so mild?
>   Huroo! Huroo!
> Where are the eyes which were so mild?
>   Huroo!
> Where are the eyes which were so mild
> When of my love you were beguiled?
> Why did you skedaddle from me and the child?
>   Johnny, I hardly knew ye!'"

"Excellent! sir," said Professor McGurk.

Encouraged, the doctor continued:

"If one were to treat that ballad with the reverence which it deserves, Dean Bernard's attention should be directed towards it, perhaps by you, McGurk, after I had translated it into Greek.   You might describe it as a writing seen in vision on a wall in Patmos by a member of the Hermetic Society.   Something like this might emerge."   He applied himself to his tumbler for a moment, then gathering his mind, composed *ex tempore*:

"'Alas, for the going of Swiftness, for the feet of the running of thee,
   When thou wentest among the swords and the shoutings of captains made shrill,
Woe is me for the pleasant places! Yea, one shall say of thy glee
"It is not!"   And as for delight, the feet of thy dancing are still.

' Also thine eyes were mild as a lowlit flame of fire
  When thou wovest the web whereof wiles were the woof, and the warp was
      my heart !
  Why left'st thou the fertile field whence thou reaped'st the fruit of desire ?
  For the change of the face of thy colour, I know thee not who thou art ! '

That is an excellent example, and an object lesson of what Dean Bernard and men of his ilk mean to the irrepressible spirit of our land.   Dulling first, then deadening it and covering its grave with a formal foreign urn."

"Huroo!"   Endymion echoed.   And his music mingled with the trees.

The lake was smoothening and beginning to reflect the few light clouds which had climbed the sky.   The ladies had tripped away and the fiddle notes receded farther and farther until they were indistinguishable from the fitful sounds of "*the wide world dreaming of things to come.*"

I removed a fruit salad that threatened to slide down and to enfillet, with crescents of orange and green, the dear old doctor's supernal brow.

The Master of Those Who Know said, with his back against a rock :

"Isn't it a nice bloody thing that when the women go off we are left here with nothing to do but go to sleep ? "

> " ' Sleep that softlier on the spirit lies,
>   Than tired eyelids upon tired eyes,' "

the doctor murmured.

For Heaven's sake don't go to sleep and leave me to keep watch here alone on behalf of intelligence which I am unable to sustain by myself.

Sleep in the sunlight, what could be better ?   It will leave the night free, bring what it may.   And by the warm rock I nodded, until there came to me the image of a little child with velvet suit and lace collar in a public-house tempted by a coachman and wondering at the drink proffered to him in secrecy, sweet and bitter, sanguine as Life.

"Would you care for another raspberry cordial, Master Oliver ? "

By 'Gis and by St. Charity if it lead to a great calm like this above the world, with friends like these, in spite of the danger of its becoming a habit, I would say 'The Same Again'! and chance again my lucky stars.

FINIS

INDEX

Other books from The O'Brien Press

SEAMUS HEANEY
Thomas C. Foster

A comprehensive critical overview of this internationally renowned poet's work.

160 pages/ISBN 199-X/£8.95 pb

AFTER THE WAKE
Brendan Behan

Collected stories, including previously unpublished material.

160 pages/ISBN 031-4/£4.95 pb

THE WEAVER'S GRAVE
Seumas O'Kelly

O'Kelly's masterpiece, and a selection of his short stories, introduced by Benedict Kiely. '*Storytelling at its best*' THE BLOOMSBURY REVIEW.

144 pages/ISBN 152-3/£3.95 pb

THE MIDNIGHT COURT
Brian Merriman, trans. Frank O'Connor

Illustrated by Brian Bourke

Award-winning edition of this outstanding translation of Brian Merriman's eighteenth-century erotic masterpiece.

64 pages/illustrations
ISBN 205-8/£6.95 pb

GREAT IRISH WRITING – THE BEST FROM *THE BELL*
Ed. Sean McMahon

A literary classic. '*A golden treasure house of great literature*' THE IRISH TIMES

192 pages/biographical notes/index ISBN 046-2/£5.95 pb

THE HAUGHEY FILE
Stephen Collins

The unprecedented career and last years of the Boss.
'Fluent, well-written account of a rollercoaster period ... an outline of Irish history ... quite simply, a must.' THE IRISH TIMES.

240 pages/photos/ISBN 298-8/£7.95 pb

SPRING AND THE LABOUR STORY
Stephen Collins

The inside story of the Labour leader by a leading journalist. A must for anyone interested in the party's history and politics.

224 pages/B&W photos
ISBN 349-6/£7.95 pb

REVOLUTIONARY WOMAN
Kathleen Clarke

A unique account of the 1916 rebellion by a Cumann na mBan activist and the wife of Proclamation signatory Thomas Clarke.

240 pages/photos, documents
ISBN 245-7/£16.95 hb
ISBN 294-5/£9.95 pb

THE LONG WAR
The IRA and Sinn Féin 1985 to Today
Brendan O'Brien

Written by a senior RTE Current Affairs reporter, an impeccably researched book with authentic material and first-hand accounts from people on the ground in Northern Ireland. Details the changes in the Republican Movement since the mid-eighties and the growth and development of their policies up to the present.

320 pages/specially commissioned
photos by Alan O'Connor
ISBN 359-3/£18.95 hb

A VALLEY OF KINGS
The Boyne
Henry Boylan

An inspired guide to the myths, magic and literature of this beautiful valley with its mysterious 5000-year-old monuments at Newgrange. Illustrated.

168 pages/illustrations
ISBN 170-1/£7.95 pb

DUBLIN AS A WORK OF ART
Colm Lincoln

From the author of the popular *STEPS & STEEPLES: Cork at the turn of the Century*. Taking the reader from east to west along the quays, and from north to south from Parnell Square to St Stephen's Green, Colm Lincoln provides a visual narrative of how the city came to be what it is today, with the aid of both archive material and new photographs specially commissioned by the National Library.

224 pages/B&W photos
ISBN 313-5/£19.95 hb

THE BLASKET ISLANDS
Next Parish America
Joan and Ray Stagles

The history, characters, social organisation, nature - all aspects of this most fascinating and historical of islands. Illustrated.

144 pages/illustrations
ISBN 071-3/£7.95 pb

PHRASES MAKE HISTORY HERE
Ed. by Conor O'Clery

A century's-worth of Irish political quotations arranged chronologically.

240 pages/index/ISBN 108-6/£14.95 hb
ISBN 108-3/£6.95 pb

A POCKET HISTORY OF IRELAND
Breandán O hEithir

Concise, insightful overview of Ireland's history from Celtic times to the present, including the North of Ireland.

144 pages/illustrations/ISBN 188-4/£3.95 pb

THE CELTIC WAY OF LIFE
Curriculum Development Unit

Social and political history of pre-Christian Ireland in accessible text.

72 pages/37 illustrations/ISBN 023-3/£4.95 pb

MARY ROBINSON
A President with a Purpose
Fergus Finlay

Fascinating account of the Robinson campaign. The making of a President as it really happened.

160 pages/B&W photos/ISBN 257-0/£5.95 pb

SLIGO
Land of Yeats' Desire
John Cowell

An evocative account of the history, literature, folklore and landscapes, with eight guided tours of the city and county.

168 pages/illustrated
ISBN 185-X/£9.95 pb

THE BIG WINDOWS
Peadar O'Donnell

A memorable novel and social document set in Donegal.
'*...timeless, the writing pure as well water*' THE GUARDIAN

211 pages/ISBN 090-X/£3.95 pb

PROUD ISLAND
Peadar O'Donnell

The struggle of an island community for survival.
'*Probably his most tremendous achievement*' THE SUNDAY PRESS

128 pages/ISBN 093-4/£3.95 pb

THE KNIFE
Peadar O'Donnell

A love story set against a background of historic conflict.
'*A wonderfully accomplished novel*' THE SUNDAY PRESS

228 pages/ISBN 0906462-037/£4.50 pb

A PLACE OF DREAMS
The Lough Gur People
Michael Quinlan

An exploration in fiction of life in the Lough Gur area in prehistoric times. Survival of an ancient village, with all the terrors and pleasures of this remote period.

160 pages/ISBN 291-0/£6.95 pb

THE PORT WINE STAIN
Patrick Boyle

Twelve outstanding short stories, introduced by Benedict Kiely. Boyle tells the haunting truth of his characters' lives with skill, compassion and sympathy.

240 pages/ISBN 010-1/£8.00 hb

GLENANAAR
Canon Patrick Sheehan

The unhappy fortunes of the family of an informer are explored in this novel set in the early 19th century. Gives a unique insight into the plight of the Irish tenant farmer. Sheehan's most famous book.

320 pages/ISBN 195-7/£5.95 pb

HERITAGE
Eugene McCabe

Tense, moving storis from a prizewinning author. Set mainly in the border counties where confusion, divided loyalties and heightened emotions are part of everyday life.

156 pages/ISBN 079-9/£3.95 pb

WHEN LOVE COMES TO TOWN
Tom Lennon

This funny and stunningly original book deals honestly with the emotions and crises faced by a gay teenager in present-day Dublin.

176 pages/ISBN 361-5/£5.95 pb

A THORN IN THE SIDE
Fr Pat Buckley

The story of the life and career of this radical priest and his thoughts on issues of contemporary life.

208 pages/ISBN 364-X/£9.99 pb

FEAR OF THE COLLAR
Patrick Touher

True account of a childhood spent under the tough regime at the Artane Industrial School. An extraordinary and moving story, and a first-hand document of social history.

176 pages/illustrations
ISBN 268-6/£9.95 pb

SMOKEY HOLLOW
Bob Quinn

Vivid, hilarious and moving account of Dublin childhood in the forties. This is fictionalised, but draws heavily on fact. Full of character and great stories.

176 pages/ISBN 264-4/£10.95 hb

ISBN 318-6/£5.95 pb

THE WIT OF OSCAR WILDE
Sean McCann

A new edition of this delightful and entertaining book on an unforgettable Irish genius.

128 pages/cartoons
ISBN 248-1/£4.95 pb

THE STUNT
Shay Healy

A no-holds-barred novel of the 'sex and rock 'n' roll' lifestyle of an up-and-coming rock band and the outrageous stunt that changes everything...

176 pages/ISBN 322-4/£5.95 pb

BLASKET ISLAND GUIDE
Ray Stagles

Illustrated pocket guide to one of Ireland's most stunning landmarks.

64 pages/illustrations, maps
ISBN 197-3/£3.95 pb

SKELLIG
Island Outpost of Europe
Des Lavelle

The past, present and future, as well as plant, animal and sea life, of Skellig Michael and Small Skellig

112 pages/illustrations/colour photos
ISBN 295-3/£8.95 pb

Send for our complete catalogue

ORDER FORM

Please send me the books as marked

I enclose cheque / postal order for £……… (+ 50p P&P per title)

OR please charge my credit card

☐ Access / Mastercard   ☐ Visa

Card number ☐☐☐☐ ☐☐☐☐ ☐☐☐☐ ☐☐☐☐
EXPIRY DATE ☐ ☐ ☐ ☐

Name: …………………………………………………………………Tel: ………………………

Address: ………………………………………………………………………………………………

……

Please send orders to : THE O'BRIEN PRESS, 20 Victoria Road, Dublin 6.
Tel: (Dublin) 4923333 Fax: (Dublin) 4922777